Culture, Capitalism,

and Democracy

in the New America

Culture, Capitalism, and Democracy in the New America

Richard Harvey Brown

Yale University Press

New Haven & London

Published with assistance from the foundation established in memory of Philip
Hamilton McMillan of the Class of 1894, Yale College.

Set in Adobe Garamond type by The Composing Room of Michigan, Inc.
Printed in the United States of America.

Library of Congress Cataloging-in-Publication Data
Brown, Richard Harvey.
   Culture, capitalism, and democracy in the New America /
Richard Harvey Brown.
      p. cm.
Includes bibliographical references and index.
ISBN 0-300-10025-6 (alk. paper)
   1. Democracy—United States.   2. Political culture—United States.
3. Capitalism—United States.   I. Title.
JK1726.B77 2005
306.2'0973—dc22
                                                        2004058501

A catalogue record for this book is available from the British Library.

The paper in this book meets the guidelines for permanence and durability of the
Committee on Production Guidelines for Book Longevity of the Council on
Library Resources.
10 9 8 7 6 5 4 3 2 1

For Remi Clignet,
in deepest friendship

Contents

1 Differences That Make a Difference: Some Exceptional Features
of the United States, 1

2 A Peculiar Democracy: Race, Class, and Corporate Power in the
United States, 36

3 Ideology After the Millennium: Problems of Legitimacy
in American Society, 67

4 Social Movements, Politics, and Religion in a
Postliberal Era, 113

5 The Dialectics of American Selfhood: Individualism and Identity
in the United States, 142

6 Transformations of American Space and Time, 172

7 Genders and Generations: New Strains in the
American Family, 205

8 The Postmodern Transformation of Art: From Production of Beauty to Consumption of Signs, 264

References, 299

Index, 343

Publisher's Note

Richard Harvey Brown died October 9, 2003, after a long illness. Before his death he completed a finished manuscript of *Culture, Capitalism, and Democracy in the New America* and submitted it to Yale University Press. To ready his manuscript for publication, a number of his graduate students stepped in to assist. The Press owes its thanks to Todd Stillman, Joey Irizarry, Jeff Stepnisky, and Tim Recuber for their tireless responsiveness to our editorial questions, and for their dedication to Richard and his work.

Culture, Capitalism,

and Democracy

in the New America

Chapter 1 Differences That Make a Difference: Some Exceptional Features of the United States

The United States is in transit from an industrial to a postindustrial society, from modern to postmodern, from national to global. But which aspects of these shifts are peculiarly American, and which does America share with other advanced capitalist states? What aspects of America simply reflect more global social processes, and which have their origin in the United States? How are general tendencies common to many nations, such as economic rationalization or changes in gender roles, shaped by unique local historical and cultural factors? How can we distinguish Americanization and globalization? Further, what is the connection between the structural shift from industrial to postindustrial society and the cultural distinction between modernity and postmodernity? These questions require an assessment of the exceptional features of the United States, such as the preindustrial modernization of American culture; its ethnic amnesia and myth of the melting pot; the coexistence of American apartheid and the dream of civic inclusion; and the tensions between the American tradition of decentralization and the extension of corporate and state power, which leads to a greater concentration of control and a narrowing of public space.

America is unlike other countries. America is like other countries. Disputes concerning the supposed Americanization of the world illustrate underlying similarities and convergences between the new American society and other states and cultures. The role actually played by the United States around the world is sometimes difficult to distinguish from the influence imputed to it. For instance, U.S. veterans returning to Vietnam have been welcomed by their former adversaries with the exclamation, "America Number One!" American journalists only ten years after the Gulf War were getting the thumbs-up in the souks of Baghdad. Perhaps these are gestures against the local regime more than an acclamation of American power, much as placing a Statue of Liberty in Tiananmen Square was a symbol of protest. People may adopt American modes of music, food, dress, or drugs to show that they are liberated from tradition or repression. To adopt American images is not simply to be Americanized. More important, it is to assert the right to be modern. "Number One" refers as much to the fact that America is deemed to be the most modern country as to America's current preeminence in relation to other nation-states.

AMERICANIZATION AND GLOBALIZATION

Like "Westernization," the very term "Americanization" masks a number of conflicting processes. Just as "Westernization" masks the plundering of the natural riches of weaker countries by strong ones, "Americanization" sanitizes the subversion of foreign governments by the CIA; the penetration into foreign markets by American-based transnational firms; or the adoption of modes of mass consumption through the use of credit cards, shopping malls, or fast food (Ritzer 1999). But "Americanization" also evokes a movement toward freedom and individualism. From Beijing to Berlin, from Poland to Palestine, the posters of antigovernment demonstrators have often been in English, which shows both the reach of the American media and the allure of American ideals. "Americanization," like its counterpart, "Westernization," has many facets.

As a counterpoint to the Americanization of other countries, the United States itself is becoming more globalized. American stock and real estate markets and more generally the whole American economy are increasingly shaped by capitalists overseas. The crash of October 1987, for example, was imputed in part to disaffection with the U.S. domestic economy by foreign investors. The economic jolt in 1997 following the fall of the Thai baht and other East Asian currencies showed a similar interdependency. The third-largest American automaker, Daimler-Chrysler, is German, as is the largest American publishing firm, Bertelsmann, which owns Random House, Bantam, and Doubleday. Americans also are adopting Thai or Brazilian cuisines, as well as Thai or Brazilian babies. They now eat formerly exotic fruits such as kiwi or plantain. The same holds true for words. The French complain about the increasing use of "Franglish" and Latin Americans of "Espanglish," and much advertising copy worldwide uses English words merely as symbols of what is attractive. But a similar borrowing goes in the reverse direction, as when words and institutions such as "kindergarten," "discotheque," "salsa," "yoga," or "zen" are converted into English. In the same way, Mexicans, Filipinos, Iranians, and a multitude of other immigrant groups are converted into American. Thus, whereas the term "Americanization" refers to the export of American culture—of Coca Cola, *The Terminator,* and blue jeans—it is matched by the symmetric globalization of the United States. Indeed, for much of what America exports, there was originally an alien cultural artifact that was introduced into what became American culture.

Moreover, "Americanization" also has a moral dimension—the spread of ideals of liberty and equality that the United States announces, embodies, and violates. Early settlers learned that there was nothing so divisive as the pursuit of intensely held values, and as early as 1641 the people of Massachusetts had determined in their code of liberties that individuals should be protected from the moral edicts of any church (Albrow 2001). With the globalization of such ideals, as Herman Melville wrote in 1849 in *Redburn,* "in some things we Americans leave to other countries the carrying out of the principle [of equality] that stands at the head of our Declaration of Independence." Even today the United States refuses to support the establishment of the International Court of Criminal Justice and other such conventions that are inspired in part by American ideals for fear that Americans themselves may be judged by non-Americans in such venues (Albrow 2001). Thus globalization continues to challenge the United States even as Americanization challenges other nations.

Economic Shifts

Emerging patterns of finance, manufacture, and trade are perhaps the most striking sign of the general globalization of contemporary life, even though citizens and government officials often do not notice it. For example, both the elder George Bush's Special Trade Representative Carla Hills and Commerce Secretary Robert Mosbacher insisted that America guard its technologies from foreign firms, subsidize sunrise industries, and force other nations to open their markets to American products. Bill Clinton and his trade representative,

Diane Barshevsky, and George W. Bush and his representative took a similar line.

But what does it mean exactly to be "American"? Ms. Hills accused Japan of excluding Motorola from its domestic markets, but Motorola designs and makes the cellular telephones it tries to sell in Japan in Kuala Lumpur, Malaysia. Similarly, General Electric is Singapore's largest private employer. At the same time, Sony exports to Europe audio and video tapes and recorders made by Americans in Sony factories in the United States; Starbucks imports Italian espresso machines; Honda sells over sixty thousand cars per year to Japan and other Asian nations from its American factories; IBM employs thousands of Japanese in its factories and laboratories in Japan and is now Japan's leading exporter of computers; and about one-third of Taiwan's trade surplus with the United States is attributable to American-owned firms that have set up operations there. When an Iowan buys a Pontiac, 60 percent of her money goes to South Korea, Japan, Germany, Taiwan, Singapore, Britain, and Barbados, though many of the contributing firms in those countries are at least partly American-owned.

A parallel situation has developed in finance, with capital raised and stock traded in a number of global capital markets. Over one-third of U.S. dollars is held abroad in non-American hands, and two-thirds of all U.S. currency in circulation is overseas. Americans own large portions of non-American firms, and vice versa. Thus, as the very concept of "American" products made by "American" firms is becoming less meaningful, the idea of the "Americanization" of the globe must be supplemented by an awareness of the globalization of the United States. In short, the process of delocalization is ubiquitous. Things are rarely produced or consumed any longer in single places. The underlying patterns of economic and cultural diffusion suggest that almost all societies are becoming more porous and open to alien but soon domesticated influences.

Demographic Changes

In the area of family life, industrialization and especially postindustrialization trigger declines in the rate of marriage and increases in the frequency of informal cohabitation. As women increasingly have paid jobs outside the home, they become more independent financially, have broader awareness and choices, and find it more costly in forfeited alternatives if they opt to be full-time mothers or housewives. Whereas industrialization and urbanization generate decreases in birthrates but rises in the relative number of children born out of wedlock, they also encourage audacious innovations aimed at preventing or facilitating pregnancy and increases in divorce rates but parallel longevity of marriages. In other words, in the United States as in other economically advanced societies, there is change in the profile of average families as well as in their differentiation.

Similarly, all economically advanced countries have been experiencing sharp increases in immigration. America has kept its doors open to Russian Jews, Vietnamese or Cuban refugees, and Latin Americans or Caribbeans looking for better standards of life. Britain, Germany, and France have been havens for the political refugees of the Middle East and have absorbed an unskilled labor force from former colonies or from semiperipheral areas such as Eastern Europe and Turkey. These workers take low-end jobs that citizens of advanced economies are now less willing to do. Similar arrangements exist in Australia and Canada, in relatively prosperous Argentina and Chile, and, more and more, in Japan. Persons registering with the Immigration and Naturalization Service in New York State in 1989 named 164 countries or dependencies as their native lands (Fuchs 1990). Moreover, whereas America continues to draw immigrants from a wide range of countries and social strata, there has been a thickening stream of Americans residing overseas. Thus there are English-language dailies in Paris, Brussels, Tokyo, Mexico City, Buenos Aires, and most large cities of the globe. Most of these Americans will return home, making the United States itself a culturally more international society.

Political Changes

On both sides of the Atlantic, definitions of the state and its functions have been subjected to similar challenges. The triumph of neoliberal ideologies almost everywhere has encouraged market-oriented social changes. Both Ronald Reagan and Margaret Thatcher denounced overgrown public sectors and supposedly counterproductive welfare, and both sought to privatize activities that formerly were conducted by the state. Bill Clinton, George W. Bush, and Tony Blair have continued these policies. The same pattern characterizes France since the return of the right to power in 1985. When the Socialists regained power in 1988 and again with Lionel Jospin in 1998, they did not change the thrust of measures adopted by their conservative predecessors. The same is true of Gerhard Schroeder in Germany. Indeed, the new administrations have kept on denationalizing enterprises, including radio and television stations—a drastic innovation for France, where for more than a century the birth of any large private communications enterprise was seen as a plot against the government. Such state devolution and market extensions have been even more dramatic in Eastern Europe, Russia, and China. This does not mean that the state is less important. It is spending more per capita than ever before. But its image and its role almost everywhere are shifting.

Thus, what is imputed to "Americanization" sometimes may be due more to structural changes or economic and technological innovations that appeared earlier or more visibly in the United States than elsewhere. The international proliferation of shopping malls or Automatic Teller Machines (ATMs) stems from new economic conditions as well as from America's particular consumer culture and marketing know-how. In one view, "Americanization" reflects the constraints, opportunities, and crises resulting from independent efforts toward modernization and industrialization and their "post" varieties. In a second view, "Americanization" results from the diffusion of institutional, cultural, or psychological traits born in the United States.

It is important, however, to note the dialectic underlying the variety of changes I have mentioned. It is one thing to describe the central tendencies of the economic, demographic, and political changes that accompany the emergence of a postindustrial order. It is another, and probably even more significant, to highlight their increased variance and the reactions that they elicit. For example, as multinational corporations become more powerful, countervailing international social movements, as well as autonomous neighborhood organizations, become more significant. Likewise, as the state's power diminishes relative to international forces, it is increasingly expected by its citizens to modify, compete with, or protect them from such forces. Similarly, trends toward more individualized lifestyles are associated with a selective restoration of extended kinship networks. In the same vein, as standardized patterns of behaviors and beliefs become more pervasive, a greater emphasis is placed on personal choice and identity.

In sum, as the world becomes more interdependent financially, ecologically, economically, and even culturally, local invention, global diffusion, and consequent relocalization become more intertwined. This shift often shows in small but significant ways. A pump invented for industrial use—say in Munich— may be adapted for rural hydropower in Togo. A plant used to ease menstrual pain in the Amazon may become a pharmaceutical manufactured in Boston. Thus, invention, adaptation, diffusion, and reinvention are always going on in diverse ways in many places and at many levels.

THE PREINDUSTRIAL MODERNIZATION OF
AMERICAN CULTURE AND AMERICAN
POLITICAL PARTICIPATION

While modernity and postmodernity today are global in scope, they play themselves out differently in different societies, including the United States. First, American culture, including a political culture of democratic participation, was largely formed *before* the Industrial Revolution. Second, ethnic and racial diversity and discrimination continue to operate in the United States amid an ethos of universal citizenship and, with this, a vacillation between ethnic amnesia, on the one hand, and assertions of particular ethnic values, on the other. In other words, not only is there a continuous tension between the ideals of the melting pot and cultural pluralism, but also the way this tension is handled keeps changing. A third important feature of the United States is its decentralized system of government, which, combined with an increasingly national and international political economy, has generated new ambiguities in Americans' attitudes and conduct toward the state. Like and unlike other countries, this decentralization reflects and stimulates a continuing diversity of regional cultures. Finally, certain ubiquitous trends often take early and extreme forms in the United States, such as the extension of corporate power and the market; the narrowing of civic space; and the decline of class politics, which has characterized the late modern period.

While the first colonists in America intended to replicate to their own advantage the system of privileges that existed in England, they also initiated some unexpected changes. In New England, the elimination of the top layers of English society enabled the middling ones to expand. Initially at least, communities in this part of the New World possessed sufficiently abundant land to distribute to virtually any unindentured white male who needed it, thereby increasing greatly the number of freeholders, which was a small class in England as a result of aristocratic dominance, the scarcity of land, and the surplus of labor (Pesen 1990). In America the opposite was true, and this encouraged more equitable land distribution, with need serving as the key criterion. Moreover, the revolution itself was to be violently contested among persons who, victorious, were to become Americans themselves. Within one generation, from the end of the French and Indian War to the election of Thomas Jefferson as president, America shifted from a religious to a secular political discourse, shed the monarchial dependency and colonial trade that had characterized the colonies for 150 years, and made a successful revolution and constitution. The word "democrat" appeared in the English (and French) language in 1789. "The revolution also yielded state governments more popular than any others in the eighteenth century world. . . . [In some states] a greater proportion of the people could vote and a greater proportion of government officials were elected than in any other country" (Wood 1980, 7). As bonds of fealty, patronage, and even extended family linkages of the colonial period were severed, people became more conscious of both their shared citizenship and their particular interests. A group of New York artisans declared that "Self Interest is the grand Principle of all Human Actions" (quoted in Friedman 1970, 789), just when Thomas Paine was declaring that "our citizenship in the United States is our national character" (Paine 1984, 1:374). By the early 1800s these (still plural) United States had become "the most liberal, most democratic, the most commercially minded, and the most modern" nation in the world (Wood 1992, 7; see also Fox 2001; Butler 2000).

Whereas a number of farmers in New York, New Jersey, and even Pennsylvania owned slaves until the eve of the Civil War (Berlin 1998), local public authorities were noting the contradictions between the continued existence of slavery and the pressures exerted on local labor markets by a growing influx of immigrants. In contrast, the southern colonies had attracted a number of individuals from noble families who were sufficiently wealthy to buy the labor and bodies of indentured immigrant workers or enslaved Africans. Early on, by about 1650, the distinction between the status of indentured servants and slaves in this part of the country became clear-cut, and with the development of large-scale plantations slavery became more systematically oppressive.

In short, while political scientists have accustomed us to distinguish systems of caste from class, the two forms of social stratification have long coexisted in the United States (Fredrickson 1997). Early democratic practices excluded slaves, women, and propertyless men. Moreover, as slavery in the South tended to justify inequalities and to reduce democratic participation among whites, Southern political leaders more easily achieved a political stability that allowed them to disproportionately influence the entire American political system. As an example, even though they denied slaves any political right, Southern political leaders still were able to count each slave as three-fifths of a citizen in order to get more seats in Congress. Similarly, in the decades since the Civil Rights Movement of the 1960s, the South has been more integrated into the rest of the country, but politically the United States has become much more "Southernized"; for example, conventional wisdom among political observers asserts that presidential candidates must run strong in the South to win an election.

Despite early differences in the respective patterns of social stratification of the North and the South, many local public positions in both regions were filled by amateurs, and most social services were provided by voluntary groups. Even today, 80 percent of American firemen are volunteers. Such amateurs established a tendency in American culture to ignore many norms and practices based on tradition, class structure, ideologies, or doctrines of the church. In their stead, Americans substituted the more universal and inclusive criterion of utility: "If it works, it's good." The shelves of George Washington's library at Mount Vernon, for example, were filled with how-to-do-it manuals for the enterprising farmer, in addition to classical political writings. Though Washington owned land and slaves and by profession had been a surveyor, he made most of his money as a pragmatic farmer-merchant. He was an avid experimenter with crops and caught eels from the Potomac River for salting and sale in Europe. The American mind was early attracted to technical and economic actions that produced practical results.

As the population grew, land pressures pushed farming colonists westward, while other farmers supplemented income from land with trade or manufactures. For example, by 1760 people in Lynn, Massachusetts, had begun to specialize in the production of shoes. Those who remained on their farms and struggled with poor soil and scarce labor sought technologies that improved efficiency. By 1850, the factory farm had appeared in the northern United States. To be sure, both its organization and its crops differed from the Southern plantation, but the general prosperity suggested that there was more than one successful economic strategy.

As Americans moved west, the opening of new horizons loosened their bonds to the old homesites, much as opportunity in the New World loosened the ties of new immigrants to their home countries, even though many returned or longed to do so. Generally, though, it was thought that the further west one went, the greater one's freedom. The settlement of the West both encouraged and depended on the development of transportation and communication. While the cultural values of mobility and equality inclined early Americans to form self-help organizations, both their diversity and their independence also encouraged them to view public and private realms as distinct spheres of interaction. More people learned to read and write, and this stimulated their taste for inventions, practical knowledge, and technology. Less educated farmers and tradesmen found political expression in the populist Republican Party, founded by Thomas Jefferson and opposed to the Federalist Party of Eastern urban elites. The election of Andrew Jackson in 1828 advanced populism and accentuated the American tendency toward anti-intellectualism at the expense of "effete" or refined culture associated with older elites of the Eastern seaboard.

This relative freedom, opportunity, and egalitarian ethos of early America facilitated a form of social mobility independent of titles and ancestry. Success was measured more by the general criterion of money, as against the inheritance of wealth or social position. As a result, male primogeniture was progressively supplanted everywhere by rough equality of inheritance. Daughters received the movable articles and cash to facilitate their conjugal lives; land was bequeathed mainly to sons. These innovations went hand in hand, especially in the North, with a commercial ethos so strong that J. Hector St. John de Crève-coeur (1782), an eighteenth-century European visitor to the United States, could praise "the bright idea of property" and the mutation of Europeans into Americans. New immigrants began to forget their former servitude and to experience the "glow" of ownership. In this sense, even before industrialization, America was modern in both its broad political participation and its ideologies of autonomy, possessive individualism, commerce, and the inherent value of every man's opinion.

This polity and culture emerged before or along with America's industrial revolution. In 1799, Eli Whitney and Simon North organized assembly lines in their Connecticut gun factory and began mass production. Such innovations soon spread to the production of clocks, textiles, and steam engines. In 1816, an American coined the term "technology," and by 1830, the assembly line with interchangeable parts became known as the "American system of manufacture." Similarly, the mass production of clocks and watches fostered a time-thrift ethos that had been first enunciated by Benjamin Franklin in 1748 with his dictum, "Remember that TIME is Money." By 1850, mass-produced pocket watches—using cheaper wooden gears instead of brass ones—were in wide distribution and used by Americans to organize household tasks and cottage industries more efficiently and to coordinate activities with others outside the home.

The early American bourgeoisie reinforced the values of entrepreneurship and hard work, and it was just this emerging indigenous class of commercial elites who led the revolution. Only the later Bill of Rights, the Jackson presidency in 1828, the Emancipation Proclamation, and the women's and Civil Rights movements extended these rights to almost all adult citizens. Unlike members of the bourgeoisie in European states of that time, however, early American leaders rarely claimed to be aristocrats or tried to preserve their privileges and traditions. Nor did they meet overt opposition to the ideals of freedom and equality from other groups already within the emerging United States, despite differences in the political outlooks of the North and South. Indeed, when the Industrial Revolution and a labor movement appeared in the latter half of the nineteenth century, they emerged within an already existing cultural consensus that equality meant legal or political equality (of white males) and that freedom meant freedom from government constraint.

By contrast, capitalist elites in Europe more often sought to join the aristocracy and frequently collaborated with it in resisting the expansion of political equality. While their strategy turns out to have been moderately successful, insofar as European capitalists eventually acquired a reasonable share of elite positions (Mayer 1981), it also reduced the chances of the new industrial working classes of Europe to enjoy much individual social mobility. This relative lack of interclass mobility strengthened class solidarity in both the elites' defense of class privilege and the working people's struggle for political equality. Thus, in Europe the ideal and demand of the new working class was for social democracy, not merely for a bourgeois democracy of individual rights, as in the United States.

Whereas the term "social democracy" has become common in Europe, it has been largely absent in America. In other words, the formal legal equality emphasized in American ideology and practice has been directly associated with a conception of individual freedom rather than with the more social or class-based conception typical of European democracies. In contrast to Europeans, who shaped a more collectivist notion of equality that fostered a socialist working class, Americans dealt with the tensions between liberty and equality by emphasizing the preeminence of private rights and decentralization. This democratic but preindustrial political culture was noted by Alexis de Tocqueville in the first volume of *Democracy in America* (1835), where he reported on the middle-class character of American populism. He observed that while the federal system of decentralization encouraged local self-government on a daily basis, private religiosity limited the necessity and role of the government in moral regulation. Thus, a radically democratic politics was practiced in a conservative social and moral context (Ryan 1989, 20; Pessen 1990).

The separation of church and state and extensive self-government also fostered a pragmatic, albeit equivocal, public secularism along with private religiosity. The sons of English Puritans longed to retrieve in New England the fading faith of their fathers in the idea that evil was a privation, an alienation from God. But in pragmatic and increasingly secular and urban America, evil had come to be lodged more in the world than in the soul, a view that was not necessarily shared by the preachers of the hinterland. People were no longer thought to be directly complicit in their own suffering as Satan now took up residence everywhere. The only way out was to rid the material world of spirits and thus make it available to be worked on in practical, instrumental ways. To be an American Protestant, and then merely an American, meant to pursue the secular salvation of an isolated, solitary self (Delbanco 1989, 1995).

In sum, openness to organizational innovation, a fascination with inventions, and the reliance on labor-saving machinery built for a short life all characterized Americans even before the Civil War. Innovations were not drawn from the cutting edge of knowledge and science. Instead, like certain industrializing nations today, the orientation was toward mass production and marketing, as American development emphasized systems of organization, storage, and transportation. Thus, America's culture and polity were already subject to the intense contradictions of modernization before the industrial revolution that came with the Civil War. This background, plus the United States' huge internal market, natural resources, and international domination for two decades after World War II, made Americans insensitive to the frequent tensions among economic productivity, culture, and traditional social institutions that are a typical anguish of most modernizing nations.

CHANGING DEFINITIONS AND PRACTICES OF AMERICAN ETHNICITY

This political and religious culture was well consolidated before non-Protestant immigration accelerated, when America began its massive industrialization after the Civil War. As newcomers began to arrive from the poor, mostly Catholic or Orthodox countries of Europe, ethnic stratification opposed newly arriving groups to those who were American born. Nativist sentiment and racial prejudice justified the restriction of these aliens to ethnic ghettos and dirty and dangerous jobs. But the second and especially third generations were able, at least in part, to keep or restore the old rituals in their homes, even while adopting new customs in public spaces; to advance economically; and to move up the job ladder and out of ethnic enclaves. "Here individuals of all nations are melted into a new race, whose labors . . . will one day cause great changes in the world," wrote Crèvecoeur (1792, 49).

African and European bond-laborers faced overwhelming common exploitation, made worse for Africans by their perpetual enslavement and that of their progeny (Fields 1990, 102). Thus, Thomas Best of the Virginia colony could write, "My Master Atkins hath sold me for £150 sterling like a damn slave" (quoted in Kingsbury 1906–1935, 4:235). From a purely economic viewpoint, Englishmen also could have been enslaved. But white owners resisted this, despite their generalized profit interests and the general cultural racism of the times. This restraint seemed to reflect a respect for the (albeit limited) rights to citizenship that English peasants had won in the civil wars of the seventeenth century in Britain. The concept and practice of slavery thus embodied not only cultural values and economic interests, but also a hard-won political status of Englishmen, however poor and indentured—a status that they were ever in danger of losing (Morgan 1975; Smaje 2001). Ethnic discrimination later melded with racism as various East and South European "others" struggled in America to become white. Indeed, beliefs in race and ethnicity transferred the social stigma attached to slavery to those who performed unskilled labor more generally, thereby coloring the social relations of the new "wage slaves" and their nineteenth-century industrial masters. Their ethnic or biological character became the explanation of their penury, not economic exploitation (R. Williams 1990). Thus non-Protestant immigrants after the Civil War were relegated to a netherworld between "white" and "black." In the vernacular of the time, these "Hebrews," "Celts," "Mediterraneans," "Iberics," "Slavs," and "Teutons" had obvious reason to disassociate themselves from blacks, and they played an active role in forging a monolithic whiteness that excluded blacks and furthered their objectification and isolation (Jacobson 1998; Ignatiev 1995). Newly white groups also changed in the process. For example, in addition to becoming more racist, Jews adopted a more Protestant, Anglo masculinity, while Catholics became more individualistic (Brodkin 1998).

America is thus defined, as Lawrence Fuchs (1990) put it, by both the *pluribus* and the *unum*. Indeed, each of these terms expresses a continuing ideal of America and its self-image as "the first new nation" (Lipset 1979, esp. v–xi, 207–348). *Unum* suggests a union or singleness, the "pot" into which all groups will melt, becoming a social and cultural "people" whose distinctions will be achieved and not ascribed. In contrast, *pluribus* suggests various peoples and a pluralist society, a mosaic of particular groups who preserve their ascribed social and cultural attributes (Lyman 2001, 1).

Immigration slowed by the third decade of the twentieth century as the Industrial Revolution matured. Since the Immigration Reform Act of 1965, however, a new wave of immigration again has altered the ethnic and racial composition of the United States. In 1900 about 14 percent of the American population was foreign born. By 1980 only 6.2 percent was foreign born, and today it is about 11 percent of U.S. residents. Most of these new immigrants are visibly nonwhite and non-European, from Central America, the Caribbean, Mexico, India, China, the Philippines, and Vietnam. Nativists, as they did a century ago, have sought with some success to limit immigration; have English as the sole official language; and exclude newcomers from public services, unions, neighborhoods, and better jobs. As before, such policies are likely to fade as members of these new groups and their children succeed economically and contribute more evidently to the democratic pluralism of the United States. For example, eighty-two different languages are taught today in the Los Angeles schools; since the implementation of the North American Free Trade Agreement (NAFTA) the area conjoining Mexico and the United States (locally called Amexica) is becoming a distinct cultural zone as the "borders" get pushed back on either side; and "pan-Asianism" is strong among second-generation Asian Americans (Min 2001).

Thus, although successive waves of immigration have induced a system of stratification based on ethnicity, this usually shifts toward class position achieved since the time of arrival. The distinctness of groups that immigrated earlier tends to blur, and the hostility displayed toward "dumb Swedes," "Polacks," or "Dagos" gets transferred to poorer ethnic groups who more recently reached the United States. Correspondingly, as assimilation has proceeded, especially among white Christian "ethnics," the sense of ethnicity itself has evolved. Ethnic identity has become more selective and refers to a narrower range of customs and affiliations. As far as whites are concerned, ethnicity often has more a symbolic than a practical meaning. For example, Alba (1990) could identify only 2 percent of white Christian ethnics who had ever been helped in business by their peers of the same origin; only 4 percent claimed to have experienced discrimination because of their ethnicity; 1 percent ate ethnic foods daily; almost none were fluent in the language of their ethnic group; 2 percent were members of ethnic lodges or social clubs; and 11 percent lived in neighborhoods that had any significant concentration of their peers. Similarly, the 1990 census revealed that after residing in the United States for ten years, a majority of immigrants mastered the English language. The children of immigrants tend to be partly bilingual and largely proficient in English, whereas their children speak English only, unless they learned a second language at college. (Hence the description of America as a graveyard for languages.) Further, by 1996 foreign-born immigrants who had arrived before 1970 had a home ownership rate of 75.6 percent, higher than the 69.8 percent rate among native-born Americans.

American popular culture and mass marketing also tend to homogenize ethnic groups with their casualness of speech and lack of social deference or distinctions. People are absorbed into a culture of consumption that was launched in the nineteenth century by department stores that democratized shopping. The new and often palatial department stores, unlike neighborhood stores or elite boutiques, welcomed everyone, regardless of ethnicity (Hall and Lindholm 1999). Mass media, advertising, spectator sports, and corporate chains of stores and eateries are other forces of homogenization.

White Americans also tend to marry outside their primary groups, thereby replacing single ethnic identities with mixed ones and encouraging self-definition merely as "American." This shift is illustrated by the views of one woman on her husband's ethnicity: "He really likes his Russian Jew part. We have a mezuzah on the front door. He converted to Catholicism when he married me. He grew up with his mother and she was Baptist, so he was kind of raised in that tradition. But he likes his Russian Jew part more, he feels close to being Catholic and that part goes together more. They are kind of similar" (Waters 1990, 91–92).

Intermarriage also is an important aspect of the blurring of racial and religious boundaries. For example, when Tiger Woods was celebrated for winning the Masters Golf Tournament in 1997, he insisted that he was not only black, but also Asian and European, since his father is African American and his mother is Thai. Foreign-born Asians and Hispanics have higher rates of intermarriage than do U.S.-born whites and blacks. By the third generation, one-third of Hispanic women are married to non-Hispanics, and 41 percent of Asian American women are married to non-Asians. Between 1980 and 2000 the number of interracial marriages tripled, from 310,000 to over 1.1 million. The number of "mixed-race" births has risen twenty-six times faster than that for any other group. Since 1960 Jews marrying gentiles has increased from 10 percent to 52 percent. Sixty-five percent of Japanese Americans marry persons with no Japanese antecedents. The number for Native Americans is 70 percent (Wong 1998). Thus Tiger Woods is not alone, for many Americans reject U.S. racial classifications, including the census category "other non-whites." They call themselves, or have been called, hapa, rainbow people, lumbees, halfies, mixed, Jackson whites, Cablinasian (as Tiger Woods does); or Caucasian, black, Native American, and Asian; or some two hundred other identities (Lyman 1998, 339–340; see also Spencer 1997; Root 1992; Sider 1993).

Similarly, particular nationalities of origin get melded into larger categories, as when Japanese and Koreans both become "Asians" or when Poles and Irish become "American Catholics." Political strategies explain the use of the term "Asian American," particularly in the Western states, where early Japanese and Chinese immigrants met with considerable discrimination (Takaki 1989). Americans of Latin American or Spanish origin also are a mixed group. Puerto Ricans were granted citizenship in 1917; Mexicans in the southwest were in the future United States before Pilgrims arrived at Plymouth Rock. Dominican and Colombian immigrants enjoy dual nationality and are allowed to vote in the United States and in their homelands. Yet increasingly, all these peoples are becoming "Hispanic." The choice of the term "African American" also reveals aspirations to assimilate, or at least to render racial classifications less dominant, especially among younger Americans (Korgen 1998). Unlike the former term of choice, "American Negro," it makes Americanness the primary determinant of identity, deemphasizes the unique experience of slavery, and implies that all persons of African origin immigrated to the United States like everyone else. Yet, as pointed out by Patterson (1997, 1998), this strategy does not always work. Racists often distinguish black strangers (Nigerians, Haitians) from the descendants of slaves, whereas nonblack immigrants of color may complain that concern about racism has been arbitrarily narrowed to cover exclusively black-white relations.

With minorities becoming more "white," these shifts have inspired fears among some whites of becoming more "black," especially to the extent that blackness is associated with stigmatized or unfree labor. The small number of Africans in early Virginia colony basically shared the status of indentured servants, with inheritable African slaves becoming the dominant form of unfree labor only after about 1680. Indeed the consolidation of the slave system created the racial category of "black," rather than racial distinctions creating the institution of chattel slavery. This is, of course, essentially the classic argument made by Eric Williams in *Capitalism and Slavery* (1961; see also R. Williams 1990). Thus the essentialization of race as a biological category was in fact a historical and political-economic process that is still ongoing, and contested, today. Indeed, white identity today still is considerably based on class, as noted by inner city children who accuse academic achievers of being "too white" or when poor whites become possibly less white because they are poor. This is shown in studies by John Hartigan (1999) of low-income whites in Detroit. Poor whites

in one neighborhood of the city, Briggs, were called "hillbillies" by more prosperous whites and stigmatized even more than poor blacks in the area, probably
because poverty is particularly threatening to normative whiteness. In another
neighborhood, Corktown, old-timer white residents distanced themselves
from the class privileges and racial attitudes of newcomers. And in Warrendale,
working-class whites who opposed the opening of an Afrocentric school were
tagged "racist" by outsiders and the local press. The concerns of these working-
class whites, though racially tinged, were complex and not altogether unrea-
sonable, but because these whites were unskilled in middle-class norms of
political correctness about "race talk," their discourse was stigmatized and dismissed as "racist."

  None of this is to say that racism is not alive and well in America. It is. But it
has diminished in overt expression and shifted to more subtle or indirect forms.
"Petty apartheid" and "cultural racism" have greatly diminished. Blacks are no
longer excluded from using public facilities or applying for housing or jobs.
Hip-hop is pursued by white teenagers in greater numbers than by blacks,
whereas black youth can be as avidly consumerist as anyone else. Moreover,
open expressions of racist sentiment have become unacceptable in public and
polite settings. Yet "structural" racism and racial discrimination continue
apace. American neighborhoods remain largely segregated, American public
schools are *more* segregated than they were thirty years ago, blacks are still three
times more likely to be poor than whites, and ten times more black males than
white aged 25–29 are behind bars. Many are there not for violent offenses but
for breaking the drug laws, which seem aimed directly at blacks. For example,
the penalty for possessing five grams of crack cocaine, the form most widely
used in black districts, is the same as the penalty for possessing one hundred
times as much of the powdered variety, which whites prefer. This harks back to
racist anti-opium laws of the nineteenth century, which severely punished
opium *smoking,* preferred by Chinese, while wholly ignoring opium *drinking,*
which was widely practiced by whites (Fossett and Seibert 1997; Mills 1997).

  One example of the decline of cultural racism is that Trent Lott stepped
down as Republican leader of the Senate in December 2002 because of racially
insensitive remarks, even though most other Republican senators, including
the man who replaced him, have voting records on affirmative action, human
rights, and reactionary judgeships comparable to Mr. Lott's. Indeed, the New
Right has brought a new discourse on race—a new racism, if you will—that is
appropriate to a lower-middle-class backlash against perceived advantages for
minorities (and women); to lower income whites' declining shares of income,

wealth, and opportunity; and to new pressures of cultural and commercial homogenization. This discourse challenges the liberal consensus that emerged during the quarter-century after World War II while simultaneously distancing itself from the explicit and essentialist racism of the past (Ansell 1997). Instead it deploys a universalist terminology, emphasizes individual achievement, opposes "reverse discrimination," and advances occasional compliant black persons—such as Supreme Court justice Clarence Thomas or National Security Adviser Condoleezza Rice—as exemplars of the new postracist policies and society. Meanwhile, institutionalized racism persists but is now denied because it is largely indirect.

To a degree, then, the very fact of cultural homogenization is often mixed with a politics of assertion of racial or ethnic identity, indirectly by whites, in-your-face by minorities. This is seen in many university programs of multiculturalism, even those that take themselves to be politically radical. For example, when Henry Giroux insists on "the necessity of creating an insurgent multiculturalism as a basis for a new language of educational leadership that allows students and others to move between cultures, to travel within zones of cultural differences" (1993, 14), he unwittingly treats cultural identity as something that one shops for at the food court, a matter of personal taste. If so, one would assume that ethnicity would go the way of most consumer commodities: mass production, lower costs, and less commitment to any particular item.

The changes that characterize the definition and the practice of ethnicity are also contradictory and diffuse, however. In 1997, for example, South Carolinians argued ferociously about the Confederate battle flag flying above the state capitol, an issue so hot that George W. Bush and John McCain refused to take a position on it during the Republican primary race in 2000. Locally, one prominent South Carolinian called the flag a symbol of "venom" and "demagoguery" and demanded its removal, while his major opponent defended the flag as a symbol of respect for one's ancestors and the sacrifices they made (quoted in Stark 1999, 6). Yet given the complexity of racial politics in America, the state's leading critic of the flag was South Carolina's white governor, while its defender was the black police chief of the second largest city, Charleston (see Pressley 2000; Nixon 2000).

On one side of such debates, champions of the melting pot plead economic and political integration into "mainstream" American skills and values. Correspondingly, they emphasize the universalistic properties of productivity and achievement. As a result, there is pressure on immigrants and minorities to assimilate and to believe that their difficulties in the United States are not caused by discrimination but by their foreign ways. In this rhetoric, the hardships of immigrants were and still are interpreted in terms of a residual otherness due to insufficient Americanization. On the other side, however, some Americans are tempted to assume that "If everything is voluntaristic, the individual is not ethnic. But if everything is clan, the individual is not modern" (Wolfe 1990, 29, 30). Indeed, rather than serving either clan or modernity, a commoditized multiculturalism may well satisfy the needs of transnational capital for "multicultural" workers with flexible personalities to go with the new flexible mode of production. Moreover, after markets are segmented in terms of age, gender, and lifestyle, the further division of people into transnational ethnic identities may well create further market niches to exploit. Thus it may be no coincidence that "multiculturalism" gained currency among American intellectuals in the 1980s, just when the Reagan administration was simultaneously promoting both international "competitiveness" and "states' rights" (Flournoy 1992). Other intellectuals argue that the partial return to ethnic identity is the unavoidable response to the growing alienation fostered by a mass society devoted to globalization (Castells 1996). The larger and more rationalized the "system" becomes, the more one feels alienated from it, and the more one retreats to peers, roots, and nostalgias.

In part because of its multiple ethnicities and their diverse connotations, the unifying culture of the United States is not ethnic but primarily political. To create themselves as a nation and as a people, Americans rely mainly on their institutions and the inculcation of their national religion, Americanism, rather than on territorial, racial, linguistic, or religious commitments, as do most other nations. American nationalism is "civic" much more than "ethnic." Indeed, because of the primarily political and institutional sources of American national identity, European intellectuals often have denied the existence of a specifically American culture. In the writings of Pirandello, Duhamel, Celine, or Gramsci, America evoked only Fordism, Taylorism, or other forms of economic production. In the sociology of Werner Sombart, American culture also was reduced to economic success, to roast beef and apple pie. The common denominator of all these European writers is to argue, with Paul Valéry, that America had and has no history but only an economic geography. In other words, its organization and its culture continue to represent immediate and ahistorical responses to a large supply of land, water, mineral deposits, rich topsoil, and temperate climate. Some American intellectuals have echoed this discourse, asserting that Americans are "born modern" and that Americans' exceptionalism has little to do with the actual history of the American nation or with its cultural and ideological elaborations.

But the political nature of ethnicity in America in fact reduces proportionately its economic components. At the same time, the vagueness of the national civic culture and the private nature of most ethnic experiences aggravate the pain of belonging to an "ethno-underclass" (Wolfe 1990, 31), since being left out is more devastating when nearly everyone else is included.

One sign of the declining class component of ethnic identification is the decrease in ethnic voting. Voting for persons of one's own ethnicity or race or voting consistently for one party that cannot be explained by other demographic factors has declined greatly in recent decades. The major exceptions are blacks and Jews, whose consistent voting for Democratic candidates, often despite economic class interests, attests both to the continuity of their political concerns since the New Deal and to continuing racism and anti-Semitism in the United States. Moreover, ethnic and racial tensions have waxed and waned over time, usually growing more intense with political and economic changes such as war, recession, increased immigration, declines in the segregation of job levels, or the displacement or redistribution of jobs or social benefits in favor of disadvantaged groups (Olzak 1992). That is, nativism, racism, and ethnic tensions (and hence ethnic voting) tend to increase with greater competition as dominant groups feel threatened by the fragility of their own position or by rises in that of subordinated groups. Generally, however, ethnic or "hyphenated" Americans begin with cultural commitments to the left of the hyphen but soon enter political alliances to its right.

Amid these various tensions and contradictions is the challenge to discover how the early cultural and political modernity of the United States leads Americans both to affirm and to forget their cultures of origin and how past and present pressures for both diversity and homogeneity interact. To view America exclusively as a modern mass society is to overlook the arrested character of the beliefs and practices of all colonizing or exiled peoples who preserve in a kind of time capsule certain forms that have since been abandoned in the country of origin (Kubler 1963). For example, some aspects of American common law look like quaint or obsolescent legalisms that were abandoned earlier by British legislatures as obstacles to further political or economic development (Horwitz 1977). Similarly, the descendants of Irish and German farmers who settled in southern Illinois continue the models of succession of their forbearers: the Irish give land to only one of the sons; the Germans share the farm equally among all children (Salamon 1980, 1994). Likewise, earlier African cultural traits persist not only among Gullahs, who escaped plantations to the islands off South Carolina, but also among other African Americans, as well as among many Southern whites. Much Appalachian music and dance, for example, combines Irish and African traits.

Traces of former cultures also continue in America through national churches (Brown and Coelho 1986). Indeed, the religious architecture and practices of American ethnic enclaves often reflect tastes that prevailed in the old countries at the time that immigrants left them. Even in the case of what became American Catholicism, its constituent Irish, Polish, German, or Italian communities each have had their own parishes, their own priests, and their own interpretations of dogmas, which are similar to those prevailing in the old country at the time of the great departure. Other practices concern the retention of words or mottos, holidays and rites, foods or spices.

Surviving cultural practices may be modest, sequestered, or reduced to folklore, but they nevertheless form important parts of ethnic and therefore American character. Thus, to see ethnicity and Americanism as mutually exclusive is misleading, as though more of one meant less of the other. Instead, we find it useful to distinguish identification and identity. On this point, Simon Herman argues that "a glance at most studies of Jewish communities in the Diaspora shows that they are at best studies of Jewish identification. They may deal with the process by which the individual comes to see himself as a part of the Jewish group. . . . But very few of them are studies of Jewish identity, of what being Jewish means, of what kinds of Jewishness develop in majority culture" (1977, 28). This difference between identification and identity also was noted by Dashefsky, who defined group *identification* as "a generalized attitude indicative of a personal attachment to the group, as a positive orientation toward being a member of the group." In contrast, he explained *identity* as "a higher level concept, as the sector of the personal system that maintains personal continuity through the coherent organization of information about the individual" (1976, 8).

In studying the various ethnic communities that make up the United States, we could attach parallel meanings to the concepts of ethnic identification and identity. Identification thereby would be treated as an important subcategory of the much broader concept of identity. This seems to be the case with many recent immigrant segments of the U.S. population, who retain a strong ethnic identity even as they acquire a firm American civic identification. But such an adaptation also depends on how that group uses its ethnic past. The transformation of American Negroes into African Americans, for example, involved both the recovery of and commitment to Africa, as well as the affirmation of a primary American identity. For others, of course, ethnic identity and national identification may be almost the same. This is true for many Anglo-Americans, but it also helps explain why a significant proportion of first-generation immigrants returned to their countries of origin and why many who stayed thought of themselves always as sojourners and never as members of American society, much as American oil workers for Arameo have neither an Arab identity nor a political identification with the Saudi state. Many immigrants to America still return to ancestral grounds to display new wealth, to discover cousins left behind, or to die and be buried. Thus, the notion of ethnicity first served to distinguish native sons and daughters from newcomers from other lands. But this has changed. For most people today, to be fully American means that one comes from somewhere else and also has the right to affirm that filiation.

In sum, pluralism and unity remain in dialectical tension in the United States as elsewhere. Despite discrimination against many and the resistance or separation of some, immigrants, and especially their progeny, have largely participated in America's system of voluntary pluralism, even as they assimilate into the political framework of civic unity based on the still-to-be realized myth of equal rights. In *Redburn* Herman Melville wrote, "You cannot spill a drop of American blood without spilling the blood of the whole world. . . . Our blood is as the flood of the Amazon, made up of a thousand currents all pouring into one." Today more Americans see this vision as a dream more than a destiny and view the United States as neither a melting pot nor a mosaic but more like a kaleidoscope, an ever-changing pattern of shifting, mutually defining parts whose members are more than strangers if less than friends, who hope for a civic culture that allows each to respect the others' quests, that permits no group to degrade others or to depose them from civil dignity.

DECENTRALIZATION AND THE AMBIGUOUS STATUS OF THE STATE

The early development of a democratic commercial culture, like ethnic assimilation and amnesia, has a particular character in the United States. So, too, the state in America has a distinct role and image. The state has no legal majesty or aura of the divine, unlike centralized societies such as France or Japan. As the colonies united, the national government was one legal entity among many and barely superordinate to others. Indeed, until the Civil War the United States were a plural, not a singular. In 1812, for example, people said that "The United States *are* at war with England." An ethos of individualism also encouraged a disregard for the state, as did the early separation of church and state, which left the first as a depository of personal morals and the latter as a largely pragmatic instrument of collective utility. Thus, Americans often use state or federal channels to advance their interests but not to overcome their estrangement.

The equivocal distinction between state and federal authorities and between public and private concerns also contributes to the ambiguous status of the state. Many Americans claim that decentralization is synonymous with democratization because it keeps elected officials close to their constituents, encourages local voluntary groups, and fosters more social innovations or experiments. They contrast the flexibility and grassroots participation of decentralized institutions to the insensitive rigidity of centralized bureaucracies. Yet historically in America, decentralization has supported privacy and the protection of property and has thereby fostered social atomization, economic inequality, and racial or ethnic discrimination.

American decentralization is thus a Janus-like figure with contradictory faces. The analysis of legal issues associated with the history of slavery offers a case in point. As shown by Tocqueville's traveling companion and friend, Gustave de Beaumont, in his novel *Marie: Ou, L'esclavage aux Etats-Unis,* the personal authority of slave owners over their labor force was not universal or absolute. Not only did some state legislatures forbid owners from teaching their slaves how to read and write, as they suspected this would undermine slavery, but they also restricted manumission—the freeing of slaves. In short, while slavery was institutionalized in order to facilitate the accumulation of private wealth, state authorities did not always trust private slaveholders in this regard. Further, the notion of "states' rights," which goes with decentralization, had ambiguous effects on the perpetuation of slavery. While slaveholders wanted to be able to cross state borders freely in order to recapture marooning slaves, they were reluctant to require the intervention of federal authorities. This sometimes led to the loss of slaves, since some states were keen to assert their sovereignty and did not want to be invaded by strangers. Similar contradictions often characterized the conduct of individual slaveholders. Some of them, at least initially, did not distinguish their slaves from their indentured servants, and a few considered that the rights they enjoyed over their slaves were not transferable to their heirs. Conversely, other slaveholders took advantage of the repressive legislation passed by state legislatures to insist that their neighbors impose equally harsh restrictions on *their* slaves. Thus, although decentralization encouraged local laws aimed at perpetuating slavery, it also sometimes undermined it.

The same holds true of the decentralization of American education. Historically, decentralization with local school boards was aimed at maintaining the control by landowners over institutions they had created with their own funds. Later, the local character of schools was supposed to strengthen local ties. Yet this function has not been consistent with economic development at the regional or national levels. Indeed, some school boards have sought to prevent economic development, which they saw as undermining their local power (Vidich and Bensman 1971). Conversely, other boards fought conservative superintendents who had been appointed prior to changes in the community that were brought by economic and social modernization (Gans 1988).

Not only are there too many school boards for efficiencies of scale, but there also are significant differences in the resources they dispose. Indeed, the enormous disparities in both the taxation rates and revenues available to different school boards often stimulate federal authorities to subsidize disadvantaged school districts. Further, politically stable and administratively efficient school districts generally are better able to make use of state or federal programs designed to curtail inequality. Since such districts are most often prosperous, however, the results of such programs may favor rich children and schools over poor ones. Thus decentralization and the corollary weakness of the federal government often serve to maintain local inequities.

The decentralization, along with the constitutional division of powers within the federal government, also heightens the difficulty of introducing reforms. Localism and the separation of powers (unlike European parliamentary democracies) mean that it is nearly impossible to impose party discipline on congresspersons, even by a president whose party has majorities in both the House of Representatives and the Senate. Moreover, the rise of telepolitics and the runaway costs of campaigning have made congresspeople deeply dependent on funding from groups that usually can block legislation they oppose. American policy in the Israel-Palestine dispute or over the ease of purchase and availability of guns have long been cases in point. The strongest interest group of all, however, has been the upper capitalist class, which today is increasingly international. Republicans and Democrats alike receive about 70 percent of their funding from corporate Political Action Committees (PACs), although the dollar amounts going to Republicans have been far larger. But even the Democratic Leadership Council, which was instrumental in moving the Democratic Party toward "the mainstream," is financed by Arco (Greider 1992).

Decentralization continues to support the preeminence of private over broader public interests, even as corporations become more national and international in scope. For example, given the increases in geographic mobility of citizens, a federalization of legislation concerning contracts and torts would reduce costly and irrational conflicts as to which state's laws and courts have jurisdiction in particular cases. Similarly, to the extent that individual wealth today involves stocks, bonds, and other assets rather than land, it would be easier for federal than state authorities to monitor movements of properties subject to federal estate taxes. The same holds true of formal schooling. Even though most Americans equate education with a form of human capital that requires personal financial investments to yield diffuse dividends, they resist federal involvement in schooling. This is particularly striking in view of the fact that federal courts are entitled to intervene whenever interstate commerce is involved, and the linkage between formal schooling and access to national labor markets is clear. Similarly, high school students' readiness for college is assessed by a private firm's test of college *aptitude,* rather than by tests of academic *performance,* which are run by the state in other advanced societies. Perhaps the most dramatic anomaly of state and federal powers was the patchwork of voting methods among different states, and among different counties within Florida alone, in the 2000 presidential election. Both Republican and Democratic candidates exploited this anomaly to their advantage. In the end, George W. Bush won procedurally, even though the total votes cast favored Albert Gore.

Elite groups, who most determine the nature and content of the law, make a selective use of decentralization. They justify it in terms of general values such as democracy or local autonomy while using it to protect particular interests such as avoidance of tax or liability. The "haves" of all institutional systems (churches, labor, universities, and most predominantly businesses) keep inventing reasons for opposing federal intervention as unjust or irrational, except when it comes to their special privileges. For example, the problem of identifying and controlling toxic substances is of great importance to chemical companies, which have learned that neither they nor consumers have the authority to determine what is acceptable. Only government can do that. But which government—federal or state? Today in contrast to yesterday, giant chemical firms with multiple locations usually have a vested interest in obtaining a national definition of the needs of the community instead of a multiplicity of local definitions. It is generally easier to respond to a single set of federal guidelines than to numerous local ones, especially when national legislation is more easily subject to national corporate direction. Moreover, enforcement is kept limited by the understaffing and underfunding of the Office of Toxic Substances of the Environmental Protection Agency. Such conditions, however, do not lessen the antigovernment propaganda of big business in general.

Similarly, American capitalists play the game of decentralization with regard to labor relations, since an institutionalized segmentation of the labor market works in their favor. But capitalists favor centralization with regard to tariffs in order to facilitate price protection and the streamlining of mass markets. And they adopt mixed strategies toward product liability, depending on whether federal standards will be stricter or more relaxed than those of each state.

In general, American leaders and citizens are ambivalent and often willfully ignorant about the role of the state. Since Franklin Roosevelt, for example, political elites have found it necessary to plan. But they have cloaked their departures from laissez-faire and attempted to make their interventions appear to be short term and merely pragmatic. That is, they have opposed statism in principle even while advancing it in practice. This obfuscates the planning functions of the state for what they are and must be. Indeed, if the role of government were more clearly understood, the federal bureaucracies might be fewer and more focused. Ironically, the American ideology of antistatism has helped to foster large and unwieldy federal bureaucracies with contradictory policies and practices.

This ambivalence parallels the conflicting strategies of private corporations. On the one hand, as noted, corporate elites have recognized that their interest usually lies in obtaining a national definition of the needs of the community (and federal subsidies) instead of a multiplicity of local definitions. Efforts of major corporations to guide the federal government's legal definitions of national needs also have fostered integration between big business and big government. On the other hand, the pretense of the limited state means that huge federal allocations are haphazard, reflecting the crisis of the moment and the power of interest groups rather than any coherent collective vision. Years ago, Ferdinand Lundberg (1969) spoke of corporate elites as "finpols"—financial politicians whose economic role and interests impelled their deep involvement in governmental life. Such an integration of economic and political spheres enables successful entrepreneurs to appeal simultaneously to the centralizing ideologies of rationality and modernity and to their decentralizing counterparts of liberty and local autonomy, depending on the corporate interests at stake.

The persistence of political decentralization in the United States also reflects the diverging evolutions of America's economic and political structures. Economic activity has been guided largely by the dynamics of market competition and oligopolies, both of which tend to expand to national and international scope. In contrast, political structures remain defined more by territory, tradition, and legitimacy rather than by efficiency and profit. Hence, political structures are more oriented toward the past and its ideological elaboration. Correspondingly, in the cultural sphere people simultaneously experience freedom as an expansion of consumer choices and as alienation, a loss of legitimacy and meaning. Such a layering of contradictory experiences often engenders a literally surreal quality of contemporary life—one layer of reality on top of another, contradictory one.

Despite conflicting trends in the evolution of the public sector, the multiplicity of governmental layers means that federal, state, and local governments of the United States together have more employees and funds in proportion to population or gross national product (GNP) than many countries that Americans have called socialist. Americans increasingly live on government largess—corporations, farmers, and schools get subsidies, allowances, and contracts, and individuals benefit from social insurance, medical care, housing allowances, and the like. Some 15 percent of the labor force works for one or another governmental agency, and despite recent declines in rates of the federal government's growth, local and state governments have increased dramatically in recent decades. So has taxation. Indeed, with the end of the Cold War and with greater efforts at "competitiveness," there has been a devolution of federal activities to state and local governments, whose spending has increased accordingly. By 1990 state and local spending—the majority supported by state and local taxes, but some by federal grants—had grown to over 13 percent of the gross domestic product (GDP) (Donahue 1992, 18).

Thus, the historical growth of state intervention has been a significant facet of the rationalization of American institutions. Despite the state's current low level of legitimacy, its involvement is of central importance politically and economically for four principal reasons. First, regardless of populist resistance, the American state has become a major economic actor in its own right, accounting for about one-third of the GNP. In the energy industry alone, for example, the state intervenes directly through tax breaks to domestic oil extractors; subsidized credit to producers of hydropower and gasohol; environmental restrictions on coal, gasoline, and nuclear power; the maintenance of strategic oil reserves; the direct production of nuclear fuel; and military aid or intervention to protect energy suppliers such as Saudi Arabia or Kuwait.

Second, the American political economy has become so complex that it requires greater guidance by the state to pay for the "external" costs of production (such as unemployment or environmental pollution), to coordinate interoligopolistic initiatives, to smooth out the business cycle, and sometimes to preserve market competition (as in the AT&T devolutions or Microsoft case). Indeed, soon after the opening of the twentieth century, leading corporate capitalists discovered how to use the authority of the state to stabilize their competitive activities and avoid some of the ruinous aspects (especially for them) of truly free competition. Reform legislation that fostered these ends was advanced by leading industrialists yet passed under the banner of the Progressives with the leadership of an ostensibly trustbusting president, Theodore Roosevelt (Kolko 1967). Such limited initiatives sufficed until the Great Depression, when it became evident that massive state intervention was necessary to restart the collapsed economy. Franklin Roosevelt's New Deal and then the war economy were the major responses, which have continued and expanded since then.

As the costs of simple labor have become a relatively small component in the total value of goods produced in the United States and as the complex interdependencies of the corporate economy have increased, there also has been a corresponding increase in the need for long-term predictability. Many corporate projects operate within a twenty-year planning horizon and require up to a decade to amortize their initial start-up investments. State coordination, subsidies, and bailouts at the national level and international agencies like the IMF or the Overseas Private Investment Corporation (OPIC) provide finance or security on such investments.

An example of continued government involvement in interoligopolistic coordination is provided by a series of actions that took place in the early 1950s: bigger, more gas-consuming automobiles were built, a national program of highway construction was initiated, and gas and oil replaced coal as the dominant fuel in public utilities and private firms and homes. The railroad and coal industries suffered as the automobile, oil, and highway construction industries enjoyed federal tax exemptions, budget subsidies, and grants (Bensman 1988, 22). In protecting and regulating the system, the state socializes risks and privatizes profit and thus becomes a corporate welfare state. Its jobs are to maintain industrial peace, civic tranquility and steady consumption, and what is called a stable climate for investment at home and abroad, all requisites of advanced capitalist economies. Criticisms of the enrichment of corporations through the corporate welfare state are stigmatized as "socialist" or "class warfare" and largely excluded from mass media. Such criticisms, in any case, generally are directed against the implementation of particular policies and their abuses, a lack of assistance to the poor, or arrogance of administration, rather than against the very existence of the corporate state. Moreover, even with efforts to curtail or discipline the social services component of government (although not welfare to corporations), these activities grew massively under Ronald Reagan's administration and continued apace under those of George Bush, Bill Clinton, and George W. Bush. All this has been despite efforts to eliminate waste and fraud in government. Thus, despite much rhetoric and some efforts to the contrary, the advanced corporate economy has required a greater (albeit more focused) role of the state.

Third, although globalization in some ways undermines national sovereignty and makes complete independence impossible, the internationalization of the American political economy also has contributed to the growing role of the state. As an increasing percentage of America's GNP is gained from international trade, the political and military activities aimed to protect this trade become more crucial. About five hundred transnational firms account for some 50 percent of international trade, and many of these are American. Similarly, half of the one hundred largest economies of the world are megacorporations, not states (*United Nations Human Development Report* 1997). Further, some 40 percent of international trade is among branches or subsidiaries of single firms, many of which, again, are American. These corporations operate internationally under the aegis of the state, whose foreign policies they shape. Indeed, during their visits abroad, American presidents act increasingly as salesmen for American firms. The repayment of foreign debt, insurance of foreign investments against losses or expropriation, provision of credits to foreign purchasers, continuity or changes in rates of exchange, and maintenance of stability internationally—all are functions of the state. Thus, even as America's military budgets have declined since the collapse of the Soviet Union, the state grows in importance as defender and regulator of America's international commerce.

Fourth, the maintenance of America's global military reach requires an interventionist role for the state. The current military-industrial complex was forged in World War II and has continued since in changing form. For example, success since 1945 in avoiding the use of nuclear weapons was bought at the price of an increased militarization of American society. Because victory in a nuclear exchange meant national disaster, if not extinction, the imperative of military policy was to avoid pushing enemies (or oneself) into situations where the use of nuclear hardware became "necessary." At the same time, in order not to be intimidated by the nuclear capacity of opponents, America (and other nations) maintained its own armaments even while disclaiming any wish to use them. But because they did not wish to use their nuclear capacity, policymakers felt compelled to build up a panoply of other military capabilities so as to have alternative choices of response. The result has been an institutionalized web of the military-industrial political interests and enterprises thought necessary to maintain this massive and now more diversified destructive potential, the most recent addition to which is the Star Wars nuclear defense system, begun under President Reagan, revived by President Clinton, and advanced by President Bush. The threat of terrorism adds another dimension and justification to this militarization and surveillance, now increasingly *within* American society. Perhaps more important, the semimilitarization of the American economy has come to be accepted as normal and permanent by virtually all sectors of society, including the academic, which depends heavily on governmental, and especially military, contracts.

The four factors discussed above have rendered ethnic and racial conflict less useful to the advanced political economy. It no longer makes sense for elites— as it did during early industrialization—to play off one group of workers against another in order to deflate wages. In an oligopolized, internationalized, and high-tech economy, labor costs are less important for production in the core states. Instead, they can be passed along to consumers, who are captives in oligopolized markets; or they can be avoided by exporting wage-competitive production to lower-wage economies such as China or the Philippines; or they can be contracted out to temporary employees, who work for low wages without security or benefits; or they can be automated or merged out of existence. Correspondingly, domestic production in advanced sectors comes to require relatively more investments of capital, technology, and skilled labor. Such labor is harder to train or replace, thereby reducing the incentive of employers to encourage discrimination and competition among ethnic or racial groups that would cut working-class solidarity and demands for better wages. This may explain the crucial role of capitalist corporations and foundations in sponsoring the assimilationist wing of the Civil Rights Movement (the Urban League and the NAACP, but not SNCC or Malcolm X), as well as their support of other moderate groups in the environmental and other movements (Brulle 2000) and their generally reformist political and legislative agendas. With the growth of income inequality for three decades since 1973, however, ethnic and racial conflict again has become useful in redirecting popular energies away from *class* consciousness and political action.

THE EXTENSION OF CORPORATE POWER AND
THE NARROWING OF CIVIC SPACE

The fiscal crisis and slow growth of many economically advanced countries in the 1980s and 1990s were brought on by increased international competition, narrower corporate earnings, and fewer tax revenues between about 1970 and 1995. Moreover, after the opening of a market economy in China in 1979 and the collapse of the Soviet Union by 1992, conservatives claimed victory in the Cold War and leftists were in disarray. During the same period conservative antigovernment and unilateralist political forces gained ideological ascendancy.

There have been two major responses to these interrelated conditions. One has been to reexamine the functions of the state and find ways either to abandon them or to perform them more cheaply through privatization, contracting out, or more entrepreneurial government (Edgell, Walklate, and Williams 1995). A second, more important response has been to give greater freedom to capital to penetrate more and more areas of social and personal life.

The main form of privatization in the United States has been to contract public services to private firms. For example, the state of Florida paroles criminals first sentenced to a jail term into the care of the Salvation Army—about twenty-five thousand at any one time. In many cities, including some big ones, street cleaning, fire fighting, and even policing are now farmed out. "In 1997 Texas passed a law enabling the state's welfare functions to be operated by private firms. The U. S. Postal Service contracts out (or computerizes) most of its internal work. In many American states, prisons are run by private contractors, the largest of which are Corrections Corporation of America and Wackenhut Corporation. Even inmate labor is being privatized—sold for below the minimum wage to such firms as Chevron, Bank of America, Macy's, TWA, AT&T, and IBM" (Parenti 1996, 11; see also Sclar 2000). Joint ventures of government and industry regarding inmate labor are attractive to businesses because prison workers are cheap, speak English, are easy to control, have no political rights or possibility of unionizing, offer fast local turn-around time, and can be used to break or weaken strikers.

The public sector also is being reinvented to be more entrepreneurial as people demand more public services while being less ready to pay taxes to fund them and as fiscal limits push governments to get more for less. Principles of business management, such as flatter hierarchies, the use of competition wherever possible, staying close to the customer, and the decentralization of authority, are now being applied in the public sector (Kanter, Stein, and Jick 1992; Osborne and Gaebler 1992, 19–20; Peters 1992). For example, electronic communications technologies, whether in private or public enterprises, enable bosses to decentralize decision making even while monitoring exactly what staff and workers are doing and when they are doing it.

Another broad response to low productivity, fiscal pressures, international competition, and political shifts has been to extend corporate control to realms of language, emotions, ideas, and activity that previously were reserved for civil society. The capitalist economy also has invaded the domestic realm, as seen in the dramatically increased participation of women in the paid labor force, the use of fast food instead of family dinners, and the commercial sale of human eggs and sperm. Indeed, the percentage of middle-class women in the paid labor force was decreasing in the United States until about 1970, when it began to rise as the middle class started to decline both in numbers and in its proportional shares of national income and wealth. The implication is that more middle-class women had to join or remain in the paid labor force in order to retain a middle level of family income. This shift has been cultural and civic as well as economic, for it also has reallocated the investment of women's time and emotional energy. In 1960 only 10 percent of married women with children under six years old worked outside their homes. Today, about 75 percent do. "As women leave the home sphere, the job culture expands at the expense of the family culture. When women stayed home, they were the guardians and champions of home and family values. [Despite its defects], this division of labor did acknowledge the existence and importance of family activities" (Persell 1994, 643).

Market activities are piercing temporal as well as spatial boundaries. For example, stocks can be traded twenty-four hours a day through exchanges in New York, San Francisco, Tokyo, or London; many more stores are open 24/7; ATMs permit around-the-clock banking; and catalogues, telemarketing, shopping channels, and the Internet bring commerce into the home at any hour of the day or night. One can shop for a mortgage at midnight or have one's car repaired when one is asleep. Kinko's, Wal-Mart, Staples, Home Depot, and other major chains are extending their hours and keeping more stores open all night. While all this brings conveniences to many hard-working individuals, it also results in less time free from market activity. As some people are working at any given time, day or night, seven days a week, and more people are "on call" all the time, fewer hours and spaces are left free from the culture of commerce. Although the average work week per person has declined in the past fifty years, the average number of hours worked per week *per family* has shot up dramatically with greatly increased female participation in the paid labor force. Some fathers work night shifts to be able to take care of their children when their wives are at work during the day. All this lowers boundaries between the commercial field of work and consumerism and the personal sphere of family, community, and play. Noncommercial social activities, including civic involvement, get squeezed out. The choice of going to a PTA meeting or a neighborhood picnic becomes a major decision if there is so little time and so much fatigue. Television, another commercial medium, becomes a preferred alternative. It occupies the children and relaxes the parents.

The market also has invaded areas of private and civic life such as emotions, leisure, and traditionally not-for-profit sectors, among them education and health care. The shift from the feelings and conduct inspired by the term "blood donor" to the practices corresponding to the label "sperm bank" illustrates these changes. The first involves a civic contribution; the latter, a commercial transaction. As more American jobs are in the service sector, people's emotions are brought more fully into the marketplace as part of sales and customer relations. Service jobs are much more likely than manufacturing jobs to require the use of feelings and facial and bodily expressions to advance commercial interests. Flight attendants are only one group of employees for whom the emotional style of offering a service is part of the service itself (Hochschild 1983, 18; Tally 2001). Phone operators, airline agents, bank clerks, and others who provide services are now trained to impose themselves firmly, but nicely, in the interests of a sale.

Social life has always required some management of emotions. We are expected to be happy at weddings and sad at funerals. What is new is that now we are routinely asked to instrumentally manipulate our feelings in the service of for-profit organizations, to sell not only our hands and brains, but also our feelings. Moreover, as emotions are more and more for hire, they increasingly become subject to intensive engineering, administration, and training by employers. As more emotional energy is captured by commerce, it is drained away from family life, neighborly engagements, or informal civic participation.

The increased control of individuals by corporations works not only through an intensification of the methods of control, but also through an extension of the arenas of social life that come under corporate aegis. Thus, Health Management Organizations (HMOs) have largely replaced private medical practices, thereby generating savings that largely become profits and shifting the governance of health services from doctors to corporate administrators and clerks. Nonprofit, community-owned, or doctor-run hospitals and clinics also are becoming business enterprises, often parts of megacorporations such as Humana, Hospital Corporation of America, or American Medical International. This trend has major implications for the cost, organization, governing principles, and quality of health care. Although profit-driven hospitals are touted as more efficient, evidence suggests that they actually are more expensive. For example, in a study of hospitals in Tennessee in 1984, the consulting firm of Booz, Allen, and Hamilton found that costs and charges were substantially higher at for-profit hospitals. While they found the for-profit sector to be more profitable than the nonprofit sector, this was not due to better cost controls, but to fewer nurses and other staff and to higher charges for medical supplies, pharmaceuticals, inhalation therapy, and laboratory services (Persell 1994, 649; see also Lindorff 1992, 130).

Corporations also have entered high culture and popular recreation as well as the emotions. Examples are the placement of museums of history in shopping complexes like New York City's South Street Seaport (Schor 1998); the explosion of business support for and influence on the arts (Naisbitt and Aburdene 1990); the naming of cultural centers after corporations; and the thorough commercialization of sports (Lasch 1978), including the tolerance of misbehavior by professional athletes and the loosening of eligibility criteria for the Olympic games. The same holds true of public rituals, which also are increasingly for hire. For example, during the Reagan presidency, corporations were invited to sponsor the annual Easter egg hunt on the White House lawn, with their products as prizes for the children. Such public dramas are mythical expressions of cultural themes whose performance gives meaning and social cohesion. Yet this civic function of public rituals is undermined as they become commercial productions for private consumption. Corporations also direct beauty contests, spectator sports, game shows, reenactments of battles fought during the Civil War, sound and light shows, and political spectacles or other events staged for a paying audience.

The intrusion of market rationality into all these formerly autonomous spheres weakens civil society in relation to the corporate state. "Moreover, the essentially authoritarian and anti-democratic character of corporate control is more difficult for individuals to understand and respond to than abuses by government. First, whereas State power is exercised primarily through balance or restriction, corporate organizations provide 'disciplinary' structures embodied in routines and technologies that appear to be empowering and apolitical" (Deetz 1995; see also Foucault 1977). Second, the corporations are thought to be private entities and legal individuals. Hence they are easily assumed to be outside the public sphere and beyond citizen control. For most people issues of democracy, representation, freedom of speech, and censorship concern the relationship of individuals and groups to government. Their usual participation in democracy is limited to occasional involvement in elections and meetings. The potential for democracy vested in everyday life is rarely a focal concern. And yet it is in the day-to-day processes of living and the formation of collective responses that democracy either exists and makes a difference or the control by dominant organizations is exercised most deeply (Deetz 1995).

To conclude, the shift of American institutional life from civic to market principles has a number of interrelated consequences. It undermines the legitimacy of the state, encourages telepolitics and media spectacles that transform citizens into spectators or consumers, and generates alienation that may yield both progressive social movements and a reactionary politics of scapegoating and resentment. The shift from civic to market principles also narrows the public space for informed active citizenship and curtails public discussion of alternatives to the culture of commerce. Finally, as both public opinion and state policies are increasingly infused with profit rationality, economic inequality both increases and is perceived as morally neutral.

Chapter 2 A Peculiar Democracy:
Race, Class, and Corporate Power
in the United States

All countries are similar; all countries are unique. Yet the United States appears to be exceptional compared to other capitalist democracies in several respects: the preindustrial modernization of its political culture; ethnic diversity, assimilation, and discrimination; a decentralized system of government; and the pervasiveness of the ideology of the market. In this chapter, we revisit some of these themes from a more political angle, focusing especially on America's history of racial exclusion, the weakness of its labor movement, the absence of a labor or socialist political party, and the extraordinary power of the American capitalist class (Laslett and Lipsett 1974; Kimeldorf and Stepan-Norris 1992, 495). As we shall see, these factors are closely interrelated.

AMERICAN DEMOCRACY AND THE
CONTINUING SIGNIFICANCE OF RACE

In the spirit of progressive evolutionism, the sociologist Talcott Parsons published an essay in 1967 titled as a question: "Full Citizenship for the Negro American?" Parsons assumed that the destiny of America was democratic inclusion of all its citizens, and he reconstructed American history around this goal. The issue for Parsons was the failure to include African Americans within the democratic polity. Just when their turn was about to come—after Catholics and even Jews had been accepted—some historical accident would occur that blocked the unfolding of this destiny.

With such an evolutionary perspective as a starting point, Parsons never felt compelled to address either the causes of racism in America or the struggles of some Americans to overcome it. Indeed, Parsons's essay is more a restatement of the dream of equal opportunity than an analysis of the racism that obstructed its realization (Lyman 1972). This dream of equality was shared by almost everyone and was offered to blacks as the bounty of progress in which they too would soon partake. The dream appears in the very title of Gerald Jaynes and Robin Williams's *A Common Destiny* and was the closing argument of *The Philadelphia Negro,* by the black sociologist and activist W. E. B. DuBois.

Sociologists like Stanford Lyman (1972) and Jennifer Hochschild (1995) and African Americans themselves have reassessed this vision of ultimate inclusion. Although whites and blacks tend to share a belief in the American dream, white satisfaction with this ideology, including its application to blacks, is increasing, whereas blacks are more doubtful, especially as to whether the dream will be realized for them. Paradoxically, poor blacks are more optimistic than middle-class blacks, perhaps because upward mobility has exposed the latter more directly to whites and discrimination by them, especially black professionals who work in predominantly white milieus. By contrast, the relative optimism of poor blacks may reflect their misrecognition of structural obstacles to their advancement. Among lower-income whites, blacks are seen as having many chances to succeed, whereas middle-class whites are only "fairly confident" in blacks' chances (Hochschild 1995). In practical terms, although black middle and professional classes have expanded in recent decades, the conditions of the lower strata have stagnated or declined compared to those of white Americans, and working-class black families remain highly vulnerable. Thus, these reported opinions may reflect mostly a fear of status loss, in that the position of low-income whites and middle- or professional-class blacks are both precarious.

The historic and continuing exclusion of African Americans from full civic and economic participation runs counter to theories of both modernization and general economics. Theorists at least since Max Weber have posited an increasing rationalization of modern societies, as expressed in a rise of laws and rules that in principle apply equally to everyone. Thus the growth in bureaucratic regulation or market forces should lead to a corresponding decline in particularism or personal ties. By this hypothesis, we would expect to find administrative practices that are indifferent to race in the "rational" matching of employees to jobs. Yet such indifference seems regularly not the case, as Mark Granovetter shows in *Getting a Job* (1995). Instead, personal contacts and connections are crucial in linking people to jobs, whether they were searching for them or not, especially higher paid positions (Cherry 2001). Information about job opportunities and how to pursue them, inside contacts, and outside references—all come through networks. This condition gives special advantages to persons with a large number of contacts or "weak ties" to people who can help them, and it disadvantages those with strong ties with fewer persons who cannot.

Since weak ties are most easily formed at the workplace itself, especially in middle-class work settings, employed persons who are constantly making contacts or networking are most advantaged. Many short-term connections—just long enough to ingratiate oneself—are much more useful than fewer relationships of longer duration or greater commitment. Women, minorities, or others whose ties are mainly to kin and neighbors tend to be more excluded from opportunities to network in occupationally fruitful (and legal) ways, especially if they live in poor or segregated neighborhoods. (By contrast, close ties are more functional for illegal enterprises and for simple survival in extreme conditions, where accords are necessarily based more on personal trust.) Although Granovetter's original work drew on a smallish sample, analyses of large-scale national surveys in the United States (as well as Japan, Germany, the United Kingdom, and the Netherlands) confirm his earlier discoveries. For example, Gilbert and Kahl (1987) found that lower-class persons interacted more frequently with fewer people and had little privacy, whereas higher-class persons had more privacy and a wider range of interactions, though with less frequency with any particular set of people.

What do such findings on getting a job have to do with American apartheid and the social and economic conditions of African Americans, particularly those of the underclass? The connection is in residential racial segregation, which tends to exclude blacks from networks that lead to jobs. Such segregation is documented by Douglas Massey and Nancy Denton in *American Apartheid* (1993). They show that American cities are generally more segregated than they were at the time of the Civil War or in the early 1900s. Once slavery and terror declined as obstacles to social mobility for African Americans, other barriers were raised. These included, and often continue to include, "the closing of hotels and rooming houses to blacks in white or mixed neighborhoods; the refusal of white businesses to serve black clients; the denial of membership to blacks on real estate boards; restrictive covenants; violent attacks on blacks who tried to move into white neighborhoods; red-lining by banks; blockbusting and screening by real estate operators; and other forms of discrimination (one study in suburban New York counted 46 separate techniques)" (Fuchs 1994, 1343). Even some blacks may acquire a stake in residential segregation—black realtors, newspaper publishers, and politicians are the short list. As middle-class whites and blacks have moved to the suburbs, overall desegregation has increased slightly since 1990. But because poorer blacks with children and whites without children tend to remain in the cities, the racial segregation of children increased in that time (Schmitt 2001).

One important technique of segregation was the policy of the Federal Housing Administration (FHA) and the Veterans' Administration (VA) before civil rights reforms of the 1960s. The FHA and VA provided loans to middle-class whites that encouraged them to move to the suburbs, but only if they moved into the same social and racial neighborhoods. Another technique was "urban renewal" (which came to be known as "Negro removal"), whereby low-income minority populations were moved from desirable urban properties into large, isolated housing projects. Even the Fair Housing Act of 1968 was negated in practice through a lack of enforcement owing to the deeply entrenched habits of discrimination by banks, owners, and realtors. These practices and their legacy continue. In Los Angeles today, for example, even poor, recently immigrated Latinos are less segregated than the most affluent African Americans.

Residential segregation not only excludes blacks from employment networks, but it also weakens the power of African American citizens to make effective coalitions with other groups to improve their lot. The overwhelmingly black election districts mandated by the 1982 amendments to the Voting Rights Act, for example, can elect black aldermen, city councilmen, and state representatives, but these districts rarely foster the interracial alliances necessary for significant changes in public policies. Moreover, neighborhoods segregated away from job networks also lose income and, with that, businesses, more jobs, police protection, and upwardly mobile members. The isolation or despair of those left behind can "defeat programs for empowering black neighborhoods. One obvious example: when children hear only black English, they are likely to be shattered in school by standard American English texts and tests and by teachers who confirm what they believe to be their stupidity when they fail. Of course, efforts could be made to upgrade early childhood education, create enterprise zones, initiate tax credits for new businesses and the working poor, and remake the welfare system to improve life in ghetto neighborhoods" (Fuchs 1994, 1343). But such interventions have little impact on reducing the minority underclass because its root cause is residential and social segregation—that is, exclusion from occupationally useful networks, especially labor unions.

The use of racial animosity as an antidote to and substitute for working-class solidarity began in colonial times, when black slaves worked alongside white indentured servants in the tobacco fields of Virginia. Lawmakers soon enacted more privileges for white servants and more strictures against slaves, finally persuading white workers and small farmers that both were equal to aristocratic planters in being "white and free" (Morgan 1975, 381). Cliff Brown finds that "both capitalist and state actors mediate conflicts between racial groups in the labor market and that employers actively contribute to racial antagonism when emergent interracial coalitions threaten to increase labor costs and polarize class struggle" (2000, 653). Other divide-and-conquer tactics included differentiated wages for the same work, the exploitation of nationalist hostilities among groups, and an ideology that defines America as an inherently white Christian society (Takaki 1989, 130; Mink 1986).

Even today, despite the passage of the Civil Rights Act in 1965, when blacks follow the rules, they still are less likely to receive the standard rewards. For example, "black men who complete college end up making $792 for every $1,000 earned by comparable whites. And black men who finish law school reach only $547 of the white figure. Nor will it do to argue that blacks may go into inferior colleges or law schools. For it turns out that black women college graduates average $916 for each $1,000 made by their white counterparts, and as lawyers they get $986 of that sum. These and other findings suggest that employers find black women more acceptable than black men" (Hacker 1988, 41), perhaps due to a residual fear of those whom whites have oppressed.

Although important gains were made in the civil rights era, these were more in racial civility than in racial equality. The difference is illustrated by the scandal and legal action surrounding the tape recording of a meeting of senior executives at Texaco who discussed destroying documents relating to a racial discrimination suit and referred to blacks as "fucking niggers" and "black jelly beans." The inflammatory remarks were headlined around the country. In the resulting controversy, Texaco's stock plummeted, two executives were suspended, two retirees had their benefits cut off, and Texaco finally bowed to public pressure and settled the suit for $115 million (Gladwell 1996, 9). Crucially, however, this settlement was essentially in response to protest against the racial *incivility* of Texaco officials, not against their deeply institutionalized practices of racial *discrimination.*

Similarly, whereas most white Americans "consistently profess good will toward blacks," 34 percent agreed in interviews that "most blacks" were "lazy," and 52 percent thought that "most blacks" were "aggressive or violent." In the same spirit, whereas three-fourths of suburbanites interviewed agreed that more should be done "to help people in the inner city who live in poverty," almost three-fourths also disagreed that *their* suburb should "work much harder at becoming more racially integrated" (Wolfe 1998). Further, though the number of black families earning over $75,000 per year (in constant dollars) since the 1970s has trebled, the number of such families in the suburbs has only doubled, and these families reside in distinctly black (not racially mixed) middle-class suburbs.

Thus, with the dismantling or nonenforcement of laws against racial discrimination during the Reagan/Bush era, civility is almost all that is left. Moreover, despite an enlargement of the black middle and professional classes, the inequalities suffered by the black underclass have increased in recent decades. Often the main response of dominant groups has been to attune their feelings and improve their "communications skills" through training in sensitivity and diversity and avoidance of "the n word." This superficial change perhaps was the most remarkable aspect of the Texaco case: even as the company was bringing in racial harmony experts to train personnel in proper jelly bean talk, only 6 of its 873 executives earning over $106,000 annually were African American.

Some American leftists hope that with greater internationalism of the American economy and greater multiculturalism in the American population, the United States will finally do away with racial discrimination, dismantle the corporate oligarchy, reduce inequalities of income, and expand opportunities for education and health care. Yet this hope is far from realization. Multicultural America is characterized by a general civility among the races along with continued discrimination, and the neoliberal policies of transnational America have been accompanied by increased economic polarization.

THE WEAKNESS OF CLASS POLITICS AND OF SOCIOECONOMIC EQUITY

In 1835 Alexis de Tocqueville warned how an aristocracy may be created by manufacturers: "In proportion as the principle of the division of labor is more extensively applied, the workman becomes more weak, more narrow-minded, more dependent. . . . The art advances, the artisan recedes. . . . Thus, at the very time at which the science of manufactures lowers the class of workmen, it raises the class of masters" (1835, 159). Tocqueville's insight became reality with the Industrial Revolution in America between 1860 and 1920. Artisanry, husbandry, and farming became less important as manufacturing and factory work increased. Workers were brought together in factories and working-class residential compounds, until the very institutions designed to exploit them also helped workers to develop a group consciousness and organize against their bosses. Thus emerged the labor movement, which eventually gained workers better wages, social protections, and the weekend.

A similar story can be told of the nations of northwestern Europe. Unlike the European industrial democracies, however, the United States has the stingiest welfare system of any rich country, the highest inequalities of both income and wealth, a weak labor movement, little overt class politics, and no significant history of a labor or socialist party. These factors make for American exceptionalism. How do we explain them? Having noted the role of racism, here we consider five further hypotheses, which can be summarized as unique cultural and political values and institutions, competition among immigrant and ethnic groups, immigration, occupational stratification within the working class, and the strength of the capitalist class and its complicity with the state.

Chief among explanations of American exceptionalism is that the ethos of individualism and individual (but not class) social mobility blocked the formation of working-class solidarities, unions, and parties. Individualism was encouraged by both the bourgeois character of the nation and a frontier that was long open to settlement or escape. Moreover, democracy in America preceded both industrialization and the emergence of a large nonslave proletariat. For these reasons, class struggle in America was limited to narrow concerns of labor (hours, conditions, wages, etc.) and largely excluded broader social, political, or class issues. Louis Hartz (1955), for example, attributed American exceptionalism to the individualism stemming from the liberal political tradition since John Locke (1632–1704). It is also a major theme in Seymour Martin Lipset's work (see 1963, 194, 202). According to Jeff Manza (1996, 760), Lipset argues that the "first new nation" emerged from the Revolutionary War with a uniquely "American creed," a core of individualistic and antihierarchical values fostered by the absence of feudal structures, aristocracies, and monarchy. Lipset invokes this American creed to explain why the crime rate is so high (lack of deference to authority), voter turnout so low (lack of citizenship norms), unions so weak (lack of status distinctions through ascription), and social provisions for the poor so meager (individualistic achievement orientation). In this view, although American workers shared an identity in their role as laborers, few of them acted in class terms within the political arena. Even as workers, Americans do not think in the usual categories of class but tend instead to blur economic differences into a gradual hierarchy with no sharp division between labor and capital. In effect, in this view, Americans subordinated their class interests and identity as workers to their conception of themselves as citizens and thus voted with the political mainstream—Republican or Democrat but not labor or socialist. Moreover, because mass-based political parties existed before mass labor organizations, the space for labor or socialist parties was largely preempted by multiclass parties. America's system of electors rather than a parliament also made it very difficult for new or third parties to gain a foothold. Thus the American left has largely failed because the working class in America is highly conservative (see especially Sombart 1976 [1906]; Hartz 1955; Lipset 1963; Hochschild 1995) and because radicalism was discouraged by preexisting values and democratic institutions.

This argument explains aspects of America's peculiar democracy, but it does not account for the weak labor movement in Britain, rising crime rates in European democracies, continued group discrimination by race, or the fact that the American working class was partly socialist and often as radical as its European counterparts since its inception after the Civil War until about 1920. Moreover, this explanation is essentially an argument for the continuity of tradition. America early had a bourgeois democratic (or "liberal" or "republican") political culture, and therefore it has remained so and not become radical. There are two reasons to question this assumption. First, as we will explore at greater length in Chapter 6 on space and time, Americans are a radically anti-traditionalist people. Thus those who argue that a conservative political culture prevails in America because democracy was achieved early must still explain its persistence over time. Second, a liberal political culture already existed in England at the time of the early migrations to the New World, and the founders of the United States were nourished by seventeenth-century British political philosophers who helped to create liberalism in England. Yet increasingly in the eighteenth and nineteenth centuries, British political culture and institutions moved in the direction of aristocratic statism, whereas American political culture remained more liberal and populist. Arguments from tradition do not account for this difference. Hence they are, at the least, incomplete.

In contrast to these explanations based on conservative civic values, other observers emphasize a strong, though largely unarticulated, working-class con-

sciousness. Ed Sadlowski, for example, the maverick steelworkers' union official, expresses this view: "There's a certain instinct that a worker has, much
more so than some candy-assed storeowner. He understands who's screwing
him, but he doesn't understand how to get unscrewed. The little chamber of
commerce storefront man, he never understands he's gettin' screwed. He's part
of Main Street America. I place my faith in the working stiff, regardless of his
hangups. He's still the most reliable guy on the street when push comes to
shove" (quoted in Terkel 1980, 267).

Further, although many workers respond positively to survey questions
about "job satisfaction," sociologists rarely try to measure *objective* conditions
of alienation and powerlessness or to distinguish between satisfaction as pleasure in work and satisfaction as resignation to what is perceived as a hopeless
situation—that is, not knowing "how to get unscrewed." When questionnaires
are redesigned to address the latter, however, "job satisfaction" plummets. Thus
most research on working-class consciousness is based on untested assumptions. One of these is psychological reductionism—the assumption that the
operative structures of society can be reduced to the expressed wishes or feelings
of its members. But even on this dubious assumption, many indicators suggest
that American blue-collar workers perceive themselves as engaged in a perennial struggle with their bosses. True, American workers are reformists, not rev-
olutionaries. But one does not need to be revolutionary to be militant. Instead,
there has been much violence in American industrial relations, most of it perpetrated by employers, but also some by labor.

Moreover, the American labor movement has not always been small and
conservative, as Lipset and others would have it. Indeed, much as in Europe,
union membership in America was rapidly expanding in the period before the
Great War.

Rising from 447,000 in 1897 to 1.1 million in 1901, the level doubled to 2.2 million
over the next decade and reached 2.7 million in 1914, approximately one-fourth of
the industrial labor force—a level comparable to what was found in Germany. In
1902, the Socialist platform was supported by 46 percent of the votes cast at the
American Federation of Labor convention, a level that indicated the rapid spread of
socialism among component unions. In 1912, a Socialist candidate for the AFL presidency secured a remarkable one-third of the votes against the incumbent, Samuel
Gompers. If these votes were in any way representative of the distribution of opinion
among the union rank and file, then it can be estimated that nearly 10 percent of the
industrial labor force—and perhaps as many as one-fourth of skilled manual workers—were in some sense socialist-minded, a level not out of keeping with what was

found in Britain or France around this time (Zolberg 1986, 426–427; see also Kimel-dorf 1999; Joseph 2000; Steinfeld 2001; Fink 1985).

At the same time, socialism was becoming a broad political movement, much as it was in the United Kingdom. "The first Socialist representative was elected to the U.S. Congress in 1910; Eugene V. Debs received 6 percent of the popular vote in the 1912 presidential election; and there were scattered victories at the municipal and state levels. The high point of Socialist electoral strength was probably reached in 1914, when in addition to the 12,000 incumbent mu-nicipal officeholders, 33 Socialist legislators were elected in fourteen states" (Zolberg 1986, 427; see also Weinstein 1967, 93–117). In sum, this growth and militancy of significant parts of labor from the Civil War to about 1920 under-cuts explanations by Lipset, Hartz, and others based on the conservative values of Americans since the revolution.

Competition among various immigrant and ethnic groups is another expla-nation for weak solidarity among workers. In this hypothesis, ethnic conflict serves capitalists while undermining labor. A distinctive feature of America's in-dustrialization was its dependence on foreign immigration, rather than the more usual domestic migration of rural peasants to urban factories. Thus, there early emerged in America a segmentation and hierarchy of the labor force based on level of skill and time of arrival, which roughly matched popular concep-tions of skilled natives and less-skilled immigrants. In 1910, when the numbers and proportion of immigrants were at a peak, about "one-fourth of the Ameri-can white male labor force (ten years of age or over) was foreign-born; but the proportion rose to over one-third in manufacturing and mechanical industry, and to over one-half in mining"—that is, in less-skilled occupations (Zolberg 1986, 442; see also Rosenblum 1973, 74).

Equally important, innovations in steam and railway transportation increas-ingly turned this foreign population into sojourners rather than immigrants. As steam navigation (and today air travel) sharply reduced the time and costs of long-distance travel, more European workers from the 1880s on engaged in a form of transatlantic commuting. As American industrial capitalism matured, about one-third of the American working class—and more than half of the un-skilled—were recently arrived Europeans who did not intend to stay (Zolberg 1986, 442). Thus the variety of ethnicities, the immigrants' status as foreign, and the transitory status of many of them all inhibited the formation of work-ing-class solidarity and political mobilization around common interests. Mi-grant industrial labor is not unique to the United States, however. Marx and

Engels observed that one-third of the inhabitants of major English industrial cities were Irish, and Marx believed that the antagonism between English and Irish proletarians was the prime cause of the weakness of the English working class, even though it was well organized (as noted in Hechter 1975, 15).

There is also much evidence that American workers since colonial times have viewed new immigrants as a threat to their wages. This often correct belief was expressed in the "Know-Nothing" movement of the 1850s and the anti-Chinese campaigns in the Western states later in the nineteenth century. Beginning in the 1860s, American labor unions pushed for legislation that would restrict and later prohibit the immigration of Asians, whose readiness to work for lower wages in bad conditions made them especially feared by white workers, much as poor blacks are feared by low-income whites today. The unions also sponsored the Foran Act of 1885, which prohibited the entry of contract workers, who were often used for strike breaking. In effect, American capitalism was formed around a labor market segmented by ethnicity and race, a condition that continues to inhibit solidarity among working people today.

The explanation that the American labor movement has been weakened by fragmentations in terms of race, gender, and ethnicity can be refined if we understand ethnic conflict (at least among European immigrants) as essentially the rivalry between more-skilled and assimilated earlier arrivals and less-assimilated and usually less-skilled newcomers. That is, U.S. labor has been stratified not only in terms of ascribed statuses such as race, gender, or ethnicity, but also in terms of levels of necessary capitalization and skill.

A two-tiered labor market also undermined working-class solidarity, and it was generated largely by the oligopolistic organization of American industrial capitalism itself (C. Brown 2000; Prechel 2000; Roy 1997). Methods of mass production began earlier in America than in other countries. These methods required relatively high costs for technological innovation and thereby provided an impetus for stable and high levels of output in order to amortize high initial costs of setting up the production line. These conditions—high start-up costs and long production runs—fostered in turn the drive toward monopolization, industrial consolidation that was so characteristic of American capitalism in the post–Civil War period (Chandler 1977, 50–78). High start-up costs themselves provide a barrier to competition and thereby encourage oligopolization, especially in large assembly-line operations that need large production runs to efficiently utilize and amortize equipment, thereby fueling a drive toward market expansion and domination.

How did this situation generate a divided labor market? As Michael Piore has shown, the oligopolization of capital-intensive production with long, stable production runs created the basis for a dual economic structure. Oligopolies in most major industries divided demand into two parts: "a stable component . . . which the newly formed trusts attempted to reserve for themselves, and which was met through modern, capital-intensive production technologies in relatively large-scale productive units, and a fluctuating component, handled by much smaller enterprises, probably in smaller productive units and using more labor-intensive techniques" (1979, 144–145; see also Roy 1997; C. Brown 2000). The oligopolies produced for the steady, predictable demand; the smaller, more vulnerable firms competed for that margin of demand that fluctuated.

This two-tiered industrial structure was matched by a two-tiered occupational structure, and the resulting occupational stratification within the working class was mapped onto the racial and ethnic segmentation of American labor. Thus the overall organization and productivity of American capitalism discouraged mass-based social movements for two reasons. It not only produced low-cost consumer goods for "the masses," but also its very organization tended to fragment labor and reinforce visible social differences of race and ethnicity. This particular deployment of capital in mass-production industries thus accounts in part for the early appearance of a "special relationship" between workers engaged in assembly-line production and their capitalist bosses (Zolberg 1986, 441; Karabel 1979, 20). The owners of capital achieved this relationship not by turning the proletariat into a bourgeoisie but by coopting strategic sectors of the working class. Meanwhile, other workers who did not share in this bounty were pacified and divided by racism. The American Federation of Labor (AFL) long stressed the difference between "industrial" and "craft" workers; was savagely racist; advocated "unionism, pure and simple"; and, under the leadership of Samuel Gompers, rejected class politics and socialism.

These points about occupational stratification within the working class also suggest that part of the debate must be over concepts and numbers, particularly the questions of who are the middle or working classes and how large or militant they are. For example, one can limit the middle class to the self-employed and professionals and managers, or one could also include additional workers who have sometimes been counted as middle class (white-collar clerical workers, technicians, salespersons, and even the more affluent crafts workers), even though the latter do not direct the work of others or even their own. If these additional workers are classified as working class rather than middle class, the working class has not declined but in fact has expanded during much of the twentieth century. By this definition, the size of the U.S. working class in 1980 was almost seventy million or 70 percent of workers, whereas in 1900 it was eighteen million, or only 61 percent of workers.

Indeed, the high productivity of the American industrial labor force went hand in hand with the rapid growth of employment in the tertiary or service sector, which included work that came to be called "white collar." Expansion of service-sector work kept pace with the growth of employment in manufacturing throughout the nineteenth century and began to surpass it in the first decade of the twentieth. In 1910, 35.3 percent of workers held service positions, as against 31.6 percent in manufacturing. By contrast, "in Britain the size of the tertiary sector labor force lagged significantly behind the secondary until the 1920s and in Germany it did so still in 1961. In short, American industrial workers constituted less of a critical mass in the United States than they did in Britain or Germany; there is little doubt that the precocious development of a large segment of white-collar workers also contributed to the formation of a more diffuse sense of class among Americans more generally" (Zolberg 1986, 441–442).

This interpretation sees American exceptionalism as lying not so much in America's values of citizenship as in its industrial and occupational organization. But the two interpretations are somewhat compatible insofar as values of individualism and personal mobility can be seen as being fostered (among whites at least) by this very economic structure. Occupational and ethnic stratification, both within the working class and among middle-class Americans, is more about individually getting ahead than about organizing for collective action.

Marxists also have struggled with the problem of American exceptionalism, with some embarrassment, for if capitalism produces its own destruction, a revolutionary proletariat should be most developed where capitalism is most advanced—the United States. As Marx declared in the preface to *Capital,* "The country that is more developed industrially only shows to the less developed the image of its own future" (1976 [1867], 8–9). Yet socialist parties are all but nonexistent in the United States, and workers there are the least revolutionary. Marx and Engels did qualify their theory, however, in ways that support our periodization and interpretation: "The class struggles here in England, too, were more turbulent during the *period of development* of large-scale industry and died down just in the period of England's undisputed industrial domination of the world. In Germany, too, the development of large-scale industry since 1850 coincides with the rise of the Socialist movement, and it will be no different, probably, in America. It is the revolutionizing of all traditional relations by industry *as it develops* that also revolutionizes people's minds" (1953 [1892], 244; Lenin 1975 [1920], 3:326) also noted that revolution was easier to start in Russia than in the more developed nations of Europe. These insights have been elaborated by both Marxists and liberals into the theory that revolutions are more likely during the early phases of industrialization and in economically backward areas of the world (Bendix 1956, 437; Mills 1963, 256; Baran and Sweezy 1967, 43; Lipset 1979, 14; Gouldner 1980, 50; Katznelson 1981, 9).

All of these factors contribute to the weakness of the American left, but perhaps most important and obvious is the one factor least discussed—the strength of the dominant class. This omission is striking since political conflict cannot be well understood by studying only one of its parties, especially a weaker one. Yet as labor historian Melvyn Dubofsky pointed out, the strength of the capitalist class determined many working-class defeats: "The Wobblies and socialists failed not because American society was exceptional, but because they reached their respective peaks when the nation's rulers were most confident and . . . united" and able to mobilize the resources of the state on their own behalf (1974, 298; see also Ostreicher 1988).

On this interpretation it is not the weakness of the working class or class politics that is noteworthy, but rather the strength of the capitalist class and its victory at crucial historical moments in getting its class politics accepted as politics plain and simple. This domination by the capitalist class was theorized by Adam Smith and other classical economists. Smith saw poverty and inequality as necessary outcomes of capitalism, but he also argued that the power of the state and the political use of the law were prime means of enforcing class domination. In contrast to most neoclassical economists, Smith knew the poverty of the Scottish highlands and was pessimistic about the market's capacity to alleviate human suffering and social injustice. Indeed, Smith noted that those "who by the products of their labor feed, clothe, and lodge the whole body of people [do not have] such a share of the product of their own labor as to be themselves tolerably well fed, clothed, and lodged" (1937 [1798], 79). Even in "civilized society," he observed, the market economy was still accompanied by the destruction of the children of "inferior ranks of people" (quoted in Conto 1999, 13).

Adam Smith noticed what Emile Durkheim ignored—that the division of labor in a capitalist economy not only increases productivity, but also divides members of society into unequal classes. Such differences, said Smith, are "not upon many occasions so much the cause, as the effect of the division of labour"

Moreover, these inequalities were not only a product of the forces of the market; they also were maintained and enforced by the "strong arm of the magistrate." "Civil government, . . . so far as it is instituted for the security of property, is in reality instituted for the defense of the rich against the poor, or of all those who have some property against those who have none at all. . . . Wherever there is great poverty, there is great inequality. For one very rich man, there must be at least five hundred poor, and the affluence of the few supposes the indigence of many" (1937 [1798], 15, 670, 674).

This theoretical formulation—that the market, when backed by the coercive power of the state, operates against workers—also applies to the United States. Such an application invokes the English philosopher John Locke, as do Seymour Lipset and others, but now in an opposite way. Here Locke's argument is not merely a precursor of the American ideals of republican democracy and individual liberty, but he is also mainly the theorist of the state as the creation of propertied persons in defense of their wealth. Both the American capitalist class and the American state were consolidated under the dominance of Northern industrialists during and after the Civil War. Each protected and stimulated the growing power of the other (Birnbaum 1971). This historical instance also accords with the sociological generalization that the development of states is usually driven by war. As Richard Bensel noted, "Union victory . . . created the American state by conferring upon it the fundamental attributes of territorial and governmental sovereignty" (1990, 2). This development was even more the case with the Confederacy than with the Union, in that most indicators of "statism" rose more quickly in the South than in the North, though the South and the North had similar constitutional structures. In the North, however, the Republican Party, despite its postbellum decay, was the "major agent in guiding administrative expansion and the most important force propelling centralization" (Bensel 1990, 367; see also Poggi 1991, 855).

With a large, fairly homogeneous internal market to support industries of mass production, oligopolistic capitalism further concentrated power in the hands of the Northern industrialists, who led and profited from the formation of the new American state during the Civil War. Indeed, the state played only a minimal role in the industrialization of the country during the late nineteenth and early twentieth centuries (Vogel 1978, 1995), with capital coming almost entirely from the domestic private sector or abroad. Though the corporate class soon learned to use the government to protect its oligopolies and other privileges, it continued its unchallenged control of almost every sector of the American economy, in contrast to other capitalist countries such as Austria, England,

France, Italy, Germany, or Sweden, where governments still owned the most basic industries such as railroads, communications, and electricity (Kerbo 1983, 170).

The work of Voss corroborates that of Bensel and others in showing how American capitalists used economic and legal power to suppress the radical activism of labor. Voss's strategy is to first show that the "exceptionalism" of the American labor movement and its political forms has varied historically. Until 1886, he argues, the development of the American working class was similar to that of the English and French working classes. But after the 1880s the political organization of the American labor movement began to differ from its British and European counterparts, although, as we noted above, the most dramatic differences were consolidated during the first two decades of the twentieth century. These differences can be largely explained in terms of the response to labor activism of U.S. employers, who enjoyed "economic concentration and state neutrality" (Voss 1993, 12). In other words, the power of American capitalists was greater than that of their English and French counterparts because, first, their resources and organization were more concentrated through oligopolies and, second, the American government did little or nothing to defend the workers and their unions.

We can adjust Voss's interpretation with insights from Adam Smith and data gathered and analyzed by William Forbath (1991) to show that the role of the state through court-made law was in fact crucial to the power of capitalists as a class. Indeed, unlike elsewhere, the government of the United States as an effective national administrative apparatus was formed only during and after the Civil War, and it was formed largely by the new American upper class of industrial and financial capitalists. Voss studied a period when court prosecutions against strikes as political conspiracies were declining and when injunctions against strikes and legal nullification of labor's political gains (such as maximum-hour laws) were just beginning. "Court-issued injunctions in railroad strikes in 1877–1895 suggest how inapt, even for the period studied by Voss, is the label 'state neutrality.' By 1920, active judicial intervention would dramatically raise risks associated with workers' class-based or radical actions, e.g., boycotts, sympathy strikes, organization, and closed-shop strikes; it would dramatically lower labor's incentives for pursuing political demands *other* than those associated with voluntarism" (Stryker 1995, 371); instead, it would encourage only those labor policies and actions that were *not* based on class politics (see also Forbath 1991).

To summarize, the failure of American socialism and the weakness of the

American labor movement—and, indeed, of the U.S. welfare system generally—have been topics of analysis by social scientists at least since Werner Sombart's 1906 classic, *Why Is There No Socialism in the United States?* For many liberal scholars, American workers are not revolutionary because the American
creed and early democratic participation have directed workers' energies toward individual mobility rather than collective protest. This directional factor
accounts for some differences between labor movements within democracies
and despotisms (where labor movements tend to be either absent or revolutionary), but it does little to explain differences between the United States and
such democracies as Britain and France, and it fails entirely to explain differences among periods within the U.S. labor movement. Some Marxist theorists,
such as Jerome Karabel (1979) or Mike Davis (1986), have argued that America's
working class is weak because of racial and ethnic divisions, in contrast to the
supposedly more homogeneous populations of European nations. We have ex-
amined these theories and supplemented them with others that focus on divisions within the working class based on occupational stratification, the early
growth of oligarchic capitalism, and the exceptional and continuing power of
the capitalist class in the United States.

RECENT TRENDS IN AMERICAN INEQUALITY
AND POLITICS

Class politics has not been strong in the United States for most of the twentieth
century. But it has declined even more with the intensification of globalization
toward the end of the Cold War, despite two decades of increasing inequalities
of wealth and income. For example, although the United States boasts the
world's third highest income per person, approximately fifty million Americans—19 percent of the population—live below the national poverty line. The
U.N. Human Development Program (2000) estimates that the total number of
Americans living in poverty increased 3 percent between 1974 and 1994. During
the 1980s and 1990s, the incomes of the top 20 percent soared, whereas those of
most other citizens stagnated or declined. Poverty is especially high among
children, female-headed households, and the elderly. One in four children under the age of eighteen, three out of every five single-parent households, and
one in five senior citizens fall below the poverty line.

While the share of national income and wealth has declined at the bottom, it
has increased dramatically at the top, reflecting an increasing polarization of incomes of the working poor and the affluent since the late 1960s (Gilbert and

Kahl 1993). By the early 1990s the average income of the richest 5 percent ($156,300) was almost ten times that of the bottom 40 percent—the greatest disparity since the U.S. Census began its annual surveys in 1947 (Gilbert 1994). Income for the bottom 10 percent fell by 10.5 percent from 1977 to 1986, while the top 10 percent gained 24.4 percent. Between 1987 and 1990 1 percent of American families received 79 percent of all the income generated (Lind 1996). In 1998 American CEOs made 489 times what their average employees earned, and the top 1 percent of the population owned 48 percent of the nation's financial wealth, while the bottom 80 percent owned only 6 percent (Gates 2000; Wolff 1996, 11). Similarly, the top 1 percent of American households owned 39 percent of the country's overall wealth in 1989, about twice the proportion of other capitalist democracies (Wolff 1996, 76) and the highest concentration of wealth since 1929. Bill Gates alone is worth more than 45 percent of the total U.S. population (Hacker 1997; Keister 2000; Blau 2001). Moreover, although the level of structurally generated poverty is about the same for the United States as for other postindustrial societies (about 20 percent), the actual levels after tax and welfare transfers remain from two to five times greater (11.7 percent poor in the United States, as against 1.7 percent for Norway, the lowest, and 6.4 percent for Australia, the next highest after the United States) (Kenworthy 1998).

One aspect of this inequality is that poverty is increasing despite growing wealth at the top. Except for some slight improvement in the late 1990s, these trends are global. The United Nations (2000) reports that incomes of the top 20 percent of nations grew three times faster than the incomes of the poorest 20 percent from 1960 to 1990. Thus, the United States is not the only wealthy, industrialized country to experience growing poverty in its population. The U.N. report notes that poverty also worsened during recent years in Canada, France, Italy, Spain, and Denmark. In Britain income inequality has deepened greatly since 1979, and while social mobility is no greater than it was during the Industrial Revolution, a new superclass is emerging from the elite boarding schools and the financial sector (Adonis and Pollard 1998; Skocpol 2000). A number of explanations are offered for these changes, including wage disparities caused by globalization and "deindustrialization"; shifts in price ratios between homes and stock; "Reaganism," including the imposition of highly regressive taxes; and the decline of class politics.

The increased nationalization and internationalization of the American economy has resulted in increased competition for wages and salaries within these now broader markets. Not only has competition put downward pressure on the wages of American industrial workers, who now have to compete with their counterparts in Mexico or Manila, but it also has put upward pressure on the wages and profits of those who hold the scarcest resources—that is, those with the still exotic skills of the new high-tech casino economy (computer entrepreneurs, international lawyers, currency brokers, and the like), as well as those deemed to be the "best" in a wider field of competition (the top surgeons, executives, physicists, and so on).

A related thesis—that increased inequality is caused by deindustrialization—argues that higher-wage manufacturing jobs have disappeared through automation or exportation to lower-wage countries, while the economy has moved away from producing goods toward services. Although part of the service sector includes jobs such as journalist, orthodontist, or executive, about 85 percent of service positions are for low-wage sweepers, drivers, data-entry clerks, hamburger servers, and the like. The shift of employment from high-wage to low-wage modes of production clearly affects the fortunes of younger, less-educated males, who have suffered the greatest relative loss in earnings. This shift explains part of the increase in wage differentials, but only part. The deindustralization thesis cannot explain why wage differentials have been growing *within* industries at least as much as among industries. That is, inequalities of earnings would have grown substantially even without deindustrialization. Indeed, the redistribution of low-skilled and less-powerful workers among industries has been a more significant cause of disparities than the growing inequality within industries (Gilbert 1994, 7; see also Blackburn et al. 1990; Harrison and Bluestone 1988).

Another source of increased inequality has been differential shifts in the cycles and ratios of stock and housing prices. Although the wealthy own most of the nation's commercial real estate, stagnation of prices for individual homes disproportionately affects the middle class, whereas rises in stock prices (over 1000 percent in the 1990s) especially enrich the already affluent, who own most of the corporate stock. Thus Wolff attributed the short-term drop in concentration of wealth between 1965 and 1976 and its subsequent reconcentration in the 1980s to changes in the ratios of prices for homes and stock. Explicit class politics also has declined since the Depression and continues to be weak today.

The effect of Reaganism, and later Bushism, on class inequality also is important but hard to measure precisely. "The champions of the Reagan Revolution virtually celebrated inequality, [and] the Reagan and Bush governments pursued many policies that widened the gap between the affluent and the bottom 60 percent of the income distribution. A short list would include union busting, regressive taxation, a depressed minimum wage, the frayed safety net, the overvalued dollar, free-trade policies, and macroeconomic policies that fought inflation instead of unemployment" (Gilbert 1994, 7). The "tax reforms" of the Reagan administration were passed in the name of increasing investment and national competitiveness. Corporate, inheritance, and capital gains taxes declined, but payroll taxes sharply increased, thus contributing to an enormous growth in inequality of wealth and income. George W. Bush's tax policies have had a similar effect (Drew 2001).

But Reaganism is far from a complete explanation either, since many of the regressive policies associated with it began much before Reagan became president and have not been much modified after. As we noted, inequalities in income and earnings have been rising since the 1970s, but policies and trends that one could identify with Reaganism are more recent. Whereas liberal pundits attributed the increasing distances between rich and poor to the policies of Republican administrations, the trend began under President Carter and was even more evident under President Clinton (Meeropol 1998). For example, the labor unions were sliding long before Reagan came to office, as was the real value of benefits to families with dependent children (Phillips 1969). Further, federal government spending and the budget deficit were at the highest levels in U.S. history during the 1980s, and most federal social programs were greatly expanded (Schwab 1991). Nonetheless, regressive policies proliferated and economic polarization accelerated in the 1980s. The main thrust of Reaganism has been a reduction of taxes for the top of the income distribution as an end in itself and the use of the resulting shortfall of revenue as a pretext to cut social benefits for the poor and middle class and to reduce restrictions on corporate profits, such as lowering standards for environmental safety. Thus the Reaganites turned a stream of inequality into a raging torrent, while the policies of President George W. Bush seek to open the floodgates further.

A final major explanation for extreme class inequality in the United States is the lack of active class politics. A key indicator is that United States ranks near the bottom of twenty advanced capitalist democracies in voting according to class position (Nieuwbeerta 1995, 53). But how can the lack of class politics itself be explained? One hypothesis is that the decentralized character of American political institutions tends to undermine the utility and hence the strength of parties as instruments of national policy. This decentralization has been especially true since the advent of two "reforms." One was the changes effected by the "good government" movement in the 1920s, with middle- and upper-class backing. The "gogos" sought to eliminate labor- and ethnic-based urban political machines, which had become instruments of working-class power and which served their lower-income constituents better than the business-controlled administrations that followed (Shefter 1994). The second is recent campaign financing legislation which, whether by oversight or intention, has permitted virtually unlimited financing of politics by corporations and wealthy individuals.

Because of these two "reforms," the output of the political system seems to have little effect on the lives of ordinary citizens. Thus, they make little effort to generate political input, at least not through the established institutions of party organization and voting. Not only is there low voting by class and relatively little relationship and identification between classes and parties, but also—and even more striking—is nonvoting among the working class and poor. Unlike in almost all of the other capitalist democracies, where lower-income citizens turn out to vote for labor, socialist, or social democratic parties, in America on election day, workers generally stay home (Burnham 1973; Piven and Cloward 1988; Kelley, Ayres, and Bowen 1967; Wolfinger and Rosenstone 1980).

As class politics declines, other political groupings become more significant. Among these, three appear to be most important: first, an emerging transnational bourgeoisie and new or strengthened international organizations; second, affiliations or social movements based on subnational cultural or ethnic features or lifestyles and consumption; third, new occupational divisions and groupings within the middle class itself.

As the solidarity and power of older local elites has become weaker, the social and economic elite is consolidating at the national level (Higley 1995), and an international class of capitalists has grown larger, stronger, and more unified and conscious of itself, as have transnational organizations that are largely responsive to its interests. The American government remains beholden to corporate and financial capitalists, as well as to other interest groups on specific issues, but this capital is now more rooted in international enterprises and transactions and less connected to local or even U.S. national values or concerns. American chambers of commerce still play a role, and their provincial values still influence the moral tone of the Republican Party. But increasingly their influence has given way to more culturally liberal and economically internationalist megacorporations that are the principal funders of both political parties.

With the weakening of the politics of class in nation-states, a sub- and transnational politics of ethnicity and identity assumes greater significance, as do so-called new social movements. "Multiculturalism" is one such movement. In its liberal optimistic version, multiculturalism is consistent with the increased internationalization of capital insofar as the opposites of multiculturalism—ethnic and racial segregations or forced assimilation—are less suited to both the emerging corporate workplace and the more sophisticated corporate niche marketing to particular groups. Of course, globalization, and with it intensified communication among groups and cultures, can lead to the greater diversity and tolerance of difference, as celebrated by postmodernists like Jean-François Lyotard, but globalization also has encouraged monoculturalism, jingoism, ethnic exclusion, and isolationist backlash. Moreover, insofar as attributes of race, ethnicity, or religion are less mutable than economic or political ones, they leave less ground for compromise and encourage a more ideological, nastier, and uncompromising style of politics, as seen in many parts of the world today. In class conflicts the key question is, "Which side are you on?" and people can choose sides and even change them. In conflicts among cultures, however, the question is, "What are you?" Here the self is at stake, a self that is often essentialized as a given that cannot be changed. Much the same is true of fundamentalist religious convictions, which also enter the gap left by the decline of either class or the nation-state as sources of identity. The meanness of the confirmation hearings on Justice Clarence Thomas, the impeachment proceedings against President Clinton, and the postelection controversies of 2000 are signs of this style of politics in the United States.

Shifts in the U.S. occupational structure, especially within the middle class, also have contributed to the decline of class politics in the United States, despite increased economic inequalities. Older economic interest groups play a lesser role as distinct entities with self-conscious collective identities, while new occupational identities have not crystallized politically to take their place. Before World War II there were self-defining social groups such as "self-respecting working people," "farmers," and "businessmen" in both small towns and big cities. These identities and values are dying out or are in transit and now lack the numerical strength, social distinctness, or solidarity to be economic estates. Instead, today's dwindling group of "farmers" is composed of range managers, dairy technicians, or agro-executives who are as computer literate as "businessmen" such as the Wall Street brokers who advise them on commodity futures. Detroit's blue-collar auto workers are still "working class" and "union men," but they also are more team workers and technicians, and there are a lot fewer of them.

Moreover, as consumption becomes a major source of identity, lifestyle is replacing working-class culture, even for auto workers, and undermining political activism based on class. Although there are class preferences for beer over wine, for example, union members' concerns now include their motor homes, power boats, and retirement pensions. They see "the same television programs as everybody else in American society, they buy the same consumer goods in the same supermarkets" (Drucker 1989, 24–25), and they often are Republican on race, crime, and "family values," even as they remain largely Democratic on issues of labor. Thus they define their status not only through their economic or class interests, but also through their lifestyle, consumer choices, and ethnic or cultural identities. As part of this shift, there has emerged a "postmaterialist consciousness" in sectors of the United States (Inglehart 1996). Seen in this light, questions of class politics and the weakness of the left today appear to many as nineteenth-century issues. In the postindustrial or postmodern economy, blue-collar assembly-line workers are replaced by or become pink- and white-collar personnel, and robber barons are replaced by netsters (computer programmers) and bureaucratic entrepreneurs (Wattenberg 1974; Naisbitt 1982).

The fuzziness of the concept and the experience of being middle class also undermine class politics in the United States, if only because the "middle class"—its composition and political alignments—is crucial in American politics of almost any stripe. Most Americans, regardless of their economic position, identify themselves as middle class; the dentist making $300,000 a year and his receptionist making $30,000 both are likely to call themselves middle class (Halle 1984; Glassman 1997; Vanneman and Cannon 1987). Further, no progressive government policy is likely to be enacted without middle-class support; as a result, the policy in question usually includes advantages or entitlements for the middle class, as well as for the working class or poor, who in any case are much less likely to vote. Social security, with the perceived success and political untouchability, is perhaps the prime example of a progressive program with broad middle-class support. Following Mills (1956, 63), Giddens (1971, 78–79), and Gerteis (1998, 641), we will use the term "middle class" simply to refer to white-collar workers.

Despite its centrality, it is difficult to characterize the American middle class, partly because it includes such a wide variety of occupations and cultural orientations (Vanneman and Cannon 1987). Thus, it is equally difficult to identify a particular "interest" of the middle class in Marxian terms, especially as its voting behavior often is highly skewed. Social scientists have sought to explain these apparent anomalies. C. Wright Mills (1956) saw the middle class as basically apathetic, with no guiding political or social interests. He may have been right, though for the wrong reasons, because during the period in which he wrote there was a sustained economic boom that broadened the middle class enormously, thereby giving rise to satisfaction that could easily be taken as apathy. Moreover, Mills wrote at the height of the Cold War, when national solidarity was especially promoted and class consciousness and interests suppressed.

Ronald Inglehart (1977, 1996), Inglehart and Abramson (1995), and Anthony Giddens (1991, 1994) try to explain the shift from class to status issues, and they see middle-class persons as defining themselves increasingly in nonmaterialist terms. The shift, they argue, has become possible with the greater affluence and freedom from necessity characteristic of the new middle class (Giddens 1991, 214; Inglehart 1977, 73–75). According to Inglehart and Abramson (1995), people's priorities are shifting from earning and spending to having a high quality of life. Inglehart's research focuses on a variety of values he considers postmaterialist. These include religion, gender, and the environment, as well as job satisfaction at the workplace. In a similar spirit, Pierre Bourdieu (1984, 1991) dissects status competition among middle-class occupational groups in France. Small business persons and professors, for example, may have roughly equivalent incomes but very different status markers and reference groups. Whether because of material or symbolic differences of interests, the result is a differentiated politics within the middle class. Thus part of the middle class may be on the left while another part is on the right. In sum, for such authors a new middle class is emerging based on ideals, morals, and lifestyles rather than traditional economic issues. Environmentalism is a favorite example of such a new orientation, which Giddens calls "life politics" and Inglehart, "postmaterialist values." And it is true that during the 1980s and 1990s support for environmentalism increased, and Americans became more liberal on women's rights, minority rights, and issues of sexual behavior (Schwab 1991), even as poverty was increasing, middle-class incomes were stagnating, and the rich were getting much richer.

Yet postmaterialist or lifestyle arguments about middle-class values and politics pose a number of difficulties. First, there is nothing particularly new about a politics of status, which is essentially what these authors describe. The revival of Protestantism in the latter part of the nineteenth century is an example. In addition, political reformers at that time fought for the vote for women, the creation of the welfare profession, the prohibition of alcohol, and other issues of status or lifestyle that were value-oriented and nonmaterialist (Gusfield

1963). Second, such a politics is not unrelated to economic position, at least in the minimal sense that protection or enhancement of group status is an excellent, albeit indirect, way of defending class privileges and excluding or coopting those thereby defined as inferior. In the example of the Protestant revival, the inferior group was a recently immigrated non-Protestant proletariat, who was thought threatening by the earlier arrived middle-class Protestants. Third, the concept of freedom from necessity—asserted as a precondition of postmaterialism—is clearly a social definition, and hence its theoretical use requires sociological justification. What are considered "necessities" by some might be "wants" for others. Moreover, as concepts such as needs imply hierarchical social relations, they should be part of the topic to be explained rather than taken unproblematically as explanations of stratification and political orientation.

Finally, many writers on postmaterialist values, lifestyles, identity politics, and new social movements tend to focus only on left-oriented groups and actions, whereas the right provides examples that are at least as compelling. One can understand the "moral majority" as a renewed kind of status politics on the right that is closely related to the economic decline of its largely lower-middle-class members, who gained little but paid a lot for liberal interventions by government. Further, most of the left-oriented political groups of the 1960s and 1970s up until today have relied heavily on conventional techniques to draw support, such as direct mail, phone banks, and the like. In other words, there is little new about their political practices. For example, the major organizations of the environmental movement are composed mainly of "checkbook members" rather than active participants, they depend heavily on corporate and government funding, and their leadership is largely unaccountable to their mostly passive members (Brulle 2000). By contrast, the Christian Coalition and other conservative groups have emerged as true grassroots organizations, much "newer" in this sense than most of those on the left.

A related approach to understanding middle-class politics, especially as a possible base for progressive reforms, is taken by theorists of the "new class," starting perhaps with Joseph Schumpeter (1942) and, for the communist world, Milovan Djilas (1957). Peter Berger (1986) and Alvin Gouldner (1979) elaborated on Schumpeter's ideas in their view that the purveyors of symbolic knowledge, or the new technical intelligentsia, would replace the proletariat as the main opponents of capitalism. Theorists of the new class also emphasize occupational divisions within the middle class and the guild character of middle-class professions, which tend to limit broader identification with others of the same economic position. Scholars like Bruce-Briggs (1979), Lipset (1981), and

Szelényi and Martin (1988) focus on differences of material interests within the middle class, especially among the liberal professions, and not only on new values (Perucci and Wysong 1999).

As a larger portion of the middle class has come to work in government or other not-for-profit organizations, relatively fewer of its members have a direct stake in the market economy. Increased levels of higher education, corresponding in part to an enlarged upper service sector, support the tendency toward liberalism within part of the middle class. Professionals, for example, are more likely to vote Democratic than managers, even though their incomes may be equivalent.

Since the collapse of a vital liberalism in the 1980s, the dominant conceptions of activist politics have been a left-wing pursuit of racial and sexual liberation and self-expression and a right-wing advocacy of "traditional values" and unregulated capitalism. The American right is composed of authoritarian traditionalists, who are usually based in evangelical religions, and libertarians or radical individualists, including laissez-faire businessmen, financers, and investors. Much of the white lower middle class that has supported "traditional values" and voted Republican in recent decades has experienced a loss of status and income. Such people tend to blame their decline on the relative increase of respect and opportunities for women, minorities, and gays and on the "cultural elite" that supports multiculturalism, affirmative action, feminism, and the like. Thus they attack "welfare queens," assumed to be black (see Gilens 1999), and internationalists, assumed to be heavily Jewish (as in Pat Robertson's 1991 *The New World Order*). As one Alabama congressman put it, the liberals desegregated the schools and then attacked Christian values (in Hodgson 1992; see also Berlet and Lyons 2000).

In fact, however, the major transformations of America since the early 1960s have had little to do with sexuality, communists, or desegregated schools. Instead, the central shifts came from changes in the global political economy and America's relative decline within it. With the economic recovery of Europe and Japan and the industrialization of many emergent economies, there was an invasion into the United States of foreign goods, "which were often better made, cheaper, and more useful than American ones. By the 1970s, this invasion would devastate much of the old industrial economy of the United States, including the high wages for industrial workers which for years Americans had taken for granted. This unprecedented competition, implemented by new technologies in transport and communication, within the once largely impregnable American market, would indeed turn the world upside down for most

Americans and contribute to the selfishness and xenophobia of the Republican right" (Epstein 1996, 31; see also Tonelson 2000). But the structural decline in American economic growth that began about 1970 was largely ignored by liberals, and its profound consequences for American society were aggressively denied by conservatives, even as growth in productivity and hourly wages stagnated or fell and the national debt increased. These trends slowed for a time only in the late 1990s, after a radical restructuring of the American social economy, which became "better" in terms of productivity and competitiveness and "worse" in terms of inequalities of income and wealth (Teixeira and Rogers 2000).

In their focus on identity politics, the left liberals and radicals also largely ignored these paired phenomena. Indeed, for both the right and the left, issues of economics and social values have become uncoupled. While this uncoupling is often interpreted as a sign of the demise of class politics, it could rather be interpreted as a victory of the dominant class: its core positions on issues of fiscal, economic, and tax politics are today largely unchallenged. In this view, lifestyles or identity politics are less a sign of the obsolescence of categories of left or right or of a postmaterialist orientation of the middle class, much less of the end of class politics. Instead, they are a sign of the capture of political discourse and agendas by the corporate elite, whose class interests have come to be defined by both left and right as the accepted and largely unchallenged middle. Thus, while significant elements of both the left and the right are engaged in a postmaterialist politics of identity or status, the state has been increasingly captured by an economic upper class.

THE ROLE OF THE CORPORATE STATE

Not only is the state being rationalized for tax savings and profit enhancement through privatization, deregulation, and downsizing, but also with the greater internationalization of finance, manufacture, and commerce, the state is redirecting its activities toward promoting the interests of the elites who are most closely linked to the transnationalized sectors of the economy. Indeed, in most states and districts, senators and representatives cannot get elected without the campaign contributions of the corporate elite (Lewis 1998). The bulk of Democratic money comes from the same source as Republican money—business (Domhoff 1972; Neustadtl, Clawson, and Scott 1992). In appealing to business for campaign funds, Democrats warn of the danger of a political system in which one party represents business and the other labor. Unlike the United

States, however, such a "dangerous" arrangement is precisely how most other capitalist democracies have been politically organized throughout the twentieth century.

One sign of business contributions in the political system in the United States is the lobbying effort of Microsoft against a judicial plan by the Justice Department and nineteen states to limit its monopoly power. Between 1998 and 2000 the software giant gave more than $750,000 to tax-exempt trade groups, think tanks, foundations, and other generators of political influence and "public opinion." Microsoft has at least tripled its lobbying budget since 1996 and gave over $2 million in campaign contributions in 2000. It also has established front groups with names such as the "Association for Competitive Technology" or "Americans for Technology Leadership" as a way to lobby for it in political and financial stealth. As David Rehr, president of the National Beer Wholesalers Association, put it, "Not many grassroots movements begin outside of Washington, D.C." (quoted in Drew 2001, 50). Fellowships for minorities also won support for Microsoft's position from members of the Congressional Black Caucus (Grimaldi 2000). The only unusual aspect of this effort is that Microsoft has entered this game quite late. For other major corporations such activities are standard practice.

Corporate influence has not diminished even as some federal functions have devolved to the states. Instead, it has intensified rivalry among states for corporate investment. Because states fear losing business and jobs and seek to attract new ones, they tend to offer corporations tax breaks, lax labor laws, and local facilities at the expense of more general social investments. Such corporate-friendly policies have often proved imprudent, however, as the public cost of each new private job created often runs into the hundreds of thousands of dollars and as less money is available for public spending on education, community development, job training, and the like, all in the name of more entrepreneurial government.

The two major political parties hardly pretend to be mass-based political organizations, having become instead national (and international) fund-raising operations. The importance of corporate financing is reflected in legislative outcomes. With greater dependence on financing by corporations and wealthy individuals, the Democratic Party has moved to the right on most economic issues. Similarly, the Republicans dominated as the 105th Congress closed in October 1998 without having even voted on major bills aimed at protecting the public, bills that had both bipartisan and broad public support. These included a "patients' bill of rights" for HMO members, restrictions on the cigarette industry, and election financing reform. However, a $512 million bill did get passed in stealth at the very end of the congressional session with virtually no public discussion. It contained four thousand pages and weighed over forty pounds—designed, in effect, *not* to be read. Most of its contents were protections, tax breaks, or direct or indirect subsidies to business, none of which were openly discussed or individually assessed. Hence it was extremely difficult for citizens to know whose special interests were being served and by whom. As Victor Crawford, a former lobbyist, explained, "That's how it's done. You never leave your fingerprints at the scene of the crime" (quoted in Nelson 1998, 9). Not only is the state largely beholden to its corporate sponsors, but it also has done little to enable the rest of society to either participate in the new global economy or defend against its worst effects.

These conditions make it difficult to advance democratic programs in core states or to consolidate democratic regimes in modernizing ones. Democracy is a system of political inclusion into a common patrimony—the republic in its conception as *res publica* or "everybody's affair." Citizen participation is conducted in the public space that exists above the level of the individual or family and below the level of government agencies or private firms, space in which all citizens are in principle equal. By contrast, poverty means exclusion and inequality. The idea that the country belongs to everyone is weakened by ample evidence that it is owned mainly by a few. The greater such polarization, the weaker is the civic community.

In this situation, what do mainstream Republicans have to offer? More free trade and freedom for global corporations, more cuts in social supports and protections (and thus more dislocation of lives and social relations), more foreign interventions, and more civil restrictions in the name of national security. And what do mainstream Democrats propose? Much the same, only with more redistribution and public assistance, especially to particular groups that claim to be victims.

> Thus neither the moderate Right nor the moderate Left even recognizes, let alone offers any solution for, the central problem of our days: the [economic decline and] personal economic insecurity of working people, from industrial workers and white-collar clerks to medium-high managers. None of them are poor and they therefore cannot benefit from the more generous welfare payments that the moderate Left is inclined to offer. Nor are they particularly envious of the rich, and they therefore tend to be uninterested in redistribution. Few of them are actually unemployed, and they are therefore unmoved by Republican promises of more growth and more jobs through the magic of the unfettered market: what they want is [better paying jobs or

at least] security in the jobs they already have—i.e. precisely what unfettered markets threaten. A vast political space is thus left vacant by the Republican non-se-
quitur, on the one hand, and [Democratic] particularism and assistentialism, on the
other (Luttwak 1994, 5; see also Skocpol 2000).

Many who enter this space are jingoists and communalists, as diverse as Ross
Perot, Jerry Falwell, Patrick Buchanan, and Jesse Ventura, whose main appeal,
like that of the early Mussolini, is in their touting of political restraints on corporate Darwinism and the delaying, if not blocking, of globalization.

Some leaders *have* advocated a "Third Way" between these alternatives, one
that preserves the efficiencies of global market competition but also includes
most of the population in the resultant economic growth. Bill Clinton in the
United States, Tony Blair in Great Britain, Gerhard Schroeder in Germany,
Lionel Jospin in France, and Massimo D'Alema in Italy have espoused such approaches. For Third Wayers, the deregulation, privatization, free (unprotected)
markets for trade and labor, and fiscal and welfare restraints initiated by the
Reagan and Thatcher governments all would continue but with a more human
face, a more compassionate conservatism (George Bush) or practical idealism
(Al Gore). This practical or humane side would focus not on welfare or redistribution but on helping those left out of the new economy to more effectively
compete within it. In this view, if people are willing to work hard, they should
have access to skills that qualify them for jobs with a living wage. If wages were
still inadequate, these could be supported through a negative income tax or
through public service positions. Health and child care also would be provided
to help parents enter and remain competitive in the new global economy.

These worthy sounding goals have little chance of significant enactment as
policies or, if enacted, of significantly affecting economic injustice. The first ob-
stacle is political: there is little constituency for the so-called Third Way since the
prosperous do not wish to pay for it, the poor or marginal and their traditional
liberal spokespersons do not want to give up the assistance that they currently receive or manage, and deficit spending to support the necessary programs would
undermine the economic growth that is the Third Way's central premise. Moreover, it is unclear that programs in job training, reskilling, and health and child
care, even if successfully implemented, would much alter the occupational structure and distribution of income. Indeed, in virtually all economic and educational policy studies, education and training are subsets of the labor market: they
are dependent variables, not causes, of macroeconomic outcomes.

The acute limitations of all these approaches, then, suggest that top-down reformist policies of any stripe will do little to address the challenges that institutionalized racism, a weak labor movement, and neoliberal capitalism pose to democracy, citizenship, and civil society. Global capitalism and neoliberal policies concentrate wealth and income at the top, limit competition over alternative social ideals and models, narrow the public sphere, turn political campaigns into expensive beauty contests, and shift the locus of the formation of decisions far from those most directly affected by them. Neoliberal capitalism both undermines the importance of the nation-state, which historically has been the framework and guarantor of citizenship, and invades the lifeworld and commercializes everyday civic practices (R. Brown 2002). Likewise, its consumer culture promotes radical subjectivism, fragments personal identity, and thereby undermines the integrity of the self. Yet in the Western tradition, to act as a citizen has meant to act as a whole moral person in the public sphere. As this public sphere is diminished and as integral selfhood becomes harder to maintain, the role of the citizen becomes more difficult to enact. Further, ethnic nationalisms and the focus on the needs or rights of other particularistic identity groups encourage the proliferation of dissonant language games, apparently at the expense of any *lingua franca* that might be the medium of a more inclusive civic discourse.

At the same time, however, global capitalism often breaks down autarkic economies and the despotisms and oligarchies that depend on them. As class politics declines in core states, it emerges in newly industrializing countries such as Thailand or Peru. In some developing nations such as India, China, or Egypt, globalization also encourages the formation of larger middle classes, which, since Aristotle, have been viewed as central to democratic cultures. Likewise, postmodern criticality and multiculturalism provide methods of resistance against political and other totalisms and imply a tolerance that could support more pluralistic public cultures.

In this context it appears that democracy in the United States, and perhaps the world, has reached a crucial juncture. While many nations and peoples struggle to develop democratic political institutions, meaningful civic participation is declining in the great state democracies. The rise of the corporation has narrowed the scope of issues that we can legitimately call "political" and widened the use of economic decision making (Deetz 1992). Personal identity, the use of natural resources, definitions of value, the distribution of goods and services, and the definition of "responsible" political opinion itself—all are increasingly shaped by capitalist corporations that have little accountability to democratic publics.

Chapter 3 Ideology After the Millennium: Problems of Legitimacy in American Society

The very bureaucratic controls, market mechanisms, and media-made consumption that foster the success of America's postindustrial economy have undermined moral authority and legitimacy in society. The means of achieving material comfort and a sense of national power have lessened civic participation and moral surety in everyday life (Scharr 1981). Many scholars and critics have noted tensions between the political economy and its ethical legitimation, as well as contradictions *within* the discourse of legitimation. Indeed, the fragmentation of public life into separate specialized spheres (such as the professional, the educational, or the religious) has its counterpart in a fragmentation of the concept of legitimacy itself (MacIntyre 1981, 1988; Heller 1987; Stanley 1981). Humpty-Dumpty has fallen off the wall and broken into many pieces.

In the United States and other societies, the ethical link between the exercise of power and people's willing acceptance of it is provided by a body of moral constructs that impose a seemingly universalistic and invariant framework upon individual or collective rights and obligations. Legitimacy is such a moral framework that has broad consensus and revolves around the right or authority to rule (Freidrich 1963, 233). Insofar as the polity is seen as the arena for the moral development of the person as a citizen, the concept of legitimacy is political in the classical sense. That is, it refers not only to individual roles and performances and not only to the obligations and privileges of the public authorities that adjudicate them, but also to the character of being human in that society.

Although the idea of legitimacy implies the existence of a moral order that authorizes conduct of both citizens and the state, this system also authorizes actions by agencies or institutions that mediate between the two. One example is the regulation of family relations. Both public and religious authorities of America (and of Western Europe) have claimed and exercised a legitimate role in establishing and enforcing status distinctions between a legitimate wife and a common-law wife or concubine. A complementary distinction is that between the testamentary rights and legal obligations of legitimate as opposed to illegitimate children (that is, those born of incestuous, adulterous, or otherwise socially unacceptable unions). By their laws and doctrinally based pronouncements, legislators and clergymen have sought to limit the range of possible domestic groups and to encourage the perpetuation of specific forms of kinship and styles of familial interaction. Thus the authority of the state realizes itself through various institutions in the legitimate regulation of everyday life and in the normative obligation of citizens to respect this regulation.

While many Americans are "antigovernment" in a general way, few are aware of the underlying sources of such sentiments. They not only suspect that others and perhaps they themselves have lost their commitment to the general norms of moral conduct and the public welfare, but they also are confronted with conflicting definitions of what this conduct and welfare entail. Yet more has been said bemoaning the crisis of legitimacy than analyzing it. Hence, our purpose in this chapter is to show how the current crisis results from an interplay of structural and cultural forces. Though rooted in American history, these forces also are those of a highly rationalized, advanced capitalist society.

Conflicts among different definitions of legitimacy correspond to conflicts among different ideologically oriented groups. The right decries permissiveness, advocates a return to traditional values, and reaffirms law and order. The left, such as it is, points to social inequities, abuses of law, and situations of injustice. And, of course, there are a variety of hues and cries in addition to these two. Politicians and entrepreneurs claim that ends justify means, while judges and bureaucrats insist that respect for procedures is what counts. Likewise, the rationalistic authority of experts, the traditional authority of religious figures, and the charismatic authority of celebrities often conflict with each other. Not only do diverse groups project differing and often antagonistic conceptions of legitimacy, each reflecting its social position and interests, but also these conflicting conceptions are often internalized within individuals, most of whom are members of, or dependent on, more than one such group.

The definition of legitimacy that each social group holds also is subject to internal contradictions. For example, many conservatives are quick to castigate intervention by the federal government, even as they advocate the control of abortion or the inclusion of prayer by public authorities. Among liberals, commitment to equality (as for women) is paired with faith in liberty (as for gays and lesbians), with little awareness of the incompatibilities that are involved. For example, many liberal women do not wish the state to dictate decisions about pregnancy, but they encourage the state to punish offensive men at the workplace.

Americans historically have used various means to deal with political and ideological threats. These include suppressing differences in the outlooks and interests of distinct classes; encouraging mass solidarity through fear of an external or internal enemy (the evil empire, the drug cartels, minorities of color); emphasizing the absolute economic gains of almost all groups; and including previously marginalized elements (such as women, blacks, or homosexuals) into mainstream political processes (Edsall and Edsall 1991). In previous decades, these strategies reduced conflict mainly because overall economic expansion masked differences in the gains achieved by distinct groups. These strategies have become less effective since about 1970, however, with greater economic globalization and increased class polarization. Policies of affirmative action for women and minorities offer a case in point. Not only do these policies seem at odds with the universalistic values underlying the U.S. Constitution, but they also have aggravated inter-ethnic tensions, especially between college-bound blacks and working-class whites.

SYMPTOMS OF THE CRISIS OF LEGITIMACY

Symptoms of the crisis of legitimacy in American society are many (for examples, see Beniger 1986; Blumenberg 1983; Crozier 1984; Connolly 1987; Habermas 1975; Offe 1984; Scharr 1981; Vidich 1991). Trust in public institutions has eroded (Caplow et al. 1991); legal action has become a first, not a last, resort in settling disputes; millionaires and millennialists join forces in railing against all forms of government; private militias and loners destroy people and federal buildings; and even ordinary persons frequently take the law into their own hands. Some investors ruined by stockmarket downturns have shot their brokers, just as farmers bankrupted by high mortgage rates have killed their bankers. Mark Burton, a stock trader upset about investment losses, killed himself after shooting more than a dozen office workers (*Washington Post,* July 30, 1999). In destroying an airborne plane and killing all of its passengers, another man who had been dismissed from the airline showed, as he put it, the same lack of pity that caused his dismissal. Disaffected students at Columbine and other high schools murder their classmates with surprising frequency and for little apparent reason. Whether people's activities involve legal or illegal maneuvers, wholesale killing, or silent withdrawal, more want to assert their power against social institutions they no longer deem legitimate.

The crisis of legitimacy is also evident in the decline of people's trust in public figures. Voter registration and turnout in America are by far the lowest of any industrial nation, and those who do vote often reject incumbent administrations. Opinion polls report people's low esteem for key institutions and leaders. This declining respect for the state parallels not only the corruption of elected officials, but also, more important, the increase in conduct that is not illegal but that is viewed by many as immoral.

Moreover, with the expansion and bureaucratization of the corporate state, political leaders increasingly become functionaries for their financial sponsors, with few personal moral obligations. Such functionary roles erode political legitimacy, as well as the notion of personal honor. For example, during the presidency of Ronald Reagan, both Secretary of State George Shultz and Secretary of Defense Caspar Weinberger claimed to have warned their president about the violations of law then being perpetrated by his national security advisers Robert McFarlane (1983–1985) and John Poindexter (1985–1986). Yet even though the president did nothing to deal with their objections, they failed to speak out publicly or to resign in the name of principle because, as each said, they had a job to do. Their role as efficient functionaries overtook their sense of duty as citizens. Such instances suggest that contradictions in the core myths and values of Americans have reached a critical threshold. These values include the involatility of private property and equal rights and access to opportunity. They include the effective management of public affairs and also a highly decentralized and hence often ineffective government. They include individual self-direction, as well as respect for expert knowledge. Right to life, but also right to guns; freedom of speech, but also the gender-neutral workplace. The conflicts of these commitments are amplified by political decentralization and the lack of majesty of the state. The very notion of legitimacy is in jeopardy whenever the core myths of a society can no longer mask an ongoing fragmentation of cultural groups, a polarization of economic classes, and the gulf between the hyper-rationalized system and the meanings to which people cling in their everyday lives.

In this chapter we explore sources of problems and contradictions of legitimacy in the United States. These include the constitutionally divided and decentralized authority of the state; rapid rates of social and technical innovation; the tension between tradition, religion, and precedent and the American celebration of the new; the contradiction between capitalism and democracy; the rise of technicism as a general ideology or habit of mind; tensions among pluralism, due process, and the celebration of results; and the role of public opinion and media images.

CONSTITUTIONAL CONTRADICTIONS AND TENSIONS IN LEGITIMACY

The creators of the U.S. Constitution feared despotism in both its democratic and monarchial forms. They tended, like most Americans, then and today, to be suspicious of institutional power in principle. "Society is produced by our wants, and government by our wickedness," wrote Thomas Paine in *Common Sense.* James Madison wrote *Federalist* 10 to show the historical importance of property. Madison clearly wanted to avoid rule by the majority and to establish a republic governed by the rich. Yet Madison also wanted to avoid concentrations of power. In *Federalist* 51, he argued that "ambition must be made to counteract ambition. . . . The great security against a gradual concentration of the several powers in the same department, consists in giving to those who administer each department the necessary constitutional means and personal motives to resist encroachments of the others. The remedy . . . is to divide the legislature into different branches; and to render them . . . as little connected with each other as the nature of their common functions and their common dependence on society will admit." George Washington echoed these sentiments in his farewell address (written mostly by Hamilton): "The spirit of encroachment tends to consolidate the powers of all departments in one, and thus to create whatever form the government, a real despotism." Similarly, what Edmund Burke said of the American colonists is no less true of Americans today: the love of liberty was "fixed and attached on this specific point of taxing," over which the "great contests for freedom" had been fought "from the earliest times" (quoted in Epstein 1996, 30).

These ideas were central to the political culture of the early United States, and they have persisted throughout American history in large part because they were directly written into the U.S. Constitution. Although the federal government has grown immensely in power and authority, the separation of powers remains among the main branches of government, and policymaking continues to be shared between the national and regional authorities. The sovereignty of particular states was of course reinforced by the differences between the North and the South, but even after the defeat of the South in the Civil War and its relative integration with the rest of the country after 1966, when desegregation, air conditioning, and manufacturing arrived to the Southern states, this relative autonomy of the states granted by the Constitution continues. For example, state legislatures rather than Congress continue to define the most significant components of legal identity, such as residence, civil status, vital statistics, and—as Americans saw in 2000—voting procedures for national elections.

This system of decentralization and separation of powers has had a number of interrelated consequences for American culture and political life. These include the relative weakness of American political parties and a corresponding civic activism through local associations, social movements, and interest groups; a lack of accountability of government; a weakness or even incompetence of government in accomplishing many tasks; and a general antigovernment attitude among the general public.

The variability of state laws (as well as the cultural diversity of the population) encouraged an emphasis on procedure or formal over substantive values. Divided power and decentralization of government may bring justice closer to where interactions take place, foster cultural diversity, and facilitate social experiments. But they also make it difficult to hold any particular unit or person accountable, for no one is wholly responsible. Moreover, by guaranteeing incapacities of each unit in the system, the division of power also reinforces negative attitudes toward government in general. Where government is centralized, dissatisfaction will more likely be directed toward the incumbent administration. Where government is decentralized and therefore inherently less competent, dissatisfaction is more likely to be directed at government itself (Barber 1983; Levi 1998). This sentiment was expressed recently by an automobile mechanic in Georgia: "I don't intend to vote for anyone up in Washington again, and I'll tell ya why. When I get to thinking about how hard I work, and how damn greasy I get, and I start thinking about how much you-all take out of my paycheck for taxes and all, an I see those people setting on their porches spending my money, why I get so damn mad I just say to myself, 'I ain't never going to vote for them sons-of-bitches again'" (quoted in Hodgson 1992). The fact that this man's payroll taxes had been raised to the advantage of the already wealthy, and not front porch sitters, had little to do with it.

Political parties have been weak in America compared to their European counterparts mainly because they are much less able to deliver the goods to those who might support them. In most European systems, the head of the victorious political party—that is, the party that wins a controlling number of seats in the legislature—becomes the president or prime minister and selects his or her cabinet ministers from winners of other legislative seats. By contrast, in the United States, the two legislative houses are strictly separated from the executive branch, and many positions and decisions remain not only with the federal executive, but also with the states. This separation diffuses power enormously, as was intended by the founders, and also makes it much more difficult for national parties to be politically effective. Similarly, the absence of unitary sovereignty makes it harder for political parties to offer a real choice of candidates who might effect significant change if elected (Gerring 1998, 12). Contributing to these factors also, of course, is the winner-take-all electoral college system, which effectively excludes third parties, pushes the two major parties toward the center, and gives greater influence to the states.

For these reasons, among others, Americans have turned historically to nonparty and nongovernmental civic activism. Since at least the early 1800s, America's vibrant civic life was said to make it unique. Indeed, the United States came to be known as "a nation of joiners." Yet this hallmark of American democracy can itself be interpreted as a product of weak government and weak parties. Civic actions such as volunteer work for community organizations, interest groups, or social movements; help in registration and get-out-the-vote drives; or protest in the streets—all are more important if government is weak. Likewise, pressure groups are especially visible in the United States partly because they know how to gain access to officials across the American government, from local council members to senators to the president (Richardson 1993).

The weakness of parties also partly explains why politics in America is considerably more "pragmatic" and less "ideological" than in Europe. Strong-party systems like those in Europe are able to "mobilize many more citizens in political life through the parties than weak-party systems, but such involvements are not likely to be perceived as the engagements of *individual citizens*—the public-spirited philosophy of liberalism. Rather, citizens will perceive themselves as partisans of a particular philosophy, and a particular political organization. It is not, therefore, to an abstract notion of 'citizenship' that such activists will appeal, but rather to ideologies. 'I am a socialist/conservative, therefore I act'" (*Economist,* August 21, 1999, 44–45).

None of these differences mean that pressure groups are less important in European democracies but only that they exercise their influence more *within* the party apparatuses rather than outside, where they perforce are more visible as pressure groups rather than parties. In both cases, of course, pressure groups tend to encourage government to do more than it can do well and to exacerbate inequalities because the influence of the rich and powerful is vastly disproportionate to their actual numbers. The strong bias against democratic majorities that the founders built into the American political system also makes it easier for privileged minorities to block changes than for majorities to enact them. Thus, the system strongly favors the status quo against reform (see Dahl 1977). In this circumstance, the victory of any majority coalition of democratic reformers depends on the support of a president so strong that he or she would have nearly despotic power.

The decentralized structure of American political and judiciary institutions also desacralizes the universality that is central to the notion of legitimacy (Litowitz 1997). The enormous variations in marriage, divorce, or inheritance laws across the nation, for example, and their apparently random distribution lower the predictability of any judicial intervention in familial relations. Moreover, the sovereignty of each state with regard to such issues enables spouses or parents to push their own interests at the expense of their relatives by moving to a more favorable jurisdiction. While Reno's fame comes from divorce as much as from gambling, its divorce decrees can be readily contested outside of Nevada. Similarly, the approval of marriages of gay or lesbian couples by the state of Vermont in 2000 elicited bans against recognizing such marriages in a number of other states. In short, high degrees of individual mobility and legal localism not only invite instability of conjugal bonds, but also encourage disrespect for governmental decrees.

The relegation of norms concerning family and marriage to the private sphere solves little, however, because there are ambiguities in the conception of privacy itself. While the term refers to the sanctity of domestic relations, as well as to one's body and one's home, it also evokes the absolute property rights of individuals to "use, enjoy, and dispose of" what they own. In other words, the concept of privacy symbolizes both the privileges of intimate relations against outside intrusions and the exclusive rights of owners over their assets. Thus the private rights and discretion of the family against the state or the public sphere are easily extended to the private rights and discretion of an individual spouse or child against the family itself. Similarly, the competitive environment of "private" firms makes openness anathema, even as these same firms maintain comprehensive information and invade the homes of "private" individuals.

The decentralized and multilayered governmental apparatus of the United States also tends to blur boundaries between public and private. The multiplicity of jurisdictions, each with its own laws and precedents, undermines people's commitment to more universal principles and, thereby, the legitimacy of the state as the bearer or enforcer of such principles. For example, in the early 1960s, in an attempt to preserve the Comstock Law of 1879 and despite recurrent confirmations of the right to privacy, the state of Connecticut sought to legislate bedroom conduct when it made the use of condoms by married couples a criminal offense. Elsewhere, states have permitted information to enter the public domain even though it had been collected on a private person for private reasons. In the litigation over Baby M, for example, the judge allowed the defendant's lawyer to make public the tapes of telephone conversations with the plaintiff that the defendant had recorded illegally. (The case hinged on whether the defendant, Mary Beth Whitehead, a surrogate mother who was carrying a child conceived by artificial insemination, should surrender the child in compliance with a surrogate parenting agreement. She lost the case, and custody was awarded to the father, William Stern.) Prosecutor Kenneth Starr's use of Linda Tripp's secret recordings of Monica Lewinsky provides a similar example.

Further, it is unclear to most Americans whether the activities of private individuals should be bound by the same principles as those regulating the conduct of public officials, who often have little or no private life of their own. In contrast to past eras, when one spoke of legitimate children and legitimate wives in the same way that one evoked the legitimacy of the state, modern rhetorics imply either that legitimacy does not concern private lives or that different moral norms govern personal and public conduct.

Thus the decentralized form and banal status of the state cause confusion about the reciprocal obligations of citizens and public authorities. For example, Americans tend to confuse whistle-blowing, muckraking, and informing. Even though whistle-blowing involves telling taxpayers and officials about misuses of public funds or authority (Nelkin 1984), whistle-blowers are usually punished as informers. Hence, the individual who revealed that the army paid an absurd price for ashtrays was banished professionally, whereas the youngster who gave away her parents for using dope was personally honored by President Reagan's wife.

The decentralization and variability of the American system also increases the number of constituencies to which political actors must respond, each with their own interests and conceptions of legitimacy. For example, is the legitimacy of judges based on their expert knowledge, the number of votes they received, their exemplary moral character, or the political orientation of their voting records? Such tensions have been present since the first days of the republic (P. Miller 1965). For another example, members of both the executive and legislative branches knew that the institution of slavery was threatening the legitimacy of the United States in the eyes of foreign powers, but they also knew that to campaign overtly for abolition would jeopardize their careers and often their wealth. Further, while they all rejected the political and civil rights of slaves, they did not fight the decision taken by Southern political actors to count slaves as three-fifths of a citizen as a roundabout way of enhancing the political representation of slave states and perpetuating their ability to limit federal authority.

Fears of conflict between legislative and executive branches of government or between state and federal authorities often invite arbitration by the judiciary partly because judges are either appointed or subject to longer electoral timetables and are therefore more resistant to the reprisals of public opinion. As an illustration, after World War II, and especially after the 1954 Supreme Court decision in *Brown v. Board of Education,* politicians at both state and federal levels understood that both de jure and de facto educational segregation was jeopardizing the legitimacy of American government. Knowing that direct action would hurt them politically, they left to federal judges the task of defining what school boards should do in order to ensure desegregation. A similarly ambiguous role was played by the Supreme Court in 2000, when it effectively decided the presidential election in favor of George W. Bush on procedural grounds, rather than favoring Albert Gore on the substantive ground that he appeared to have received more votes.

In sum, America's institutionally mandated system of checks and balances and decentralization has tended to weaken the state as the legitimate embodiment and effective executor of shared universal values. Instead, this system has engendered a skeptical, antigovernment attitude among many Americans, as well as weak parties and a lack of governmental accountability, and the use of alternative means of political activism such as community service, social movements, or interest group lobbying.

SOCIAL AND TECHNICAL INNOVATIONS
AND LEGITIMACY

Some weaknesses of legitimacy inhere in the U.S. Constitution. Others are products of the basic, defining orientations of modernity itself. These include rationality, the cult of efficiency and profit, ethical relativism, egalitarianism, secularism, and rapid rates of technical and social innovation.

Emile Durkheim showed that changes in social structure invite changes in the collective sense of moral bondedness and hence in the character of the law. Changes in social structure and culture are not necessarily synchronized, however, and the resultant disruptions that Durkheim saw as transitional seem, instead, to be chronic conditions of societies with high rates of innovation. The faster these rates, the more likely there will be inconsistencies between institutional structures and their cultural and moral justifications. And given such inconsistencies, contradictions will appear between the legitimacy of innovations and the legitimacy of existing institutions and conduct. For example, the globalization of commerce or the thinning of the ozone layer, like the conquest of space or the exploration of the deep seas, challenges principles of property and national sovereignty. Thus American authorities did not know how to respond when the debris of a Soviet satellite fell on American territory, when a French research team lifted parts of the sunken *Titanic,* or when other French researchers identified the wreckage of a Confederate battleship off the coast of Cherbourg. Similarly, biotechnological innovations expand the ways to mark or measure more exactly the beginnings and ends of human lives, thereby challenging existing definitions of human death and human rights. Such technological revolutions create conflicts between the rights of comatose patients and their relatives; of mothers and their fetuses; or of an older recipient sibling and her younger donor sister, who was conceived for the purpose of providing an organ for transplant. Such conflictual situations undermine the individual body as a sacred receptacle of inalienable natural rights, even as they fragment family solidarity as a moral basis of society. Other social and technical changes, such as the AIDS epidemic or the intergenerational transmission of genetic defects caused by nuclear radiation, may create uncertainties in social relations that cannot be resolved in terms of existing moral beliefs or legal precedents. In such contentious conditions, neither elected officials nor bureaucrats or judges can offer much reasoned ethical guidance, and there are no neutral or objective processes to rely upon because there is no consensus about what in these cases is neutral or objective.

Rapid change also accelerates the obsolescence of legal statuses, thereby undermining a sense of the permanent validity of the law. For example, in 1965 Congress excluded sexual deviants from visiting the United States and stipulated that homosexuals were included in that category. But public norms have changed since then, and in 1979 the American Psychiatric Association stopped listing homosexuality as a psychiatric disorder. Bureaucrats in the Immigration and Naturalization Service and federal judges watching over them accordingly have made new laws, granting admittance to avowed homosexuals (Inglehart 1991, 1; see also Reich 1991a, 40). True enough, laws may catch up with changing technologies, norms, or administrative practices, but time lags between changes in the law, new but still informal norms, and people's actual practices undermine the legitimacy of each of them. In short, technological innovations heighten the dilemma of deciding when to rely upon existing definitions of fairness or justice and when to create new working concepts, thereby destabilizing the concept of legitimacy.

Threats to legitimacy also result from the greater division of labor and social complexity of modernity, which makes it more likely that each sector will claim the preeminence of its own standards. For example, in the arts, norms of both propriety and property must be defined to guide and safeguard cultural production and use. The legitimacy of the relevant aesthetic and legal norms underpins artistic paradigms and conventions and ensures the property rights of individuals with respect to cultural products (Becker 1984; Brown 1995; Clignet 1985; Wolff 1981). Whereas artistic *propriety* is largely sanctioned by and within artistic communities, *property* is defined and controlled by public courts of law, and each of these may hold different conceptions of legitimacy. In other words, the authority of the artist or critic is pitted against that of the judge or politician who claims to be the *vox populi,* speaking in the name of laymen. This position is evident in the debates concerning the conservation of buildings considered as historical landmarks by some and as urban decay by others (Thompson 1979). Such debates refer to rules of aesthetic propriety, norms of historic significance, and laws regarding private property. Such diverse norms of legitimization also apply to new buildings that appear to some as challenging experiments and to others as visual pollution. The removal of Richard Serra's innovative artwork, *Tilted Arc,* in downtown New York, for example, pitted the public, in the form of the inhabitants of the immediate neighborhood, against the state, represented by its experts located far from the actual site (Merryman and Elsen 1987).

Moreover, as each distinct sphere of activity—such as art, medicine, or education—develops its own specialized vocabulary and rationales, tradition becomes less useful as a guide in the face of rapid change. Thus the particular notions of legitimacy of each distinct sphere of activity get further removed both from the others and from everyday conceptions of fair play or justice. This deficit of common sense encourages recourse to litigation and the proliferation of attorneys in the United States. Moreover, in their efforts at professionalization and in response to the needs of efficiency, many law schools have sought to turn law into a formalistic technique. Such efforts too have widened the gap between official legal practices and private moral judgments. While the increasing incomprehensibility of the law to ordinary citizens enhances the need for lawyers and fortifies their claims to financial and symbolic privileges, it widens the gap between law and ethics. With the formalization of the law and the growth of legal actions and legal workers, justice tends to be reduced to legality, and whatever is not judged to be illegal by courts becomes therefore not unjust. Thus the law loses its legitimating function as the procedural embodiment of justice and becomes instead a scholastic exercise in the occult or an arbitrary exercise of power that is largely monopolized by lawyers and their wealthy clients—or, in the case of five justices of the Supreme Court favoring Bush over Gore, conservative judges favoring conservative politicians. In Habermas's terms, the system again takes over the lifeworld.

Increasing technological development and division of labor also accentuate geographic and social mobility and, hence, the flaccidity of social commitments, which in turn undermine the homogeneity and stability of lived moral frameworks and relativize all of them. Thus, as the sociologist Georg Simmel (1971 [1903]) noted a century ago, social pathologies increase in the metropolis. Today, however, it is possible for many people in suburban or even rural areas to engage in varied and ephemeral experiences, at least in their personal lives, and then leave them as soon as their needs or curiosities are satisfied. Such possibilities undermine the stability of the lifeworld and indirectly the legitimacy of the social order that is supposed to secure and stabilize it. "Thus a paradoxical situation is created: the value of law has always depended on its stability and its ability to predict conformist behavior" (Szabo 1973, 16–17). Yet when changes are too rapid, the law loses these essential attributes because fast-changing conditions and conduct can hardly serve as bases for seemingly permanent legislation. Indeed, with rapid technical and socioeconomic changes the law becomes more reactive and more redundant. It is more reactive because it is more difficult for legislators to predict changes that will require new legislation, as, for example, in the emergent areas of cybernetic or genetic technologies. Yet because rapid change also accelerates the obsolescence of earlier legislation, the law paradoxically also comes to appear more redundant or irrelevant, as, for example, legislation concerning technologies that are no longer much in use. Thus the law, and legitimation more generally, are often either outdated or too late.

As rapidly changing situations cause standards to seem ad hoc or arbitrary, these standards themselves appear relative and open to manipulation. Sometimes such effects of technological or social innovations on specific norms are counterbalanced by the use of cost-benefit calculations as a more general source of legitimation. But this usage implies that as everything has a cost, it also has a price. Such a reduction of all values to money is a triumph of means over ends and, hence, a devaluation of moral ends in general. The generalization of the expression "the bottom line" epitomizes this expansion of market calculations at the expense of substantive values. Max Weber (1978) had seen the danger inherent in the generalized use of money as a standard means of evaluation. The expression "formal rationality," which he coined in this respect, should be contrasted with the notion of "substantive rationality." Parallel concepts are "procedural justice," usually understood as "due process" or correct legal procedure, and "substantive justice," which refers to outcomes of legal proceedings that can be taken as just. Thus there emerges a large gap between legality (of procedures) and justice (of conditions or outcomes). Such gaps violate the moral bases of solidarity, which, as Durkheim showed, must be prior to any effective democratic law. In such circumstances the legitimacy of the legal system, and of government in general, is subverted. To speak of "healing" such ruptures is trivial or obfuscating because it personalizes and therapeutizes what are essentially political and social structural problems.

Something similar is occurring in the world of work. As technological change increases the division, temporal turnover, and geographic dispersion of labor, the product (the end) becomes more distant from the labor (the means) that achieved it. As the substantive purpose of people's work becomes less visible, it becomes more difficult to reconcile the moral agency of the individual worker and the procedures of the overall system. The person (the worker) becomes a cog in an ever more complex machine. This shift erodes the links between personal decisions and collective moral life; in the workplace, it is expressed in such sayings as "It's just a job" or "I only work here," connoting psychological and moral disengagement.

Theories of modernization assume the progressive rationalization of laws and legal procedures. One can imagine such an ideal improvement in the sys-

temization of multiple and mutually exclusive legal customs, as with the
Napoleonic Code in the nineteenth century. However otherwise desirable such
rationalization might be, it also fosters new frameworks of meaning that not
only threaten traditional views of the cultural, political, and moral orders, but
also are often, paradoxically, inconsistent with each other. Indeed, one might
say that the greater the pace of modern and especially postindustrial rationalization, the more it generates a postmodern culture that disturbs the normative
bases for its own acceptance. In other words, even though rationalization can
reinforce the stability of the system, it thereby limits the space and validity of
agency in the lifeworld and thus deepens both anomie and alienation and reduces the system's legitimacy. Moreover, as separate spheres of the lifeworld—
work, family, health—also get rationalized, these rationales may compete with
each other. The profit rationality of the corporation, for example, might nullify
the ethical rationality of friendships. As we shall discuss below, the shift toward
enclave cultures, lifestyle groupings, cults, gated residential areas, and other
communities of similarity appear to be a reaction to this. Though they offer a
partial solution, such enclaves also reestablish the problem: the distance between universalism and rationalization of the system and the particularism of
new lifeworld communities.

Whereas modern industrial societies justified themselves in terms of metanarratives of progress, freedom, or a better material life, postmodern societies
appear to lack an intrinsic justification. Their institutions come to be seen as
wholly artificial, to be constructed and deconstructed at will. As the activities of
technicist culture become more complex and specialized and as rates of technical and social change accelerate, there is a growing sense that the late capitalist
economy is at once inescapable, impenetrable, and irresistible. And because of
this, there is no close connection between what an individual actually does and
the social structural forces that shape his or her life. Free human activity increasingly becomes a matter of adjustment, adaptation, or "personal growth"—
all ethnically vacuous responses to situations that are often morally overpower-
ing.

On the one hand, the world is more abstract and unreal because increasingly
it becomes accessible only through abstract statistics, technical symbols, or
monitor screens. On the other hand, a new subjectivism pervades the realm of
private existence. The private (and increasingly the public) realm is given over
to personal feelings and expressions of emotion, which accounts for the tendencies to both psychological awareness and self-absorption. It was these qualities of both calculation and emotivism that characterized Bill Clinton's presi-

dency, accounting for its successes and enabling him to salvage it from self-created crises. Similarly, although a considerable majority of Americans favor Democratic policies and respected Albert Gore as more competent in this area, many also preferred the folksy affect and seemingly more accessible persona of George W. Bush.

A telling example of systems rationalization and radical subjectivism is offered by the explosion of the *Challenger* space shuttle on the chilly morning of January 28, 1986. Before the explosion, two engineers of the private firm that built the defective "o-ring" had opposed the launch because of the effects on the boosters of the unusually low temperature on the launch pad. The higher-ups in their firm and the authorities of the space agency invoked two managerial motives to overrule them, one fiscal, the other image. First, despite frequent and long delays in the execution of the program, the budget should not be overrun. The abstract definition of the fiscal year and the space agency's timetables that were built around it stood against the concrete constraints of the weather. Second, accumulated delays could be interpreted as caused by mismanagement and could therefore jeopardize the further growth of the agency and its private contractors. Officials disregarded the warnings of the two engineers and the concrete risks of losing human lives, to say nothing of highly expensive equipment and highly trained personnel. Instead, they favored the abstract concerns of budgetary timetables and public relations. The final decision was taken after consultation with persons located far from the launch site itself, persons whose information therefore suffered from reality anemia. Further, the formal appearance of consensus carried more weight than the concrete conditions under which it was reached or the direct knowledge of the people at the site.

When the warnings given by the two engineers became known to the public, both were punished for having jeopardized the welfare of the company. Even though the sanctions taken against them were eventually abandoned, their careers after the catastrophe illustrate how objectivized rationality can coopt subjectivized moral commitments. Apparently unable to cope with the tragedy, the first engineer asked for a long-term sick leave and then sued his former employer for several million dollars for emotional damages. The guilt generated by an ineffectual protest became in effect another source of profit. The second engineer became the company's official spokesman for all the improvements made on the o-rings since the ill-fated launch. His new role may be seen as a bribe he accepted from the firm as much as the result of remorse or of lessons belatedly learned.

In this instance, the bureaucratic system seemed to have a life of its own. The human purposes that the machines were designed to serve were forgotten, while the moral protest of two lone engineers was transformed into rationally calculable litigation or organizational advancement—personal gain on the one hand and corporate legitimation on the other. Worse still, the report of the presidential commission that investigated the disaster, led by William Rogers, as well as the comments on it by academics, emphasized the technical and procedural aspects of the incident. It thereby reproduced, rather than criticized or even noted, the hyper-rationalized discourse that underlay the failure of moral judgment that generated the disaster (Gross and Walzer 1997). As distinctions between good and evil cease to be grounded in personal experience or ethical judgment and instead are reified in electronically supported procedures or calculations, public actions become displays of either impersonal rational efficiency or moralistic posturing.

TRADITION, RELIGION, AND PRECEDENT
AGAINST THE SECULAR THRILL OF THE NEW

Americans conduct much of their activities through market exchanges, and they value both cultural pluralism and radical individualism and freedom. These attributes undermine any transcendental or universal values that support social conformity. Instead, Americans govern themselves through nontraditional, rationalistic legal systems that are geared toward efficient system maintenance rather than toward the fostering of any general ideology or morality except, of course, a patriotic commitment to the "American way of life." Religion tends to be more private and removed from public life, which is largely secular. Indeed, religion may become secularized as a kind of morally driven social reformism or personal therapy or, failing these, an intense eschatological religiosity that sees itself as deeply estranged from the dominant secularized world.

The United States has always been this kind of society more than other nations. From the beginning Americans rebelled against authority in their flight from the Old World, even as they affirmed the moral sanctity of their dream of a new one. The partly exiled populations of settlers and immigrants have oscillated between excessive doubts and unwarranted assertions about themselves, torn between forces that pulled them away from former homes or pushed them toward new horizons. The Puritans and Catholics of Britain nourished images of God and His grace unlike those that were preached by the official Church of England and that were adopted by the majority of their countryfolk and required by Britain's elites. Early immigrants felt relief and honor in avoiding the prosecution of the crown and in bearing a just cause when they landed on American shores. The same tension between an older authority and a newer mission also plagued last-born children of mighty families, who were unable to gain wealth within European rules of inheritance and so sought new wealth by new means in America. In addition, early American society was a plurality of religiously distinct cultures, many of which conceived of themselves as voluntary legal associations, such as that posited in the Mayflower Compact. The function of religion as a source of legitimacy was undermined, however, by the multiplicity of zealotries that have been typical of American religion since the earliest days of colonization (Eitzen and Timmer 1985, 521). And with a plurality of competing sectarian faiths, after a time the emerging public sphere became a religiously neutral ground not dominated by any particular religious dogma.

In brief, the very circumstances of the founding of the United States and the symbolic parricide by those Americans who created the republic suggest why, from the outset, successive waves of settlers were tempted to define legitimacy in terms different from those prevailing in their original cultures (P. Miller 1965; Ditz 1986). The foundation of America thereby established a tradition of anti-tradition, a legitimacy based on challenges to earlier forms of legitimation. This, along with American pluralism, individualism, and secular democracy, fostered the emergence of rationality, efficiency, newness, and profitability as criteria of the moral validity of practices and beliefs, since these appeared to be independent of any specific religion, culture, or national tradition.

Yet the boundaries between the profane and the sacred, or between the human and the divine, are more ambiguous than official rhetorics induce us to believe. The American republic has always overtly separated the state and the church. But the official proclamation of Thanksgiving by the president; the addition of the words "under God" to the Pledge of Allegiance; the references to God on currency and in civic, political, and academic rituals; the fact that oaths are taken on the Bible; the recurrence of religiously motivated movements of moral and social reform; and the diffuse religiosity of the American populace—all suggest that the secular state continues to derive part of its legitimacy from religious feelings that are not officially approved. Religion also manifests itself in public life in smaller ways, as when the two teams competing in the Super Bowl pray jointly before the game, or in the official rituals of Christmas.

Despite such residues of religiosity, the dominant American tendency toward secular politics and government undermines any divine legitimation of official power or even the ability to blame God for human failings. Secularism, part of what Max Weber called disenchantment, came with the rationalization of society and was justified as bringing increased freedom, affluence, and social justice. Without God to blame for persisting poverty, misery, and injustice, however, the fault could only be attributed to people and their institutions. "If equality, rights, and privileges were man's making, not God's, then all men were entitled to these social rights" (Bensman 1988, 17). Thus, the new secular dispensation has generated a demand for "responsible" or "effective" leadership, accountable to a historically new political entity—the people.

Yet this demand presented new and more complex problems of legitimation. The Enlightenment, having achieved a full, if distorted, rationalization of society, now turned back on itself by undermining the very principles that once sustained the legitimacy of the modern state. One example of the subversion of legitimacy through rationalization is the rise of social welfare programs, mainly during the Depression, to help restart the economy, smooth out the ups and downs of the business cycle, and placate the proletariat. While such welfare programs partly achieved their purposes, they also imposed more burdens on democracy. First, the passage of welfare legislation required a strong and energetic president who could concentrate and expand all the political resources of his office. Indeed, one could say that the imperial presidency began not with Andrew Jackson or with Richard Nixon but with Franklin Roosevelt. Roosevelt's reformist presidency disarmed those who otherwise would have been most opposed to the undemocratic concentration of power that was needed to enact those reforms. The welfare state also needed extensive governmental bureaucracies to be effectively implemented, and these new agencies further extended the president's power to persuade, manipulate, or coerce. Moreover, the expanded bureaucracies are hierarchic and controlling and, as such, inherently undemocratic in relations with both their members and their clients (Dahl 1977).

As long as traditional moral opinion and officially administered justice are in close correspondence, there is no crisis or fragmentation of legitimacy. The problem arises when morality, mores, and law are divided. In such a circumstance, there is little agreement on how ethics and mores can be translated into legislation that people accept as morally right. This is the case in contemporary America, not only for so-called moral crimes, such as President Clinton's peccadilloes, but also increasingly for property crimes, as seen in debates over the Internet about whether tariffs should be placed on foreign content or intellectual property. Moral and legal boundaries become unclear even in cases of violent crimes, as in the case of date rape or recovered memories of childhood incest. "Victimless" crimes are even more morally ambiguous, but so are "perpetratorless" crimes such as environmental pollution, faulty product design, or dangerous foods and drugs, where it is extremely difficult to identify culpable individual actors. Terrorism as crime or as political act is also ambiguous, as is contemporary war itself, where over 80 percent of casualties are civilians. In all such cases, traditional standards of legitimacy are inadequate, and each of the alternate standards proffered renders the others less believable.

Like other peoples, Americans endow particular aspects of their past with a legitimating power. At the extreme, *any* contemporary interpretation is seen as a deviation from an original sacred truth. Salvation is thought to require submission to the immutable power of the original political or religious text. For Americans these texts are the founding documents of their nation and its institutions. Thus the strict constructionist approach to the Constitution illustrates the appeal to tradition or precedents. For strict constructionists, all interpretations of the Constitution are suspect unless they focus on what the text "actually says." The ensuing debates are practical as well as doctrinal. For example, appointments or elections to judgeships have been blocked by conflicts over whether the right to privacy is legally protected, even though it is not explicitly mentioned in the Constitution, or whether the constitutional amendment barring the police from entering private homes without warrants includes protection from electronic surveillance.

In the political or legal arenas, however, Americans have encountered difficulties that often are alien to other peoples. Although common law was initially abhorred by some American settlers because of its British origin, in the nineteenth century it was viewed as an embodiment of the accumulated wisdom and best approximation of natural rights and duties (P. Miller 1965). Thus, cases of maritime insurance were adjudicated by federal rather than state courts, not for the logical reason that the federal government should be responsible for conflicts regarding ocean transport, but because American jurists drew on precedents created by the British admiralty. The struggle of some Protestant sects to ban theories of evolution from schools because they conflict with the Bible also illustrates the continuing legitimating influence imputed to the past, in this case an inherited sacred text. Similarly, in the secular sphere, Colonel Oliver North of the Iran-Contra scandal referred to heroes of the American War of Independence in order to justify assistance to Nicaraguan "freedom fighters," whom the United States supported. Yet the invocation of precedents as a legitimation of current actions is always shaky. Appeal to historical precedents may recall events or actors that many people would prefer to forget. Thus, the legitimacy of the past has enabled Native Americans to justify their claims on the basis of near forgotten treaties and the anteriority of their presence in America.

Appeals to reason may further complicate attempts to resolve conflicting interpretations of precedents or traditions. When Allan Bloom (1986; 378) accuses deconstructionists of valuing the interpreter's creative activity more than the text itself, he forgets that there are always competing interpretations of a text and that history is constantly rewritten to fit the needs and visions of dominant or aspiring groups. Which precedent, which original text, which framework of legitimacy to invoke are ever-present questions. For example, a wide range of different precedents is invoked by alternative legal metaphors used in adjudicating cases of surrogate mothering. One can rely on precedents governing conflicts over rents. Cast in this interpretive tradition, the renting of a womb is akin to renting an apartment. Conversely, one can extend to surrogate mothering the principles used to deal with prostitution, principles that forbid women from making money by using their sexual organs. One also can generalize the precedents of slavery to surrogate mothering and assert that selling one's own infant is even worse than selling a stranger. Finally, one can base decisions concerning surrogate mothering on the reasonings used to deal with the sale or gift of human organs for transplant, in which case donors or their surviving relatives are engaged in a charitable act.

The availability and use of such alternative interpretive traditions suggest the fragility of attempts to eschew interpretation in the name of some direct representation of an original truth. Instead, both the maintenance and innovation of precedents inevitably involve selective retention. In choosing an appropriate precedent or tradition, one undertakes a journey into the collective memory, and each such journey has its own duration and itinerary. Each may bring back different gifts (or curses) from alternate pasts. Each such version of the past seems to relativize the others, thereby promoting a postmodern view of all traditions as alternative rhetorical performances, none of which corresponds to any historical essence.

In more general terms, whereas the manipulation of precedents and traditions helps to advance immediate instrumental ends, such instrumentalism subverts the very conception of tradition that it exploits. Indeed, the principles of instrumental efficiency, rationality, and progress are the antitheses of tradition. Thus the more that tradition is used instrumentally to win arguments or justify positions, the more it is uprooted from its taken-for-granted normative contexts, and the less it can serve as a stable source of meaning, identity, and motivation. With the growth in technical efficiency of the means of mass destruction, for example, patriotism may become a call for collective suicide; with the success of demographic engineering, appeals to motherhood may be anachronistic. Family planning replaces instinct or religion as a vocabulary of sexual motivation, now directed by pharmaceutical enterprises instead of the church. Indeed, the practices of policy analysis or social planning announce that what once was accepted as traditional can be otherwise, that traditions can be used or abandoned, and that the choice is not in correctly interpreting the legitimate tradition but in accepting or rejecting it in terms of administrative criteria that themselves have no traditional legitimation. As the Islamic jurist and theologian Abu Hamid Al Ghazali observed many centuries ago, to be a traditionalist, one must not know that one is a traditionalist. Thus, competing invocations of the past in contemporary society undermine tradition as a source of legitimacy even while deploying it as a justification. In this process, the life-world becomes more rationalized and, hence, more available to penetration by the market, state, and corporations.

LEGITIMACY AND THE RISE OF
THE SUPERCORPORATION

Contradictions between the requirements of the state to protect capitalism and to govern democratically also undermine legitimacy. Contemporary capitalism needs state intervention to preserve the conditions of profit taking, regulate markets, maintain domestic order and the stability of labor, and defend the interests of capital at home and abroad. In avoiding economic crises, for example, or in schooling a new generation of workers, the government takes on an increasing role, even as this role is modified through corporate partnerships, outside contracting, or privatization. While the state has the task of sustaining accumulation, however, it also must maintain a certain degree of mass loyalty and acceptance of discipline. Although compliance with the rules and laws is secured partly by coercion, excessive coercion suppresses the innovation that is a requirement of global competitiveness for advanced economies. Moreover, the stability of societies claiming to be democratic depends more on the existence of a widespread belief that the system adheres to principles of equality, justice, and freedom. Thus the state in capitalist democracies must act to support the accumulation process and at the same time conceal much of what it is doing in order to protect its image as fair and just. As this contradictory stance itself threatens mass loyalty, it too tends to foster delegitimation (Held 1982, 184; Habermas 1975).

For many decades, a major resolution of this contradiction was the corporate welfare state. In this model, capitalist democracies depend on the state to maintain markets for labor and investment capital and also to provide policies and programs for welfare, social control, and legitimation. Marxists have argued that this model does not resolve the contradiction, however, because the interests of profit are basically inimical to those of welfare and popular self-direction. Instead, the state becomes unable to reconcile the popular demands transmitted through democratic institutions with the requirements of the national and international capitalist class, and the result is disorder and delegitimation. Ironically, a parallel view of populist democracy and social movements has been developed by conservative political theorists who assert that rising expectations will result in an "overload" of state bureaucracies and hence a breakdown of government authority, thereby proliferating further demands, further delegitimation, and further "ungovernability." Thus in both radical and conservative theory, the modern capitalist state contains a contradiction: its role as a neutral and objective mediator that defends the public interest conflicts with that of the interventionist state and violates its claim to legitimacy. The liberal state is an object and arena for struggle because it announces a promise it cannot keep: "Democracy, equality and liberty, within the context of capitalism" (Bowles and Gintis 1986, 225).

For conservatives, the recommended response to this contradiction is to suppress demands for wages and social consumption by strengthening discipline and restraint and by altering both cultural values and administrative practices (Offe 1984, 164–165). Conservative elites also try to limit or bypass the democratic values and processes that they believe are the causes of overload and delegitimation of the system. Thus elites may resort to extra-legal, nonpublic, corporatist, informal, collusive, or other poorly legitimized forms of policy making. In parallel, citizens may withdraw from official channels of political expression into social movements or even extra-legal forms of protest or social control, such as the Weatherman militia or other illegal violence. By either elites or popular forces, official political institutions are bypassed and hence delegitimized. Social movements of course also may function to renew and *rele*-gitimate democratic institutions such as the party system and elections, but if they fail, antidemocratic elite and populist reactionary elements grow stronger.

The role of the state and its interdependency with business advanced greatly in response to the Depression. The interventionist state and the process of corporate-state integration accelerated further during World War II. The acceleration continued in the postwar period, when the functions of government shifted from the passive role of night watchman to the positive role of enhancing the well-being of the American people through mass-consumption capitalism. This "unrecognized revolution"—as the London *Economist* (August 8, 1964, 550) called it—was epitomized in the Employment Act of 1946, which established the Council of Economic Advisers and led to active management of the economy by the state. The preamble of this act legally instituted the corporate state under the rhetoric of employment and general welfare: "The congress declares that it is the continuing policy and responsibility of the Federal Government to use all practicable means . . . to foster and promote free competitive enterprise and the general welfare . . . to promote maximum employment, production, and purchasing power."

Business leaders also were clear about what they called the "government-business partnership." As one leading industrialist stated, "Since the early part of this century we have been developing a new form of public-private society. . . . Call it what you will, the fact remains that this kind of government is here to stay, and those who would accomplish almost anything of public interest must work with the government" (Baker 1959, 12). This sentiment was often repeated by business leaders in their trade publications.

Many observers have noted the potential of great corporate and governmental bureaucracies to thwart individual freedoms. The founders were wary of the potential of democracy to become mob rule, but they also worried that even representative government could become despotic. Alexis de Tocqueville issued a complementary warning: that the rise of great manufacturers (today's corporations) would one day threaten democracy. What almost no one noticed, however, was the potential for a rise of both a powerful executive state and huge corporations working in tandem, largely to the exclusion of ordinary citizens. In shaping policies of the national government, for example, the major corporations are far more influential than the fifty geographic states. Indeed, in many areas of policy the latter are significant mainly as administrative districts for policies that are established by corporate and federal actors. President Woodrow Wilson asserted in 1908 that the relation of the states to the federal government was the cardinal question of the U.S. constitutional system. But this is not the case today. Instead, the cardinal question today is the relation of the supercorporations to the federal government. Federalism continues as the form, but it has little of the political or economic content that it had in 1800 or even 1900. Instead, "the supercorporations have produced a national economy which is superimposed upon a decentralized formal political order, and in so doing, have warped the federal system and undermined its legitimacy" (A.

Miller 1968, 19). In the new corporate state, the historical meaning of "social-ism" is inverted. Today, state protection, subsidies, and benefits are for "the al-ready rich and affluent, while the poor and the disadvantaged, who tradition-ally have plumped for socialism, are told to pursue the elusive path of rugged individualism" (A. Miller 1968, 73).

Yet the supercorporation has only a thin claim to legitimacy. Under the Con-stitution and in American cultural values, power, to be legitimate, must derive from the consent of the governed, through the vote or other forms of public ac-countability. But the corporate elite is in fact a largely self-appointed and self-perpetuating oligarchy. How then do the corporate oligarchs legitimate them-selves? First, they do so because they have delivered the goods to many Americans. Despite great inequalities, most Americans lead relatively affluent lives. Second, though the Constitution guarantees freedom of speech, highly concentrated media conglomerates restrict freedom of communication; thus the major media exclude viewpoints or criticisms they do not consider "reason-able" or "responsible opinion." The "culture industry" thus promotes citizens' passivity and acceptance.

The corporate elite also has legitimated itself through an ideological shell game. John Locke, the thinker with most influence on American political phi-losophy, conceived of the state as the defender of property. This conception supported democracy more in the early nineteenth century, when most Amer-icans were engaged in agricultural production and many were landholders. Af-ter the Industrial Revolution, however, Locke's arguments were applied intact to the new corporate concentrations of enormous wealth. This ideological tri-umph protected corporations not only from nascent socialist attacks on the pri-vate ownership of the means of production, but also from traditionalists who defended the old agrarian order. Socialism was largely crushed or coopted in America, and agrarian conservatives conflated the autonomy of the farmer with the autonomy of the corporation. They bestowed on the corporation respect that had previously been reserved for people who worked the land, in spite of the questionable connection between the two (Dahl 1977).

These changes had two major consequences that undermined democratic culture and the legitimacy of the state. First, although the new corporate order greatly increased wealth, it also polarized the society by wealth, income, social esteem, education, and skills. Moreover, the occupational structure itself sepa-rated the mostly white, Anglo-Protestant male owners and professionals from more recently immigrated "ethnic" wage-earning workers. These differences converted readily into political resources, with power now more concentrated in the new industrial class and away from an earlier agrarian demos. Second, the new industrial firms and government agencies were (and still are) hierarchic and often despotic. As large percentages of the population came to work in such organizations, Americans lived much of their lives in antidemocratic environments. Thus the space in everyday life for active democratic participation was radically reduced, and the habits of citizenship diminished. Although in the 1980s and 1990s there has been a growth of smaller firms and the percentage of total national production by the five hundred largest firms has fallen, a great number of these apparently independent small businesses are in effect subsidiaries of the major corporations, established to fly under the radar of regulations intended to protect workers from excessive exploitation.

TECHNICISM AND THE CRISIS OF LEGITIMACY

The rise of gigantic firms and the corporate state, with their avalanche of policies, programs, and experts, also fostered a new ideology of governance that may be called technicism. As the term implies, this orientation values the use of technique, or the means of achieving something, over whatever ends are to be accomplished. It thus gives a special place in governing to professional experts, the masters of technique. Citizens are still thought to have a role in setting ends, but this role is diminished as experts increasingly are looked upon to define which ends are reasonable or could be possibly achieved. Means are considered morally neutral, since they are now viewed as a matter of technique. Since the technicist language is inherently incapable of ethical self-reflection, it eschews substantive moral criticism. Thus, reasoned moral judgment about both means *and* ends is little by little excluded from the public sphere.

In using calculated rationality to advance profits or programs, corporate firms and governmental agencies also become the quintessential vehicles of modern power. Such organizations use information (more than knowledge) to control both their members and their clients. The roles of both functionaries and consumers are defined and shaped in terms of system efficiency, profitability, or organizational expansion or reproduction. For example, McDonald's has trained its customers to be their own waiters and busboys, as other firms have trained their callers with phone prompters to be their own service representatives.

This technicist way of thinking and being is, seemingly, highly effective in the operation of large, information-driven organizations, as well as for the day-to-day performance of the people who inhabit them. But it also has profound consequences for humane and democratic values. For when such a way of being becomes dominant in a society, corporations and bureaucracies are seen as having a life of their own. The human purposes that they were designed to serve are easily forgotten, and the cybernetic system comes to generate ends and purposes of its own. The relevance of freedom of speech and democratic action is thereby diminished, as is the public space for their enactment. In such a world, freedom becomes confined to a narrower and narrower sphere of private life.

Experts such as shamans and priests have always been a source of legitimacy because they possess sacred knowledge. Usually they are allied with political authorities or are such authorities themselves. In the modern period, lawyers, administrators, social scientists, and other professionals have been added to this list, and they too are used by secular elites (Haskell 1984). For example, American industrialists were keen to substitute expert arbitrators for lay juries in the administration of common law. In their eyes, such experts were more likely than the common man to advance elite interests. The role of experts has grown further in the postindustrial political economy, with its large-scale bureaucracies, global networks, high division of labor, knowledge-intensive production, and the apparent difficulty of individuals and groups to make informed decisions unaided by specialists. As expertise takes precedence over lay knowledge, even the most trivial statements come to be prefaced by references to the professional affiliations of their authors or disclaimers such as, "I'm no expert, but . . . ," which reduce the reasoned judgments of citizens to mere opinion. As expertise proliferates, reasoned public debate and shared civic consensus decline.

One can distinguish those who are *in* authority because they hold a mandate and those who *are* authorities because they have expert knowledge. Thus elected officials are authorities on nothing in particular but nevertheless are in authority, whereas plumbers are authorities on pipes and drains but nowhere are in authority except, perhaps, in flooded basements. In advanced societies, however, this distinction becomes blurred as specialized knowledge appears to be necessary for more and more activities. This necessity partly is due to the greater complexity of society as a whole, where a high division of labor makes many people specialists and almost no one generally competent.

The growth of expertise also is a function of the weaker links among the generations and, hence, a reduction of socialization into informal knowledge and practices. For example, large, extended, intergenerational households had little need of Dr. Spock or other experts in childrearing because such knowledge was acquired informally at home. Advanced economies also are more knowledge dependent in both production and consumption, creating more need and positions for experts. Thus, increasingly, experts are *in* authority because they *are* authorities—in medicine, management, accounting, law, education, and dozens of other domains. Social practices and institutions thereby come to embody an ethos that is less democratic than technocratic (Ball 1984, 743). Indeed, the very number and types of experts today are staggering. The media also have created a demand for expert commentary or at least punditry; there is even a *Directory of Experts* written explicitly for such authorities (Davis 1988). There also exists a voracious demand for self-help books written by self-named experts.

One sign of the importance of expertise is the pervasiveness of testing. Americans are undoubtedly the most tested people in human history. Testing often begins before birth, with amniocentesis. Americans also have their intelligence tested periodically when young, and their job aptitudes are tested a little later. If deemed suspicious, at work they may submit to drug and lie detection tests. And at some point they will likely check the status of their love lives, career adjustment, and development of their children with "objective" tests designed and evaluated by experts.

Another sign of technicist tendencies is the increased power imputed to machines, whose outputs are taken as trustworthy because of their neutral inhuman qualities (Beniger 1986). This position was an effective argument of the Bush campaign in 2000, despite compelling evidence of the fallibility of voting machines. Computer results also are thought to be insensitive to personal bias. Thus, Americans tend to place greater trust in the results of lie detectors than in live detectives (Hearne 1986). Similarly, many teachers assert that grades given to students on the basis of multiple choice examinations scanned by computers are more valid and legitimate than those given on essays assessed personally by instructors. Administrators see student assessments of teachers in the same light. This faith in machines contrasts to Catholic countries, where teachers and students tend more to respect hierarchic authority even while acknowledging the foibles of human judgment and where the analogy of the confession is used to legitimate the activities of examiners.

This resort to expertise has several internal contradictions. Since being wrong with the pack is much less damaging to one's reputation than being wrong alone, experts fear risk and innovation, and such fear reduces the variability of the judgments they offer in public forums. Competition among experts for public visibility may encourage some to innovate, but generally competition accentuates only the most marginal contrasts among viewpoints. Moreover, since expertise is expensive, the advice of experts as a whole tends to reflect the assumptions of their usually prosperous clients. In consequence, the range of insights, perspectives, and choices available to the general public is narrowed. Indeed, one way for elites to deflect and literally bankrupt an insurgent social movement is to seduce it into a "battle of experts," which the better-funded group almost always wins (Brown 1998, ch. 9). At the same time, the skepticism of ordinary citizens and divergences in the testimonies of experts undermine their collective claim to apodictic knowledge.

With the growing division of labor in society and in the academy, disciplines narrow into specialties, and individual experts no longer know much outside their domains of expertise. As their opinions are invoked in an ever-wider spectrum of ever-narrower fields, however, the relative distance that separates each of them from some common ground of shared experience keeps increasing. Then space is created for a plethora of how-to books. The creation of generalized ignorance is seen in the popular definition of the expert as "the person who knows more and more about less and less" or of the professional as "the person who doesn't care why or where she is going as long as she gets there competently." Thus, the privileging of expert technique denudes public life of reasoned ethical considerations and turns moral-political concerns into policy options, business decisions, and cost-benefit ratios, on the one hand, or unreasoned personal opinion, on the other (Farrell and Goodnight 1981). As a consequence, the notion of "public" comes to refer to the publicizing of expert opinions or the aggregate of individual sentiments, rather than to the public as an informed citizenry collectively forming reasoned political judgments.

Modern leaders must often make decisions based on technical knowledge that they little understand. President Franklin Roosevelt had to rely almost entirely on experts in his decision to develop the atom bomb, just as President Clinton did to assess the prospects of an air war in Yugoslavia. Yet experts often do not know the broader implications of their recommendations, and often they disagree—circumstances that rarely can be resolved by further expertise.

Nonetheless, champions of expertise advocate the technical application of scientific knowledge to all political decisions (Brown 1989). Their hope is that a scientific politics will eliminate the anarchy of conflicting opinions and interests and thereby enhance society's operational efficiency. In this form of legitimation, the discourses of engineering or medicine are taken as models for public life. In these applied disciplines, it is thought that disagreements are settled without reference to personal wishes or group power, but instead on the bases of objectively measurable preconditions and outcomes. Similarly, in a politics of expertise, "decisions" are expected to have the same neutral characteristics as those of engineering (Fay 1975, 23). This notion of how important disputes are resolved in medicine or engineering is empirically dubious at best, but it highlights key features of legitimation through expertise: the reduction of rationality to instrumental calculation, the separation of means and ends, and the disavowal of a rational consideration of values.

The technicist orientation has been elaborated into a full-blown theory of postindustrialism, with its own vision of the future and a set of strategies to realize its objectives. Though its lineage can be traced to Auguste Comte, leading thinkers include Daniel Bell, Zbigniew Brzezinski, Amatai Etzioni, and Philip Rohatyn. Technicism and the technocratic society have been discussed with varying degrees of complacency or alarm by Hannah Arendt, Niklas Luhman (1982), James Coleman (1982), Manfred Stanley (1981), and Jürgen Habermas (1975). Technicism also has been adopted as a basic orientation by top political leaders of most Western political parties, as well as by such formidable political economic organizations as the Tri-Lateral Commission, the IMF, and the World Bank. For these adherents, postindustrialism has brought forth an unprecedented societal formation that is so differentiated, complex, and interdependent that it requires, and to some extent has created, a new scientific form of governance and a new class of professional experts. These experts are to produce the appropriate types of policy-relevant knowledge deemed necessary for "societal guidance," thereby eroding the function, power, and relevance of both politicians and citizens. Thus, in the interest of efficient governance, technicist ideology and practice depoliticize democracy and largely exclude citizens from "public" policy.

One strand of technicist ideology that encourages this depolitization is the "end of ideology" thesis itself, especially as espoused by its two major American advocates, Daniel Bell (1991) and Seymour Lipset (1979). In place of traditional ideologies of the left and right, these new (anti-)ideologists substitute technicism, without noticing the concomitant growth of the corporate state and its penetration into sectors from which it had been excluded. Scientists and scholars are accomplices in delivering our pluralist society into the hands of big and bigger government to the extent that they affirm the privileged role of specialized knowledge in the guidance of public affairs. In *The Coming of Post-Industrial Society*, for example, Bell wrote that "Post-industrial society is organized around knowledge, for the purpose of social control and the directing of innovation and change; and this in turn gives rise to new social relationships and new structures which have to be managed politically" (1973, 20). In this new society, according to Bell, capitalist values associated with property, wealth, and production will gradually give way to values based on knowledge, intellect, and education. In place of the entrepreneur, the expert emerges as the new ideal.

Far from an end of ideology, however, experts and professionals themselves have crucial functions for a new kind of legitimation in postindustrial society. First, professionals and experts claim to be objective and disinterested in their service to society, thereby removing politics from the passions of the proles and putting governance on an objective, scientific basis. Second, the ideology of governance through expert technique obscures distinctions between who rules society and who runs it. It is true that more social activities are directed by persons with professional training and pretensions, but it does not mean that they themselves are not directed. And, indeed, though experts and professionals have become more important in running advanced societies, these societies continue to be largely ruled by corporate elites who themselves now reproduce their class advantages more through advanced professional education than through mere inheritance. Thus, technicist ideology announces the end of ideology even as it both obfuscates and justifies the continued domination of the corporate state.

Moreover, paradoxically, as state and market come to govern more and more areas of life that were formerly thought of as traditional or private, social conditions and personal fates are demystified and viewed more as the outcomes of political-economic management (or mismanagement) and less as the result of individual failings or natural causes. In effect, the visible hand of the state comes more to supplement the invisible hand of the market. Thus, people come to see more and more areas of life as political—that is, within the potential control of the state—though this politics has been shorn of its traditional or ethical legitimation. Further, more demands are made on the state, not only to make fair and efficient decisions over a wider scope of issues, but also to accommodate more and more varied constituencies. This "excess" of democratic demand, along with the demystification of the state, invites a legitimation crisis when the state becomes unable to either avoid economic downturns, on the one hand, or fails to provide adequate social benefits, on the other. Of course, class inequalities of wealth and power are crucial in these processes since the state must secure the loyalty of most of the populace while mainly serving the few. Yet as the state's role expands and these inequalities become more transparent, the state's further interventions stimulate even more popular dissatisfaction and delegitimation.

In America more than elsewhere, modernity implies the diffusion of the ideologies of rational calculation and possessive individualism across all groups and arenas of social life. But these two ideologies promote competing versions of legitimacy. And as the system becomes more rationalized and pervasive and people withdraw more into their personal or enclave worlds of emotion, this conflict deepens. The principle of rational calculation links legitimacy to objectivity, but the principle of subjective individualism links it to subjectivity (Macpherson 1962). Originally these two sources of legitimation joined in the notion of money or profit, which underlined rational calculation and measured the success of the acquisitive individual operating in a market economy. In postmodern society, however, with its oligopolistic public and private bureaucracies, its casino capitalism, its consumer culture, and its fragmented moral orders, these two earlier sources of legitimation have lost their common existential basis. Rational calculation and subjective individualism now represent two distinct strategies of individuals and organizations and two distinct and often competing principles of legitimation.

Though the subjective private realm of personal relations serves as a haven from the rationalized worlds of markets, corporations, and the state, extreme rationalization continues to erode boundaries between the two. The ethos of bureaucratic or market calculation encroaches constantly on the private sphere, producing reality anemia by reducing or reifying personal experience into generalized impersonal categories useful for managing others but not oneself. Correspondingly, the definition of freedom as the right to participate in civic life is transformed from a positive value into a negative one: freedom becomes the right to withdraw from civic life. As citizens become bureaucratic functionaries or private consumers, responsibility shifts from the individual as a moral being to impersonal rules, regulations, and calculations of efficiency, on the one hand, or to personal tastes and lifestyles, on the other. Morally committed action is thereby rendered merely subjective, if not irrational. In both the abstract system and the personal lifeworld, reasoned ethical and emotional judgments appear to be oxymorons, seemingly arbitrary and anachronistic because they are dysfunctional to the emerging techno-system. Thus, "rationality" itself becomes the ideological catchword for the mystification of a curtailed individual participation in public affairs and for the ensuing political dominance of elites and their experts.

PLURALISM AND THE TENSION BETWEEN DUE
PROCESS AND THE WEIGHT OF RESULTS

American concepts of legitimacy have been influenced by America's extraordinary abundance of land and resources, as these encouraged a plurality of widespread, distinct communities of belief. Decentralization, radical individualism, and the myth of the frontier, combined with a millennialist Protestant tradition, encouraged nonconformists to move further West, where they could join or create communities more to their liking. In the proliferation of utopias throughout American history, from that of the Amish or Oneida to more recent hippie, New Age, and militia communes, each utopian community stood as a challenge to both established sources of legitimation and those of other utopian groups.

The plurality of cultural origins of Americans has made it difficult to define the consensual basis necessary for political and social life. To be sure, the effects of this plurality have been counterbalanced by the myths and partial realities of the melting pot and equal opportunity. But earlier immigrants, such as the British and the German, enjoy clear advantages over groups that arrived later. The rank-ordering of Americans in terms of their time of arrival has undermined the timeless and transcendent quality of American culture as a moral order. Moreover, as social assimilation and mobility can often be bought only at the price of abandoning or even betraying one's national or provincial origins, "successful" individuals often experience social and emotional losses that erode the ideals of pluralism and the melting pot (Cuddihy 1974; Fuchs 1989; Vidich 1987). Even this cruel choice—ethnic loyalty and marginality versus assimilation and cultural betrayal—has long been denied to persons of color insofar as they bear highly visible physical markers of origin and stigma.

Thus, American nativism, on the one hand, and cultural pluralism, on the other, oppose each other as distinct legitimating principles. One attempt to resolve such tensions is to consider American beliefs or conducts as proper to the official, objective, or public spheres of life and to consign ethnicity to the subjectivity and particularism of the private realm. But such a stance makes public life impersonal, while it turns national, ethnic, or religious backgrounds into idiosyncratic folklore, thereby creating a seedbed for alienation and subversion of the legitimate order.

In response to pluralistic conflicts over basic ends and values, Americans have elaborated the concept of due process and of justice as procedural rather than substantive. Unable to easily reach consensus on substantive values, they assert that a correct procedure for making decisions should itself generate respect for its outcomes. As the popular expression puts it, "It's not whether you win or lose [that's important]; it's how you play the game." As the preeminence of self-interest and pluralism in American ideology reduced moral stability and consensus, the social contract was limited to focus on the formal procedures—rather than the substantive justice—of social transactions. One example of acquisitive individualism is that since the initial phases of industrialization, American legislators have increasingly abandoned the notion that the law should dictate the lower and upper limits of what individuals can offer or demand in contracts (Horwitz 1977). The variability of state laws accentuates the effects of this triumph of formal over substantive values.

The preeminence of procedure over substance is related to American conceptions of individual free choice; the pursuit of personal happiness; and the polity as a marketplace for labor, goods, feelings, votes, and ideas (Bensman and Lilienfeld 1985). In the absence of a broadly accepted vision of a commonweal or the good society, persons are thought to be free to pursue their own private interests, as long as these do not interfere with the freedom of others. But what then can be the basis of moral solidarity and political participation within the society? And why would people have a moral interest in fulfilling the private obligations of their various deals? In this situation, the concept of fair play has emerged in which legitimacy is not based on equity of outcome but on equability of process.

Given their individualistic and market orientations, Americans are slow to accept any general and transcendental ideal of justice that might ground this procedural conception of legitimacy. On the contrary, definitions of substantive democracy or justice are often seen as ideologies that serve one or another interest group. For example, critics have argued that the focus of the administrations of Ronald Reagan and George Bush on legalistic and procedural issues helped to shift public discussion away from substantive concerns about inequalities of class, race, and gender. An emphasis on procedure also legitimized the electoral victory of George W. Bush in 2000. Similarly, concern over official misconduct in the Iran-Contra and Whitewater scandals were reduced to the question, "What did he know and when did he know it?" Questions of the morality and appropriateness of the operations were thereby pushed aside. Likewise, debate over the Clinton health reform focused on questions of cost and access and not on the more substantive question of who should live or die—a striking omission given that over 80 percent of health costs are incurred in the last two months of patients' lives.

A focus on due process rather than moral substance also served to mask growing inequalities of wealth and power that emerged with the rise of great manufactures in the nineteenth century and have accelerated since 1970. For example, in dealing with conflicts about contracts, American courts for a long time retained the notion of fair price and the underlying sense of *noblesse oblige* associated with stable social and economic arrangements. Later, the courts began to selectively underline the importance of compliance to formal criteria and procedures that make contractual agreements binding (Horwitz 1977). Using arguments inspired by Social Darwinism, jurists sought to legitimate increased inequalities in the bargaining power of different economic actors. The courts simultaneously minimized the substantive limits that laws could impose on contractual obligations and maximized the significance of contractual procedures. Eventually, the law could hardly restrict the terms of bargains but only review the correctness of their forms.

Legality, as represented in documents such as constitutions, bills of rights, and statutes supported by judicial procedures, is, in Weber's terms, the basis on which legitimacy is claimed under a system of rational legal authority. Thus legitimacy granted by the electoral process is limited and restricted by the parameters of the law. When engaging in actions for which routine legal acceptance cannot be expected, leaders have been careful to find or create in advance explicit legal justifications—as, for example, in the Gulf of Tonkin resolution during the Vietnam War. When legality cannot be adhered to, clandestine actions are possible through agencies such as the CIA and FBI or through the subcontracting of illegal work to private businesses such as the Mafia. Since these latter actions are kept secret, they can be thought either to not exist or to represent only an occasional lapse into illegality. "Legitimacy is thus ultimately based on claims of legal rationality supported by rhetorical invocation of 'government of laws, not of men'" (Vidich 1975, 781). Mass communications, image management, spin, leaks, disinformation, and other forms of propaganda are also activities of government that are not part of the traditional language of the rule of law. Because government must resort both to propaganda and to extra-legal and covert forms of action, legitimacy based on due process is thereby put at risk.

Conflicts thus arise between legitimacy based on effective performance and legitimacy based on fair and acceptable procedures, because desired results sometimes can be achieved more easily if proper procedures are ignored. The conflict is illustrated by the hidden tension between law and order. The strict enforcement of the law may stimulate disorder, and the maintenance of order may require the selective enforcement, or even violations, of the law. Frequently in ethnic neighborhoods local police might permit (for a fee) community practices such as gambling because to prohibit them could generate resistance and disorder. Similarly, both the Weatherman underground organization and the CIA have claimed moral legitimacy for illegal armed attacks on the institutions of their own or other governments. The need to sometimes claim legitimacy for all varieties of political action places the politician in a precarious position when political choices involve severe moral compromises (Vidich 1975, 809). In these circumstances the legitimacy of rulers is easily challenged. Thus universalistic legal procedures, which emerged to manage cultural diversity, are undermined by illegal (non)enforcement in the interest of order, which also accommodates cultural differences.

In sum, emphasis on legal forms renders many Americans insensitive to the distinction between legitimacy and legality and, hence, between substantive ethics and procedural norms. This gap is fertile ground for the growth of cynicism (Goldfarb 1992). Thus legitimacy through due process and fair play ("how you play the game") is modified by a contrary focus on whether the action gets results. As Vince Lombardi, the coach of the Green Bay Packers, put it, "It's not whether you win or lose . . . , it's whether you win."

Legitimacy gained from the results of actions draws on the American traditions of utilitarianism and pragmatism. Americans distrust state power and believe that it can be given directly to private citizens or private firms that the state has legally created. Repeatedly throughout their history, Americans have attempted to empower the people directly or through their representatives and at the same time to limit the scope and power of state bureaucracies. The effect has been ironic: government in America is both big *and* weak. Thus legitimation through popular democracy generates conditions that undermine governmental effectiveness and, hence, legitimation through results (Morone 1991).

Further, in contrast to legitimacy through expertise, legitimacy through results is a lowest-common-denominator concept. Much like political mandates or opinion surveys, legitimacy through results emphasizes the significance of good numbers, such as the body count, the square miles of territory conquered, the amount of taxes collected, or the number of clients served. Like the formalism of due process, such aggregate numbers support the process of rationalization because they decontextualize and universalize any individual or collective claim to achievement by restating it in calculative, bureaucratic language. Measures of results in *outputs* of specific programs, however, rarely reflect the *impact* of such activities on overall goals or success. High body counts did not win the

Vietnam War, nor do high rates of job placements by federal employment agencies notably affect overall rates of unemployment. Hence, legitimation by results often involves conflicts in the meaning of success and which results are to be measured.

The invasion of Iraq in the early 1990s, for example, derived its legitimacy mainly from its battlefield success, including its limited American casualties, but lost legitimacy by the staying power of Saddam Hussein. Similarly, public failure to assess the legitimacy of the Vietnam War is partly due to the lack of positive results for either the right or the left. For the right, America lost the war; for the left, the rebels it championed turned out to be despotic killers. Hence, neither side could claim positive results to legitimate its position. Instead, the entire war is now discussed in the language of psychotherapy, as a "trauma" or "syndrome" that needs a process of "healing." Again, a radically subjective discourse of therapy is invoked when the hyper-rationalized system reaches its limits.

At the individual level, the importance attached to results—the bottom line, it is said—highlights the role of money as an embodiment of formal rationality (Weber 1978; Simmel 1978). The emphasis on results entails the substitution of utilities for meanings and, above all, the replacement of commercial for civic values. Once all meanings are either dispensed with or translated into comparable utilities, all values become subject to market or bureaucratic calculation, and legitimacy comes to be measured in terms of practical results. Absent from such calculations, however, is a grounding or context for the agent who is doing the calculating. In other words, what is missing in such conceptions of legitimacy is a cultural basis for moral agency and citizenship.

Since money is the most universal measurable sign of results, the sheer quantity of wealth or material possessions becomes an indicator of legitimacy. Such abstraction is also a subtraction, since universalization of measures hides the variability of what they indicate. Thus, the universality of money as a criterion of success is qualified by such distinctions as "new money," with its connotation of avarice and vulgar consumption, and "old wealth," with its implications of genteel inheritance and refinement of taste. Here older elites emphasize inherited breeding at the expense of acquisitive achievement.

The use of wealth or consumption as a measure of success and legitimacy reaches entropy, however, when further production and consumption exhaust scarce motivational and material resources. People want more and more things since the inherent value of any particular thing has been emptied by its character as a commodity and its use in status competition. Yet they want to work for these things less and less, since there is a proportionate decline in the inherent value of work. As motivation decreases relative to the supply of consumable rewards, legitimation again becomes problematic.

In some circumstances, legitimacy is maintained because the results of action are too disturbing to accept. Thus inertia by fear of the unknown can sustain an otherwise dubious legitimacy (Krugman 1991). Challenges to existing structures of power are costly, not only because of the repression they might trigger, but also because they may reveal the obsolescence of entire political institutions and make it necessary to build lifeboats for the deluge *après moi*. For example, President Clinton regularly "put his presidency on the line" for particular issues. Similarly, officials of the Reagan administration banked on public fear of a constitutional crisis when they fought for the candidacy of Judge Robert Bork for the Supreme Court, hoping that such fear would limit the Senate's scrutiny of the nominee. The Iran-Contra hearings also illustrate how fear of the unknown can legitimate action or inaction. President Reagan and his aides believed that both their opponents and the public would judge the costs of a new presidential scandal and impeachment to be too high coming so soon after Watergate (Vidich 1975). And they were partially right; presidential aides were more deceitful and congressional investigators more timid than they otherwise might have been, and the perpetrators went unpunished. A similar fear probably restrained some senators in the proceedings to impeach President Clinton and also encouraged the concession of Al Gore. Because of the fear of unknown results, actors in such crises may limit the scope of conflicts and avoid general confrontations.

In sum, the pluralism of belief systems characteristic of American culture has inclined Americans toward a legitimacy based on due process rather than on substantive general values. Yet due process itself is jeopardized when it yields unjust results, even as the achievement of useful or admired results (or the fear of bad ones), if achieved through illegitimate means, also can undermine legitimacy based on proper procedure.

LEGITIMATION BY MANDATES THROUGH ELECTIONS, PARTICIPATION, PUBLIC OPINION, AND MEDIA IMAGES

For a long time the franchise enjoyed by Americans had a limited scope. Even though the republic was founded on the ideals of liberty and equality, these were initially enjoyed only by free, propertied, white adult males. Former slaves received the right to vote only after the Emancipation Proclamation in 1863 and the Civil War amendments to the Constitution. Direct election of senators was enacted only in 1918. The electoral college continues to block direct election of presidents today. Women gained the right to vote only in 1920. To this array of exceptions one could add the recurrent blindness of both judicial authorities and public opinion to violations of universalistic values through open discrimination and even political terror such as the rape of women or the lynching of blacks. All such instances undermine the supposed indivisibility of liberty and equality, subjecting them to challenges and bargains incompatible with their alleged majesty as basic principles of legitimacy.

Legitimacy nonetheless is conferred by mandate. Mandates may be gained from public elections or from appropriate nominations. In the public sphere, actions of elected officials are presumed to be legitimate because the votes they have gathered entitle them to speak on behalf of their community—that is, the electoral community that constitutes them as authorities. Such mandates too are bound by notions of correct procedure. For example, the mass support of Mao Tse Tung by the Chinese was not accepted as legitimate by Americans because it had not been gained through free and fair elections. Some Americans question the legitimacy of George W. Bush's presidency for similar reasons. In the private sphere, the election or the appointment of the chairman of the board according to the corporate charter endows that person's decisions with legitimacy.

Similarly, husbands and wives are presumed to behave legitimately on behalf of each other and their children owing to the mandate they elected to give to each other when they married. Legitimacy derived from domestic mandates helps to explain the reluctance of public authorities to intervene in cases of family violence or of national governments to do the same in the cases of other countries' domestic strife. Of course, the domestic mandate has been undermined as the public has become aware of its role in perpetuating sexism and family abuse. Nonetheless, the Supreme Court decision of 1989 exonerated individual states from any liability for victims of domestic violence, thereby confirming not only the preeminence of the domestic mandate, but also the frequent lack of fit between public and private sources of legitimacy in this regard. Moreover, the decreased solemnity and increased secularization of rights of marriage or divorce jeopardize the notion of domestic mandate, which was already made fragile by the diversity of rules of the various states.

The role of political mandates as a source of legitimation has been eroded by a number of factors. First, the notion of representativeness of political mandates is increasingly attacked. Political representatives, whether congresspeople, governors, or presidents, are often nominated by pluralities of unrepresentative social groups for their own particular interests. The popular and electoral votes may be different, as in the presidential election of 2000. With increasing costs of campaigning and with most of the funds coming from economic elites, those with greater financial resources can effectively buy their own political representation (Neustadtl, Clawson, and Scott 1992; Qualter 1985; Rothman 1979). As in the cases of Malcolm Forbes or Ross Perot, some wealthy people can personally finance their own political candidacy or party. To the extent that electoral shifts reflect the success of opinion management through private money, however, the legitimacy of any possible mandate is thereby weakened.

Second, since the turn of the century the legitimating power of electoral mandates has been eroded by significant declines in levels of political participation (Neumann 1986; Piven and Cloward 1988). As a result, the electoral mandate may be more easily subject to errors, manipulation, or challenges (Dugger 1988). For example, the election of John Kennedy over Richard Nixon was contingent upon the votes of the Chicago machine, the absentee ballots of California, and the possible Mafia involvement in the countings from polling places in West Virginia. When Nixon did win the presidency in 1968, it was by a plurality, not a majority, as was the case with Clinton's victory in 1992. The victory of various presidents also has different meanings depending on whether one counts the electoral votes or the popular votes (as in 2000) or if one compares the percentage of votes won to the percentage of eligible voters who stayed home. For example, Reagan's 1980 majority victory represented a minority (only 48 percent) of the eligible voters, thereby undermining the legitimacy of his mandate. A similar story unfolded with the presidency of George W. Bush.

Last, preelection allegations of character weaknesses hurled by office seekers at each other—such as womanizing, mental troubles, religious sectarianism, or past use of drugs—erode further the legitimacy that successful candidates can claim after their elections. These may be combined with postelection charges and inquests, as in the case of Senator Robert Packwood, who was investigated for sexual harassment and forced to resign in 1992. Indeed, the diffusion of such charges spreads suspicion to all candidates and induces the public to suppose that innocence is only an appearance engineered by a temporarily successful cover-up. All these ambiguities make mandates a problematic source of legitimacy.

Engineered participation is another way that organizations and states have sought to generate mandates and also to link the workings of the political system

with moral meaning in people's lifeworlds. The collapse of traditional legitimations and the moral vacuity of both technicism and consumerism present elites
with heightened problems of social control that in turn have had two basic solutions: repression or cooptation. Often both these solutions are attempted at
once. Radical dissidents are suppressed, and moderate critics are coopted, and
an apparent mandate is generated by the local "machines" of national special-interest groups. In advanced capitalist societies, such cooptation has become an
integral part of sophisticated planning processes themselves, as evidenced by the
movement for citizen participation among liberal policy elites.

Yet the effects of greater participation are equivocal. On the one hand, it may
slacken the radical energies necessary for significant change, result in the cooptation of movement leadership, mystify differences of class interests by merging
them in a planner's vocabulary of efficiency and cost-effectiveness, or ratify a
materially exploitative class structure in exchange for mere status acceptance.
On the other hand, increased participation may also increase demands rather
than mollify them or result in an elitist backlash against participation that engenders long-term popular resentment, delegitimates elites, and reduces guidance of the system.

Despite its ambiguities, popular participation has become necessary to overcome resistance to technocratic guidance and to thereby stabilize the system.
Hence, efforts are made by elites to guide and coopt participation, rather than
to merely resist and suppress it. These efforts explain in part the rise of mass
opinion and money-driven electioneering. Indeed, public officials are tempted
to use mass opinion polls to both measure and gain additional support for their
decisions (Wheeler 1976). As an illustration, President Reagan, who was elected
partly for his anticommunism, sponsored surveys during the visit of Premier
Mikhail Gorbachev in 1987 in order to assess how Americans evaluated the
daily performances of the two leaders. Jack Valenti, a former presidential aide,
joked that Gorbachev was running third in the Iowa primaries. Such media images and opinion polls are used to indicate what political actors need to do or
avoid. The use of focus groups, polling, and Hollywood media consultants was
further refined by the Reagan and Clinton administrations. Candidates Steve
Forbes and Robert Dole in 1994 and George W. Bush and John McCain in
2000 used "push polls" in their Republican primary campaigns to covertly dis-
seminate negative information or lies about their respective opponents. Journalistic accounts also contribute to this image mongering, insofar as the apparent self-evidence and hyper-realism of televised news discourage reflection or
verification on the part of the viewer.

Media manipulation and impression management have become indispensable tools for successful politicians (see Bennett 1984; Edelman 1988; Entman 1989; Laufer and Paradeise 1988; Rosen 1988; Vidich 1990). Leaks of privileged information are a means of guiding media attention and hence public opinion. The belated "discovery" and publicity of the crimes committed during World War II by Kurt Waldheim, former president of Austria, are an example, since Waldheim's actions were certainly known and covered up long before they were created as topics of public concern. Likewise, General Manuel Noriega was allowed by the United States to become the strongman of Panama in the 1980s and was used by Colonel Oliver North as an arms runner and drug dealer, but this latter role was leaked only when Noriega ceased to be sufficiently useful. On the domestic scene, during the Reagan administration damaging information previously known to insiders, including perhaps some journalists, was published against Senator Joseph Biden just in time to lower the plausibility of his attacks against Judge Bork, then a candidate for the Supreme Court. Similarly, a journalistic report on George W. Bush's driving while intoxicated was published days before the presidential election in 2000. The late appearance and role of Anita Hill in the confirmation hearings of Judge Clarence Thomas also can be understood this way. Similarly, presidential advisers, from President Reagan's Michael Deaver to President Clinton's Dick Morris, are essentially managers whose job it is to create pseudo-events or to repair happenings that get out of control. As President Reagan's chief of staff Donald Regan put it, "Some of us are like a shovel brigade that follows a parade down Main Street cleaning up. We took Reykjavik and turned what was really a sour situation into something that turned out pretty well. Who was it that took this disinformation thing [American plans to attack Libya] and managed to turn it? Who took on this loss in the Senate and pointed out a few facts and managed to pull that? I don't say we'll be able to do it four times in a row. But here we go again, and we're trying" (quoted in the *Economist*, November 22, 1966, 27). The 1998 fictional film *Wag the Dog*, which shows master media manipulators creating a war in order to boost a president's ratings, has today merged with actual events.

The increased role of media images and opinion polls underlines a shift in the notion of legitimacy through mandates, which today are based less on the stability of the past than on images of the current moment, as suggested by the growing use of terms such as "spin doctors," "sound bites," and "handlers." Indeed, this shift is openly acknowledged by a television news show called *The Spin Room*, where spinners and pundits eagerly appear. Yet the mandate of legitimacy given today can be withdrawn tomorrow because reality anemia and historic amnesia have shortened the lifespan of public attention, knowledge, and ideas. Indeed, knowledge itself gets reduced to information and thence misinformation or disinformation, thereby narrowing the role of responsibility and consistency of any individual knower.

Through such processes, civic participation in a shared institutional life is reduced to the exercise of narrowly specialized functions or the consumption of reified and segmented images of the media. "The grandchildren of men and women who once stayed late in the night at the Grange Hall or the union hall, talking intensely with each other about what kind of society they wanted to build, now stay home watching TV [or surfing the Internet]" (Harrington 1985, 18). Media executives and website designers conceive of screen watchers not as citizens, but as segmented audiences and markets, each with its own demographic or socioeconomic characteristics, lifestyle, and pattern of consumption. This commercial culture supports the moral minimalism of many Americans, a solipsistic tolerance whose eleventh commandment is "Thou shalt not be judgmental" (Hall and Lindholm 1999; Wolfe 1998). Making collective judgments about shared moral/political issues, however, is precisely what deliberative democracy is about and what makes mandates democratic. Thus, much of media, marketing, and consumerism in politics subverts the classical meaning of the "public," reduces the reasoned judgments of citizens to mass opinion, and thereby undermines legitimation through mandates (Atlas 1984; Brenkman 1979; Geiger 1969; Mills 1963). Hence, whereas mandates formerly required public *actors* who either acted or actively abstained, they increasingly have become contingent on the *images* generated by the media. Even though people have become more suspicious of official information, distinctions are harder to make between actions and announcements and between announcements and advertisements. Indeed, the difference between action and image has narrowed as more and more of what officials do is done simply to be reported on, and being reported increasingly is what turns some occasion into an "event." Increasingly in postmodern society, the image *is* the action or event.

The theatricalization of civic life is made evident in the now famous question inherited from Watergate: "Will that play in Peoria?," as well as in the actions and reactions of the American TV networks and their publics to the Iran-Contra hearings and, later, to the presidential scandals surrounding Whitewater, Paula Jones, and Monica Lewinsky. Some viewers liked the Iran-Contra hearings because their repetitions enabled them to recognize the same players and procedures, the same challenges and strategies, that often were like those they had observed in the media coverage of Watergate and, later, the

Lewinsky affair. Yet other demographic segments of the audience were either bored or hostile, which induced the networks to lessen their overall coverage. Similarly, the dramaturgical styles used by congresspeople to ask questions of Oliver North shifted in response to the opinions that were reported to be held about him. And since Congress granted immunity to participants that protected them from later criminal indictments by Special Prosecutor Lawrence Walsh, theater did in the end triumph over justice. In turn, this triumph of theater has undermined legitimacy, as shown by the sympathy of many Americans for the "bit players" (notably Susan McDougall) that Special Prosecutor Kenneth Starr indicted in order to squeeze her for testimony damaging to President Clinton.

Americans' conceptions of the importance of public knowledge for democratic government are institutionalized in laws protecting freedom of speech and freedom of the press. "The right to freely transmit information and news was thought of as a powerful instrument not only for resisting the tyranny of government but also for the creation of an educated political community. The safety and well-being of democracy were thus linked to an intellectually enlightened public. With the advent of mass media and highly complex institutions of opinion formation, the slogan freedom of speech and press has been extended to cover these newer media. However, the media are highly complex bureaucracies which specialize in gathering and transmitting news and information" (Vidich 1975, 784). Often these organizations are the size of whole government agencies. Conversely, Starr's $70 million budget generated a prosecutorial bureaucracy on the scale of many of the news bureaus that were covering it. Both entities were primarily engaged in manipulating images and appearances, yet their own processes of manipulation were largely hidden from the public. "Thus, in both government and the institutions of the mass media, there is a backstage of administrative process which is managed by political and administrative bureaucrats who make laws and break them at the same time they manage the appearance of legality. So long as frontstage and backstage are kept apart—in our terms, so long as the propaganda remains intact—crises of legitimacy are not likely to occur" (Vidich 1975, 785).

In sum, media imagery, opinion surveys, and impression management increasingly are used to create facts and define outcomes, to create mandates for aspiring elites or to show existing leaders as rats. As such, they have become significant sources of legitimacy. Captains of industry now work through captains of consciousness (Ewen 1976; Qualter 1985); kingmakers and imagemeisters converge. Such image making pushes the political hyper-reality of the media further away from the lived experience of citizens. Whereas legitimacy always requires the presence of rituals and hence of social theater, the erosion of public space for active citizen participation in civic life reduces most citizens to passive witnesses of spectacles. The voyeurism caused by mass media undermines the active participatory rituals required for civic legitimacy and electoral mandates.

LEGITIMACY IN POSTMODERN SOCIETY: A REPRISE

The problems of legitimacy reflect basic tensions between the personal and institutional levels of American life. Social forms are always in tension with personal experience, but such tension is especially acute in fast-changing, culturally heterogeneous, and highly rationalized societies. An emphasis on stability maximizes predictability but impedes change, whereas a faster rate of change heightens the need for predictability and also reveals the fragility of links between social forms and personal experience. And since most social and ideological forms are also forms of domination, their character as obstacles to a more equitable allocation of material and symbolic goods also becomes more evident when their pretense to universality is relativized by rapid change. It is history, more than literary critics, that deconstructs ideological absolutes. While change heightens the need for legitimacy, it also makes any form of legitimacy more transparently ideological.

The crisis of legitimacy results not only from the accentuation of change, but also from the coexistence of contradictory time orientations of different social groups and their respective ideologies. Thus, the sources of legitimacy discussed above reflect the diverging time orientations of postmodern societies. Electoral mandates, religious judgments, due processes, and precedents all reveal the sacred quality imputed to the past. By contrast, the role assigned to experts expresses the myth of progress and a future necessarily better than the present and the past.

In an ideal past, the dominance of a single moral and political paradigm, and hence a single source of legitimacy, enabled authorities to identify and tolerate at least a modicum of conservative rear-guard and progressive avant-garde actions. In postmodern America, however, the moral center has not held, and there is now a proliferation of rear and avant-gardes, each claiming to be the old or new mainstream and each advancing its preferred form of legitimation. Hence, it has become more difficult to distinguish normal from marginal, progress from regress, or good from evil as the proliferation of competing mainstreams and avant-gardes encourages each to undermine the credibility or legitimacy of the others.

While accelerated rationalization, social change, and media images have multiplied the number of interest groups and individual commitments, they have not mollified the loyalties and attachments that already existed. Hence changes in the political economy generate contradictions both within and among ideologies and groups and a multiplicity of incommensurate political and moral language games. The ensuing crisis of legitimacy not only undermines the authority of institutions such as governments, schools, or families, but also induces self-doubt, or alternately self-glorification, in individuals who are now uprooted from stable moral meanings. Indeed, the erosion of legitimacy and the spread of narcissism are coterminus.

The centrifugal forces at work in postindustrial, postmodern societies are particularly visible in America because the high commitment of Americans to social change; their rejection of antecedents; their separation of church and state; and their faith in science, individualism, pluralism, and decentralization have always thwarted efforts to develop a coherent moral basis for social life. With the rise of the corporate state and the increased role for experts and professionals, the ideology and practice of technicism has grown, with all the problems for democracy and legitimacy that we have described.

Ironically, when public consensus concerning standards of legitimacy erodes, a politics of narrow and extreme interest groups emerges, along with efforts to rationalize legitimacy itself, in formal codes of ethics, review boards, legalistic insistence on procedure, and various instrumental tactics to simulate the appearance if not the actuality of legitimacy. All such efforts reflect the disjunction between an increasingly abstract, distant, and hyper-real social structure and a radically subjectivized and anomic (or liberated) individual existence. What disappears in this dialectic is any ethically reasoned sense of legitimacy or public good. When all versions of the public good are radically relativized, organizational legalism seems to be the only source of stability as legitimacy fragments.

Yet the changes discussed may be as much a source for hope as a cause of despair (Bartel 1996, 31). Those cultures may be the richest—in resources and potentials, in complexity of ideas, in experimentation and critique—that display tensions within their discourses of legitimation rather than a hegemonic dominance of any one of them.

Chapter 4 Social Movements, Politics, and Religion in a Postliberal Era

In light of the difficulties of reforming the American political economy through conventional means, many observers and activists, of both the right and the left, have put their hopes in grassroots social movements, especially what have been called the "new" social movements (NSMs). Yet as we shall see, these new (or renewed) social movements are as often reactionary as they are progressive, they are readily coopted by the corporate state, and they often turn to a radical subjectivism or emotivism that is more a symptom of the established order than a serious effort to change it. Nonetheless, renewed social movements have often been politically innovative and influential and a source of sustenance for cultural values and identities.

"Social movements" (what sociologists used to call collective behavior) refer to sustained group or mass political action outside the boundaries of established institutions. Earlier views of social movements were mechanistic. For example, in the decades after the French Revolution, the social philosopher Henri de Saint-Simon spoke of social movements as akin to celestial movements in a Newtonian social universe. Thus he viewed workers' movements as a natural adjustment to the dislocations created by industrialization.

As the state, market, and private spheres became differentiated in Western societies, social movements emerged as a legitimate form of political action. Since then, the boundaries of what is a "social movement" have been much contested. For example, Eli Zaretsky (1976) posited a broad definition in arguing that the highly bureaucratized War on Poverty had a rhetorical career much like that of a social movement. Michael Calvin McGee pushed the concept back to Elizabethan England, at least as a rhetorical style. "In studying public address in England from 1550–1800, I have observed literally every technique of persuasion that prescriptive theorists have associated with so called 'social movement rhetoric.' . . . Books, witches, Catholics, and threshing machines were cremated in much the same spirit that the Berrigan brothers destroyed selective service records. . . . After about 1750, the world was gradually democratized [and] mobs were symbolically transformed into civilly-disobedient citizens demonstrating grievances by breaking unjust laws . . . and discourse that was once seditious libel became public address. After the turn of the nineteenth century, all of these symbolic transformations came to be associated with social and historical 'movements'" (1983, 75; see also 1980). In a similar skeptical spirit Klaus Eder (1993) asks whether the NSMs are moral crusades, political pressure groups, or *real* social movements. Others, such as Claus Offe (1985), exclude religious movements from the category because he deems them nonpolitical, whereas Rhys Williams (1992) believes that religion is often a cultural resource for social movements that themselves may be essentially political in character.

It does seem that NSMs are not historically unique. In the United States, for example, NSMs concerned with reenergizing religious beliefs, freeing slaves, protecting occupational interests, prohibiting alcohol, and stirring up patriotism (among others) date as far back as the early nineteenth century (Calhoun 1994). Further, many of the traits associated with NSMs characterize most social movements in their early stages (Tarrow 1989; see also Ashley 1997, 69–70). An example is the lesbian and gay movement, which often is considered to be the quintessential NSM or identity movement (Melucci 1989; Duyvendak 1995; Kriesi et al. 1995). To overcome the stigmas borne by homosexuals has required assertions of self-value and struggles against cultural stereotypes. Yet this movement, which at first focused on transformation of self and social norms through sexual liberation, is becoming one that seeks to advance its political rights through a narrower, interest-group politics, sometimes through the generally homophobic Republican Party.

The category of social movement can contain a wide range of collective agitations for social or cultural change. Indeed, the particular aims and repertoires of collective action used by social movements in the West have varied historically. In the eighteenth century, the dominant movements were localized peasant efforts to resist the intrusion of capitalistic economic relations. With the consolidation of capitalism and the working class, this form of protest was replaced by the politics of labor movements and socialism in the nineteenth century. By the mid-twentieth century, however, the welfare state reoriented class conflict into a more diffuse politics over distribution of benefits. Finally, the decline of work as *the* determining feature of social life and the intrusion of both the state and commercial processes into everyday life have given greater importance to a politics of lifestyles and identity in the NSMs in the United States and Western Europe (see Melucci 1996; Dalton and Kuechler 1990). In the first decade of the twenty-first century, however, social movements increasingly address collective issues such as poverty or pollution and increasingly are global, or at least international, in form and operations. International nongovernmental organizations (NGOs) expanded from fewer than one thousand to eighteen thousand during the 1990s.

The approach taken by social sciences to social movements has varied with these changes. During the relatively calm 1950s, for example, explanations by structural functionalists such as Neil Smelser seemed adequate. The vast expansion of social movements in the 1960s, however, led to a reconceptualization of social movements in terms of conflict and a focus on political opportunities and the resources that groups could mobilize to exploit them. The prominence of social movements organized around lifestyles or identities since the 1970s and 1980s has encouraged an emphasis on the symbolic cultural and discursive aspects of social movements and how issues are framed rhetorically for various publics (for example, Larana, Johnson, and Gusfield 1994; Klandermans 1997; Johnston and Klandermans 1995; Stryker, Owens, and White 2000). Today, processes of globalization increasingly provide a context for the study of social movements.

As a result of these shifts in both practice and theory, the study of social movements can draw on a wide range of theoretical approaches. For example, Marxists tend to view social movements as extensions of class politics, such as the labor movement or socialism. Writers in the utilitarian tradition of John Stuart Mill might see them more broadly, and less radically, as part of interest-group politics, within which class interests are only one element. Followers of Max Weber or Emile Durkheim interpret social movements as charismatic or symbolic rejections of the rationalization of advanced modern societies or a particular group's place (or displacement) within it. Indeed, a focus on the psychocultural and symbolic aspects of social movements seems particularly illuminating today, when class politics is in relative decline and interest-group politics has been thoroughly institutionalized through well-established local and national associations. By contrast, many of the NSMs—both religious and secular—are less based in specific classes or driven by specific group interests.

MODERNIZATION, SELF, AND COMMUNITY
IN SOCIAL MOVEMENTS

In premodern communities, identities as well as labor processes are more oriented toward families, clans, and intergenerational relations of patronage and fealty. With the rise of modern capitalism and the modern bureaucratic state, however, persons emerged from the bonds of kin and estate as discrete economic, psychological, and legal individuals who interacted with each other more through anonymous markets, firms, and government agencies than by direct personal relations. Central in both the mental and practical orientation of modernity was its secular, instrumental rationality, which brought efficiencies in economic and political realms but which also seemed to atomize individuals and undermine any collective ends or meanings. This condition has been described as alienation by Marx, as rationalization and disenchantment by Weber, and as anomie and egoism by Durkheim.

Social movements, both religious and secular, are partly generated by the central aspects of modernity itself. One of these, the weakened cohesion and continuity of families, neighborhoods, and communities, renders individuals more in need of new group filiations that can support their identities. In this sense, social movements provide a source of meaning, identity, and community that may be otherwise unavailable in modern societies except through religion. Indeed, many modern social movements have a religious style if not an explicitly religious belief. For example, the abolitionists argued that slavery was not merely economically inefficient, but also unholy and immoral. Alcoholics Anonymous (AA) is another religiously infused secular social movement. While the public rhetoric of AA emphasizes the economic and social damages caused by the "disease" of alcoholism, the group's primary thrust is personal redemption.

Conversely, although Americans are the most committed church-goers in the West, religion itself has become largely secularized, privatized, or individualized and often reduced to feelings, emotions, or therapy. Partly in response to this increasingly private and therapeutic character of established religion, charismatic cults and religious revivals, like those of the Pentacostals, have emerged as efforts to recover a more integral and sacral sense of selfhood. Membership in or identification with mainstream Protestant and Jewish religious organizations has declined significantly, whereas affiliation with evangelical or New Age organizations has grown rapidly since the 1950s. The paradox is that as religious groups respond to modernity by becoming more ecumenical and therapeutic, they become less religious, whereas if they stress religious faith and enthusiasm, they tend to become more cultic and committed. Thus, as mainline denominations have become more secular, therapeutic, and bureaucratically organized, they have lost their share of a giant market for *religiosity* to more enthusiastic, absolutist, and participatory sects. While membership in Episcopalian and Methodist churches declines, Southern Baptists and the Assemblies of God have increased. A part of this growth can be attributed to a strong social solidarity that is generated by high demands for members' time and high standards of personal conduct (Finke and Stark 1992).

For most Americans, religion of the first kind is a retreat into a private sanatorium for the soul; for others the second provides the ideological and organizational resources for collective agitation. At the same time, many members of the increasingly secularized mainline (sometimes called oldline or sideline) churches find emotional engagement, solidarity, and communal identity through secular but religiously infused progressive social movements. In other words, the decline of mainline churches and the rise of sectlike ones both feed NSMs. In this light, the growth of conservative fundamentalist churches may not be due to their conservative ideology per se but to the fact that they create closer, more cohesive communities.

Thus many religiously infused social movements can be seen as a kind of symbolic politics—some by progressive blacks organized by or around churches, others by small-town, middle- and working-class whites to maintain or recover an eroding social status and respectability in response to secular modernity. Examples of the latter are the Moral Majority and Liberty Foundation, founded by Jerry Falwell; the Christian Coalition, founded by Pat Robertson in 1989; and Promise Keepers, led by football coach Bill McCartney. Such organizations have opposed the Civil Rights and women's movements; deeply distrust the new national technical and professional elite; and view the AIDS epidemic as a confirmation, both objective and divine, of their critique of modern permissiveness and moral decline, especially sexual. Sometimes these movements organize and express great fury, as in beatings against gays or abortionists or against blacks who symbolize the decline of white supremacy (Patterson 1998). These are blows against modern individualism, with which local police, themselves mostly white and working class, are often sympathetic.

Resistance to the rationalization of modern societies also may be formed on the basis of ethnicity or race as alternative sources of identity and community. New, often transnational, ethnic movements are creating extended forms of blood communities that formerly were associated with primitive kinship groups and clans. These neo-ethnic communities often are reactions to the very institutions and technologies of postindustrial society that make such new, extended tribes possible. Examples are militias, skinheads, and white, black, Christian, or Muslim nationalist movements. Indeed, the more encompassing the scope of the rationalized system, the greater the appeal of small-scale, chiliastic, and particularistic affiliations. What is at stake in such movements is not the defense of a traditional society, however, but a lifeworld that is already modernized yet incompletely or inadequately so (J. Cohen 1985, 710). Societies or groups in which these movements occur are usually well into a transition from communal, ascriptive, and functionally diffuse roles to ones that are already individuated, achievement oriented, and highly differentiated.

While awaiting the coming of their respective kingdoms, fundamentalists often are busy disciplining the wayward and punishing those who refuse the true faith. In this, their demonizing stereotypes in many ways replace those of the Cold War, in which evil Soviets were pitted against pure Americans. Such movements thereby offer new forms of social solidarity and psychological succor against real or imagined enemies, like those who would forbid prayer in public schools or "creationism" in science. Such populist religious mobilization has local variations and causes but is part of a broader pattern of discontent with the alienating and anomic rationality of modernity. Whereas modernity relativizes traditions, redefines inherited beliefs as unreflective prejudices, disconnects people, and relies on impersonal markets and large bureaucratic organizations, social movements reinforce basic truths, inspire commitment, and reestablish group cohesion through direct participation. Instead of alienation there is solidarity; instead of rationalization there are shared emotions; instead of anomie and egoism there is common meaning and purpose.

Social movements also can form on the basis of (rather than in reaction to) the expanded range of interactions that comes with the breakdown of traditional communities. Modern persons can easily associate with those who are neither family nor neighbors. Industrial civilization concentrates vast numbers of people in metropolitan and suburban regions; thus, the labor movement was the product of cities, not villages. Over a century later, postindustrial technologies of communication and transportation expand the boundaries of shared experience even further, creating new forms of both solidarity and atomization, subverting traditional communities and fostering new ones that have no spatial boundaries at all and can be formed around an agency as evanescent as a website (Vidich and Hughley 1988). For example, diasporic Palestinians in America and elsewhere play a key role, through over 150 websites, in both domestic ethnic organization and in their national liberation movement (Stillman 2000). With the ease of entering and leaving such communities, relationships and commitments also become more fragile and mobile, more far flung, and more easily shaped by each individual in a quest for an ideal world. The Internet, for example, was the prime medium through which Jody Williams organized a worldwide movement against the use of military landmines; the effort eventually led to international regulation by most nations and a Nobel Peace Prize for Williams in 1998.

In this sense, protests such as those over abortion or the environment are puzzling to (or labeled "infantile" by) orthodox Marxists, who have viewed progressive action as occurring only at the point of production, with workers as the vanguard. From the Marxist perspective real power was economic and industrial, and significant change required control over production, for which unions and labor movements were the primary instruments (Poulantzas 1982). The shortsightedness of this perspective is illustrated in the polemics directed at Frantz Fanon, who argued that farmers of the developing world might be the symbolic equivalents of the workers of the early phases of industrialization. Their assumptions also blinded many Marxists to the progressive possibilities inherent in citizens' initiatives around local community issues or around gender, ecology, or religion, because the local community was often viewed as inherently conservative.

It is true that class politics is difficult to organize at the national level, except of course ruling-class politics. The two major American political parties must ignore certain constituencies in order to retain the support of their major funders—corporations and wealthy individuals. In such conditions, nonelite class interests are at least partly expressed through cultural movements rather than through the party system (Offe 1985). The result for most citizens is either to withdraw from civic involvement and to redefine liberty as the right *not* to participate or, conversely, to mobilize politically through means outside the state or party. Just as elites bypass democratic procedures and turn to alternative, behind-the-scenes mechanisms for decision making, so individual citizens either cease to vote (or do so only ritualistically) or engage in extra-institutional political action. Citizen action is then based in churches; universities; labor unions; groups oriented around ethnicity, gender, or lifestyles; and other nonofficial and nonparty bases of social mobilization.

These developments are more likely in the United States than elsewhere since the American electoral college effectively excludes parties that are not mass based and therefore includes only those that are heterogeneous and non-ideological. Moreover, as the political economy shifts from production toward consumption, political parties with a base in the working class give way to social movements based more on lifestyles and identity. For example, Alain Touraine (1981) noted that the movement for civil freedom was central in mercantile societies, whereas the workers' movement was its fulcrum in industrial society, and we have now entered a postindustrial phase with new forms of social movements. Thus, the intrusion of the state into the lifeworld or civil society is matched by the expansion of social resistance into domains outside of the political economy strictly defined. Those domains concern ecology, housing, health, education, transport, and the like; as a result, the function of the relevant social movements is to foster and mediate an improved reflexivity regarding the construction of both reality and social identity as a whole.

Such analyses of social movements turn us from an orientation toward economic interests to a more Weberian or Durkheimian focus on meaning. In this view, social relations are no longer merely reflections of class positions and interests but are now seen as interactions soaked with values within a cultural field of contested identities, statuses, and meanings, as well as interests. Social action is not analyzed as driven by an inner logic of the system but as the means through which society and its history and members are constituted. This way of seeing social movements as sources of identity, solidarity, and community offers, in effect, a structural account of the religiously secular and secularly religious social movements discussed in the next section. Moreover, rather than a concentration on essentially class issues of productivity or even distribution, for both religious and secular NSMs what is at stake is the very arena in which struggles now take place—civil society itself. Indeed, the concept of civil society is central even when negated, for it constitutes both the normative continuity of modern societies and the terrain of their social struggles. That is, civil society is the main bearer of such values as tradition, liberty, patriotism, or justice, as well as the principal arena in which they are contested. In these terms, modern societies *are* modern precisely because they have been institutionalized through democratic revolutions and ongoing social movements as *civil* societies, which are distinct from yet related to families, corporations, markets, and the state. From this standpoint, the defense and extension of civil society provide both a narrative structure for the project of modernity and the norms for judging whether particular actions of markets, states, or social movements are "reactionary" or "progressive."

Such changes in the articulation of politics in the United States have made Marxian analyses problematic, especially those concerning the class basis of politics and its instrumental nature. For example, identity-based social movements are more "expressive" than "instrumental." For many actors in NSMs, values are more important than interests, direct participation more important than "checkbook membership," solidarity more important than efficiency, and process more important than product (Touraine 1981; Melucci 1996; Calhoun 1994; Kriesi et al. 1995, 84–85). Once the new collective identity becomes recognized and consolidated, however, action becomes less expressive and more instrumental, and direct participation gives way to representation, though not necessarily based on class membership (C. Cohen 1995). Contemporary social and political movements are thus hard to understand in terms of accepted theories of modernity and modernization, in which politics are supposed to be pragmatic, technocratic, instrumental, and driven by specific class or group interests.

Although modernity remains the dominant mode of political life, antimodern and postmodern challenges have emerged that articulate the feeling that modernity no longer provides adequately for human meaning or species survival. Instead, NSMs—often devoted to feminism, peace, and the environment, but also sometimes to religion or ethnicity—generally advance a less instrumental and alienated future by pursuing and practicing ecological wholeness, community, and spirituality. Although usually secular and nontheistic, they draw on religious pantheism and sacred views of human nature and destiny to seek a transformed humanity more than interest-specific reforms.

In sum, continuing class conflict and economic injustice are being supplemented by other issues that are more difficult for the liberal bureaucratic state to absorb or reconcile. These issues—ones of cultural identity, not only of economic class—have been described as "postmaterialist" or "postacquisitive," as opposed to issues of income or material security. Postmaterialist values such as community or self-development are especially important among new urban groups with relatively high disposable incomes, for whom "material" concerns about wages and jobs are not urgent, except perhaps in cyclical periods of economic crisis or recession. Animated by postmodern political sensibility, many of today's social movements engage in a secularized religious politics but not from any theological or churchly standpoint. However, NSM values of community, solidarity, and identity may as well be called *anti-* or *pre*modern insofar as they also characterize the Christian right. These changes, especially evident in the United States since about 1970, suggest that the American political economy and culture are entering a postmodern condition (Lyotard 1988; Harvey 1989), a shift also implied in the concept of "old" versus "new" social movements. NSMs themselves have been called postmodern in the sense that they often reject grand narratives, especially a universal modernist one, and instead focus on particular changes and worlds of meaning. In both their reactionary and progressive forms, such movements favor an antimodern primitivism in their propensity for direct, simple, and emotional forms of expression, at the center of which is a "return to the self" and to issues of feelings and community.

SOCIAL STRUCTURAL AND CULTURAL BASES FOR NSMS

The corporate state has broadened political participation as a form of legitimization and cooptation even while confining it to established ritualistic channels and narrowing the range of viewpoints that can be given air time as "responsible opinion." In turn stability and predictability have been enhanced, and thus a better economic climate for planning and investment has been created. For example, after the defeat of socialist and radical unionists early in the twentieth century and especially after World War II and during the Cold War, "business unionism" became the dominant mode of labor activism. Unlike those who saw the union movement as part of a larger struggle for social and economic justice, the business unions focused narrowly on wages, working conditions, and benefits for their members (Gerson and Armbruster 1997). This model was effective, at least for union members and business elites, as long as most of American industry was oligopolized and hence could pass on wage increases to consumers without reductions in profit.

This system began to change about 1970, with social structural and cultural shifts toward a globalized, postindustrial, postmodern society. For example, the U.S. share of global trade following World War II was 48 percent. But in the 1960s, as the economies of Japan and Western Europe recovered and again became competitors, America's share of world trade began dropping to its current, historically more usual level of 28 percent. With greater global competition came squeezes on profits, greater resistance by capitalists to compromises with labor, and union busting by the federal government under President Reagan. One reflection of this change has been the decline of the labor movement (Brecher and Costello 1990).

Other symptoms of systemic changes since 1970 include a decline in class voting and support for the two major parties and the rise of new political forces, such as nonaligned, independent voters and various reactionary or progressive social movements. Other changes that have undermined the old alliance between capital and labor, which was the precondition of the success of business unionism, include new modes of flexible production; a harsher, two-tiered labor market; the automation or exporting of many industrial jobs; management policies of cooptation (such as worker participation programs and flatter hierarchies in business organizations); a greater entry of women and minorities into the full-time paid labor force; and the rise of the media (as opposed to the family or the workplace) as primary sources of socialization into consumerist rather than class ideologies (Gerson and Armbruster 1997; Brecher and Costello 1990; Harrison and Bluestone 1988; Harrison 1994; Piven 1992). With these changes, older class divisions and identities have weakened, thereby undermining the political cohesion of most economic groups and, hence, class politics.

The unions, parties, and other mediators of popular interests or dissent responded to these challenges largely by further narrowing their scope and focus, centralizing their managerial control, and using mass techniques rather than grassroots participation for recruiting and mobilizing members. These essentially bureaucratic responses ultimately weakened the appeal of both the labor unions and the parties and made them vulnerable to crises of legitimacy. Weber's exhortations against lackluster bureaucratic politics and Robert Michels's warning about "the iron law of oligarchy" in labor organizations seemed to be confirmed.

NSMs can be seen as a response to these changes and an attempt to resolve them by expanding private morality to the public sphere or, conversely, reclaiming the personal as political. The Moral Majority, for example, was "founded . . . in direct response to new initiatives by the state" (Wuthnow 1988, 317). As noted, such groups promote emotional involvement, personal participation, and local organizational autonomy, and they use the affective language of religion, community, family, and human rights. These factors do not necessarily make their politics reactionary or irrational. Instead, the NSMs pursue a *value rationality* that uses moral principles to assess political actions and outcomes, often leading to moral absolutism and cultural, if not political or programmatic, radicalism insofar as the affirmed values provide the bases for condemning existing institutions and practices (see Offe 1985; Melucci 1996; Misztal 1985). Thus the NSMs depart from class politics or the traditional socialist critique of capitalism. Instead, members of NSMs are skeptical about technology and its ideology—technicism—and they oppose bureaucracies and a strong role for the state (Hulsberg 1988, 109). Radical protests in 2000 against the World Bank and IMF are examples, but so are reactionaries' critiques of the U.S. Census, particularly the "long form" that supports the state's social research and planning.

Another structural change that gives rise to new (or renewed) social movements is postindustrial shifts in the occupational structure, which have increased the polarization of wealth and income. In addition to greater concentrations of wealth and income at the top, there also is an apparently permanent class of unemployed or only marginally employed citizens at the bottom, including especially youths, women, and minorities. Such persons, who cannot establish viable identities and incomes through the labor market, suffer from both poverty and social exclusion (Dahrendorf 1988). Nonetheless, this development is accepted by most Americans as the "price one has to pay" to remain "competitive" in global markets. This now seemingly inevitable underclass also poses a threat to those just above it, who fear that they too might be pushed downward by "restructuring," "globalization," or "competitiveness."

New class and status groups and new political alignments among them began as America's industrial economy matured. At the same time, there was a separation of corporate ownership from management and a parallel differentiation within the working class. This differentiation was based mainly on differential skills, new affluence for parts of the working class, the assimilation of white ethnics, and a growing diversity of styles of consumption. The growth of the welfare state expanded the roles of government agencies and the dependence of people on them instead of on the union hall or political club. The increased number of government employees (including professors in community colleges and state universities) also enlarged that part of the workforce whose employment, status, and identity were not directly dependent on corporations or markets, as the older working class had been. Increased economic, geographic, and status mobility also tended to erode class boundaries, class identification, and class consciousness, as did the expansion of rights and entitlements to women, minorities, and others.

Although most members of progressive NSMs come from the "new middle classes" (Offe 1985), their class background does not determine the collective identities of the actors or the stakes of their actions. Indeed, the "productivist" model of the Old Left, as well as its modes of organization, seems less relevant today. Instead of forming unions or political parties of the socialist, social democratic, or communist type, contemporary activists generally focus more "on grass-roots politics and create horizontal, directly democratic associations that are loosely federated on national levels. Moreover, they target the social domain of civil society rather than the economy or state, raising issues concerned with the democratization of structures of everyday life and focusing on forms of communication and collective identity" (J. Cohen 1985, 667). In practice, of course, with an increasingly global division of labor and diffuse postmodern culture, it becomes more difficult to create or sustain a unitary identity even as more people seek to do so.

Another shift in the occupational structure has been the emergence of a new class of "knowledge workers." These are the upper members of the so-called service sector—the technicians, consultants, managers, financial analysts, and the like—but not those whose service is serving hamburgers or cleaning office buildings at night. The explosion of the knowledge industry is itself linked with the shift toward knowledge-based, capital-intensive production, which requires a more educated workforce and more flexible employment. Many members of the secular NSMs are either members of this new class or college students who expect to join it.

A further consequence of shifts in the occupational structure is that gaps of income and wealth widen among various parts of the service sector and the middle class in general—for example, between the office staff, made up of low-level employees, and the upper professionals and managers whom they support. Though a secretary makes $30,000 a year and a bond trader makes $300,000, both work in the same office and both consider themselves middle class, even though the secretary's salary has stagnated while the bond trader's has advanced.

Several further phenomena follow from the increased polarization of national shares of wealth and income within the middle class. One is a politics of scapegoating and resentment by substantial parts of the lower-middle or upper-working classes. One example is institutionalized racism, which is partly masked by the rhetorics of state rights, meritocracy, and competitive individualism. Others on the list of scapegoats in addition to blacks are liberals, feminists, the undeserving poor, homosexuals, and lefties of all sorts. From the viewpoint of the Christian New Right, such groups have impeded the natural unfolding of America as a divinely inspired Christian nation (Lienesch 1993).

By contrast, on the part of students and the new professional groups, there simultaneously emerges a libertarian or therapeutic politics of personal entitlement, as well as some broader NSMs that advance more general values. These latter social movements are more fragile, however, because their members are mostly from relatively weakly organized or weakly bounded occupational groups that give them less autonomy and legitimacy than more strongly organized professional groups such as those of lawyers or doctors. Moreover, the resources of such members tend to be cultural credentials rather than financial or economic capital. "Whereas financial or monetary capital can be invested or liquidated by private individuals without organizational or group support, cultural or symbolic resources (i.e., claims to expertise) usually cannot be cashed in without access to organizational structures or professional groups" (Ashley 1997, 75). Leaders of progressive NSMs may like money as much as anyone else, but their access to it depends on their ability to perform cultural tasks for those who command administrative and financial resources. Hence, their social movements are relatively weaker and more vulnerable to state or corporate manipulation. For example, almost all of the larger organizations in the environmental movement depend on corporate or governmental contracts and grants and thus tend to limit their agendas to "renewable" or "sustainable" growth, rather than to the radical reductions in levels of consumption that would seriously address environmental problems but also would threaten the established order (Brulle 2000).

Another source of renewed social movements is the decline of oligopoly in certain American industries, at least at the national level. With greater competition from low-wage economies, many industrial firms have survived by automating their assembly lines; shifting to more specialized, knowledge-intensive production; relocating plants and jobs abroad; and buying major shares of "foreign" competitors. The result has been a decline of industrial workers to about 11 percent of the total U.S. labor force in 2001. With this, the core membership of labor movements also declined, which also diminished the importance of class politics in favor of identity politics. Government policies have facilitated this trend—not only by granting largesses to business (such as protection of overseas investments or restrictions on labor), but also by recognizing and providing entitlements for particularistic identity groups. All these trends encourage people to think of themselves as women or minorities, say, rather than workers or citizens, which in turn undermines both class politics and broader conceptions of civic obligation. Instead, by defining themselves as particular or even unique "communities of meaning," such groups, at least initially, have more difficulty in forming working political coalitions and in recognizing economic limits or value conflicts in the satisfaction of their demands (Gitlin 1996, 737; see also Pizzorno 1978, 293). In other words, they become less pragmatic and more ideological.

Another key precondition for the growth of NSMs, both religious and secular, is the increased importance of electronic media of communication. The mass media shape NSMs because gaining legitimacy and the ability to influence policy require that one be noticed by the public at large (Gitlin 1980). Abbie Hoffman and other left activists of the 1960s and 1970s were among the first to use the media to their advantage. The New Right learned from the 1960s, however, and also benefited greatly from the centralization and concentration of media ownership. "Whereas 'old' evangelicals operated small churches and conducted old-fashioned revivalist camp meetings, the New Evangelicals rely on the latest technologies in mass marketing and mass-mediated communication (Wuthnow 1988, 197ff.). These include religious TV stations, computerized mailing lists, rapid-response networks, and monthly strategy updates that can be beamed by satellite to hundreds of meeting sites around the country. The member roles of fundamentalist Christian organizations have increased as a result. As the number of Christian radio stations rose from about 350 in 1972 to nearly 1,600 in 1994, so did the number of fundamentalist Christian voters. By 1994, their ranks grew to one-quarter of all U.S. voters (Ashley 1997, 77–78).

In adapting "old-time religion" to the exigencies of mass-mediated proselytizing, the New Evangelicals posit an other-directed viewer who is oriented toward external messages and thereby ignore the inner-directed believers whom the early modern Protestant sects addressed. Thus the Christian New Right participates in the subversion of the "inner" resources that Weber believed were central to Protestantism and a midwife to the birth of modernity. Whereas liberals contribute to the death of the inner-directed subject by encouraging greater public assistance and statist regulation, the Christian right often does so by replacing the active and "knowing" conscience with the passive viewer of religious spectacles. Both left and right thereby advance the post- or antimodern tendencies described by Lyotard, Jameson, and Foucault. In this sense, Evangelicals are antimodern in outlook but postmodern in method (Ashley 1997, 78). Indeed, what is most new about NSMs may be their use of media such as television and the Internet for both their internal communication and public exposure. Contemporary social movements also use new media to create new kinds of communication. Messages of movements appear on banners, bumper stickers, graffiti, billboards, trees, buttons and balloons, and even the finger-painted faces of children. The conventional media of printed programs, plat-forms, and newspaper ads are passé.

With such renewed social movements, boundaries separating religion, mo-rality, and politics have become ambiguous and more uncertain. For exam-ple, the widening division between more established churches and the newer fundamentalist sects has created two versions of American civil religion—one conservative, one liberal (Wuthnow 1988, 266; see also Ashley 1997, 77). Yet un-til about 1970, mainline or liberal Protestantism—Presbyterian, Episcopalian (Anglican), Methodist, and Congregational—enjoyed a religiocultural hege-mony in the United States (Neuhaus 1999). Groups traditionally called "lib-eral," such as the Unitarian Universalists, supported a separation of church and state, a more ecumenical and less dogmatic outlook, and a belief that matters of conscience and salvation were essentially private. In contrast, conservative fun-damentalists are dogmatic about basic values, which they regard as authorita-tively given, and they try to enact "private" morality into public policy. More-over, for fundamentalists, commitment to values does not require individuals to give a reasoned or even a formally consistent account of personalized voca-tion and commitment. Instead, having "values" means that true Christians have a moral right to demonize those who deviate or disagree.

With "success," however, such movements may become more institutional-ized or rationalized, and leadership may be removed from its political base. Running a political advocacy office is not much different from running a cor-poration. Both rely on managerial skills and professionalism; both require in-strumental orientation, pragmatism, and organizational competence (Crook, Pakulski, and Waters 1992). Movement politics thus can become an elite poli-tics because it relies on specialized managers, lobbyists, and their professional staffs to guarantee stability and optimize the chances of a group's success. Such rationalization may in turn generate alienation and, hence, give rise to more participatory and direct social activism.

In sum, with the formalization of politics at the institutional level comes greater differentiation in informal politics and social movements. For example, groups without formal representation may become imagined political commu-nities, as Benedict Anderson used that term, because "the members of even the smallest nation will never know most of their fellow-members, meet them, or even hear of them, yet in the minds of each lives the image of communion" (1983, 15). Today the nation is diminishing as the most significant political com-munity and so also are classes, which in modernity were the "real" foci of political identification and action. Yet in postmodernity political communities are becoming both hyper-differentiated and hyper-reified through the mass media. People may come to view themselves as members of multiple, highly particular communities characterized by shared attributes portrayed or discovered through mass media. But such imagined communities do not depend on actual shared experience or even dense interpersonal networks.

Thus the "postmodernization" of politics involves a shift in patterns of inequality from the social to the cultural sphere, from life chances to lifestyles, from production to consumption. Social distinctions become more fluid as status rather than class becomes more important and multiple status identities emerge to replace a smaller number of enclosed social selves. NSMs, which are central to this emerging political configuration, differ from earlier liberal-bourgeois and socialist-labor movements in being "apartisan or even apolitical in the sense that they reject the conventional institutional idiom of politics; they aim not to capture the state but to ignore or even abolish it. Also, unlike the student revolts of the late 1960s, they have proved to be persistent, widespread and politically fertile. They cannot be treated as a residuum of conventional politics, or dismissed as transient outbursts of collective protest" (Crook, Pakulski, and Waters 1992, 133).

The success of rationalized, corporatist-bureaucratic politics depends on a high level of elite autonomy and a low level of public involvement, which in turn establishes an unresponsive leadership, on the one hand, and an apathetic public, on the other. It also results in the reduction of citizens' power in favor of social groups that are able to articulate their interests through an organized political lobby within existing structures of the corporate state. This kind of politics has been paralleled by changes in the major American political parties. Though originating as social movements with strong ideological orientations into the twentieth century, both the Republican and the Democratic parties gradually transformed into vote-catching, highly centralized managerial apparatuses that became tightly integrated with executive agencies of the state. "Initially, this helped to open up the political system and guaranteed political success by means of electoral victories and consequent influence on policy making. Ultimately, however, bureaucraticization weakened the substantive appeals of the parties and made them vulnerable to legitimation crisis. . . . The new movements can be seen as a response to these tensions and an attempt at their resolution. They promote involvement, participation, self-organization and group autonomy, and reject the legitimacy of sectional interests as the basis of political demands. Moreover, they challenge the corporatist-bureaucratic model of intermediation in the highly charged language of general social values and universal human rights" (Crook, Pakulski, and Waters 1992, 150, 151).

The novelty of NSMs rests not only in the value-laden, anticentralist orientation they engender, but also in a new organizational form and a specific counterculture that they generate. The organizational structure of movements is often an exact opposite of the corporatist-bureaucratic model. As noted, this contrast makes new movements radical in a social, but not necessarily political or programmatic, sense. In their very organizational form and methods of mobilization, they pose a challenge to old politics that is both damaging and difficult to neutralize (Crook, Pakulski, and Waters 1992, 151–153). In contrast to traditional forms of political organization, NSMs typically do not rely "on the organizational principle of differentiation, whether in the horizontal (insider versus outsider) or in the vertical (leaders versus rank-and-file members). To the contrary, there seems to be a strong reliance upon de-differentiation, that is the fusion of public and private roles, instrumental and expressive behaviour, community and organisation, and in particular the poor and at best transient demarcation between the roles of 'members' and formal 'leaders'" (Offe 1985, 829). If we look beyond the specific political content of renewed social movements, their social form becomes more visible as a largely communitarian and subjectivist reaction to the instrumental rationalization and pervasive alienation of the late modern corporate, market, and government system.

UNDERSTANDING CONSERVATIVE PROTESTANT SOCIAL MOVEMENTS

Conservative Protestants belong to a congeries of denominations and do not agree on any one set of beliefs or approaches to social activism (Dayton and Johnson 1991; Marsden 1987; Kellstedt et al. 1996). Terms such as "fundamentalist," "evangelical," "born again," "conservative Protestant," and "religious right" are often used indiscriminately by social scientists without regard to important distinctions, including those made by members of such groups themselves (Kellstedt and Smidt 1996). The phenomenon of conservative Protestantism also is complex. Some groups are highly conservative on some issues of theology and ritual but often innovative on others (Oldfield 1996, 49; Dayton 1991; Woodbury and Smith 1998, 25–26). Theologically orthodox clergy (mostly from evangelical denominations) have an individualistic worldview, resulting in a "moral reform agenda." In contrast, theologically modernist clergy (mostly from mainline denominations) have a communitarian perspective, leading to a "social justice agenda" (Guth et al. 1997). Similarly, in the first half of the nineteenth century, Northern evangelicals, now socially conservative, were activists for temperance, abolition of slavery, and similar social reforms and were early advocates of the separation of church and state (Carwardine 1993; Marsden 1987; T. Smith 1957; McLoughlin 1978). After the Civil War, Northern evangelical leaders argued over Darwinism and higher biblical criticism, whereas Southerners remained unified against both (Marsden 1980, 1991). Many Southerners thought that defeat in the Civil War was God's punishment for their lack of faith, so they sought to redouble their belief in the fundamentals of Christianity. Revivalism swept through the South, showing in effect that Southerners were morally and religiously superior to Northerners, who had strayed from the true word into secular social reforms (Hill 1980, 106; Ammerman 1990, 38–39). Thus, for example, Southern Protestants generally have supported prayer or Bible reading in public schools (Shibley 1996; Woodbury and Smith 1998, 31). Since the Civil Rights era and the greater integration of the South with the rest of the country, conservative Protestants have become more visible politically. "Traditionally, Catholics, Jews, minorities, and Southerners voted Democratic, and white non-Southern Protestants voted Republican. However . . . liberal Protestants have moved strongly toward the Democratic party and conservative Southerners into the Republican party. This has radically shifted party coalitions and rhetoric. Thus, blacks, Jews, secularists, and social liberals have become the new core of the Democratic party," yielding greater power to conservative Protestants as the core of the Republican party (Woodbury and Smith 1998, 43–44; see also Manza and Brooks 1997; Green et al. 1996, 4).

In the early twentieth century fundamentalists argued for the authority of Scripture, the strict literal interpretation of the Bible, veracity of biblical miracles, and salvation through Christ alone. They claimed that these doctrines were so fundamental to the Christian faith that those who denied them were outside the Christian tradition (such as liberal Protestants and Catholics) (Marsden 1987, 1991; Ammerman 1987). Many fundamentalists also viewed the rise of Bolshevism as the natural outcome of a barbarous modernism, much as Jerry Falwell and Pat Robertson saw the 2001 attack on the Twin Towers as a punishment for New York's licensciousness and homosexuality. Society was becoming worse, not better, and sin could be overcome only through personal rebirth and embrace of the true faith.

Evangelicalism is the strongest major Christian tradition in America, encompassing about twenty million citizens. Christian Smith notes that Evangelicalism "thrives on distinction, engagement, tension, conflict, and threat" (1998, 89). Its very tension with the secular cultural environment gives Evangelicalism its identity as a movement and allows it to provide strong personal identities to its individual members. Their politics are diverse, however, reflecting contrasting theological orientations, further modified by social, contextual differences. "Charismatics and Pentecostals comprise approximately 12% of the U.S. population and have had a profound impact on African, Latin American, and Asian Christianity. They are the fastest growing segment of Christianity worldwide, and yet social scientists have paid little attention to them" (R. Anderson 1987). Most research surveys do not ask even a single question that would identify them (for example, questions about speaking in tongues or religious movement identity or detailed denominational categories). Thus, most scholars and journalists did not realize that in the 1988 presidential campaign Pat Robertson's political support was limited almost exclusively to the "Spirit filled" (Green 1996; Oldfield 1996; Smidt and Penning 1990). Similarly, although fundamentalists have some loose national associations, such as Jerry Falwell's Baptist Bible Fellowship, power remains predominantly with individual pastors.

Since the 1976 election national Republican strategists have sought to consolidate conservative Protestant support for their party. At the same time, there was a conservative Southern response to desegration, the women's movement, and other liberal policies or government programs, all of which made conservative Protestants more supportive of right-wing Republican politics and coalitions. Part of this change reflected a generational shift of experiences from that of the Great Depression and World War II to the current postwar generation. For example, adult activists in progressive NSMs

> experienced a period of sustained economic growth, political stability, social reform and an "educational revolution" during the 1950s and 1960s. This halcyon period generated high expectations and idealistic orientations, but it ended with a series of economic downturns and political turbulence during the late 1970s and 1980s. Such a historical sequence, reminiscent of Davies' (1962) "J-curve," had radicalizing effects, especially among those sections of the postwar generation which had benefitted from educational expansion but whose skills, mainly in the areas of humanities and social science, were less marketable under conditions of economic contraction. Most of these people found employment in the public sector, which was badly affected by economic downturns and contracting opportunities. Reduced career prospects, combined with low market power, made these categories more receptive

to social criticism, especially criticism adopting an idealistic, anti-corporatist idiom of value-rationality" (Crook, Pakulski, and Waters 1992, 146).

Something parallel may be said of activists in conservative religious NSMs. Their social base consists mostly of persons and groups whose class and cultural identities have been destabilized or destroyed by the nationalization and then globalization of American capitalism since World War II and especially since about 1980. The national and homogenizing reach of capitalism after World War II helped to break down barriers of region, race, and gender, including the delegitimation of racism, patriarchy, and, more generally, conservative and insular Southern religious culture. In addition, the restructuring and increased globalization of the U.S. economy destroyed many industrial and lower supervisory jobs that had been the mainstay of the lower-middle classes, for whom conservative churches and NSMs have largely replaced the labor union as vehicles for political activism. Finally, new opportunities for education and employment in the upper service or professional sectors were less available to Southern whites, and the rise of the women's and Civil Rights movements resulted in a loss of status respect, especially for poorer white males.

NSMS: SECULARIZED RELIGION AND
SACRALIZED POLITICS

NSMs, both of the right and the left, can be seen as issuing from advances made by class movements in advanced capitalist countries. Many of the claims of working-class groups were met during the post–World War II boom through social insurance programs, most of which were paid by workers' tax dollars and involved little challenge to capitalists' control of the economy. These measures and others helped to smooth out booms and busts, placate social dissent, stabilize demand, and maintain capitalist accumulation. Since about 1970, however, the welfare state compromise has been undermined by weak economic growth, the fiscal limits of the state, and the official promotion of a culture of greed. In response, the right has proposed neoliberalism, protectionism, or laissez-faire, whereas the statist left advocates a more comprehensive state that provides more regulation of capital and more assistance for the working poor.

In contrast to both these positions, the programs of the renewed secular and religious social movements challenge the idea that the state ought to promote unlimited economic growth and instead focus on values, community, and quality of life, even if this stance slows economic growth or requires basic societal changes. Moreover, unlike conflicts over the distribution of material goods, conflicts over the form and quality of life are organized around symbolic and institutional conditions that are not directly tied to individual incomes. For example, a central goal and process of social movements is solidarity within primary groups and communities, as opposed to efficiency of bureaucracies or other formal organizations. Further, greater equality of life chances often depend on collective goods that cannot be adequately produced by the market, such as safety or health. Thus, for many people, economic growth or even increases in personal income do not necessarily enhance collective or even personal well-being.

In this context, NSMs arise that are more concerned with religious, moral, or cultural issues, such as equal rights, family values, or shared social bonds or conditions such as community or a clean environment. Moreover, both conservative religious and progressive secular social movements generally oppose modernity and challenge institutionalized economic and political rationality or technicism. Further, both define the "enemy" not as social class so much as a dominant culture of calculative rationality. Movements of both the right and the left also tend to be "postideological" (Dalton, Kuechler, and Bürklin 1990; Dalton and Kuechler 1990; Offe 1990), at least in the limited sense that neither advances a unified alternative vision of relations of production or political authority. Lack of such an ideology makes it more difficult for these movements to make alliances with older labor groups, and their value (rather than class) ideologies inhibit pragmatic accommodations with existing parties and programs. Veen and Inglehart, among others, see such movements as reflecting value orientations rather than class-based economic interests:

> Inglehart's studies reveal a generational shift in value orientations in all major Western societies. This value shift or, more precisely, changed hierarchy of preferences, has resulted from both increasing affluence and historical changes in formative experiences. The ascendancy of new postmaterialist values represents an ascendancy of new, "higher" ethical and aesthetic needs among the post-Second World War birth cohorts which grew up during a period of economic prosperity, political stability and peace. The new generation rearranges value priorities by stressing the importance of freedom of speech, participatory democracy and quality of life. Their value priorities are, in turn, reflected in the new politics, especially in the "participatory revolution" and the rise of new social movements (Crook, Pakulski, and Waters 1992, 145–146).

Assertion of these values leads, in turn, to a political reaction by the New Right, the religious elements of which have often been left out of the material and status enhancements enjoyed by the liberal professional class. They more often are white, male, Southern, and working class or working poor. The national Republican leadership has coopted much of this vote by attacking liberal "cultural elites" and stressing noneconomic, "moral" issues such as "permissiveness," "family values," and "reverse discrimination."

Although the renewed religious right seeks to return to an idealized premodern condition and the new secular left heralds postmodernity, the "religious" enthusiasm of the right can be seen as well in "secular" social movements on the left. For example, ecological activist Gary Snyder, drawing on Buddhism, parodistically converted Marxist-Maoist rhetoric into an ecological pantheism. Such a sensibility endows all of nature with a religious aura, so that it becomes worth dying for the sake of dolphins and whales and perhaps even on behalf of rivers, mountains, and forests. Illustrative is the Rainbow Warrior incident, in which French intelligence agents exploded two bombs on a Greenpeace ship while it was docked in Auckland, New Zealand, on July 10, 1985, killing the photographer Fernando Pereira. The ship and its multinational crew were seeking, on behalf of the Earth and all of its inhabitants, to protest and disrupt French nuclear testing in the Pacific. "Recourse to political violence by France . . . represented a modernist effort to destroy the postmodernist kind of challenge being mounted by Greenpeace. . . . There was a kind of muted silence by most governments about such a terrorist tactic" (Falk 1988, 389). Perhaps this silence was in solidarity with France, another modern state that, though terroristic, was fighting postmodern anarcho-protestors, however pacific.

One example of a quasi-religious but ostensibly secular social movement is that for animal rights. Although 65 percent of respondents in a readers poll of *Animal Agenda* claimed to be athiest or agnostic, the movement itself is characterized by "overwhelmingly religiously styled moral outrage, concerns with purity, foundational moral orientations, and moral resources that inform the animal rights movement. As a belief system, 'animal rights' provides activists with a conception of morality, symbolic boundaries for their daily micro-social interactions, motivations for their involvement in organizations and protests surrounding animal rights, and provides an overall cosmology or world view that informs both the perceptions and motivations of the participants" (Lowe 2001, 46). This apparent contradiction between the professed secularism of adherents and the religious style of their beliefs, literature, motives, and conduct is all the more striking given that 90 percent of Americans say that they believe in God, 70 percent that they are members of a church, and 60 percent that they attend church services once a month (Jasper and Nelkin 1992, 38). Moreover, persons with higher levels of religious affiliation and church attendance tend to be less accepting of animal rights and less opposed to medical testing of animals.

Nonetheless, the animal rights movement has its sacred texts, such as Peter Singer's *Animal Liberation* (1975); its "religious virtuosos" (Weber 1958), such as members of the Animal Liberation Front; its occasions for moral outrage (slaughter, vivisection); and its implicitly religious vocabulary of cruelty, suffering, and compassion (Lowe 2001, 42–43). Moreover, like members of renewed religious movements, believers in animal rights are not irrational but pursue a Weberian value rationality for the sake of an ethical principle (Weber 1978, 24–25), which itself becomes sanctified as a religious object for believers (Durkheim 1995). Indeed, animal rights groups have rejected instrumentally rational political negotiations in favor of protecting the "purity" of their ethnical beliefs and feelings (see Linzey and Cohn-Sherbok 1997; Linzey 1999; Parker 1993).

Bizarrely, however, the vast majority of writers on NSMs focus on feminist, environmental, antiwar, or ethnic movements, whereas the study of contemporary religious movements is addressed by specialists in religious studies or Middle Eastern politics. Perhaps this exclusion reflects an ideological bias insofar as, in the generally liberal orientation of social scientists, NSMs appear to be progressive, whereas religious movements, whether in the United States or in India or Iran, are usually viewed as reactionary. Yet given our guiding definitions of social movements and their origins in certain social structural and cultural changes, there is no reason to rigidly distinguish between the religious and the secular. As noted, many secular NSMs have strong sacral aspects, and most religious NSMs have at least implicit political agendas. Both are formed around issues of identity or status more than issues of class; both are non- or antibureaucratic in ethos and often in form; both seek to create morally committed bonds of solidarity and status; both claim to reject modernist, statist, or class politics in favor of grassroots mobilization and individual transformation through solidarity and commitment; and, in all this, both are in transit toward a postmodern politics (Gibbins 1989, 1–2; Brown 1998, ch. 9).

Grievances, however ubiquitous, become political causes only when articulated as changeable through morally imperative action. And religiously based social movements are especially well endowed with latent symbolic capital that can easily affect such mobilization in pursuit of social change. The involvement of churches in the Civil Rights Movement in the 1960s (Morris and Mueller 1992), the influence of the religious right on the Republican party and the federal government since the 1980s, and turnout for George W. Bush in the Republican primary election of 2000—all attest to the continuing power of religion in American political life. Religious theology is readily transformed into political ideology that can justify the activities of social movements, and revivalism can energize people with rituals of salvation through righteous action. As Mayer Zald notes, "Transformation of theology and ideology provide a base for *justifying* social movement activity. . . . Revivalism changed the *meaning* of souls and salvation . . . [and the] conception of right action. Religion may by the opiate of the masses under some conditions, but under other conditions it serves as a sword of assassination" (1982, 325, emphasis in original; see also 1988).

Effective moral arguments must resonate with an already available cultural and rhetorical tradition that provides a repertoire of commonplaces from which versions of the public moral good can be fashioned. In social movement theory this is called "framing." As American cultural history is redolent with moral and religious themes, these are frequently used by both secular and religious social movements to frame and legitimate themselves and their goals. Such moral themes might be the sanctity of property or human freedom, whether these are deployed around issues of slavery or abortion. The rhetorical "moralizing" of an issue may give a social movement "ownership" of that problem and control of the terms in which it is debated, including what the problem *is*. But it also can open that movement to counterlabeling as femi-Nazi or Christian fascist, depending on what is at stake and who does the labeling.

Moreover, much like older religious movements such as those of the Shakers, Quakers, Pentacostals, and other (originally) enthusiastic sects, secular NSMs increasingly are a collective embodiment of the identity and goals of their members. That is, the form of an organization is not chosen only according to its utility for achieving that organization's goals; the organizational form also embodies and expresses the goal itself; the ideological commitments of that group are displayed in its very methods and practices of social change. Hence organizational arrangements, as well as strategy, cannot be justified in terms of instrumental efficiency alone (Ammerman 1990).

Like secular NSMs, renewed religious movements also tend to be diffuse in their goals and organization. Even while claiming universality or revelation, these goals are interpreted differently by members who are differently located in the space-time of highly diverse sects that characterize American religious history. Recently, however, the processes of forming goals and gaining consensus on them has been accelerated by the new medium of electronic interaction. Moreover, both religious and secular activities in America are infused with larger individualist and consumerist ideologies, according to which persons pick and mix their own causes and religions, a process that began with the spiritual individualism of the Protestant Reformation and continues in contemporary New Age spirituality. Indeed, both secular and religious renewed movements see themselves as creating an exemplary politics (Offe 1985; Dalton, Kuechler, and Bürklin 1990) and present themselves and their own conduct as a model of the transformed society. They build base communities as representations of the ideal polity and reject mere calculations of efficiency or material success. Given that the personal and the political are one, community building is itself both moral witnessing and political action. In such a "magical politics," concessions to instrumental strategic thinking can undermine both a movement's internal cohesion and its external impact. Thus, both leftist and Christian radicals seek to overcome the dichotomy of public and private spheres that is central in liberal capitalist society. That the personal is political and the public is (or should be) moral are parallel projects. Indeed, the leftist goal of unmasking domination and the radical Christian goal of ethicizing public life are convergent (Ashley 1997, 76).

These observations encourage a critique of theories of secularization that have tended to take Western Europe as the norm and to view the religious vitality of the United States as yet another aspect of American exceptionalism. Such theories posit a necessary connection between modernity and secularization: the more modern a society, the less religious it will be. The very modernity but also vibrant religiosity of the United States then becomes an exception that has to be explained (Neuhaus 1999, 35). For example, Christian Smith (1998) tells us that "Evangelicalism has been more successful than any other contemporary American religious tradition." Evangelicalism is "embattled and thriving"—and in some ways thriving because it is embattled (Neuhaus 1999, 35). But perhaps some theorists have it backward. In a world that is becoming simultaneously more modern and more religious, the oddity to be explained is the "exceptionalism" of Western Europe, which appears to be on an unremitting course of ever-greater secularization.

One example of the convergence of religious and secular social movements around a political issue is Christian fundamentalist and radical feminist views of both pornography and what in the 1980s and 1990s were known as repressed memory syndrome (RMS) and multiple personality disorder (MPD). Many religious fundamentalists and radical feminists see the other group as the source of many evils. Yet they have collaborated on some crucial issues, as when in Indianapolis religious conservatives generated decisive grassroots support to pass an antipornography ordinance that had originated with radical feminists (see MacKinnon 1992). Similarly, for Christian fundamentalists on the right, RMS and MPD were products of the new permissiveness that was undermining American society. For feminist fundamentalists on the left, RMS and MPD were the results of predatory males again victimizing women (Acocella 1998, 74).

Moreover, although the ideologies of religious fundamentalists and radical feminists seem antithetical, they display some similarities of structure and logic, especially in their mutual opposition to pornography and to certain doctrines of laissez-faire liberalism. Both ideologies assume that contemporary society is deeply flawed morally; both are shaped by and try to influence the mass media; both collapse private into public or public into private; both claim to know the root cause of our moral or political corruption; and both offer policies as temporary treatments for a deeper disease that, they believe, can be cured only through fundamental individual and social transformation. Finally, both depend on the tolerance offered to dissenters by the very liberal society they oppose. Of course, these parallels and the alliance between Christian and feminist fundamentalists on pornography issues do not imply a general or continuing agreement, especially on such concerns as abortion, wage equity, or affirmative action. Indeed, given their respective absolutisms, each group inclines toward absorption or elimination of the other.

In sum, religious and secular NSMs share a number of features that emerge from modernity itself and its anti- or postmodern reactions. Closely following Ashley (1997, 76–77, 93) and Crook, Pakulski, and Waters (1992, 148), we note that these include:

- A rejection of metanarratives of any large-scale "project of modernity."
- A rejection of the authority of the intellectual-as-legislator.
- The view that new kinds of selves, or personal rebirth, are crucial to social transformation. In this sense, both types of NSMs help create the kind of plastic and flexible personalities that are compatible with the new requirements of postmodern capitalism.
- An emphasis on culture over structure, status over class, and cultural consciousness over class membership.
- The recognization that knowledge and power are intimately entangled. For example, both types reject totalizing metanarratives of progress through instrumental rationality and science because these kinds of knowledge empower males, Jews, or financial or technocratic elites.

- A reliance on mass media and other new technologies of communication, even while advocating grassroots participation.
- An orientation more toward lifestyles and consumption than toward work or production.
- An avoidance of direct challenges to the state. Instead, both types seek to capture the resources and authority of the state for devolution to their own purposes.
- A preference for a decentralized politics of transformation or witnessing over a centralized politics of compliance.
- Motivation and goals oriented toward moral concerns rather than instrumental considerations. This characteristic is encapsulated in such labels as "antipolitics," "counterpolitics," "symbolic or lifestyle politics," "politics of moral protest," or "citizens' poilitics" (for example, see Misztal 1985; Melucci 1996; Dalton, Kuechler, and Bürklin 1990; Schmitt 1989).
- The new politics is not based on centralized and bureaucratized intermediation of interests through the "pillars" of corporatism. Instead it relies on self-organization and utilizes semi-institutionalized forms of pressure.
- The key activists are openly suspicious of the established elites and centralized state apparatuses, whose effectiveness, rationality, and ability to represent the collective good are all doubted.

Further, the distinctive features of the language of renewed social movements can be summarized in five points:

- It relies on "imagined communities," which can be shaped by new cultural entrepreneurs using mass-media technologies. The media need movement activities for news events, and movement activists stage such events for maximum media exposure.
- It is critical and expressed in an adversarial mode of opposition, rejection, and protest. Appeals use such expressions as "stop" and "ban"; symbols make use of proscriptive signs; icons stress danger (of war, damnation, nuclear radiation, etc.). Such shared symbolism opposition forms a broader basis of cooperation than an explicit ideology or program.
- It is iconic and therefore general and unspecific (Brown 1989). Iconic symbols "stand for themselves" and thus are always ambiguous, multivocal, and open to new interpretation. This ambiguity suits the ideological and programmatic vagueness of social movements, and it is useful for articulating general value concerns. At the same time, it merges well with other symbolic elements such as modes of dress, body decoration, aesthetic

taste, and dietary habits into a recognizable and distinctive countercultural lifestyle.

- Movement symbols are simple, syncretic, didactic, and compact. They draw from popular repertoires, including road signs, folk traditions, and national symbols, and from different historical and sociocultural contexts. Symbols and icons are highly condensed, infused with purpose, and often simplified so that they can be easily used in graffiti, banners, chants, bumper stickers, or T-shirts. Such an economical form of presentation facilitates dissemination and is highly suitable for mass media (especially TV) consumption and amplification.

- The media become messages as form and content collapse into each other. Protest marches, rallies and sit-ins, festivals, music concerts, and street performances—all appeal as "happenings." Their very form is compelling as unorthodox, informal, critical, and infused with values.

Chapter 5 The Dialectics of American Selfhood: Individualism and Identity in the United States

American conversations about the self have pessimistic and optimistic positions. Pessimists portray rootless and narcissistic contemporary persons against an imagined backdrop of the warm and secure communities of an earlier period. Optimists see these same persons as free from the suffocating constraints of provincial communities, confronting the challenges of modern social and psychological mobility with considerable success. Whereas some decry the current fragmentation of lifeworlds and contexts for self-presentations, others celebrate the new breadth and richness of identity choices. Once more, American self-images are torn between the ideological forces that regret the loss of an Edenic past and those that celebrate the possibilities of an endless future.

This disclosure is closely bound to American culture itself. Indeed, it is more an expression of that culture than an analysis of it. For Americans, the division between individual and society is near absolute, along with a nostalgia for community that once brought the two together (Stryker 1994, 888). Modernity has created far larger social and political units than the segmented and isolated clans and villages of former times, and, in this context, the multidimensional self is a mark of cosmopolitan sophistication, not an enfeeblement by diffusion. Just as Marx saw the diversity of hunter, fisherman, and writer as realms of freedom, so we could add teacher, parent, golfer, Virginian, and investor. Such a person would have a more varied and diffuse identity than his or her counterpart in a traditional society. Yet while some would celebrate this increase in the degrees of freedom as a new richness of personality with a plurality of options, others would bemoan it as a splintering of self and a corresponding source of alienation or estrangement.

Such discussions of identity focus on whether social differentiation and identity diffusion have led to declines in personal agency and democratic self-direction. Pessimists, like writers of the Frankfurt School of critical theory, dissect these declines. But in dialectical fashion, they also recognize that alienation created the need and possible conditions for emancipation. Persons who articulate their selves in various discrete contexts and fast-changing roles experience anomie and a relativization of values, but this very condition of estrangement is a resource for mobilization in support of emancipatory praxis. Leaders of anti-imperial resistance, for example, from Thomas Jefferson to Ho Chi Minh, usually have the inner estrangement of colonial elites who have been deeply exposed to the dominant metropolitan culture. Similarly today, empowered classes tend to participate in wider ranges of selfhood and to be seekers of "who they really are."

Modernity brings a more complex division of labor, more specialized and differentiated social roles, and, hence, more complex and differentiated selves. Modernity as differentiation has been a crucial theme since Hegel, developed by Maine, Marx, Tönnies, Durkheim, Parsons, and, more recently, Luhmann, Habermas, and Bourdieu. Lifeworlds, status groups, and taste cultures become more plural, and differing subjectivities can therefore be expressed in multiple contexts of interaction that have indistinct boundaries. As a result, the conditions for contradictory expressions of the self, or even different selves are created—single parent, film buff, and lawyer may all be aspects of the "same" person. As kin and community diminish as the core institutions, a split emerges between a public world of large institutions and a private world of atomized selves. Within and between these worlds, however, the person often has a wide range of networks that may be wholly disconnected from each other. Electronic technologies multiply, segregate, and individualize these networks even further into a potential infinitude of time, space, and psychic zones (Gergen 1991). In the global system of faxes, bulletin boards, cell phones, and answering machines, the self can be virtually in many places at once.

Thus, central to American discourse on identity is whether the self remains unified or is in fragments. For "conservatives" the question is how the self can be protected from fragmentation, which they read as cultural decline or moral pollution. For "progressives," the question is how a stable selfhood can be maintained amid its many performances, read as freedom. Ambiguity and fragmentation of self are typically very American and particularly hard for Americans to bear. The very success of America's instrumentally active and success-oriented culture has generated a pervasive ambivalence that seemingly contradicts the instrumental rationality that brought it about. Within the success ethos of America, "tough mindedness and surety of purpose is a cultural imperative. Thus failure to resolve ambivalence may be interpreted as a lack of a strong ego identity, or even as pathological self doubt" (Weigert and Franks 1989, 211; see also Bellah 1975; Blumer 1969; Mead 1934; Schutz 1967; Erikson 1959; Lifton 1976). For hard-striving Americans, doubt is dysfunctional because it interferes with imagining positive scenarios, weakens motivation, blocks action, and creates anxiety. Thus the integral, stable, and unified self that was a core cultural ideal of American modernity is undermined by the pursuit of success itself, which increasingly involves rapid changes of roles, social and geographic mobility, and multiple contacts with less than significant others (called "networking")—all of which subvert any stable core identity. Indeed, as shown in the characters of the wife and her lover in the film *American Beauty*, the solid "core self" increasingly becomes a set of calculated performances, representations to inner and outer publics that are necessary and calculated for "success."

This historical development generates a typology of American selfhoods, as noted in Diane Bjorklund's (1998) study of a sample by decades of eleven thousand autobiographies written in the United States from 1800 to 1980. An early and prerevolutionary model was the self as a religious passion or "morality play." These autobiographies were mostly by Protestant clergymen who wrote of their inner struggles between good and evil, their state of sinfulness, need for change, and hope of divine forgiveness. A second model of selfhood arose with the growth of industrial capitalism after the Civil War, where self-made men presented themselves as "masters of fate." Here the self prevails individually, much as dominant classes won out over weaker ones according to Social Darwinist beliefs of the period. The turn of the century saw a third model: the "uncertain self," which lasted into the mid-twentieth century. Here questions of primary family relations and motivations (especially unconscious or irrational ones), as well as the quest for one's true or essential self, come to the fore. The elusiveness of objectivity and illusions of memory also are acknowledged. The fourth model, the contemporary one, is the "beleaguered self." It focuses on the role of social institutions and discourses, not so much in shaping what one is or in finding one's true self as resources for constructing the self that one wishes to become. This self is beleaguered as it becomes apparent that relationships, self-creation (or even maintenance), and life itself have all become an implacable, inescapable form of work.

CONCEPTS AND VALUES OF INDIVIDUALISM
IN AMERICAN IDEOLOGY

In America, individualism is more than a social construction about self, feelings, others, and objects. It also is a moral principle in which freedom of individual action is a virtue, even if the consequences are painful, whereas constraints on it are sinful. Thus the possession of guns is seen by many as a God-given or con-stitutional right, even if schoolyard killings occur as a by-product. Individual freedom also is the central trope in cultural battles between "pro-life" and "pro-choice" over abortion. In these battles each contestant claims moral legitimacy for his or her particular version of individual freedom—that of the fetus versus that of the mother (Langman and Harold 1989, 14). When American individu-alism is at odds with American religious absolutism or with secular ideals of equality or community, the issues usually are resolved in favor of personal rights and freedoms.

For the earliest American citizens, the autonomy of the individual was the ideological link between property and liberty and, later, between capitalism and democracy. For example, Thomas Jefferson wrote that cities make a wise and virtuous politics impossible because urban workers rarely are independent economically and thus are unlikely to rise above "subservience and meniality" (1954, 164–165; see also Fox-Genovese 1993). Moreover, freedom was not so op-posed to equality—not only because the gaps between rich and poor (except for slaves) were much less dramatic than in Europe, but also because for most eighteenth-century persons in the New World, political terms like "public good," "liberty," "slavery," and "individual liberty" were understood in the con-text of a reformed Protestant communalism (Shain 1996). Equality thus re-ferred mainly to the innate capacity of all men for moral virtue within a na-tional universe. Indeed, this belief in a universal innate goodness and moral sense was, for early Americans, a precondition of democratic freedom because it appeared to be the only resource through which social order and national defense could be secured without the coercive authority of a monarch. Only natural goodness and a spirit of self-sacrifice could guarantee security in the new republic of personal freedom. Liberty and autonomy in this period still referred to the self-government of families, villages, and towns, not to individual persons (Shain 1996; Taylor 1983).

A more modern American conception of individualism crystalized only later, when Alexis de Tocqueville invented it from the French *individualisme* to describe what was exceptionally American in the new country's ideology and culture. Tocqueville, like Louis Hartz (1955) or Seymour Lipset (1979) over a century later, theorized that the absence in the United States of traditional European institutions such as monarchy, aristocracy, and an established church permitted an extraordinary degree of individual freedom for (white male) citizens. As the republic became more secure, especially after the War of 1812, new elites rejected the eighteenth-century doctrines of public virtue and Protestant communalism and adopted the view that government was the mechanism for accommodating individuals, whose basic nature was self-seeking.

About the same time that Tocqueville was touring the United States, Ralph Waldo Emerson resigned his Unitarian pastorate to adopt the radically individualist creed of the God within. Soon after, Walt Whitman was to write *Songs of Myself.* Whereas Tocqueville used the concept of individualism to describe a social reality, "Emerson intended his variant, 'self-reliance,' as a spiritual prescription for his politically liberated but religiously and morally conformist countrymen. 'Let me admonish you, first of all,' he told his Harvard Divinity School audience in 1838, 'to go alone; to refuse the good models, even those which are sacred in the imagination of men, and dare to love God without mediator or veil.' He exhorted each American to assert his personal independence as forthrightly as the rebels of 1776 had asserted their collective independence. 'In all my lectures,' he wrote in 1840, referring to the influential addresses he had delivered in the aftermath of his conversation to the new faith . . . 'I have taught one doctrine, namely, the infinitude of the private man'" (Marx 1987, 36).

Thus individualism was understood differently in different times. Yet until the twentieth century, Americans like Jonathan Edwards, Benjamin Franklin, Abraham Lincoln, Horace Bushnell, Horace Mann, Margaret Fuller, Henry David Thoreau, Dorothea Dix, and Frederick Douglass all felt that powerful but base passions must be mastered by reason in the service of public virtue (I. Howe 1986; Appleby 2000). Individualism was thereby linked to democracy, for it was long thought that independent, self-reliant persons were the natural members of a democratic society. Thus Henry Thoreau asked not what civil disobedience was, but *who* could be disobedient to civil authority. For Thoreau, "civil disobedience was rare because individuality was rare. Both are scarce because the process of forging a self into a true individual is arduous and precarious, requiring continuous effort" (Bennett 1990, 560). Thoreau thus was a technologist, an architect or sculptor, of the self: "Every man is the builder of a temple . . . to the god he worships. . . . We are all sculptors and painters, and our material is our own flesh and blood and bones." (Thoreau 2000, 147). Similarly, for Thoreau loneliness did not express a need for sociability but was a weakness of character. "In proportion as our inward life fails, we go more constantly and desperately to the post office. You may depend on it, that the poor fellow who walks away with the greatest number of letters . . . has not heard from himself this long while" (quoted in Bennett 1990, 561). Sociability, especially as a medium of prejudice and platitudes, is an enemy to robust individuality, for such companionship tends only to incline the self toward conformity with convention. For this very reason, Thoreau commands his readers to "Exclude such trespassers from the only ground which can be sacred to you!" (ibid.).

Individualism was also seen to have its down side, chiefly its tension with the needs of community. "In America," wrote Tocqueville, "I have seen the freest and best educated of men in circumstances the happiest to be found anywhere in the world; yet it seemed that a cloud hung habitually on their brow and they seemed serious and almost sad even in their pleasures" (1945 [1835]). What Tocqueville observed seems echoed in our day by the singer Judy Collins: "Lately I can't help thinking / I reap what I sow. / For all of my holy freedom / What have I got to show? / These are hard times for lovers. / Everyone wants to be free. / Ain't these hard times for lovers? / Everyone singing I gotta be me / —without you."

Freedom, clearly, is not the same as happiness. Indeed, the aggressive and acquisitive individualism that contributed to America's growth and prosperity also has tended to produce emotionally retreatist and inexpressive persons. George Miller Beard's treatise on American nervousness, published in the 1880s, remains a classical effort to link such sentiments to social structure (see Langman and Richman 1987). It described neurasthenia as a mixture of tiredness, vague psychic discontent, and depression, which is the malady of American civilization. Since Tocqueville's insights and Beard's elaborations, many psychiatrists have accepted Freud's ideas not only that neurosis is a product of civilization—that repression of erotic desire makes social life possible but miserable—but also that various forms of civilization breed differing types of neuroses. For example, Robert Bellah and his colleagues (1991) discovered that

Americans were unable to express and accept anything but the self as a dominant reality or significant value, even though they often sensed that the credo of individualism was a source of deep malaise. Those with whom the authors spoke seemed at an impasse: individualism produces a mode of life that was not viable, while a return to tradition would be perceived as unacceptable penury and oppression.

Bellah and other researchers also have found that the transcendental morality and civic life of an earlier era have been largely supplanted by bureaucratic regulations, corporate acquisitiveness, and amoral self-interest. Communities of memory are being replaced by taste cultures and lifestyles promoted by corporate advertising. The former are exemplified by the small towns of nineteenth-century America, inhabited by people for whom the community was an inclusive life with a collective history constantly retold in ritual and story. In contemporary America, some ethnic communities, religious groups, or even families continue to be committed to such a set of values. But "where history and hope are forgotten and community means only the gathering of the similar, community degenerates into life style enclaves" (Bellah et al. 1991, 154). Such enclaves cannot offer the avenues of interpersonal commitment, public service, or civic principle that the authors believe nineteenth-century Americans took for granted. Their twentieth and twenty-first-century counterparts cannot cope with the diversities of American life except as the negotiation of claims among self-serving members of various interest groups or social movements (Gusfield 1986, 8). Indeed, in contrast to the notions of Durkheim, who believed that organic solidarity came necessarily after mechanical solidarity, the existence of the enclaves noted above suggests that excessive social complexity does not breed solidarity among differently placed persons so much as a return to forms of association based on similarities. That is, such memberships involve different and often incommensurate cosmologies that also carry deeply patterned forms of selfhood, which, when challenged, are defended with angry social protest. These actions themselves recreate values, feelings, and social groups or movements as diverse as feminism, black nationalism, and Christian fundamentalism.

At the personal level, the cosmology of community and the cosmology of individuality involve different norms of identity, emotions, and action, and they require and are limited to different forms of social organization. In the earlier pattern, the discipline of impulses and the control of emotions was paramount as a virtue if not as a fact. In the current dispensation, to express and be true to one's feelings is what counts.

JOHN WAYNE AS AMERICAN INDIVIDUALIST

One form of American individualism, especially for working-class males, is ruggedness or toughness, termed "aggressive individualism" by Hsu (1983). This toughness may have antecedents in "English cultural traditions of knightly valor, the difficulty of survival in the new land and the highly masculinized forms of Protestantism that were associated with economic individualism and entrepreneurship" (Langman and Harold 1989, 10–11). In effect, American Protestantism sequestered Mary, marginalized Jesus, and elevated God as an all-dominating *male* father. In this way it gave an aggressive cast to individualism and made toughness, in the pursuit of righteous virtue, a sacred value.

Whatever its sources in American history and culture, a prime icon of rugged individualism is the screen persona of John Wayne (born Marion Morrison). According to biographer Garry Wills, in 1993 pollsters asked a representative sample of more than a thousand Americans, "Who is your favorite star? John Wayne came in second, even though he had been dead for fourteen years. He was second again in 1994. Then, in 1995, he was number one, getting more than twice the votes that put Mel Gibson in the third spot and nearly six times the number of Paul Newman's votes" (1997, 11). With a kindred enthusiasm, in 1979 the U.S. Congress voted to strike a special gold medal to honor him, bearing the superscription, "John Wayne, American." The John Wayne International Airport in Orange County, California, is adorned with an enormous statue of him. Would-be macho men and convicted multiple murderers John Wayne Hearn and John Wayne Gacy bear his name. Ron Kovic, the Vietnam veteran who became a paraplegic in the war and later denounced it in *Born on the Fourth of July,* said it was war movies with John Wayne that got him to enlist. "Yes," he reflected, "I gave my dead dick for John Wayne" (quoted in Wills 1997, 12). As did, for a while, John Wayne Bobbitt.

John Wayne's often xenophobic, even genocidal, roles and imagery have been especially popular on the political right. This is no coincidence. "Individual masculine 'virility-hardness' is inevitable if men are going to contribute force to a power organization" such as the military or a fascist state (Spindler 1948, 276). These same qualities, however, along with the rifle and the ax, also symbolize the pioneer who *conquered* the *virgin* frontier. Such symbols train young Americans in aggressive courage, domination, and direct destructive action—to fight the Evil Empire or the Axis of Evil. Though not a member of the John Birch Society as was Wayne, the pudgy, bespectacled Henry Kissinger compared himself to the Duke: "I've always acted alone . . . Americans admire that enormously. Americans admire the cowboy entering the village or the city alone on his horse" (quoted in Hitchens 1997, 20; see also Roberts and Olson 1997). This association worked much better for Kissinger's boss, Ronald Reagan, who often dressed Western, rode horses, and "was introduced to the Republican Convention in 1994 with a specially made film that included clips from Wayne's performances" (Hitchens 1997, 20). The social consequences of this credo of "aggressive individualism" include the personal greed and public squalor of much American life, as well as the tendency to locate all social maladies in individual shortcomings.

This macho Protestantism operated on the psychological level to help engender a highly productive economy, which has now come to depend on consumption for its dynamism and, indeed, for its very existence. Ironically, however, the new consumerism favors indulgence more than discipline and validates the desires of the self, its feelings, its expression, and its fulfillment, especially as these can be gratified in consumption. Inner-directed restraint gives way to other-directed hedonism (Inkeles 1983; Reismann 1950). Only now these valued desires, feelings, and self-expression are increasingly nourished, commercialized, and controlled by corporations, experts, and the state. Individualism is now expressed through exquisite hedonism and therapeutic searches for the true self and through the incorporation of images and desires made available by ads and spectacles that are manufactured far outside the control of those who consume them.

Of course the personality style of John Wayne varies by gender, race, and class. Nancy Chodorow, for example, argues that "growing girls come to define themselves as continuous with others; their experience of self contains more flexible or permeable ego boundaries. Boys come to define themselves as more separate and distinct, with a greater sense of rigid ego boundaries and differentiation" (1978, 169). Others (for example, Dickson) argue that "the cool pose of the Black male . . . the ability to present oneself as emotionless, fearless, and aloof . . . functions to preserve the Black male's pride, dignity, and self-respect" (1993, 481). But observers also find that the John Wayne persona may be dysfunctional to forming stable intimacies, not only with women, but also with other men. Black men, of course, generally are not fans of John Wayne as (racist) hero, but their "cool dude" posture has much in common with that of the Duke.

Similarly, working-class men distinguish themselves from the talkativeness and emotionality of women. They value more the hand and body intelligence that is likely necessary for their often physical labor and hold the belief that the pink-collar activities of their wives and daughters in offices are not really work (Halle 1984). Moreover, they have less of the income and leisure that are usually required for the cultivation of feelings. Thus, working-class males tend to possess or deploy fewer of the skills of feedback and reflection that are necessary for intimate communication. Instead, their model is more the strong, silent type—like Wayne (Illouz 2000; see also Hall 1991).

Perhaps professional-class liberals and neoconservatives also are following Henry Kissinger and embracing the John Wayne image, at least after they have been mugged. The most noteworthy aspects of Bernard Goetz, the John Wayne of New York's subways, was not that he shot menacing black teenagers, but that in the rest of his life he was a nerd who suddenly was seen by most New Yorkers as an avenging hero.

FROM SPIRITUAL QUEST TO PSYCHOLOGICAL SICKNESS: THE INDIVIDUATION OF THE AMERICAN UNCONSCIOUS

Central to the history of American identity are changes in Americans' conceptions of the unconscious. This term does not belong to various schools of psychology only. Before that and more important, it had been a symbol of aesthetic spirituality that is deeply rooted in American thought. Indeed, this American idea of the spiritual unconscious has roots in the pantheism of Jonathan Edwards, the transcendentalism of Emerson, and the metaphysics of William James. It can be traced from nineteenth-century philosophical writings, tracts on natural theology, and popular demonstrations of hypnosis by Mesmerists to humanistic and existential psychologists of the twentieth century. In its psychotherapeutic and New Age forms the discourse of a spiritual unconscious still enables persons to define and pursue modern and postmodern forms of selfhood. Contemporary humanistic and popular psychologies continue the nineteenth-century legitimation of the spiritual by making the harmony-seeking unconscious the vital core of the psyche, giving it factual status, and reconciling scientific and religious convictions.

The idea of the psyche as our unconscious pathway to higher spiritual realms has been challenged by psychoanalysis, behaviorism, structuralism, and other intellectual and cultural movements. Thus, Freud's concept of the unconscious, with its connection to instinct, conflict, sexuality, and other "lower" urges, was incompatible with the American idea that the unconscious is a transcendental, integrating function of the psyche. The behaviorists' dismissal of a nontangible inner life and their focus on behavioral management and control also threw the spiritual legacy of Emerson and James into disrepute, especially among the new academic psychologists (Brown 1998). The earlier spiritual meaning of the unconscious was resurrected only in the 1940s, "when the neo-Freudians (especially Horney and Fromm) reinterpreted the Freudian concept of the unconscious in American terms, emphasizing vitality, play, and growth. . . . This interpretation was extended by Maslow, May, and Rogers, and later by popular psychology, including est, New Age cults, and parapsychology" (Westkott 1988, 226; see also Fuller 1986, 17).

As the spiritual unconscious developed in response to the secularization of Western culture, it converged with the trajectory of the Catholic confession in the United States. Although initially a sacred ritual of the church, confession in American expanded from a means of spiritual redemption to a resource for secular emancipation. The Americanization of confession also took place *within* the Catholic Church. For example, Rita Melendez found the following:

> When confession was seen as liberating it was likened to therapy; however, confession was seen as oppressive when placed in the context of a mandatory ritual set within a hierarchical institution without a large amount of individual control. . . . By likening confession to therapy, [respondents construed confession as a therapeutic] process of personal disclosure. . . . [For example,] Victor . . . saw confession as "a way of repressing people," yet when asked about his own personal experience in the confessional, he answered using psychological terms and reasoning: "Freud wrote that religion is a parental figure which humans have created. Going to confession is like psychology. You feel relieved because you have been pardoned. The first thing I felt [after confession] was relieved because I felt that I had done something wrong and that I had gotten pardoned, in psychological terms" (n.d., 10).

This comparison with therapy also highlights how important it is that disclosures be on the individual's own terms and not hierarchical or communal.

Not only have secular values come to infuse and shape the religious sphere, but also the religious confessional has moved from a booth in a church to offices, meeting halls, TV shows, and presidential addresses. For example, an emphasis on control by the individual has appeared in the views of gays and lesbians questioned about the forced public revelation of another person's "true" sexual identity. Most saw outing as oppressive because "power did not rest with the individual being 'outed,' which meant that a personal matter about an individual was revealed without his or her consent and understanding. 'Coming out,' on the other hand, is the voluntary revelation of gay/lesbian identity. . . . 'Coming out' was seen . . . as tremendously liberating for the individual and group at large" (Melendez n.d., 2, 5). Confession, whether to a priest, a psychiatrist, or the general public, can bring personal relief and liberation. But now the locus of power to regulate the psyche is relocated from religious institutional discourse to a more diffuse, individualistic, secular discourse of liberation. Yet as Foucault (1978, 3–13) noted, power operates precisely where people think they are liberating themselves from domination.

Parallel to the reshaping of confession from canonical penance to personal counseling or public pronouncement was the emergence of psychotherapy as a distinct profession. Originally, "profession" involved an intense commitment to the sacred that enabled priests and others to help lay people. Usually their service was gratuitous, and they were rewarded with an honorarium that ideally expressed devotion. But the term "profession" itself had changed in meaning from venerable faith to vendable expertise. This is evident in the changes undergone by psychotherapy, which arose as a profession in the decades after 1860, when the emergence of modern states, industrial capitalism, and legally and psychologically individuated persons began to generate the new problems of personal autonomy and social control upon which psychologists were to work. Early attempts to address these problems within traditional clerical or medical frameworks were often ineffective, especially with persons who responded to problems with physical complaints that could not be readily understood in purely physiological terms. Eventually the earlier theological, then physiological, and then "neurological construction of personal problems turned into the modern concept of neurosis as a psychically generated, psychically diagnosed, and psychically treated phenomenon" (Abbott 1988, 313). The concept of neurosis has dominated discussions of personal problems ever since, even though the kinds of relevant practitioners have changed with shifts in demand or mode of payment.

The language of therapy was not confined to therapists and their patients or clients. It is used, for example, in pastoral counseling, presidential apologies, parole board hearings, and TV talk shows such as those of Oprah Winfrey or Montel Williams. Many of the persons whom Robert Bellah and his colleagues (1991) interviewed also used therapeutic language in describing the self as the source of all values. For such persons therapy was the model of the institutionally adjusted, contractual character of the ideal self. Socially deviant conduct was redefined from wicked or indecent to neurotic or dysfunctional (Gerth and Mills 1953, 123). All this has made values other than those of the improvement, fulfillment, or interests of the self difficult to defend or even imagine.

The anticivic and narcissistic aspects of this therapeutic discourse have been criticized by Philip Slater (1991), Philip Rieff (1990), and Christopher Lasch (1978). One place to observe this discourse is at meetings of Alcoholics Anonymous. AA was founded by white, Protestant, small-town Americans, partly in response to the repeal of Prohibition in 1933.

> Instead of political action, AA followed its spiritual progenitor, the early-twentieth-century Oxford Group, in preaching a species of personalized moral rearmament. . . . There is nothing new about recovery except the packaging, they tend to say, insisting that the search for "inner children" and such are only the latest in that long series of enthusiasms for self-improvement to which Americans have been drawn since at least the middle of the nineteenth century. . . . Indeed, few Americans . . . live untouched by the conviction that they can change almost anything about themselves if they really want to do so. For Americans, self-creation has from the beginning been the essential act. The great American stories, from James Fenimore Cooper to Philip Roth, are about busting free, finding some way of shucking off the bonds of family and tradition, not so much with the purpose of winning the freedom to *be* oneself as out of the conviction that only the act of lighting out for the territories ensures that one will ever *become* onself (Rieff 1990, 53, 52).

One measure of such individualism is the term "codependency," which defines as an illness the reliance on any opinion other than one's own for a sense of self.

The continued economic success and social rationalization of the United States has generated new insecurities but also provided resources for the medicalization of deviance and for the democratization of reflection on one's own suffering. Thus many more Americans, often well into middle age, can afford to dissect their feelings and divine the sources of their discomforts in the inadequate care given to them by their parents (Rieff 1990, 56). Perhaps the expansion and narcissistic aspects of therapy stem from the fact that many Americans today feel *entitled* to more—not just to the pursuit of happiness, but also to happiness itself (Acocella 1999; Irvine 1999). For example, formerly Americans wanted a job, then a "decent" job. But according to studies by the University of Michigan, Gallup, and UCLA, greater percentages of young people today—compared to their counterparts in the 1950s, 1960s, and 1970s—want "jobs that pay a lot," second cars, swimming pools, vacation homes, and "clothing in the latest styles." "Their first priority is themselves," concluded the UCLA survey of college students (noted in Georges 1993).

This focus on the self and on personal feelings as a basis for morality also spills into the civic and legal realms, especially those most frequented by the professional classes, for whom a therapeutic worldview is both affordable and politically comfortable. One instance of this is the original guidelines for the University of Michigan's antidiscrimination code, which insisted that "students must be free to participate in class discussion without feeling harassed or intimidated . . . by a professor's remark, even if no one else in the class saw anything objectionable" (quoted in Leo 1992, 28). In other words, the feelings of the self become the socially acceptable gauge for ascertaining whether there is a basis for litigation. Pennsylvania State University, the University of Maryland, and other campuses are striving to banish from campus anything that makes people uncomfortable about sex. Law professor Catherine MacKinnon (1987) also asserts feelings to be the basis of both legality and morality.

Such regulations and remarks collapse the former borders between public and private realism by insisting that a person's negative feelings create and define an offense and its victim. This individualism of feelings in the name of tolerance destroys the deliberative discourse of democracy more insidiously than despotism. Child abuse, rape, or sexual harassment are reduced to whatever anyone feels they are. Since such phenomena are increasingly viewed subjectively, definitions of these acts can and are being expanded indefinitely (Acocella 1999; Irvine 1999). For example, John Bradshaw, a leading author and lecturer on the recovery circuit, asserts that almost everyone has suffered some form of child abuse insofar as a whopping 96 percent of us are supposed to be the products of dysfunctional families. Such early abuses are said to foster "addictive" adult behaviors that can be cured, so experts claim, through twelve-step programs, weekend workshops, and extended psychotherapy. One twelve-step group, Codependents Anonymous (CoDa), differs from AA in that it attributes adult problems to abusive parents rather than to a disease. Since such abuse, past and present, is said to result from the lack of a nurturing environment, one way to correct it is to ensure that all environments are nurturing. Founded in 1986, Codependents Anonymous—"a fellowship of men and women whose common problem is an inability to maintain functional relationships" (Irvine 1999, 7)—now has over four thousand groups in the United States. Members learn "to get in touch with their true feelings" and discover the "real self." And the bodily experience of "sharing": confession and release; the support and endorsement of fellow members; the almost always available meetings with groups of different strangers/comrades—all create a feeling of authenticity and relatedness without the usual burdens of commitment. In a twist on Max Weber's famous assessment of modern life, we slide, slowly, from the iron cage toward the padded cell.

The emergence of the right not to be offended explains why insensitivity has become a highly damaging accusation. Since there are apparently few social rules that anyone wants to defend, our constant duty—let us call it chore—"is to guess what will trigger negative emotions (sensitivity) and accuse ourselves ruefully when we accidentally step on another person's emotional land mine and set it off (insensitivity)" (Wills 1997, 78). This focus on feelings indeed was the central theme of *Seinfeld,* the most popular TV comedy of the 1990s, where virtually every episode centered around the fear of offending someone or the consequences of having done so. This focus also is seen in the evasive non-apologies of public figures caught in misconduct. William Aramony, stepping down as head of the United Way amid clear evidence of malfeasance, apologized for a "lack of sensitivity to perceptions." The board, in turn, accepted his "thoughtful and sensitive offer" to resign immediately (Leo 1992, 28). In such a way of thinking and feeling, "utility replaces duty; self-expression unseats authority. 'Being good' becomes 'feeling good'" (Bellah et al. 1985, 77; see also Hewitt 1998).

Transformations in adult education offer another illustration of both the rationalization and fragmentation of the private sphere and the new sovereignty of the self. Initially conceived as a means of upward social mobility for the masses, or at least the middle classes, adult education is now often the way to acquire a "more positive self-image." For example, the New School for Social Research, which once sponsored the courses by W. E. B. DuBois on race and by Hannah Arendt on politics, today offers classes on "How to Educate Your Dreams to Work for You," "Body Awareness," and "Personal Growth." Hofstra University, a relative newcomer to the identity market, teaches "Masculinity" and "Pitfalls and Possibilities: A Couples Workshop."

Another example of the seeping of the therapeutic ethos into the public sphere is the state's assumption of the role of adjucator of emotions or even the role of therapist or counselor itself. Thus "a family in Hawaii recovered $1,000 in compensation for the emotional distress incurred from the negligent death of their dog Princess" (Nolan 1998, 62; see also Polsky 1991). Similarly the state becomes the last resort when convicted drug users or spouse beaters receive counseling, rehabilitation, group therapy, and emotional support along with their punishment, provided by people who care.

Workshops and how-to-do-it manuals now cover topics from mourning to masturbation. Such courses, essentially without content, offer an experience of participation to people whose isolation is very real. Yet the participants can get little satisfaction since such workshops, courses, and manuals, like "authenticity" or "spontaneity" themselves, have been rationalized along with everything else. Thus one may achieve competence in expressing one's feelings in settings devoid of moral commitments, but such activities reproduce rather than counterbalance the new amoral professionalism of the public sphere. In both cases, personal or occupational distress, shortcomings, or aspirations are no longer transformed into collective moral and political narrations. Instead, the reverse is true. Public issues are often reduced to technical problems or personal troubles. Metanarratives having been disposed of, everyone has his or her own story to tell, a story that is more a calculated confession derived from media spectacles than a moral witnessing for political solidarity. As a result, what might otherwise have become self-directing, action-oriented communities remain passive audiences or transient associations of individuals bound only by the similarity of their fleeting impulses and desires.

The sovereignty of the individual, and today of the individual's feelings, is illustrated by a contretemps in 1997 over recollections of childhood by Senator Robert Torricelli, then freshman Democrat from New Jersey. Torricelli, now a convicted felon, served at the time on the committee investigating campaign irregularities.

> [He] gave a tug to the nation's heartstrings when he advertised his sensitivity about insensitivity towards Asian-Americans. Sensitivity-mongering has special éclat when coupled with a boast of victimhood, and Torricelli managed this coupling. He remembered how pained he was by unflattering Italian-American stereotypes that he recalls being fostered by Sen. Estes Kefauver's televised hearings into organized crime. "It is among the first memories I have of government of the United States, and probably the first hearing of the United States Senate I ever witnessed. It was only on a flickering television screen, but I will never forget it, and even if I tried, my family would never allow me." "Among?" "Probably?" "Witnessed?" He was five days old when Kefauver's hearings ended in 1951. When a journalist asked Torricelli about his prodigiously early interest in public affairs, Torricelli upbraided the journalist for missing the larger point, about "insensitivity" (Wills 1997, 78).

With such an emphasis on feelings and sensitivity, the speaker "is judged for his attitude toward the audience, an attitude that is either sincere or insincere, rather than by his . . . honesty and skill. [But] just because such a premium is placed on sincerity, a premium is put on faking it" (Riesman 1950, 194, 196). With such an emphasis on personal feelings and perceptions, reality anemia readily ensues. For example, President Clinton's former labor secretary, Robert Reich, fabricated events recounted in his book, *Locked in the Cabinet,* which he called a "memoir." Among other things, Reich recalls being bombarded by rude questions hurled at him through dense cigar smoke at an all-male lunch of the

National Association of Manufacturers (NAM). But as Gary Wills points out, "it was breakfast; at least a third of those attending were women; NAM rules forbid smoking; the transcript records no questions remotely like those Reich recounts. Asked about this, Reich breezily noted . . . 'I claim no higher truth than my own perceptions. This is how I lived it'" (1997, 78). Thus Reich and many other public figures seem to have adopted what "feels right" and "satisfying" as a standard of judgment. In pursuing such nostrums, much of American culture has been recast in the mold of therapy. Self-esteem as a goal replaces achievement, and feel-good stories about each ethnic and gender group replace accounts of conflict, struggle, or tragedy. The individualism of Thoreau, defined in terms of engagement in democratic society, shifts toward an unbounded postmodern freedom from any fixed definition of what is real or true.

From the earliest days of America, the "immigration in time" typical of voyagers to the New World induced many newcomers to reject any community of memories. Since immigrants believed in the priority of the future and the obsolescence of the past, they abandoned tradition often in favor of progressive (that is, rational and instrumental) models of behavior (Shils 1981). This rejection of the past as a source of legitimacy facilitated commercial and technological innovation as long as individualism remained "instrumental" rather than "expressive" (Bellah et al. 1985). In other words, the pursuit of selfhood contributed to society as long as individualism implied the pursuit of excellence and the challenge was to build one's character by *being* or *doing* good.

For a great number of Americans this is no longer the case. Postmodern individualism means to *feel* good (Rosen 1985). It implies the pursuit of personal needs or pleasures that are unrelated to civic virtue or attainment. Such withdrawals into inward spiritual or emotional states themselves contribute to broader processes of rationalization and, with these, the depersonalization of one's emotional control of others and the emotional manipulation by others of oneself (Langman and Kaplan 1979, 27). In this context, once deeply emotional acts such as parenting are increasingly becoming instrumental projects. Feelings and relationships become purposive and calculated in terms of their utility for certain goals, whether these goals be success or adjustment. But as such calculations enter personal relations, people become more estranged from one another and, hence, more likely to retreat into a purely inward realm. For example, the more that sexual intimacy becomes an explicit bargain calculated in terms of the frequency, intensity, or quality of orgasms, the more elusive intimacy itself becomes (Bejin 1985). Indeed, with the elevation of individual feelings and the downgrading of intersubjective experiences, autoeroticism may gain status relative to alloeroticism, and so may voyeurism, exhibitionism, pornography, or Internet sex in relation to direct human contact.

In short, postmodern individualism involves the transformability not only of feelings or ideas, but of partners and friends as well. Indeed, the influence of familistic or religious vocabularies and their stress on essential relations and communal obligations have declined in favor of individualist discourses—a romantic discourse of love and personal growth and a commercial discourse that emphasizes egocentric pragmatism (Hirschman 1977; Lyman 1978; Nelson 1968). In both these discourses, for example, each spouse is declared innocent in the breakup of a marriage since neither passion nor commerce are about social obligation. This declaration of mutual innocence is captured in the expression "no-fault divorce" and also implies the elimination of alimony, regardless of the differential involvement of males and females in the paid labor force or in unpaid child rearing. Thus, both the positivist conception of ethical neutrality and the romantic view of the higher morality of passion invite the assertion of formal equality and moral equivalence of all individuals, regardless of their particular merits or circumstances. In this sense, both the positivist vocabulary of systems and its romantic counterpart of feelings express the overarching processes of de-essentialization. Instead, as selves become more transformable, people and relations become more interchangeable.

HYPER-RATIONALIZATION AND RADICAL SUBJECTIVISM: PENETRATIONS OF SYSTEM INTO LIFEWORLD AND SELFHOOD

Max Weber characterized modern societies as those in which calculations of utility were systematically applied to social interactions. Such "rationalization" clearly is evident in the marketplace and the world of business, where profit is the guiding principle and all else tends to become an instrument toward that end. Government agencies also are rationalized in the sense that they are designed and exist to more efficiently pursue some end. Unlike the church or families, firms and bureaus are not legitimated as ends in themselves. Hyper-rationalization, then, is the extension of these processes to an extreme, to all areas of social life, so that there is little space left even to discuss purposes or ends—when, for example, child rearing becomes mostly a matter of expert guidance, as in much of the upper-professional class, or when justice is reduced to cost-benefit analysis or economic calculation, as it is by some sitting judges appointed by President Reagan.

In postindustrial and postmodern societies, hyper-rationalization creates new tensions between macrosocial structures or processes and microsocial patterns of interaction and also between public and private spheres and their respective discourses. The public sphere is reified into the language of scientific rationality, as in scientific marketing, scientific warfare, or scientific management. As this vocabulary of utility and efficiency comes to dominate the public world, it empowers experts, managers, and techno-administrators, whether these be university presidents, hospital directors, or corporate CEOs. At the same time, the everyday world (to the extent that it escapes domination by the hyper-rationalized system) is emptied of substantive rationality and reduced to mere feelings or opinions. It becomes the sphere of peak experiences and the search for authenticity. This private sphere complements the emotional sterility of both impersonal bureaucracies and interactions of citizens or consumers who must deal with, or dwell within, such organizations.

One consequence of the hyper-rationality of the system and the privileged status of feelings in the lifeworld is reality anemia. Reality anemia occurs with the standardization of the criteria by which economic performance is assessed and also with the decline in the scope and duration of such criteria. It also involves a much narrowed conception of accountability. For example, the assessment of college teachers through students' evaluations of them places students' feelings above their own possible improvements in performance. Similarly, as the assessment of corporate executives comes to be based on quarterly earnings or the price of the company's stock, accountability is reduced to narrowly defined impressions the executives make during an increasingly limited period of time. What often counts is the effectiveness of their short-term role playing, management of information, or "creative bookkeeping," rather than the long-term consequences of decisions they have taken. In such ways, reality anemia subverts the grounding of the self in stable experience and achievement.

Reality anemia invades politics as well. In the Iran-Contra affair, for example, both witnesses and suspects invoked ignorance and amnesia to cover up illegal actions. Thus, President Reagan, the most powerful American political actor, could successfully assert his *powerlessness* because the audience easily identified with it. As human shortcomings become more uniform and abstract, deniability of misdeeds replaces verifiability of achievements as the benchmark for judgments on individual conduct. In such conditions, where all is transformed into appearance, the virtual and the real are collapsed into each other, and "virtual reality" does not seem oxymoronic.

The bureaucratic ethos, with its standardized procedures and ways of thought, and the marketplace, with its calculations of deals and profit, also encroach constantly on the private sphere, thereby reducing or reifying personal experience into general categories and creating reality anemia. As citizens are replaced by functionaries, public space for their critical reflection and ethical action is thereby reduced, and responsibility shifts from the individual as a moral being to impersonal rules, regulations, and calculations of efficiency. Thus, in their rhetorics and practices, contemporary bureaucracies favor the "objectivity" of instrumental rationality to the "subjectivity" of moral commitment, which is decried as dysfunctional, capricious, or anachronistic. Rationality thereby becomes the ideological catchword for the mystification of a curtailed individual participation in public affairs and for the parallel political dominance of existing elites (Arendt 1951; Belohradsky 1981; Marcel 1962). Correspondingly, the definition of freedom as civic participation is transformed from a positive value into a negative one: the right to *withdraw* from civic life into a world of personal desires, fulfillment, or frustrations.

People react to indeterminacy and to the collapse of stable meanings in many ways. Some may surrender passively to their circumstances, whereas others may plunge into the stream of ideologies that are increasingly implausible in their very proliferation. These responses may go with a tendency to form opinions based on sentiments, associations, and magical formulas—each of which favors simplification and overstates the orderliness of experience. The mass media aid in this by their need for brevity, dramatic images, and reduction in presenting the news. Many people withdraw into isolation or sameness. In the case of isolation, individuals in hyper-rationalized society respond to the diversity of social encounters by turning would-be friends into contacts and contacts into hoped-for contracts. They thereby limit their commitments in the public sphere and maintain an emotional aloneness as they manipulate others. This isolation is expressed by the poetic image presented by Edwin Arlington Robinson of Richard Cory, the affable young man who went home and put a bullet through his head. It also is seen in the transformed ethos of *Nole me tangere,* which was once on the American flag. Formerly it was a warning to foreign powers to tread carefully with America; today it is a more subjective, "Don't step on me, buddy."

In the second case, withdrawal into sameness, individuals respond to social diversity and its consequent emotional overload by withdrawing into solidarities based on similarity of appearance or origin, at the expense of solidarities based on complementarity (Sennett 1978). This celebration of sameness is perhaps the most common link between the twinlike appearance of gay or lesbian couples on Sundays in Washington, D.C.'s Dupont Circle, the specifications for membership of proliferating gated communities, and the "gender neutral" egalitarian ethos of many young cohabiting couples. Each participant wants to find himself "the other," but that other is already himself. In this sense radical identity movements and reactionary fundamentalist ones both withdraw affect from a common civic life and attempt to create meaning with resources under their control. In both there also is a focus on one's body—its pleasures, its vices, its color, its organs—which, presumably, neither the alienating other nor the rationalized systems can or should control. The modernist commitment to *civitas,* or solidarity of citizens, is thereby replaced by the postmodernist celebration of *difference,* which invites solidarities of sameness. Features such as race, gender, sexuality, or lifestyle are highlighted as social distinctions and core aspects of identity. Awareness of difference with others is matched by enforcement of sameness within one's own group. Though often hailed as democratic diversity, such social fragmentations and reconsolidations also contract the space for forming more inclusive identities as citizens. For example, the programs on many college campuses to encourage cultural diversity often result in an array of self-segregated social environments of similar persons who stick with their own (Brown 2000).

Rationalization also generates a greater division of labor and often greater specialization of each person's roles, greater distance among them, and less identification with any of them. The sociologists' terms "role conflict" and "role distance" express this. In order to maintain some degree of integrity, the self withdraws commitment from (and then consciously performs) these diverse, fragmented, and often conflicting social roles. In this "inner-worldly asceticism," the drama of grace of the early Protestants is replaced by the graceless melodrama of contemporary role players. Ultimately the self may lose connection with any social experience and become a purely inner essence, thereby separating external organizational actions and inner moral consciousness even further. Such a self reduces persons' commitment to any social role or system of authority (Benn and Gaus 1983; Valadez and Clignet 1987; Ostereicher 1979). It is akin to the "inner migration" of many Germans during (and after) the Nazi regime. Such withdrawal can be seen in the evolution of language concerning work. Consider the concept of a job. Initially, the term referred not only to a specific occupational role and to its demands and advantages, but also to occupational attainment, as in "a job well done" or "nice job." As this usage has diminished, the term now connotes an indifference to work, responsibility, or achievement, as in the expression "It's just a job." Correspondingly, the term now has a mainly pecuniary implication, as in, "It's a $40,000 a year job."

There are many other indications of the declining importance of work and achievement as major determinants of identity. Thus, a clerk in a shopping mall says, "I can't exchange this; I only work here." Similarly, a Smithsonian biological researcher considers the Pacific Program to be a successful field study in spite of how the Defense Department used it (Gup 1985, 9–12). The advice of a prospective CIA employee is in the same spirit: "You can compartmentalize. . . . If I am an analyst with the [CIA], they may knock off a Chilean leader, but I didn't do it" (quoted in Rothschild 1984, 18). This parallels Vietnam-era pilots who said they flew missions but did not think about targets (Kahn 1973). In each of these cases, the moral dimensions are "compartmentalized" out of the task. Fighter pilots become service providers akin to social workers or alcoholism counselors, since in the new abstracted language all are now "service workers" who are "just doing their jobs."

These expressions also reveal the divorce of the self from "them" (managers, but also fellow workers, customers, or clients). As Hannah Arendt put it, there is a "rule by nobody" in a society where "there is no one left who could answer for what is being done" (1970, 38–39). Formerly, when the work ethic was a trademark of American public ideology, work was a means to worth and not just to wealth. But today, those in most sectors of the economy who seek a positive moral identity from their workplace are increasingly destined to be frustrated, manipulated, and exploited. The shift of the meaning given to the word "professional" further illustrates this. Against a historical tradition that emphasizes the ethical and intellectual obligations of those who have something to profess, current specialists endow the term with more privilege and less responsibility. Such a change confirms the declining contribution of occupational commitment to the definition of the self. Only those least powerful, like welfare recipients, are expected (or compelled) to gain dignity through labor.

The expression "It's just a job" suggests much of this situation. Both the adverb "just" and the noun "job" suggest that individuals split off their occupational activities from the remaining parts of their lives. Such psychic absence at the workplace, though a response to the hyper-rationalization of organization life, also induces workers to give priority to their own private concerns (Bellah et al. 1985). This psychic absence is illustrated by the increase in side conversations in which bank tellers or cashiers engage while attending to their clients and the increased, and increasingly alienating, efforts of employers at surveillance and control. The rise in accidents caused by the use of drugs among bus drivers or railroad engineers and the complimentary drug testing of job candidates by major corporations suggest that occupational roles are more than ever defined in terms of expedience, not ethics. In their legal contracts employers and employees both stress their rights and minimize their obligations both toward each other and toward others who are not explicitly part of their legal agreement. This again narrows the scope of the self and encourages moral and psychological atomization.

In "advanced" societies like the United States, but elsewhere as well, the more that relationships are consciously constructed—that is, entered and exited in a purposive fashion by individuals—the less stable and secure will be their normative basis. With more scope and freedom for individuals to shape selves and relations, norms are more likely to be up for grabs, and actors are more likely to wage microscopic wars in the zone of everyday life. Because individuals—pinioned beneath the state and the market—have to turn themselves into the center of their own lives and because ready-made recipes no longer can guide action, actors are left to haggle and bargain over the norms that should underpin their relations. Paradoxically, at the same time that "intimate relations" and "feelings" become paramount to one's identity, actors entering relations for a variety of purposes, interests, needs, and values are likely to argue vehemently about these relationships. As love, family, and parenthood are undermined by the state and assaulted by the market, people increasingly are faced with contradictory demands. On the one hand, we are expected to make ourselves the center of our own life plan, even at the cost of estrangement from our intimates; on the other, because of the "homelessness" entailed by fading communities and traditions, we are in an ever more urgent need of intimacy and personal relations to alleviate these losses in social solidarity. Thus, the same forces that drive us to seek intimate personal relations are also those that undermine those very relations and drive us to talk about them incessantly, all with an every-growing frenzy.

As Eva Illouz (2003) argues, these conditions are found in microcosm on talk TV. Indeed, highbrow views of American talk shows miss the fact that they are a kind of deliberative moral discourse about identity in late liberal societies. Critics of "trash talk shows" have decried their alleged thirst for sensationalism and shock, much as nineteenth-century reformers campaigned against popular recreations. But the appeal of talk shows may be explained by their cultural meanings. In particular, talk shows conflate aspects of the private sphere with the claims and modes of argumentation of the public sphere. Thus, talk shows mimic the deprivatization and embattled character of the lifeworld and simulate an "ideal speech situation" to cope with the increasing contentiousness of everyday life. Talk shows can be seen as attempts to retrieve the meaning against the backdrop of contradictions in contemporary political ideas, recent trans-formations of the family, changes in the psychology and roles of everyday life, and the impact of the media on the formation of identity. Indeed, it is precisely these forces that account for the intense dramatic staging of emotions in certain talk shows. The shows not only perform the ritual claim that personal and inti-mate relations are of paramount importance to daily life, but also confirm that they are difficult because there are no preestablished normative guideposts on which individuals can lean to resolve their disputes. Intimate relations have be-come central to the constitution of late modernity, yet the impossibility of knowing and deciding in advance how such intimate relations should be con-ducted leaves actors peculiarly vulnerable to others, as well as to the nay-saying voices within themselves.

Hence, talk shows deal symbolically with a basic question of late or post-modernity: how should we talk—and argue—about ourselves and others when no moral foundation can preside over our discussions? Paradoxically, the answer that talk shows give to this question is generally the same one that is offered by Jürgen Habermas, Richard Rorty, and Jean-François Lyotard: speak sincerely and honestly; listen; be open and fair about the rules; do not silence the other; keep the conversation going. Thus the linguistic format of the talk show itself provides a response to our cultural conundrum. The world of talk shows is underlain by the assumption that language is the paramount reality of personal relationships; that these can and in fact *ought* to be argued over; and that they exist, or can be made to work or continue, only through conversa-tion. Moreover, even if the principal parties cannot agree, in the end there usu-ally still is a decision—by the audience. Thus the staging of talk shows as con-frontations and disputations is also a staging of the populist democratic assumption that social bonds can be discussed, negotiated, and repaired through arguments and communications in which the *public* is the ultimate judge.

In sum, the hyper-rationalization and radical subjectivism of advanced cap-italist states diminish the space for fulfillment of oneself as a rational ethical agent in more than purely personal relations. As it becomes more difficult to act as a citizen outside of talk shows—that is, to act as a whole moral person in the public sphere—the Enlightenment metanarrative of progress and freedom through reason also is delegitimated. The collapse of such metanarratives of democracy and selfhood in postmodern society—or their reduction to John Wayne imagery or talk shows—undermines individual and collective memory of either affluence or scarcity, victory or defeat. Without such shared historical and moral frameworks, persons lose the ability to reflectively define collective goals and forge the bonds of solidarity needed to achieve them.

ASSESSING AMERICAN INDIVIDUALISM

Modernity, especially its capitalist forms, has encouraged the breakdown of ties to kin and community and fostered both the retreat and expansion of the self. On the one hand, the self retreats into the small circles of friends, family, and personal wants and feelings; on the other, it expands into abstract collectives such as class, nation, or civil society. In modernity, persons move as individuals in wider public spheres, albeit from a much narrowed social and emotional base. Such individualism has been most broadly spread and is still deepest in the United States. For Tocqueville and his intellectual heirs the danger of individualism was in its excess, that it could become what Emile Durkheim (1951) called "the social pathology of egoism." As Tocqueville noted, "individualism, at first, only saps the virtues of public life; but in the long run it attacks and destroys all others and is at length absorbed in down-right selfishness. . . . Every man seeks for his opinions within himself [and turns] all his feelings . . . towards himself alone" (1945 [1835], 98). But Tocqueville also distinguished individualism from the vice of ordinary selfishness, or *égoisme,* and thereby showed how the particular self-centeredness of Americans was egalitarian and democratic—a calm, mature, socially authorized feeling.

The strains that an earlier Protestant individualism had placed on communal ties were exacerbated as America became more urbanized, more mobile, more rationalized, and more democratic. Individualism came to be associated with wealth and mobility rather than with civic virtue, as it had been for Alexis de Tocqueville, Frederick Douglass, or Henry David Thoreau. Americans remain joiners, but the groups they now join usually have the most limited ties and obligations. They bowl with other people, for example, but not as clubs or leagues (Putnam 2000). Thus Americans generally are socially transient, their life consisting more than before of a series of handshakes in the hallway, short-term friendships, and serial marriages. Such social transience is consistent with high rates of geographic, occupational, and lifestyle mobility and also with an agile, flexible form of capitalism. But it also tends to subvert traditional values of community and kinship. It is an aggressive individualism of agile, flexible people who burn the social fabric.

In assessing modern and then postmodern selfhood, social theorists and critics tend to be pessimistic or optimistic. In the modern period after World War

II, David Reisman (1950) argued that a reorganization of personality occurred in the transition from nineteenth- to twentieth-century capitalism, from inner-directed to other-directed persons of the postwar years. Similar personality configurations were described as the "organization man" (Whyte 1956), the "market-oriented personality" (Fromm 1974), and the "neurotic personality of our time" (Horney 1937). Arnold Gehlen described "a weakening of self, [and] an invasion or saturation of social forces that have made it more and more difficult for people to grow up or even to contemplate the prospect of growing up without misgivings bordering on panic" (1980, 195). Reisman, however, also hoped for the emergence of a new "autonomous" personality. In postmodern capitalism, however, seduction and surveillance have replaced bribery or coercion as the tools of choice for controlling consumers, workers, functionaries, and voters. Thus Reisman's autonomous personality seems little in evidence. Other thinkers, such as Minson (1985), Rose (1989), and Foucault (1977, 1978), who focus on the social-structural sources and implications of these changes, are more pessimistic. For Richard Sennett (1978) and Christopher Lasch (1978) subjectivism turns inward, away from the world, in order to concentrate on the cultivation of the self and its inner life. This self-absorption, Lasch (1978, 25) argues, defines the moral climate of contemporary society.

While many thinkers have viewed contemporary individualism as a social malaise, others describe it as a new liberation. For example, Kenneth Gergen (1991) and Robert Fuller (1986) assert that the postmodern saturation of information, transformative technologies, or psychotherapies opens up a new freedom for self-definition and even community and expresses not narcissism but the urge for harmony, empowerment, or transcendence. Optimists like Gergen tend to see a new freedom emerging from the increased rapidity of change; of social, occupational, and geographic mobility; and of communication. For Gergen, new and accelerating technologies for the disbursal and exchange of information are creating a social saturation that fundamentally alters the meanings of knowledge and identity. The postmodern self is not merely a dissolution of earlier typical selves, nor is it sheer emptiness. Instead, the new saturation by technologies of communication intensifies relatedness and feelings of connection. The new intimacies may be distant, but they are no less powerful, thereby infusing new communities of postmodern selves with potential for unlimited, multiphrenic connections.

Gergen focuses on academics and other professionals like himself. With other groups and classes the degrees and effects of "saturation" are somewhat different. For example, Philip Wexler (1992) found a similar dissolution of earlier social and self certainties among youths of lower strata, but these youths did not receive it with optimism. Instead, for those with fewer economic and cultural resources, everyday life becomes a struggle to secure an integral self-identity in the face of social contradiction and disintegration. Similarly, when Herbert Gans (1991) studied the distinctive individualism of working- and lower-middle-class Americans, he discovered at the core of American individualism a spirit of self-reliance on the part of people who have little influence over the political and economic institutions that play so great a part in their lives. Unlike the more therapeutic individualism of privileged groups, working-class individualism is a response to social domination and dissolution.

There is thus a temporal and social distribution of both modern and postmodern forms of individualism. As America remains a land of disparities, even today the individuation of people who live in ethnic enclaves or remote communities differs from that of persons who dwell in more complex systems. The former may appear to have greater integrity or self-consistency, if only because their world is one of greater consistency between and among its roles and values. Similarly, newly arrived immigrants often have been social pioneers who seized opportunities offered by an industrial or postindustrial economy to redefine their acquired identities and their inherited cultures (Ewen and Ewen 1982). Individualists of the popular classes often preferred a grimace followed by a right hook to talk therapy or a stiff upper lip. Their aggressive/defensive individualism and the frequent rejection of refinement and intellect that it implies were noted by Tocqueville and discussed by Richard Hofstadter (1963). Their heroes are John Wayne or Mike Hammer, not Hercule Poirot or Sherlock Holmes, two very non-American characters (Langman and Harold 1989, 11).

In contrast to past psychological theories that underlined the stability and immutability of human nature, current rhetorics assert the right of the self to change at will (Adorno 1973; Trilling 1971). As the increased mutability of the person has made it easy for almost everyone to imagine him- or herself in differing personas and situations, the ensuing vision that "anything is possible" becomes both an article of faith and a cause for dread. Indeed, the very ease with which one might choose one's identity or form of life condemns *any* commitment to be partial since no particular choice can be the sole, ultimate one (Fingarette 1963, 236). A surfeit of choices devalues and relativizes any identity that might be chosen. Reality anemia and overchoice encourage people to assume that the promises of tomorrow can be realized today. As it takes less time and effort to fulfill one's desires, there is less investment in hopes and ideals, as well as in disillusions. In short, a postindustrial political economy goes hand in hand with a postmodern culture of calculation and narcissism and the celebration of individuality over the accomplishments of individuals.

One can see all these tendencies in the popularization of psychiatric therapies and modes of thought, the spread of New Age spirituality, the proliferation of techniques for self-help and self-enhancement, the therapeutization of the confessional, the iconography of John Wayne, and the socialization into selfhood through electronic media and the culture of consumption. All these are signs of a new subjective individualism, now more corporate directed, that collapses the ego even as it liberates the self. Thus the assertions of individualism, the will to explore, to transform oneself, to "grow," are simultaneously admissions of the loss of a center, of narcissistic self-absorption, of a loss of civic involvement, and of our difficulties in coping with what used to be called the adult world.

Yet the social class distribution of these tendencies remains important. For example, many investigations based on reported attitudes and values have shown that "persons of higher social classes, that is, with higher levels of occupation and/or education, [are] consistently more likely than those in lower social classes to value self-direction and concern with inner psychological processes" (House 1981, 549; see also Kohn 1969; Pearlin and Kohn 1966; Wright and Wright 1976). Other studies, more ethnographic than statistical, reveal something similar. For example, Adrie Kusserow (1999) conducted extended interviews with white working-class and professional-class mothers and teachers in Queens and Manhattan. The individualism of the working-class mothers was "rugged" or "tough." These were strong women, without husbands, raising and supporting kids on welfare, exhibiting a strength and resistance that was palpable in their voices and bodies. For these women, "individualistic values were woven into discourses about how they had made it through difficult events. Theirs was a philosophy of the lone individual standing tough against a world which threatened to undo her, knock her down. Individualism's *raison d'être* was usually an attempt to deal with something 'tough,' perhaps the most common word used by these mothers. . . . Independence, self-reliance, minding one's own business and a dogged self-determination where the traits that would help their children buck up, toughen, harden and keep going through some challenging situation that would arise, when 'things don't go right for them.' . . . Mothers also used images of war and fighting, e.g., 'defend yourself,' 'fight it out'" (1999, 14, 15).

In contrast, the professional women in Manhattan practiced a "soft psychologized individualism." In discussions about rearing their children, for example, talk of autonomy, uniqueness, individuality and self-confidence was intertwined with talk of the importance and rights of the psychological self (emotions, feelings, desires, tastes, personality) to emerge and be the best it can be. Children must fully acknowledge and honor their emotions and desires so that they can find the right social outlet for them. The energy of true desire, authentic preference, unique feelings and tastes will naturally motivate them to be good at what they love. . . . Hence, an individualistic and independent child was felt to be a happy child insofar as independence was proof that feelings were not being stifled or blocked. Happiness came about when psychologized uniqueness was able to flow freely. . . . Raising an individualistic child was akin to gently assisting the child in emerging, unfolding, flowering, self-actualizing his or her own qualities, thoughts and feelings. . . . One of the most common metaphors used to speak of this unfolding process was that of the child as a "flower" in which images of growing, blooming and blossoming were invoked (Kusserow 1999, 20, 21).

Of course, class is not the only factor that accounts for different styles of individualism in America, but it helps dissolve the paradox of a John Wayne–style "hard" individualism coexisting with a therapeutic "soft" individualism. Unlike working-class persons, members of the upper-middle class have more control over the external conditions of their existence: they can more easily change jobs or neighborhoods, avoid violence or illness, and defend themselves against injustice or bad luck. But such persons buy these advantages by acting in accordance with normatively sanctioned patterns of behavior. They are what Robert Merton (1957) called "conformists." The low-income person, by contrast, is more vulnerable to changes in his or her conditions but has more control over existential actions. Low-income persons usually work in more physically dangerous, demanding, or unsanitary jobs. An office worker can still perform with a broken leg, but a bricklayer cannot. And the bricklayer is unlikely to have health insurance to cover injuries or illness. Such vulnerability extends to many other areas besides health. Thus the low-income person needs to be quick and tough in order simply to "survive." Hence lower-class persons display existential qualities of rugged individualism—spontaneity, daring, physical courage, loyalty to peers, resistance to authority, and toughness—that Miller, Kohn, and Schooler (1977); Trotha (1974); Whyte (1956); Bernstein (1971); Brown (1987, ch. 1); Kusserow (1999); and many others have noted in urban low-income groups.

By contrast, soft, therapeutic individualism seems equally adapted to middle- and upper-middle-class life and occupational roles. Whereas the work of lower-income persons usually involves handling things, middle-and professional-class jobs more often require the management of symbols, people, and feelings, especially in the upper sectors of the information and service economy, where "bosses" have become "team leaders," hierarchies are flatter, gender distinctions are blurred, and sensitivity to others (and hence to oneself) becomes a prerequisite for effective performance. In addition, of course, more privileged groups have more resources to devote to "self-development," and the tendency to cast all problems into psychological (and not social structural) terms certainly serves their ideological and political-economic interests as a class.

Yet few theories of American character or individualism are cast in historical or social-structural terms. Once we add these dimensions, we see a civic individualism emerging from an earlier ascetic and religious Protestantism (and particularly Puritanism), in both England and early America. In the twentieth century this civic individualism, exemplified by Henry David Thoreau, was largely replaced by a John Wayne–style rugged individualism, on the one hand, and a softer, therapeutic individualism, on the other, both of which have correlates of class, gender, and other social-structural factors. Rather than simply celebrating or decrying these forms of individualism, social thinkers must first show how these cultural forms of selfhood both reflect and shape their historical and social-structural contexts.

Further, rather than taking positions *within* popular debates on identity and individualism, we might note the limitations of all such positions, even on their own terms. Rugged individualism, however useful as an orientation for low-income persons, also serves as a cultural ideal for political reactionaries, who tend obdurately to oppose working-class interests. Moreover, the defensive toughness and isolation of this identity inhibits the formation of the solidarity and collective action that could turn personal troubles into political issues. Somewhat in parallel, upper-middle-class persons who pursue self-development or personal authenticity, in opposition to the demands of society, nature, or history, create selves that are shallow, hedonistic, and narcissistic, as critics have avowed, because depth, significance, or authenticity themselves can be created only in the dialogical process of social engagement. Closing off demands that emanate from sources beyond the individual person destroys the very conditions under which a more fully realized selfhood can be shaped. Thus the question of how to build democratic identities within the context of postindustrial, postmodern society remains acute.

Chapter 6 Transformations of

American Space and Time

As bulldozers, cranes, and cellular phones reshape American cityscapes, new configurations of space and time also reshape bodies, ideas, and feelings, but at different rates and often in conflicting directions. As change becomes more rapid in some spheres than in others, some temporalities speed up while others lag. Not only are present spaces and times more different from those of the past, but they also are at once more homogeneous with and more distinct from each other. This makes it harder for Americans to assess the beginnings and the ends of change and to know what kind of space-time they are in. Is such confusion of space-times common to all societies that go through successive phases of late capitalist development? In other words, are accelerating times and shifting spaces the by-products of movements from industrial to postindustrial patterns of organization? Or do they reflect the "exceptional" historical development of the United States and the diversity of histories of America's ethnic groups (Clignet 1990)? The first assumption stresses the universality of the social and psychological turmoil caused by economic and political dislocations. The second highlights the cultural relativity of human responses to structural upheavals.

In this chapter we develop a framework for assessing how changing material and ideological conditions affect the definition and manipulation of the spatial-temporal dimensions of American life. We first discuss the social character of space and time, how all peoples deploy temporalities and spatialities to organize their behaviors and beliefs. We then examine how American space-time changed with changes in capitalism, from early industrialization to late corporate capitalism to the current postmodern capitalism of consumption. We argue that the emergence of postindustrial or postmodern capitalism fosters shifts in temporality and spatiality, such as that from a future-oriented ideology of production toward a present-oriented rhetorics of consumption. Further, whereas there is a growth of simultaneity in postmodern experience, existing cleavages in the space-times of social interaction also are exacerbated. Even as space-time becomes more uniform, universal, and rationalized, it also becomes more particular, local, and subjective.

We focus also on Americans' faith in the future and show how industrial capitalist development shaped Americans' centripetal and centrifugal conceptions of temporality and social mobility or, more precisely, how Americans have conceived of the movement of persons in social space and time. This was a future-oriented spatiality and temporality of optimism. The horizon was ever expanding, the future was contained in the present, not the past, and the present at each moment gave birth to the new.

We conclude with a discussion of the coexistence of multiple American spatialities and temporalities and their contradictions, as well as the strategies of stabilization that Americans have invented to cope with them. These strategies seek to naturalize social life by marking certain events as constant and significant through rituals that endow the present, past, and future with more stable and reassuring meanings.

THE SOCIAL CHARACTER OF TIME AND SPACE

Nineteenth-century theorists discussed the social character of time and space. Karl Marx dealt with time and space as resources for profit making in his theory of surplus value (1973 [1857], 399). Emile Durkheim addressed time in his sociology of the *conscience collective* (1965 [1912], 21ff., 488ff.). In pursuing his program to show the essentially social character of Immanuel Kant's a priori synthetic categories of the mind, Durkheim revealed temporality to be a collective representation. Max Weber also discussed social time orientations in his study of the cultural sources of capitalism, noting that for Puritans the "waste of time is . . . the first and in principle the deadliest of sins" (1958 [1904–1905], 157). Pitrim Sorokin (1943) and Georges Gurvitch (1964) also contributed to a sociology of time, although until recently more ample studies of time and space were the purview of philosophers, physicists, psychologists, linguists, and anthropologists. These scholars showed that there is not a physical, objective time or space but a multiplicity of social ones, including those that are considered physical and objective.

The social sciences themselves emerged from the Enlightenment project of modernity and progress through reason, and their analyses of social time thus focus on the organization of the modern West into the objective time of the clock (Moore 1963; Young 1988; Zerubavel 1981); the management of time (Marx 1976 [1867]; Nguyen 1992; O'Malley 1992; E. P. Thompson 1967); and the global standardization of time (Kern 1983; Adams 1990, 377; 1995). Such Western approaches to the study of time are usually committed to an objectivistic, rationalistic, and Eurocentric conception of temporality. Hence, even though major social thinkers have been aware of the social relativity of time and space, they generally have analyzed it within the assumption of a Newtonian space-time that is universal. All these studies, however, could constitute the beginnings of a sociology of time as such (see Moore 1963; Roth 1963; Schwartz 1975; Melbin 1978; Zerubavel 1977, 1981; Maines 1983; Aminzade 1992; Nowotny 1994; Flaherty 2000).

Time is both a resource and a constraint in forming individual attitudes and behaviors. As a resource, different temporalities provide standards for evaluating peoples, lives, and works. There is mystical time; sacred and profane time (Durkheim 1965 [1912]; Eliade 1954, 1959); existential time (*conscience de soi, durée*); Newtonian absolute space and time; and Einsteinian relative space-time (Gregory 1988), each of which helps define a particular world of meaning and possible agencies or actions. Far from unitary and pervasive, there are and have been many kinds of time. Different places have different space-time. "Street life has its circadian and seasonal rhythms. The street wakes up in the morning with a spurt of business, relaxes mid-morning, gathers momentum toward noon, calms down once more in the afternoon, becomes roily between the end of work and dinner, and settles into a steady pace of activities in the evening. Street life tends to be lazier in the summer, bracing in the fall, restrained in the winter, and exuberant in the spring. In a well-lit, air-conditioned, twenty-four-hour supermarket, however, time decays into a featureless flow that feebly reflects the changes of the real world outside" (Bergmann 1993, 131).

Different peoples also have their differing spaces. The Plains Indians of what is now the United States conceived of space very differently from the white colonizers, thereby making "territorial" treaties into agendas for misunderstanding and conflict. Adults and children also live in different spatialities with differing conceptions of "territorial rights." Studies by historians and anthropologists reveal how variables are concepts of space. "The spacial worlds of . . . the mentally ill (particularly schizophrenics), oppressed minorities, women and men of different class, rural and urban dwellers, etc. illustrate a similar diversity" (Harvey 1989, 203). The Apache teach geography through experience, so that visiting certain places becomes a lesson or reminder of how to conduct oneself.

Space-times also may shift for a given people, as occurs for overseas Chinese with diaspora or for indigenous peoples with conquest. When would-be developers sought to build a hydroelectric system in Ashe County, North Carolina, local space-time representations of self and community shifted from family and genealogy to larger conceptions of a way of life that was worth preserving (Foster 1988). Borders also are negotiated, even when they are legally fixed. The U.S.-Mexico border, for example, is both guarded and porous, a symbol of imperialism and hope for Mexicans and defilement or cheap labor for Anglos (Liera-Schwichtenberg 1996).

Once spatial and temporal systems are seen as socially produced, they also can be seen as resources for political domination, "a means of power at all levels from the personal to the international" (Sack 1986, 1). Similarly, various rulers have designed their capital cities to symbolically and physically link their kingdoms with the cosmos and so legitimate their rule, as in Borodubor in Java, Tenochtitlán in Mexico, or Kandy in Sri Lanka (Duncan 1990). Foucault (1977) has written eloquently on the manipulation of space and time to create docile bodies easy to control. This further suggests that the use and manipulation of time are differently located hierarchically, with greater time constraints on servants, than on masters for example, or on "female" occupations than on "male" ones.

Modern conservatives may sacralize the past, underline the binding power of tradition and precedents, or extol a golden era prior to subsequent decline. In their space-time, loyalty to one's origins and forebears is a primary virtue. In contrast, standards of progress, such as those of the Enlightenment, may stigmatize the past as a haven for superstition and hail a future against which the present should be judged. Terms such as "forward-looking" or "expansive" and their negatives, "backward" or "narrow," fit this space-time. Another temporality may push aside both past and future to emphasize the significance of the ever-present moment. Such is the temporality of mystics and hedonists (Mannheim 1936), whose eternity is always now. There are also the space-times of work versus family, of short business cycles versus the longer Kondratieff cycle, and the durée of intimacy versus the turnover time of commerce.

As a macrohistorical example, the shifts in Western Europe from Aristotelian thought and the theocracies of the Middle Ages to the rise of modern science also were shifts from the cyclical and embracing space-time of being to the linear time of becoming. "During the Middle Ages man was seen as a microcosm within the macrocosm. One did not see space as a geometrical or physical extension, but as an organic connection. One was mythically connected to the stars, psychologically conjoined with others, symbolically united in archetypical experiences, and metaphorically bonded in consciousness—the feeling of being embedded in the cosmos" (St. Clair 2002, 202). One was not in space but *of* space as a single body with others. "A glance at medieval maps tells us that cartographers of the Middle Ages divided space differently than we do today. In the great *mappae mundi,* for instance, Jerusalem takes center stage, with an image of the crucified Christ separating one place from another. The architects of medieval cathedrals manipulated space to clarify the roles and status of anyone who crossed the threshold" (Hanawalt and Kobialka 2002).

Medieval time also tended to be passive, more like a deep lake than a running stream. One did not race against time so much as simply exist in it, without worry or effort at control. Space-time, like a living creature, could be fossilized into a stable hardness, filled with commonsense, everyday meanings. But changes like Descartes's dichotomy of mind/body and the Protestant separation of a transcendental soul from a now mundane worldly experience uprooted human beings from the synchronicity of space. Descartes articulated a mathematical model of a spatial extension that avoided the experience of merging that is often suffocating to moderns. However much we disavow alienation, most moderns prefer it to the dissolution of separateness into oneness that was part of medieval spatiality. Indeed, the modern cogito negates this oneness by delimiting objects and isolating them from one another in such a way that space no longer means oneness but extension, distance, apartness, and isolation (St. Clair 2002, 202).

Space-times may be individual as well as collective. Persons learn to evaluate the succession of their experiences in relationship to an ideal biography or movement through life stages (C. Brown 2000; Lukács 1971; Turnbull 1983). The same is true of collective memory and group self-concepts. Collective temporalities embody broad material and ideological conditions, including what might be called eschatological time—the collective temporalities from which peoples deduce a "meaning of history."

We do not just exist in time and space; we embody the spatialities and temporalities that shape us and that we have shaped. Not only do persons, entities, sentiments, values, and actions exist in space-times, but they also derive and create the prehensive and modal qualities of space-times that are prior to knowledge or understanding (Whitehead 1953, 64ff.; Heidegger 1980). Temporality gives order to life cycles and histories to peoples, just as spatiality gives order and specificity to our ambient or imagined environments. Thus space-time facilitates the integration of appearances and happenings into persons and events of the here (or there) and now (or then) (Kubler 1962).

While space-times help create and organize individual or collective activities, they are themselves shaped by specific societal contexts (Halbwachs 1950; Zerubavel 1981). Thus we could say that "History occurs within time" but also that "Time occurs within history." The first formulation defines natural and social events as occurring within a cumulative and universal temporality. Here time is a continuous and homogeneous integument that contains every history and every geography and, indeed, all that anywhere occurs. Conversely, the second construct stresses the role played by narratives, as well as their discontinuities and successions, and the meanings they give to individual and collective experiences, including the experience of temporality. In this formulation there is not history or nature or humanity within one universal time, but a multiplicity of peoples with diverse histories, each of which shapes or contains its own temporality as part of its particular experience.

In this view, current witnesses and subsequent observers keep reconstructing temporality retrospectively as well as prospectively. There are multiple histories, and not one History, because natural and social events become experience only when they take a narrative form (1998; Moscovici 1968; Rouse 1987). Manhattan's Lower East Side stands for Jewish experience in America, as does Harlem for African Americans. As Hasia Diner (2001) shows, no other ethnic groups have been so thoroughly understood and imagined through a particular chunk of space. Despite the fact that most American Jews have never set foot there—and many come from families that did not immigrate through New York, much less reside on Hester or Delancey Streets—the Lower East Side is firm in their collective memory. Whether they have been there or not, people reminisce about the Lower East Side as the place where life pulsated, matzoh tasted better, relationships were richer, tradition thrived, and passions flared. This was not always so. During the years now fondly recalled (1880–1930), the neighborhood was only occasionally called the Lower East Side. Though largely populated by Jews from Eastern Europe, it was not ethnically or even religiously homogeneous. The tenements, grinding poverty, sweatshops, and packs of roaming children were considered the stuff of social work, not nostalgia and romance. It was only after World War II that the Lower East Side was enshrined as the place through which Jews passed from European oppression to the promised land of America. The space became sacred at a time when Jews were simultaneously absorbing the enormity of the Holocaust and finding acceptance and opportunity in an increasingly liberal United States. Particularly after 1960, the Lower East Side gave often secularized and suburban Jews a biblical yet distinctly American story about who they were and how they got there. And because such space-times are cultural creations, they are inherently relative and plural. In this sense, natural and social events *become* history insofar as they are made evident repeatedly in specific space-times through different narrative forms, as, for example, through "The Midnight Ride of Paul Revere."

Mutations undergone by the concept of modernity illustrate the dialectic between these two ways of time. On the one hand, modernity is seen as a world-historical force that shapes polities, economies, and identities. On the other hand, modernity also has a particular history and histories. Originally rendered synonymous with progress in contrast to tradition, modernity also suggests the cleavages between immediate experiences and what can be imagined (Fuentes 1986; Kundera 1983). Historically, modernity was the ideology of imperialistic Western elites; then of their clients, the indigenous bourgeoisies of developing nations; then of revolutionizing nationalists in those new states. Today, the history of modernity is almost over, or, at the least, its meaning is changing again. The term now suggests genocide, irrationality, and ecological disaster as much as humane progress through reason.

To sum up, as space-time is structured by the social life that it organizes, it exerts both centripetal and centrifugal effects on the representations that Americans and others elaborate of who and where they are. The subsequent sections seek to specify the changing spatialities and temporalities associated with different forms of capitalism in the United States and, particularly, how the current political economy has generated both greater bureaucratic unifications and greater personal fragmentations of space-time.

TEMPORALITY AND THE EXPANSION
OF CORPORATE CAPITALISM

Modern time, as Louis Mumford observed, is produced by "The clock, a piece of power-machinery whose product is seconds and minutes: by its essential nature it dissociated time from human events and helped create the belief in an independent world of mathematically measurable sequences" (1963, 15). The introduction of clock time responded to and encouraged the abstract coordination of diverse habits, practices, and ideas into coinciding abstract spaces. Such coordination began in the medieval European monasteries and spread from the fourteenth century across Europe and later the world, enabling far-flung persons and objects to move and be moved in synchronic organization. Man and machine became more integrated through clock time and then through time scheduling and accounting. Increasingly, the clock and not nature served to order one's daily routine. With the predictability of timekeeping, punctuality and efficiency became paramount social values. Timekeeping synchronized individuals with machines and whole communities with industries. It became imperative to be on time and on schedule as modern society adapted to the quickstep of the clock (Luke 2003; see also Kern 1983; Bartky 2000; Landes 2000).

The clock released time accounting from nature (the sundial) and enabled the multiplication of ever-finer distinctions of sequence. Now the runner would always be second, even though he had lost the race by only 3/100ths of a second. In the emerging positivist habitus, time could be both measured and embodied in persons, and because measurements and persons were embedded in social organizations, the new temporality was real and meaningful (Young 1988). Thus Benjamin Franklin's expression, "Time is money," was more than metaphoric since in the emerging capitalist world to save time or to work faster was to save money or make more of it. The factory system took work out of the home and placed it in a space especially organized for profit-efficient production. The time flows of industry were regulated by bells and whistles, timekeepers, and punch clocks. A secular discipline of labor replaced the religiously governed rhythms of an earlier agrarian life, despite resistance by both religious authorities and an emerging working class. The time discipline of Catholic monasteries was extended to the Protestant world of work.

Competition compels capitalists to accelerate processes of accumulation, whether these be in production, marketing, or consumption. The top speed of travel or transport in George Washington's day was that of a horse at gallop. But open space was already rapidly collapsing into regulated time in 1875, when America's transcontinental railroads instituted regulations to synchronize their hauling services. "Human pregnancies still lasted nine months, but the tempo of almost everything else in life was speeded, [and] the span was contracted" (Mumford 1963, 197). Plantations of the American South also became industrialized with the imposition of time consciousness and the regulation of slave labor by the clock, which increased productivity substantially after 1830 until 1865 (Smith 1997; Eltis 1987). The adoption of clock time not only increased profits for slave owners, but also facilitated greater discipline and control over slaves. Indeed, control of labor by the clock was a way to increase profits *through* increased domination.

All these changes accelerated turnover time and augmented the value and return on investment. Of course, there are barriers to such acceleration. Workers resist speedups, but payments for land, factories, and machinery also resist acceleration insofar as they are fixed and must be amortized over time; slippages also occur in inventory control, deliveries, and the like. Yet the manipulation of space-time to accelerate profit still includes everything from physical processes like fermentation or genetic engineering to assembly-line production of car batteries or chickens; credit systems and electronic banking; and planned obsolescence in consumption by product (mis)design, fashion shifts, or advertising of the new.

Firms deal with changes in space-time by reducing their risks, spreading them geographically, and colonizing the future. Firms subcontract, resort to flexible hiring, or go offshore to discount the potential costs of future market shifts. They also deal with seasonal or cyclical fluctuations in demand by using two-tiered structures of production and employment. The constant part of demand is handled by oligopolized firms and full-time workers. The variable part is handled by a more competitive sector using more part-time or seasonal workers (Piore and Sabel 1984). Techniques for discounting the future into the present also include insurance hedges of all kinds; futures markets in everything from corn and pork bellies to currencies and government debt; and the "securitization" of all kinds of temporary and floating debts.

In this context the adaptability and flexibility of workers become vital to late capitalist development. After peasants were taught the work time of factories, their children demanded the ten-hour day and fought for the weekend, while the third generation struck for pay at time-and-a-half for work beyond the requisite hours. Workers and owners battled and still struggle over minutes, hours, and years of required time, overtime, vacations, and retirement (E. P. Thompson 1967, 90) Yet even those who resisted speedups came to accept the basic equation that time is money. Thus, despite much resistance, "most work schedules are extremely tightly ordered, and the intensity and speed of production have largely been organized in ways that favor capital rather than labor. In industry, just-in-time methods of production save the firm paid time that workers might otherwise waste waiting. Instead workers may be waiting unpaid at home, perpetually on call and available for work. Telephone operators working for AT&T are expected to deal with one call every 28 seconds as a condition of contract, lorry drivers push themselves to extremes of endurance and court death by taking pills to keep awake, air traffic controllers suffer extremes of stress, assembly-line workers take to drugs and alcohol, all part and parcel of a daily work rhythm fixed by profit-making" (Harvey 1989, 231). Today, instead of acquiring a skill for life, workers can expect multiple bouts of deskilling, unemployment, and possible reskilling in a lifetime.

The commodification of time as money is expressed when Americans use terms such as the following: Don't waste my time; That was time consuming; We saved time on that project; I can't give you the time right now; He spends (or wastes) his time; They are running out of (or losing or making up for lost) time; or Thank you for your time (Lakoff and Johnson 1980). Americans plan, budget, manage, schedule, and rent time, as when working for hourly wages (Sack 1986). They also rent, buy, and schedule space, as when renting rooms, paying for mortgages or parking meters, or reserving a seat on the train. Moreover, as market activities penetrate into everyday life, time is further sped up and turned into a commody to be bought or sold. As noted in chapter 1, these changes reduce space-time for noncommercial family care, community involvement, civic participation, and fun.

Employers demand more hours, including "billable hours" from professionals, as workers are expected to assume more responsibilities to make up for "downsizing." Moreover, with the decline of unions and the growth of white-collar jobs that are not covered by the Fair Labor Standards Act, employers have less resistance to squeezing more hours and labor from their workers (Kalleberg and Epstein 2001; Jacobs and Gerson 1998; Yakura 2001). For example, Americans worked 1,966 hours annually per person in 1997, up from 1,883 in 1980, whereas Japanese worked only 1,889 hours in 1997, *down* from 2,121 in 1980.

Though corporate systems have invaded the shrinking private or personal sphere, there are, paradoxically, more people with time to use at their own discretion. Americans live longer and thus have more active years of retirement.

The average life span in 1920 was fifty-four years; today it is seventy-six. People also marry later and have fewer children (and have them later if they have them at all), thereby freeing time from family duties (Robinson and Godbey 1999). Work time for men dropped between 1965 and 1985 from forty-seven to forty hours per week and for women from thirty-seven to thirty-one hours. Since then, however, the average work week for Americans has gone up to forty-four hours, not counting longer times for commuting. Full-time workers now spend more hours on the job (an average of one month more per year) than their parents did. In the two-tiered labor market, more hours are squeezed out of those who are fully employed, even as the number of people doing part-time work is expanding. Recent decades also have seen a breakdown of both traditional limits and institutional constraints on letting some people's work expand to saturate every pore of their lives while others have no work at all. For example, night and weekend work (which includes the Sabbath) has expanded, while unions, which have always wanted to expand the number of jobs (and members) rather than the number of hours worked, have declined from about 35 percent of the labor force in 1940 to some 12 percent today. Similarly, with automobiles now equipped with computers, bubble jet printers, and wireless Internet connections, cars are no longer associated so much with Lovers' Lanes or getting away from it all. For real estate agents, insurance claims adjustors, sales representatives, and other mobile workers, cars have become work stations on wheels. "Home" for many hi-tech nomads is where the phone is (Garreau 2000).

Some companies have become more flexible, allowing time off for an employee to take a spouse to the doctor or a child home from school. Yet observers find that employees rarely avail themselves of such choices. Instead they spend ever-longer hours at work, often putting in a lot of overtime. As one climbs the occupational hierarchy, there is more pressure to put in longer hours and to display a total dedication to the job. Thus, the "executive lunch" of the 1950s has shrunk to the "working lunch" of the 1990s—a sandwich and coffee at one's desk or in a meeting. Whereas the number of hours worked by men has remained fairly constant, married women with children nearly doubled their working hours, from 622 per year in 1969 to 1,197 in 1996. Such women often need the earnings. Moreover, with the relative decline of most Americans' incomes after 1973, plus the propagation of an ethic of consumption, people now work more to service their debt, which has risen from $5,000 per household in 1947 to about $50,000 today, after correction for inflation but not for the fact that households today are smaller, a fact that indicates an even greater debt per person (Hochschild 1997). But often, confronted with a choice between stress at work and stress at home, both men and women choose work, where at least they enjoy contact with colleagues, are taken seriously, and get paid, whereas at home they often feel isolated, taken for granted, and ground down with never-ending demands. As Hochschild has noted, work has become home, and home has become work. Moreover, most employees feel (correctly) that taking time off, even if permitted, will likely make them appear less dedicated and dependable and hence less worthy of raises or promotions. In consequence of work demands, couples interact far less with each other than they did a decade or two ago (Rogers and Amato 2000). As one in five workers is on a nontraditional shift and commuter marriages become more common, as does "tag-team parenting" (Salman 1998, A1), couples eat fewer meals with each other, go out together less, and experience more conjugal tension and higher rates of divorce.

Some firms and families respond to this time bind through "domestic outsourcing" to agencies that provide a corporate concierge or dial-a-wife for people too enervated by work or too estranged from home to manage domestic chores, from carpooling the kids to choosing a nursing home for grandpa. Because such services are now available for an hourly fee, they have become accessible to the middle class. Some firms, like Xerox, Hewlett-Packard, AOL, and Marriot, have on-site versions of some of these services; others provide loan assistance, breast feeding, wedding arrangements, counseling to teenagers, bill paying, surrogate shopping, free family dining in the corporate cafeteria, and on-site massages and saunas (Talbot 1997; Grimsley 2000; Specter 2000, 97). All this of course makes people all the more available and dependent on the world of work.

The 24/7 society is more attractive for those who do not have to be in it all the time. For example, e-mail lets you communicate when you want or shop at three in the morning and withdraw when you wish. But Americans increasingly are scheduled up or at least "on call." Even children ages 3–12 have less leisure. Their free time after sleeping, eating, personal hygiene, and school or day care dropped from 40 percent of the day in 1981 to 25 percent in 1997. Their parents seem at least as busy. Of two-income couples with children, 57 percent have at least one spouse who works evenings, nights, or weekends. One effect of split-shift families is that fathers often become more involved with their children. Children in two-income and male breadwinner families spend twice as much time with their parents as the children of single mothers (Spain and Bianchi 1996; see also Epstein et al. 1999). Although parents of both sexes are spending less time with their children than they did in 1960—an average of ten or twelve hours less per week—time spent per child is about the same because families are now smaller.

In 1971, 73 percent of adults (persons over eighteen) said they were "always" or "sometimes" rushed, whereas by 1995, 83 percent so reported. For many, time is not only scarcer, but it also is more filled through "multitasking." In the kitchen one not only cooks, but also watches the news and helps children with homework. In the car, one drives but also learns Italian with audio tapes, takes cell phone calls, and stimulates the gums with a rubber tip (Glick 1999). Perhaps being hurried or busy is simply an intensification of a business civilization. Tocqueville observed that Americans are "always in a hurry. . . . Besides the good things that [an American] possesses, he every instant fancies a thousand others that death will prevent him from trying if he does not try them soon. This thought fills him with anxiety, fear and regret" (1945 [1835]).

In this view, time stress is a dysfunction of democracy due to an excess of ambition, overchoice, and the American dream society of high expectations. Where almost everyone feels he or she must at least try to improve, there is little excuse for doing nothing at all. As Tocqueville noted, Americans brooded over advantages they did not possess and often strove to achieve them. Moreover, with the early elimination of an aristocratic caste and elite cultural values, the marker of achievement became mainly money—a near-universal value for which large numbers of persons could compete. Such competition results in status anxiety, compulsive striving, and time stress, especially today, as previously marginalized persons are more included in the race for time and money and as neoliberal practices and values have penetrated further into all realms of American life. Thus, many individuals and families create the very time binds in which they feel imprisoned. Americans seem to keep themselves hurried, even if it is to watch TV. Indeed Americans spend some 15 hours each week in front of television sets, compared to 6.7 hours socializing, 2.2 hours in outdoor recreation, and 8 hours reading.

Another cause of time stress is the fragmentation of roles and activities and hence of the allocations of time. For example, Robinson and Godbey (1999) found that an increasing amount of free time now comes in tiny portions—a half-hour here, an hour there. With such small chunks of time, it becomes much easier to watch a rerun on TV in the evening than to begin working in the garden or arranging dinner for friends. Time-saving technologies do not seem to help, since the newly freed time can be used for other rushed activities, such as a paid full-time job for former homemakers. Employed women at the opening of the twenty-first century do twenty hours less housework than unemployed women did in the 1960s, whereas men do only four hours more.

Indeed, the very pervasiveness of science and its derivative technologies suggests that laboratory time is extending into areas of life that formerly were less subject to close calculation, and such areas thereby demand more time than they actually free. As Helga Nowotny (1994, 93) argues, in the laboratory it is possible to accelerate things and slow them down; unique temporal events are possible as well as varied repetitions. Such temporal processes are being introduced into the larger society as laboratory time leaves its mark on the "normal world." For example, the use of such artifacts as voice mail, beepers, car phones, faxes, e-mail, and other applications of science has increased geometrically since 1990. In coordinating space-time through such devices, we thereby train ourselves to be always sending or receiving, on hold, online, or on call, just as though we were running a continuous laboratory experiment in which we ourselves were the subjects.

This new temporality and spatiality is very hard to leave or switch off. For some persons, always being "in touch" is an antidote to alienation, a sense of connection with someone, anyone, who can remind us that although we are alone at midnight, by checking on our portfolio in front of our screens, we also confirm that we exist. Indeed, it is now possible in principle for anyone to "be with" anyone else on the planet any time one wishes, for corporate profit, personal pleasure, or statist control.

SPATIALITY IN CORPORATE CAPITALISM

Capitalism also transforms space. The dynamic of competition compels the social and geographic expansion of capitalist markets. The pursuit of profit, which is necessary if the capitalist is to remain a capitalist, requires a search for cheaper labor and supplies and new outlets for one's products, and eventually capitalist markets expand to include all aspects of society and the entire globe, from the rental of wombs to the purchase of organs, from Kalamazoo to Kamchatka.

As capitalism expands in space, it also must contract time, insofar as profit is reduced if returns on investments are delayed. Moreover, as space is measured largely in time, travel or transport, one way to expand in space is to shrink time. For many purposes, Tokyo is only as far away as the telephone, fax, or computer. Indeed, the rapid extension of market economies in the post–Cold War era has been due in part to the acceleration of communication, which enables safe, controlled, and almost instantaneous transfers of capital or credit or data on prices, inventory, sales, design, or targets of production. To a great extent, space collapses into time.

Space shapes time even while merging with it. For example, the shorter the time between the investment of capital and the receipt of returns on it (turnover time), the greater the profit (rate of return on investment). Thus capitalism provides an incentive to organize space for optimum profit efficiency, including optimum turnover time. One sees this in the history of innovations in the organization of production and consumption, such as the factory system; assembly lines; divisions of labor by skill or territory; the creation of industrial cities and towns; new systems of transportation and communication, such as the railroad, highway, jet plane, telegraph, radio, and phone; and new modes of consumption such as supermarkets, shopping malls, telemarketing, and credit cards. All these innovations have been central in the history of capitalism, turning it into a history of transformations of space and time.

Where time differences are imposed by space, these often are capitalized upon by national or global corporations. For example, because Hawaii is five hours ahead of Tokyo and six hours behind New York, Hawaiian offices of Japanese or American firms can do business with both sides of the Pacific on the same day (though the dates differ). New York law firms e-mail document files at the end of the working day to document processors in Hawaii and get them back by morning with value added. National polling organizations hire Hawaiians in the daytime to telephone mainland Americans at home at night. So do telemarketers—the 1990s high-tech equivalent of the traveling salesman (*Economist* 310, no. 7589 [1989]: 28).

Configurations of space-time also change with shifts in the spatial and legal boundaries of public and private. For example, the number of private police began to exceed the number of public police in the United States in the 1970s (Shearing and Stenning 1983). Cyber-policing is done almost entirely by corporations. One reason for the enormous expansion of private policing is the privatization of what formerly was public space in American towns and cities. To go shopping fifty years ago, one went to town and walked from store to store on a public sidewalk. Today one more likely enters a mall, along with teenagers hanging out and elders taking a stroll. Here one is in a private space monitored by hidden cameras and private, often disguised, police. It is of course "public" in the sense that many people are there, but it is legally private, designed and controlled by a corporation for the maximum extraction of profit. It is a "single-minded" space, to use Michael Walzer's term, designed for similar, single-minded people. The lighting, the Muzak, the lack of clocks that might remind one of duties elsewhere—all guide persons to the single purpose of consumption. By contrast, "open-minded" spaces, like public plazas or parks, are available for a multiplicity of civic activities and a wider range of persons. Open-minded space is "designed for a variety of uses, including unforseen and unforseeable uses, and [is] used by citizens who do different things and are prepared to tolerate, even take an interest in, things they don't do" (1986, 470). Most important, private, single-minded spaces are governed by the "laws of commerce," whereas public, open-minded spaces are governed by the Constitution and its guarantees of freedom of speech and assembly (Jacobs 1984; Gabel 1984, 268).

The privatization of public space into single-purpose, single-age, or unique lifestyle communities accelerated after the 1970s for several reasons. Residents of rustbelt cities moved to sunbelt suburbs, more cars and highways created more options for commuting (for a while), independent elderlies became a larger part of the population, and innovations in technologies such as telecommunications made it easier for businesses to choose nonmetropolitan locations. At the same time, the neoliberal economic policies initiated during the Reagan administration, plus a growing antipoor, antiminority ideology, fostered a rise in economic inequality, a decline in public services, and a weakening of older forms of social discipline. Private enclosures, single-minded gated communities, and private clubs all grew, even as older neighborhoods and public recreational facilities declined, especially in inner cities with shrinking tax bases and more marginalized populations.

In the 1970s and 1980s, along with the shift from Fordist to flexible modes of production, white middle-class people began to retreat to private enclaves that were often protected by walls, guardhouses, entrance gates, and surveillance cameras—first in Florida and southern California and Nevada, then in Arizona and Texas, then in the Northeast. Many residents of such enclaves say that they know they are trading diversity and a sense of community for security but that they are not interested in making new friends. Most residents agree with the strictly imposed rules and covenants of these private enclaves and want to live in a controlled, well-maintained environment. Some such environments insist on being "child-free" and even limit visits by the residents' grandchildren (Hacker 2000, 12; Low 2000; see also Caldeira 1996; Ellin 1996; Davis 1990).

But perhaps this is not so new. Richard Sennett (1970) noted that affluent suburbanites were reluctant to address either problems in their communities or conflicts within their families. Others have attributed such unwillingness to the transience and impersonality of suburban life, including weak bonds with both neighbors and family members. The lack of both resources and motivation for resolving conflict suggests, paradoxically, that the apparent harmony of suburbia, like that of more recent gated enclaves, depends on people not caring very much for each other. A premier sunbelt city, Houston, provides an example. "The idea that the city should take care of people is only partially grasped here. In Houston, you wall yourself off in a private enclave. You get services if you pay for them—private police, private fire departments, private garbage collectors. And if you don't have the money, you suffer. That may sound cruel, but in Houston the word entrepreneurism makes this an exciting place" (Louv 1983, 66). One result is that civic life and democratic government decline in favor of more corporatist, private arrangements, where the rule of one-person/one-vote gives way to the practice of weighted voting, which depends on how much stock one owns. At the national level, such community associations exceeded the number of small-town and other local governments in 1980 by about fifty thousand to about thirty-eight thousand, and since then their disproportion has grown in both numbers and financial power. Increasingly there is public distress and private comfort, safe enclaves for some and unsafe streets for most.

There is, in sum, a move toward the privatization of formerly public space, especially for the prosperous—from sidewalk shopping to shopping malls, from neighborhoods to gated enclaves, from the street corner to Starbucks. This new spatiality reflects a turn toward neoliberal policies and practices in the larger political economy. These policies have generated greater overall wealth but also greater social and economic inequality, thence a greater threat of both physical danger and status contamination in public places, thence a felt need for spaces for "people like us" that are deemed safe *because* they are private and exclusive.

As in earlier capitalist societies, today's built environment displays patterns of standardization and specialization that are driven by capital investment and market demands. For example, the post–World War II suburbanization of the United States involved standardized housing within easy driving access of shopping malls, whose controlled environments of shops and eateries underminded many central business districts (Checkoway 1986; Kowinski 1985; Mintz and Schwartz 1985, 43). The shift from steam to electric power and from rail to highway transportation also facilitated the removal of better jobs to suburbs located close to where interstate highways crossed urban ring roads, just as minorities and unions were becoming stronger within the older city centers (Gordon 1978). This trend appears to be peaking, however. As commutes become longer and suburbs more urban and as more people remain single or without children, metropolitan areas become relatively more attractive and gentrified. Moreover, within private corporate spaces of the "new economy," where many upper-service technical personnel are employed, space is being redesigned to enhance networking, to open communication, and to create a semblance of community that no longer exists in those parts of life conducted outside the workplace. Gone are the closed offices or even semiprivate cubicles. Old office buildings are redesigned to serve as warehouses, and old warehouses now serve as communal work spaces, complete with gyms, espresso bars, grand pianos, gourmet cafeterias, and bunkbeds—so comfortable, in fact, that one rarely needs to leave "home."

The centralized city of early industrial capitalism was built around the railhead or port and powered by steam. As noted above, a later capitalism shifted to suburbias near ring roads and truck transportation, and then to the present megamalls, with cinema multiplexes, shops, and food courts; to industrial parks; and to service plazas that constitute a dispersed set of metro-centers, in which the functions of the former city centers are replicated in miniature along the highways. These new clusters of "edge" or "plug-in" cities remain connected to the larger cultural whole through intricate networks of freeways, telephones, and computers (Bukatman 1993, 122). The trend, as the Federal Committee on Metropolitan Statistical Areas reported as early as 1983, has been toward "sprawling urban areas with no clearly defined center," Los Angeles being a prototypical first (quoted in ibid.).

This decentering or multiplication of many similar centers has brought more homogeneous yet segmented spatial-temporal experiences. For example, the simultaneous sharing of events through television generates what are taken as collective memories (Ferguson 1991). With more integrated production and marketing has come a greater compartmentalization of time and culture. Even this segmentation, however, tends toward uniformity in the manufactured quality of its particular units, which can be reconfigured depending on shifts in demographics, taste cultures, and innovations in styles of consumption. Similarly, with air conditioning, deep freezing, and cooled (or heated) malls, there has been a commensurate disappearance of seasons and regions as markers of social distinctions. Increasingly people can live and eat as they similarly and individually wish around the clock, the year, and the nation, without regard to time, region, or custom. Within this unity, however, has come a greater diversity, though it is now based on market and lifestyle segments and increasingly guided by corporate stratagems.

SPACE-TIME AND SOCIAL MOBILITY IN THE
CONSUMER SOCIETY

The growing importance of consumption relative to production invites the celebration of the current moment and a commensurate reduction of both past and future, which are now seen as a drag on enjoyment of the present. Thus the expression "Don't put off for tomorrow what you can do today," which used to be a Puritan prescription for work as an investment, today means that we should take our pleasures right now. Postponement of gratification does not make sense if "you only go around once," as a beer commercial insists. Similarly, and unlike Palestinians and Israelis, when Americans say, "That's history," they mean that the object of discussion is not paramount but irrelevant.

With the postmodern collapse of both past and future into the present, there have been further changes in the sentimental bonds of family and gender relations. For example, the care of children is now more oriented toward present feelings than toward future achievement, or, rather, it is oriented toward managing present feelings for future success since "relationship skills," "communication," and "emotional intelligence" have all become more important for success in the postmodern economy (Hochschild 1993; Hage and Powers 1992). Analogous shifts have occurred in the meanings assigned to the successive stages of the life cycle. For example, feminist ideology, itself fostered by late capitalism, entitles women to denounce not only the faults of their successive male partners, but also their own preceding roles; for some women, past commitments to femininity or to being a housewife are now rejected as patriarchic mystifications (Hughes 1993; Nadesan 1997). For both (major) genders, the stress placed on the current moment modifies the meaning attached to marital continuity and change. Successive spouses are more accepted than before as symbols of successive steps in the march toward success, though now success is seen more as personal fulfillment or growth in one's permanent present.

The rise of target marketing to specific age groups also affects conceptions of the life cycle and time and encourages an increased segregation of age groups. Not only are there retirement communities from which children are excluded, but there are also singles' events, apartment complexes, or cruises that cater to unmarried adults. Social scientists, demographers, and marketers mirror this practice in their focus on "cohorts" and "peer groups" (Ryder 1965). Once the latter term referred only to adolescents; now it refers to the entire life cycle. Each cohort or peer group is assumed to have its own routines and haunts, each its space-time distinct from that of others.

Capitalism also erodes *intra*generational solidarity, as suggested by distinctions such as "fast-track" versus "mommy-track" workers. Sustaining or increasing consumption requires more family members to work, and this may disrupt the temporalities of intergenerational relations. Many teenage girls and boys work to buy clothes or cars respectively, thereby taking time from family activities. Similarly, the lack of coordination between the schedules of firms and schools, or of different schools, creates disparities in the timetables of parents and their young children, especially as mothers increasingly work outside the home or are the sole parent in residence. Declines in the quantity of co-temporality and co-presence also reduce social interaction among family members and thereby accentuate the individuation of cognitive, emotional, and moral styles. As latchkey children proliferate, "quality time" is emphasized, as if parents were able on demand to compensate their offspring for a lack of generally available attention. Humming a lullaby on a cell phone does not quite replace co-presence with a child abed.

Americans' criteria of social ranking also have changed with the greater emphasis on consumption. Whereas formerly social mobility referred to changes of occupational roles, in the consumer society it evokes changes in styles of housing, clothing, furniture, or vacations. It is true that all groups and societies elaborate criteria of rank or status that tend to shift with patterns of social mobility and modes of production. For example, high rates of upward mobility tend to encourage an emphasis on newness and on universalistic standards of social evaluation such as money. Thus, relatively open class societies will have a faster, more future-oriented temporality than societies ordered by caste, lineage, or estate. In the new casino economy, however, ups and downs become more frequent. Thus the part of the personal property of rich Americans that comes from their forebears declines, and there is a more rapid turnover of what even one generation may possess. As objects such as furniture or silver become markers of the successive steps of one's ascension (or decline) rather than symbols of a cherished and continuing past, they also become more fungible in time—readily dispensed with or purchased in the secondary market, as needed. Geographic or social mobility requires traveling lite. In this context, a renewed interest in roots, family values, and traditions appears as a sign of searching or nostalgia for more stable space-times in a faster changing world (see Rochberg-Halton 1986, 173; Harvey 1989, 292).

The perpetual postmodern present is composed of patches of simulated times past and places elsewhere. The poignancy of nostalgia derives from its implied contrast of the golden days of yesteryear with a distressing present and disturbing future. Reinvented space-times of nostalgia themselves may become novelties as the multiple temporalities and spatialities implied by historical slumming and retro-tourism coexist harmoniously. Thus the icons of the counterculture have long been adopted by Madison Avenue. Mercedes-Benz has appropriated the peace symbol as its logo, Jimi Hendrix can now be heard as Muzak, the newest blue jeans from the Gap are called "1969," and there is still a call for "Revolution—by Nike."

In the same spirit, in 1999 an archaeological dig commenced in Guadeloupe, California, to unearth the remains of the plaster sets of Cecil B. DeMille's 1923 movie *Anthony and Cleopatra.* Cultural waste becomes spiritual nourishment as "old products and forms are consumed with the pleasure of the new: Woodstock II, platform shoes, The Sex Pistols, the Volkswagen Beetle. . . . All that has been stored [is] revived and refashioned as 'retro' and 'vintage': swing dancing, lounge music, martini bars and cigars; the fashion and costume of hipsters, beats, hippies, disco, punks, the 'new wave' in music; even obsolete computers are resurrected, signified, and circulated as nostalgia" (Murphy 1997, 9). History too is often packaged in televisual images, newly built landmarks, or political slogans. Trips aboard restored railroads and paddle boats, to Williamsburg or Sturbridge with their candle-lighted inns, or to Disney parks and their presentations of American historical themes—all seem to fix the past as past but also as available on demand for mixed-media consumption in the present.

Similarly, food courts and mall restaurants portray multiple cultures and historical periods side by side. These images reflect both the class of the diner and the class to which he or she may aspire. More exclusive (expensive) restaurants may use the decor of Louis XIV or the antebellum South, when self-confident aristocracies prevailed. Fast-food restaurants may glorify periods or personages that suggest the survival or achievements of rugged individuals. Long John Silver's and Popeye's celebrate the pirate or seaman; Roy Rogers, the cowboy (see Shelton 1993). Through such simulacra, the past itself is modified. The past as "referent" (as in poststructuralist linguistic theory) is increasingly annuled, leaving us with little more than traces.

Many features of the new corporate space-time are illustrated by consumption at McDonald's. Once an icon of American society, whether in Buffalo, Beijing, or Buenos Aires, the McDonald's establishments have been increasingly "indigenized" and claimed as their own by adults who grew up eating in them throughout the world (Watson 1997). When entering "a McDonald's" (it is hard to characterize it as a restaurant, coffee shop, or diner), one is not ushered toward a table or the bar. Indeed, one is not ushered at all. One waits in line. Personal interactions among cook, waiter, and client have become bureau-cratic exchanges. The fixed menu is on the marquee above; the customer is sep-arated from the uniformed employees by a stainless steel counter. The exchange of food for money is initiated by the impersonal, "Can I take your order?" and closed with the innocuous, "Have a nice day" (Shelton 1993, 16). This is part of the service sector that has moved from craft to industrialized production/con-sumption. An older, hierarchical master-servant relationship is replaced by a more egalitarian and instrumental exchange between single-minded persons in streamlined roles (Wexler 1983). The back-stage Fordist preparation is inte-grated with the front-stage Fordist presentation. Space-time is reorganized into an experience designed by corporate planners (Shelton 1993, 20). As the corpo-ration comes to mediate between the raw and the cooked, social exchanges at meals are replaced by the cash nexus.

In sum, in the modern period and especially since the Industrial Revolution began in the United States about 1850, spatial organization and time regimes have been increasingly ordered around mechanized modes of production and profit extraction. Time became a series of standardized, arbitrarily divisible minutes, hours, and weeks. People accepted conformity to the new temporality as virtuous (punctuality) and adopted new goals (such as saving time). They lived in the fu-ture as their aspirational home, where things would be newer, better, faster. Ex-perience was shared more broadly but less deeply, since simultaneity of experi-ence could now occur even when people were not together in the same place.

Beginning about 1945 and accelerating since 1970, an electronic mode of in-formation (Poster 1990) became relatively more important in the computer-coordinated, more globalized, postindustrial consumer economy. With the greater globalization of capitalism in the post–Cold War period, several changes in spatiality occurred: first, toward a concentration of centers of finance, coor-dination, and investment in the new downtowns of many American cities; sec-ond, toward the decentralization of production, as in the export of jobs or even whole factories abroad; through optic cable and computers, these can be coor-dinated in "real" time (*Economist,* Feburary 2, 2002, 3–19); third, toward a greater standardization of consumption, though now more nuanced and stratified by class and more targeted to demographic or lifestyle niches. With these changes, the ever-expanding future becomes an ever-enlarging present. Social rhythms and space allocations are still influenced by the market and the interests of capital, but the roles of science, technology, and the state grow even more rapidly as the time structure of the laboratory radiates out to the rest of the world.

SPACE-TIME AND AMERICANS' FAITH
IN THE FUTURE

The founding of a New Jerusalem and then a new nation, the conquest of a continent, and the creation of new industrial wealth—all bred a sense of unlimited potential. Thus for most of their history Americans have been oriented toward the future. Alexis de Tocqueville, visiting the United States in the late 1820s, saw America as the first country to display the benefits and vices of the new age. Another Frenchman, Georges Duhamel (1931), touring the United States a century later, felt that America offered an image of the life in the future. Americans also viewed their way of life as a preview of what other countries would encounter later on. Yet other observers, such as Charles Dickens (1978), have underscored the provincial and quaint qualities of Americans and their penchant for naive or absolutist views. These qualities combined in the optimistic belief that Americans could shed their past and invent the future—that they could, in effect, recreate time and live outside of history.

Unlike Canadians or Australians, whose lands were harsh and where settlers remained loyal to Britain, and unlike Africans or Native Americans, who were enslaved or conquered, most Americans claimed to create a present and future liberated from any past. Moreover, whereas Canada was settled more by Anglo elites and Australia by the lower social orders, early Americans were largely middle class. American society thus was formed and has always remained conscious of itself as the Great Experiment in a land whose history is antihistorical and ever-open to reinvention. In this sense, America is founded on a contradiction of temporalities. Its history is that of a denial of historicity; its time has been spent in the abolition of temporal constraints; its notion of space is one of infinite expansion—from the Eastern seaboard; across the Appalachians, the plains, and the Rockies; on to global power, to the moon, to Mars, and beyond.

The space-times of agrarian, commercial, and then industrial capitalism in America expressed a faith in the endless availability of land on the frontier and, later, in the endless growth of markets. Americans learned to coordinate activities of production and exchange according to the clock, to hold the flow of goods constant through the use of successive shifts of labor, and to control workers for greater profit efficiency through time and motion studies. The engineer's stopwatch, the executive's wristwatch, the factory workers' punch clock—all symbolize the social control inherent in Americans' use of time. This utilitarian control of time present also implies control over time future. The various forms of insurance, the futures market in commodities, the purchase of options on various goods, and the institution of credit in general—all reflect the colonization of the future by instrumental calculation in the present.

But spatial mobility and a progressive sense of time also imply a historical amnesia, as in the assimilationist ideology of the melting pot, which equated success with Americanization and the abolition of the desire to return to a home that had become foreign. The past, especially a past located outside of America, spelled oppression, prejudice, and failure. This, notion, however, has not prevented many Americans from remaining committed to their particular pasts, even while aspiring to a more homogeneous American future. Many groups have retained their own parishes and clerics, their own newspapers, their own radio or television stations, and their own grocery and butcher shops, at least for a while. Sometimes they did so quietly, as with recently immigrated Asian Indian groups (Brown and Coelho 1986); sometimes, with the support of political figures and public funds in exchange for votes, as with earlier immigrating non-Protestant whites; sometimes, as a countermilitant form of status acceptance, as Anglos have done with Hispanics; sometimes, with ambivalence and anger, as with El-Hajj Malik El Shabazz (Malcolm X), who insisted that blacks were "victims of Americanization."

Until the nineteenth century few people thought of the historical past, and when they did, they imagined it to be much like the present—not a foreign country but their own. But then, especially in America, the past came to be viewed not as a source of lessons but a far away place from which one had fortunately departed. "This new past gradually ceased to provide comparative lessons, but came to be cherished as a heritage that validated and exalted the present. . . . Our own more numerous and exotic pasts, prized as vestiges, are divested of the iconographic meanings they once embodied. It is no longer the presence of the past that speaks to us, but its pastness" (Lowenthal 1985, xvi–xvii). Now a foreign country with a booming tourist trade, the past is a place we visit rather than the place we live. Moveover, with the enormous increase of historical knowledge, no individual can apprehend more than a tiny part of it. Hence, while oral societies combined meager knowledge of the past with a shared consensual history, in modern society a great mass of knowledge is fragmented among clusters of experts, and consensual history shrinks to a veneer of media-dominated images.

One implication of the ideology of progress is that the American ethnic hierarchy generally followed the order of arrival of various groups in the New World, with Anglo-Saxon Protestants on the top rung and subsequent waves of immigrants imitating the earlier arrivals and deriding their successors. As ethnic succession occurred in the occupational structure, especially its lower margins, crime, boxing, and neighborhood grocery shops were dominated successively by people of German, Irish, Italian, and Jewish origin and, more recently, peoples of color.

The American belief in progress also is associated with the myth of Horatio Alger or the self-made man, which precludes any recognition of the debts owed to preceding generations. It also implies that upward mobility means leaving one's class or ethnic group of origin and moving into an individualistic future by rejecting an ethnic past (Whyte 1943). In this ideology one makes one's own destiny and rejects one's heritage. In the ethos of individual achievement, inheritance and other bequeathed advantages are suspect. Such suspicion accounts for the asymmetry in popular images of testators and their heirs. To bequeath is a sure sign of success and civility, a symbol of commitment to property and propriety. In contrast, to inherit is to violate the ideology of individual self-reliance and is thus viewed as a sign of possible weakness (Clignet 1992; Gouldner 1972). Like beauty, inheritance, especially in men, is a benefit of birth and not of effort, and, as such, it is a source of embarrassment in a culture of equality, individualism, and achievement. Inheritance favors past accumulation over present and future accomplishment and thus gives unearned and hence unjust advantages to the children of the rich.

The effort to tame the future also is seen in educational reforms such as free, universal, mandatory schooling and the emphasis on practical rather than speculative studies. Such reforms are partly explained by the absence of a national aristocracy in America and the corresponding dominance of middle-class culture and values in a decentralized system of schools. The resulting orientation toward the future and emphasis on calculation are symbolized in the concept of an academic credit, which marks the accumulation of cognitive and social capital to be invested later in a future open to individual advancement. As farmers became factory laborers and their children became white-collar workers, each generation received more schooling than the last, schooling that served as a socialization into the future. In this context, each successive wave of immigrants is expected to change its spatial and temporal bearings.

The stress placed on social and geographic mobility also supports the view of schooling as a continuous progress that is transferable from the present to the future and from one place to another. In this perspective, formal schooling is no longer an ordeal that one goes through in order to be confirmed by familial or professional elders, but rather it is a set of steps toward individual mobility through self-improvement. In contrast to European traditions of sponsored advancement, within which individual trajectories have fixed starting points and preclude crossovers, American education permits many points of entry and exit and much experimentation until one finds one's personal direction, as well as many second chances (Turner 1960; R. Brown and Clignet 2000). The ideology of mobility as individual achievement also presupposes that students attend college or graduate school away from their parents. For those who attend local institutions, it is more acceptable not to live at home. For the same reasons, it is generally considered better to do one's undergraduate and graduate studies in different institutions. American temporality is made shorter and faster, spatiality more shifting, and space-times more universal as they become individual possessions within a rationalized system and not part of more local, intergenerational processions.

The concept of mobility, which may encompass whole lives and lifetimes, is captured by the expression "A rolling stone gathers no moss," a saying that has different meanings in the United States and Europe. In Europe, the stone (the self) derives its virtues from its stability beneath the river's currents. The moss that it gathers symbolizes the succession of experiences that socialize and hence humanize the self. Conversely, for Americans, what makes the stone and the self more valuable is the very process of their movement, of being on the loose and ready for action, untouched by moss (history, attachments) that inhibits one's progress. In America, then, socialization generally has shifted from preparation for traditional roles to preparation for new ones to preparation for ever-present change.

DIVERSITY AND CONTRADICTIONS IN
AMERICAN SPACE-TIME AND STRATEGIES
OF STABILIZATION

There is still great diversity in American space-time despite the massifying tendencies of media and market culture and the shrinking and speedup of space-time through new modes of transporting goods, information, and selves. The diversity is shown in Americans' ambivalence about individualism and community, which also takes a spatial form. At one end of the continuum, there is the myth of the frontier, of rugged individualism, of cowboys, sailors, and other wanderers who seem to escape from social restrictions. At the other end, this very openness or malleability of space has provided room for closed, homogeneous social enclaves that have little contact with one another. Given the diversity of these places and origins, any description of the medians or averages of

American space-time as a whole is misleading, since it necessarily masks such varieties in American life. To talk well about America is to talk about contrasts and oppositions underlying an almost common code. For example, the distinctions between rural and urban time did not become widespread before the nineteenth-century Industrial Revolution (Whitehead 1953, 64ff.), nor did it affect simultaneously or equally all arenas of social or cultural life. Even today, "seasons" are not the same for automobile workers as for workers in the fashion trade. One can get lost in the crowd in America or simply hide out with one's own.

Certain American economic, social, or geographic communities remain small and fairly constant, however anachronistic and obsolete they may appear in the eyes of others. Some of these enclaves are the geographical expressions of racial segregation, group stratification, and ethnic self-selection. Other enclaves are based on different criteria. But like the Amish communities of Pennsylvania or the Hopi of New Mexico, these groups may be packaged and folklorized as tourist commodities even if they wish to be let alone.

Such cultural enclaves permit or force people to live with others with whom they share a significant sameness. Such urban enclaves express distinct forms of community, whether they be based on race, class, or ethnicity. One can walk miles in the Bronx, for example, without hearing a word of English. South Central (Watts) and Baldwin Hills are respectively poor and prosperous African American areas in Los Angeles. Miami's Little Havana is organized around ethnicity, Brooklyn's Hassidic Crown Heights around religion, the Castro district of San Francisco around sexual lifestyle. These enclaves may be relatively self-contained economic units or, more likely, the foci of a vital subculture and strong emotional attachments, be these centered in synagogues or bathhouses (Abrahamson 1995; Rosenzweig and Thelen 1998).

Until a recent past, some parts of Indiana lived with Eastern Standard Time, others with Central Standard Time; railroads and airlines kept schedules that had distinct organizational principles. Dates fixed for local, state, primary, and national elections also are diverse. Similarly, unlike the idle rich or poor, the middle classes long took pride in a time orientation that postponed gratification and got the job done. Whether the sameness within a given space is chosen or imposed, it can reflect sharp differentiations of space-times, social stations, and stages or styles of life.

Regional differences also are expressed through space-time orientations, as well as other cultural traits. For example, Southerners have stronger religious and historical commitments than Americans in the North and West (Naipaul

1988). Indeed, after the Civil War, which transformed the "Union" into a distinct national state, two contradictory interpretations emerged of the American past: the Northern, Puritan Yankee myth of progress and the Southern Cavalier version, with its clear references to seventeenth-century England (Zelinsky 1988; Franklin 1975; Taylor 1979; Grant 1997). Interracial relations in the South are interpersonally richer than those of the North, but (or because) opportunities for social mobility are fewer. Hence the expression, "In the South you can get close, but you can't go high; in the North you can go high, but you can't get close." The North rejected slavery with indignation, a moral stance that persists today among many Northerners who are loathe to recognize the grace of some Southern ways and relations. The Civil War has few memorials in the North. In the South, the War Between the States has many monuments to the memory of soldiers who died for what many whites still deem to have been the cause of liberty, tradition, and honor. In general, the South has a closer relation to its past than the North or West. Whereas the North has only recently found use for residues of its economic history—say, by making obsolete warehouses or factories into studios, theaters, and eateries—Southerners have long cherished and preserved their historical remains. Early on, people have used history consciously as a source of self-definition, and many Southerners, as in Charleston or Savannah, speak eloquently about the successive cycles of prosperity brought by the cultivation of indigo, rice, cotton, and tobacco and the expression of their respective cycles and cultural styles in the built environment. Whereas in cultural terms the North exploits its workers by denying them long-term commitments, in the South until recently one found domination through an enduring rural patriarchy. Whereas the North is about cold and calculating rationality, the South has been about romantic enthusiasms and despairs. Thus, for Southerners today the practice of civil rights is more likely to be based on religious belief than, as in the North, on secular values.

Although at the opening of the twenty-first century, the South looks much more like the rest of the United States, at least in the affluent parts of its urban centers, many Southerners have been sacrificed for economic victories. Although newly opened automobile plants have gained the attention of the national media, the South is also home to many food-processing plants that offer only low wages and hazardous working conditions to cash-strapped communities (Applebome 1996). It is not surprising that Southern elites are deeply, and effectively, anti-union.

Southerners, black and white alike, not only live in a distinct region, but they also have had a distinct temporality. They are more likely to accept the weight that the past exerts on their lives, and, regardless of their diverging life chances, Southerners retain an intergenerational solidarity alien to the North. For many Southern blacks, the link to the past is to a world of slavery but also to one of solidarity and survival. For Southern whites the link may be to an image of a genteel way of life and also to the memory of the Northerners' invasion. Until it was changed in 1994, the word "darkies" in the state anthem of Virginia was hotly contested. The anthem was a song of slavery to blacks and liberal whites and a sign of prebellum harmony to conservatives, who pointed out that the anthem's offending words were penned by a former slave. The flying of a Confederate flag over the state capitol of South Carolina likewise became a topic of national discussion during the 2000 Republican primary race. Thus Southerners' sense of their past reflects the wounded pride not only of enslaved or defeated peoples, but also of successive planter elites who have been displaced by recurrent political reforms or economic booms and declines. Such a division and layering of histories by class and race and region reveals the contradictory character of temporality in America.

Americans also have differing space-times, attitudes, and systems of life in small towns, cities, and suburbs. Some hamlets still are keen to survive in mass society, even though they may have lost either economic autonomy or a language of community or have been effectively colonized by postmodern escapees from the city (Vidich and Bensman 1958; Bellah et al. 1985; Foster 1988). "Small-town folks are more satisfied than others, do not recognize that suburbs exist, fear cities, and congratulate themselves all over the place on their neighborliness. City folks disdain suburbs and small towns as stifling, boost their own cities but not always city life in general, equate all that neighborliness with nosiness, are often vaguely dissatisfied, and think urban crime problems are much overrated even as they pat themselves on the back for the nimbleness with which they avoid muggers. They also value cities for being liberal and tolerant, zones of freedom. . . . As for suburbanites, a minority promote the best-of-both-worlds line," while the rest see themselves as living either in a small town or a city (Griswold 1992, 1753–1754).

For almost all Americans, however, the myth of the frontier has always made it easy to believe that conditions of life are better elsewhere in the states and that one should hedge one's present bets. The phrase "community of limited liability" expresses this theme (Greer 1962), as does its opposite, "America, love it or leave it." The first concept suggests mobility, a readiness to pick up and leave; the second implies that this can be done legitimately only within the United States. This tension also is contained in Americans' concepts of freedom and the pursuit of happiness. For most Americans, freedom involves geographic or social mobility as part of one's success. Conversely, the pursuit of happiness involves the acquisition of property and a slower pace of life, which connote stability and permanence. In sum, if American space-time fosters social and geographic mobility, it also longs for stable, homogeneous, property-owning communities.

While many American standards are stated in apparently universal and value-neutral terms such as utility, efficiency, or mobility, usually measured by money, the very impersonality of such standards encourages a longing for personal authenticity, a permanence of place, and a remembrance of origins. This tension is seen in the two major approaches to the interpretation of the U.S. Constitution. One approach bases validity on an earlier historical acceptance; the other, on logic and the universality of procedure. In the more historical view,

> logic and consistency in principle play little part in identifying constitutional rights. The fact that the Court has recognized one right—a right to abortion, for example—provides no argument why it should also recognize any other right—for instance, the right of homosexuals to sexual freedom or of dying patients to control their own deaths even if no principled reason can be given why people should have the former right but not the latter ones. The only issue is whether the particular right in question has been historically recognized, and that test must be applied independently to each suggested right, one by one. . . . The opposite party in the constitutional wars—the party of principle—denies that order of priority. It insists on integrity in constitutional law: it argues that the abstract constitutional rights acknowledged for one group be extended to others if no moral ground distinguishes between them. In 1961, a conservative justice—John Harlan—offered one of the strongest judicial statements of this view. . . . The liberty protected by the due process clause, Harlan said, "is not a series of isolated points. . . . It is a rational continuum which, broadly speaking, includes a freedom from all substantial arbitrary imposition and purposeless restraints" (Dworkin 1996, 45).

Of course these two temporalities and principles of interpretation are not always applied consistently. In its 5-4 decision on the 2000 presidential election, the majority of the Supreme Court stretched the concept of due process to condemn variances in local voting procedures. Usually, however, this same majority had been "strict constructionists."

Such "archaic" or "progressive" times can be spatialized, mixed, or changed in different degrees and directions, as the above example shows. The changes may generate a multiplicity of space-times, each of which tends to destabilize the others. For example, the histories of Coney Island and Las Vegas respectively show how spaces of public amusement are coded differently over time by class and race, by forms of capitalism, and by changing public values—from a spirit of urban populism of Coney Island to one of capitalist speculation and spectacles of Las Vegas (Zukin et al. 1998). Such changes suggest that the future is not what it used to be. No longer an endless progress, it is now more an object of bittersweet irony, as in the expression "the end of history" (Fukuyama 1992), which refers both to the demise of the Evil Empire and the collapse of any redemptive individual or collective project in the West. The instability of time past also is evidenced by the saying "Nostalgia isn't what it used to be" (it has been recycled for consumption) and the expression "It's *déjà vu* all over again," implying that the past, like a movie, can be edited, cut, rerun, or canned at will. The ironic neo-ruins by postmodern architects express a similar porousness and malleability of what will be and what has come before.

As both past and future and near and far are collapsed into the here and now, experience of events, even historical or imaginary ones, no longer depends on being physically present when and where they occur. Simultaneity of virtual experience replaces sequence of actual experiences so that there is now a global present (Friedland and Boden 1994, 15). That is, through postmodern simultaneity people in different local places and times can exchange information, conduct business, or share certain experiences without being co-present in the same space-time. Such hyperspace-time exceeds the present capacities of individuals to locate themselves, psychologically or perceptually, in a mapable external world or, indeed, to map the global and decentralized network of capital and communication in which we find ourselves today. Of course there is a social distribution of these changes. Poor people and poor countries tend to have slower times and more local spaces. They may not be saturated with information so much as undernourished. Further, in advanced sectors and societies experiences and emotions that require greater personal co-presence, such as affection, solidarity, and empathy, are in retreat. The space-times for mourning or for mutual joy and pleasure are becoming remnants of a former life.

The greater the demons of social change, the greater the craving for stability. Indeed, the illusion of permanence reduces fear of a world in which change destroys markers of meaning and prevents the integration of successive experiences in a common and stable identity and community. Americans have developed strategies to cope with such contradictions, strategies that seek to freeze the relativity of space and time, even to freeze their seemingly irreversible flow. At work people have schedules, however infrequently these are followed, and make lists, however often ignored. Some Americans seek to deny or explain the uncertainties of time with the metaphor of development. This metaphor treats discontinuities as stages of predictable progress and emphasizes the cumulative, irreversible, and continuous properties of homogeneous and rationalized duration. For example, parents of children acting badly may say, "She'll get over it; it's just a stage." Thus, developmental orders seem to protect individuals from the risks and changes that pervade their lives and those of their communities. At the level of personal development, every disaster can become a "learning experience" or an "opportunity for growth," as in the actor Kirk Douglas's book on his brain aneurism, *A Stroke of Luck*.

Despite the instabilities and efforts to rationalize them, Americans have remained faithful in imagination to the rural life of their forebears. For example, although American breakfasts remain more suited to the workdays of field hands than of office dwellers, they still are celebrated as a model of family bonding, at least on Sundays. Similarly, many Americans continue the rural tradition of early dinners, even though it no longer has any occupational justification. In other words, in both the timing and the composition of their meals, many Americans retain a rural tradition.

Americans also repair the fragmentation of their social relations by linking types of food, drink, dress, interaction, and visits to places of memory with seasons of the calendar year. Despite the diverging paths of the memories and aspirations of different social groups, most Americans mark the passage of seasons with rituals that help to neutralize the centrifugal yet homogenizing effects of hyperspace and time. Autumn is the season when children go back to school, the time for the start-up of football, for fall colors, wearing sweaters, and taking walks. Winter, too, has its rituals of intra- and intergenerational solidarity, of sociability toward one's relatives and friends. Thanksgiving marks the survival of a culture of the heart that is especially American, in contrast with the Christmas celebration of consumerism, on which retailers depend for nearly 40 percent of their annual sales. Though ritualized and commercialized, Christmas also brings an apparently spontaneous generosity toward colleagues, friends, and strangers. Spring, with Easter, means home cleaning, new clothes, and romance or weddings. With daylight savings time, individuals return to the practice of their favorite sports and take more advantage of parks and gardens. Spring marks the restoration of neighborhood contacts that loosened during the short days of winter. Finally, summer begins with Memorial Day and finishes on Labor Day. Summer for many is still the season of barbecues; pastel clothing, tank tops, and shorts; wine coolers and white shoes; and either getting in shape or abandoning bikinis for one-piece bathing suits. American couples may shift their usual division of labor on weekends, as husbands grill meat and work in their yards. In contrast to Europeans, for whom the recovery of informality requires clearly marked vacations and a change of decor, Americans become informal at home simply by changing their greetings, as well as the people whom they greet. Summer is the time for neighbors and pals more than workmates and contacts. These routines are fairly general throughout classes, ethnic groups, and regions. As such, they provide a shared yet personalized space-time that helps to stabilize a sense of American identity and community despite the postmodern fragmentations.

Chapter 7 Genders and Generations: New Strains in the American Family

The American family is heralded as a haven in a heartless world and decried as a snake pit of abuse and oppression, a refuge from late capitalism as well as its victim. Today only about half of American children live in a "typical" nuclear family—two married parents, their biological children, and no one else. Other households are single persons; unrelated groups; single parents or grandparents or unmarried couples with children; gay and lesbian couples; persons living together; and other arrangements. Yet the normative ideal of the nuclear family broadly persists despite its increased disconnection with the way most Americans actually live.

This diversity of conditions and the confusions about their normative justifications generate new choices for and strains between genders and generations. For example, women may now follow careers of their choice, control conception, adopt children, conceive them with the sperm of their lover or the stranger of their dreams, or implant in their wombs ovules fecunded elsewhere. Thus women as well as men are able to differentiate pleasure from loyalty, birth from conception, sexuality from affection, and financial autonomy from commitment, and so experience both the stresses and the satisfactions of independence. They enjoy and are bedeviled by a wider range of choices than preceding generations, in a society that celebrates freedom, youth, and the pleasures of the moment. All these options affect women's relations with men, as well as what it means to be a "woman."

Yet the dreams of today may become the disillusions of tomorrow. Personal liberation seems to foster a decrease in rates of marriages; an increase in rates of divorce; and rising reports of incest, battered wives, and abused children. New freedoms also have unleashed physical evils that erode familial bonds. The diffusion of AIDS is caused in part by the disruption of familial bonds and gender roles and by the resulting increase in multiple sex partners, especially among homosexual men who formerly remained discreet because they were married. The fear of AIDS has led to the outcasting of entire families, including children, whose very tears are suspected by some of carrying the deadly virus. Within families, the arrival of children often widens the gap between romantic expectation and harried reality, as time for candlelit dinners and pillow conversations grows even scarcer. Thus, greater personal liberty within and without familial units also brings greater risks of loneliness and disappointment.

We argue here that changes in the life chances of individual family members and in the profile of familial groups reflect short-term changes in material conditions that correspond to the development of modern and postmodern society. But these short-term changes should not mask the recurrent tensions between self and system—between the radical subjectivism of American culture and the rational calculation needed for the maintenance, predictability, and integration of the social order and the maximization of profit. In effect, cultural and economic changes give new twists to the long-term ambivalences in relations of genders and generations and new variations of these relations according to class, race, and ethnicity.

HISTORICAL PATTERNS AND RECENT TRENDS

We can order the development of gender relations in the West into three ideal-typical stages. The first is exemplified by ancient Greece: extreme patriarchy with a high degree of male sexual freedom, including homosexuality, infidelity, and illegitimacy, combined with many restrictions on female sexuality. A second stage is represented by certain Roman and then Christian ideals, where men's sexual action was more restricted within the norm of companionate marriage (Ariès 1979). In this mainly Christian ideal, sex is less important, and each spouse is supposed to find emotional fulfillment in the other. Though men are expected to be monogamous, there is still gender hierarchy insofar as males continue to control family wealth, have superior (or even exclusive) legal standing, and are permitted more de facto sexual freedom. Thus the pursuit of equality in the American Revolution fell short of recognizing the full rights of women. "Women were excluded from any share in formal public power; and even in the privacy of the family a woman's very identity was subsumed in her husband's: any property she brought to the marriage was his, any debt she owed was his, almost any tort she committed was his" (Morgan 1996, 67; see also Gordon 1978; Norton 1996; Basch 1999; D'Emilio and Freedman 1989; Hartog 2000). Despite its limits, the division of labor of the ideal-type family in this second phase acknowledged the existence and importance of family activities. Indeed, some Americans still think that a return to that era is a practical panacea despite changes in the global economy that make this unlikely and, for most, unattractive.

The nineteenth-century bourgeois Victorian family ideal exemplifies the second stage. This modern family type was closely associated with such virtues as self-sacrifice, devotion to children, modesty, and piety. As an article in *Harpers Magazine* put it in 1909, marriage meant self-discipline and was not for the individual, but for the race. This value orientation was probably aided by the steady drop of America's spectacular fertility during the eighteenth century (Juster and Vinovskis 1987; Degler 1980). Victorian marriages were explicitly devoted to the maintenance and transmission of religious values and social order and in that respect demanded that men and especially women subordinate themselves to the accomplishment of these higher goals and values. If such marriages were happy, it was not primarily because a man and a woman had realized their "inner selves" in daily shared intimacy, but rather because men and women, who had distinct roles, gender identities, and spheres of action, managed to make their family a microcosm of a higher social and spiritual order. Middle-class Victorian courtship could be quite exalted (Lystra 1989), even exhibit a certain emotional fervor (Gay 1986), but by and large, intimacy as a self-referential project was unknown (Illouz 1997a).

Indeed, Victorian Americans saw sexual pleasure as threatening to love, then as essential to love in the early twentieth century, and then as legitimate for its own sake in the late twentieth century. Victorian culture spiritualized marital love and attempted to separate procreative sex (which was necessary to marriage) from erotic pleasure. Then, from about 1890 to 1960, sex was imagined to be a chief motivation and sustaining source of love. Soon this sexualization of love legitimated sexual pleasure for its own sake. "By the post–World War II era, pleasurable sex outside of an intimate relationship was widely accepted, alongside the contradictory belief that sex was integrally related to love and intimacy" (Cancian 1994, 907; see also Seidman 1991; Laumann et al. 1994). Still, duty long was felt to be paramount: young men "did the right thing" by marrying their pregnant girlfriends, and couples stuck together even if their love declined (Hacker 1997, 35).

Even before the 1920s, however, popular magazines had begun to voice a new meaning of marriage, especially for women. Marriage progressively was less about security, leisure, and social status and instead was viewed more as a joint emotional enterprise in which feelings should be freely expressed to achieve sexual, verbal, and emotional "intimacy." For example, in 1908, a writer explained why she would not marry her husband again: "I am very sure that my husband was first to speak the cross, impatient word: to exhibit carelessness of the little niceties and considerations necessary to happiness in housemates. I am sure that he deliberately showed me the other side of his nature with utter tactlessness and unconcern as to how it may affect my love" ("Why I Would Not Marry My Husband Again," August 1908, *Ladies' Home Journal*, 38).

Thus, by the turn of century, women had begun to demand from men what they had until then demanded only from other women: support, sympathetic listening, and affection (Smith-Rosenberg 1986; per contra, see Melody and Peterson 1999). Indeed, as Francesca Cancian (1994) argues, there occurred a "feminization of love" by mothers and wives in the privatized family. Naturally this change caused considerable anxiety on the part of "sexually respectable men," who sought to conform to these new standards (Hall 1991). It should be added that with the new economic importance of the service sector and with more jobs requiring emotional skills, there also has been a feminization of work.

This second model of marriage fell apart in the late twentieth century, mainly with the greater economic and sexual independence of middle-class women and new democratic expectations regarding marriage (Griswold 1982). Recent changes affecting women—their greater share of jobs, declining birth rates, and the changing nature of work and leisure for both genders—have undermined women's monopoly on loving and on the emotions in general, and new standards and expectations of conduct are emerging that apply more equally to men and women: economic independence, self-development, assertiveness, emotional and sexual fulfillment, and the pursuit of friendship and intimacy. Because they depart significantly from traditional and bifurcated images of the sexes, they become androgynous blueprints for "relationships," not "marriages" (Cancian 1987, 40). In this new ethos, men as well as women should be nurturing, attentive, and empathetic, and they should emphasize "self-fulfillment," "flexible roles," "intimacy," and "communication" (McCarthy 1988, 827; see also Jamieson 1998).

Fatherhood and childhood also changed with the maturation of the Industrial Revolution in America, the separation of home and work, and the growing role of the state in family matters. Especially in the decades between World Wars I and II, there emerged a deeper and broader father role and tensions between two kinds of fatherhood: father as pal versus father as male role model. Correspondingly, there has been an increasing intervention of the federal government in children's lives, a rise of child-care experts, an increased social importance of the peer group as children spent more and more time with others of their own age, an emergence of new family forms in response to new economic challenges, and the direct participation of young children in the market economy as consumers. There also are much greater numbers of programs designed for children, as well as of people making their livings doing something with, to, or for children. Today there are planned activities for newborns, infants, toddlers, preschoolers, and adolescents, both after school and in the summer. There are special television series for children of all ages and marketing strategies designed to identify and tap the buying power of specific groups of children and young people. These developments suggest that "childhood" has expanded as a social construct and that children growing up today face very different and often more complicated conditions, choices, and responses than did children of earlier times.

The changes discussed above suggest that a third ideal type of family has emerged, at least in the wealthy countries and classes of Western postindustrial societies (Chambers 2001). It has emerged mostly since 1950, when only 10 percent of married women with children under six years old were employed outside the home; by 2000 70 percent of such women had joined the job culture and were spending less time at home as guardians of family values. In this third ideal type, commitments are more tenuous, and there is greater economic, legal, and sexual parity of the genders. Companionate marriage remains, but it is more voluntaristic and undertaken later and less often. The influence of the extended family becomes negligible, the functions of the family become narrow, and the ethos of individualism is more important. For example, in this third type, production and education are conducted outside the home, and women move into the workplace and thereby become financially independent and have more opportunities for meeting and mingling with males who are neither kin nor neighbors. Hence the needs and benefits of pledging their chastity in exchange for male financial support are fewer. Men also have less to gain from marriage, since spousal loyalty is now more conditional, and even "respectable" women are more available outside of marriage. Hence marriage tends to give way to temporary, tenuous, nonconjugal forms of companionship and cohabitation, with or without children. Between 1970 and 1998, for example, non-marital births rose 224 percent, the numbers of women and men ages 40–44 who had never married rose 83 and 108 percent respectively, the number of single-parent families rose by 190 percent, and the number of children living with unmarried couples rose 665 percent (USBC 2000). Indeed, marriage is becoming increasingly irrelevant to parenthood. In the early 1990s, 53 percent of firstborns of women ages 15–29 were conceived—and 41 percent were born—out of wedlock. That is triple the figure for premarital conceptions and five times that for premarital births since the early 1930s. The U.S. Census for 2000 found that only 23 percent of today's young, pregnant women decided to marry before the birth of their first child, in contrast to 54 percent sixty years ago.

Kinds of sex, sexual relations, and sexual identities that formerly were deviant flourish along with the decline of patriarchy, conjugal exclusivity, and sexual propriety. Much thinking and conduct has shifted since the 1960s. During the 1960s, premarital sex became statistically normative, occurring with increasing frequency outside of serious courtship. Similarly, "nonmarital cohabitation by the unmarried and formerly married is now sufficiently conventionalized to earn acknowledgment in the obituaries of the *New York Times*. And while extramarital acts, if made public, can still damage the careers of politicians and clergymen, in most other spheres they occasion little by way of stigma, particularly if they can later be reclassified as premarital. Lastly, despite the early manifestations of moral panic associated with the current AIDS epidemic, expanding acceptance—though far from complete—of both homosexuality and homosexuals is quite evident" (Simon 1991, 1299; see also Klassen, Williams, and Levitt 1989; Sullivan 1998).

Conduct in this third ideal type of gender relations is regarded by many as grossly immoral, whereas others see it as a new freedom and tolerance. In more neutral terms, it is an adaptation of men and women to a society in which lineage and patriarchy have given way to postindustrial social organization and postmodern patterns of identity and conduct. The family is shifting from a preindustrial, cohesive unit of production to a postindustrial, fragmented unit of consumption, creating in the process new strains between the genders and generations. But this is not to say that things have gotten worse. Indeed, despite liberal critiques and conservative nostalgia, by many indicators the conditions of the American family have improved since earlier times. For example, in spite of the strict rules of early American families, one-third of brides in rural New England at the time of the revolution were pregnant. With short life spans, the average marriage lasted only twelve years. Likewise, earlier American middle-class families enjoyed many comforts—but their fine clothing and household goods depended on the labor of slaves or poor immigrants. Before the Civil War more than half the workers in some mills and factories were children. Moreover, with Americans today living much longer, children have more living grandparents for a longer period of time than ever before (Bengtson and Robertson 1985).

Perhaps because of Ozzie and Harriet and other family TV shows of the 1950s, many Americans mistakenly assume that earlier generations lived idyllic lives and that nontraditional family arrangements were rare. Yet in 1940, some 30 percent of American children lived without both parents, in part because of higher rates of death. "In the 1940s a quarter of Americans lived in poverty—without food stamps, Medicare or widespread subsidized housing. In two-parent black families, the poverty rate was more than 50 percent. Women's economic status and independence declined from the preceding war years, and many middle-class women led lives of cocktails, card games, and country clubs" (Coontz 1998). Thus we should not idealize bygone eras. Though families have always been diverse and fragile, today's family life is improving. Although cohabitation and divorce are more common now than formerly, the increase is "due in part to our much longer life spans. More Americans have living grandparents—and are close to them—than ever before, and 54 percent of all adults see a parent at least weekly (and 68 percent talk by phone)" (Seligmann 1992, 67; see also Coontz 1988, Farley 1996; Skolnick 1998). Ninety-six percent of American children lived with at least one parent in 1990, compared with 90 percent in 1940.

Still, many changes are seen as problems. One of these is the break in the normative link of sex and marriage that occurred in the 1960s and 1970s. After the contraceptive pill but before AIDS, friendly or even casual sex became more frequent and socially acceptable, as did cohabitation, especially among the young. Between 1960 and 1970 the number of adults cohabiting increased almost tenfold, and it jumped another sevenfold between 1970 and 2000. Similarly, the U.S. rate of divorce doubled between 1966 and 1976 (Weitzman 1985), though after 1980 it began to level off. Moreover, cohabitation usually does not end in marriage, and cohabitors who do marry have higher than average rates of divorce. Indeed, the longer or more frequently one cohabits, the less likely is it that one will marry or remain in wedlock if one does. Also contributing to the rise in the incidence of divorce is the fact that in some 45 percent of all current marriages, one or both of the spouses have already been divorced, compared to 1970, when the proportion was 27.2 percent. As a result, the overall pool of couples on which the divorce rate is based is in greater peril, since people who remarry again are half as likely to break up compared with first-timers (Hacker 1997, 35). Americans who marry do so later and divorce sooner and more often, yielding by far the highest divorce rate (about 50 percent) in the industrial world. More people have children without marrying or even without a steady companion. More births out of wedlock and more divorce also mean that more children spend at least part of their youth in one-parent families. In America, one in four babies (and 60–65 percent of black babies) is borne by a single mother, and about 32 percent of children live with only their mothers or in some other nontraditional arrangement. Conversely, over two-thirds of American children live in households with two parents, though not necessarily their biological parents (Casper and Bianchi 2002). More persons live alone today than formerly (over 25 percent in 2000), though the number of openly gay or lesbian households is rapidly increasing (up 72 percent from 1990 to 2000).

Other kinds of "nonfamily" households, such as roommates or cohabiting couples, grew from 1.7 percent in 1970 to 5.7 percent in 2000. This growth is matched by a steady decline in family households—that is, residential groups composed of people who are related by blood, marriage, or adoption. In 1970, more than 81 percent of the sixty-three million U.S. households were family homes, almost half of which were traditional families of two married parents and their children. In contrast, by 2000, not quite 69 percent of households were family homes, and of these, the largest portion, 28.7 percent, were married couples without children. In just three decades, "traditional" families dropped from half to less than one-fourth of American households (Casper and Bianchi 2002). The decisions of millions of young men and women to delay marriage and childbearing are major factors in these household shifts. In 1970, for instance, 64 percent of women and 45 percent of men were married by the time they reached the age of twenty-four; by 2000, barely 27 percent of women and 16 percent of men were married by that age. The median age for first marriage has risen by roughly four years, to 25.1 years for women and 26.8 years for men in 2000.

What has caused these changes? Some analysts note the decline of religious morality, the rise of secular materialism, cultural or sexual "permissiveness," and the growth of the welfare state. Others point to expressive individualism, the legal changes that made divorce easier, or the rise in women's paid employment. These hypotheses have varying logical and empirical support. For example, changes in attitudes, welfare policies, and divorce laws often accompany or follow rises in divorce rather than cause them. A stronger correlation of these changes is to shifts in the economy—first, toward a consumer capitalism that emphasizes personal gratification above social obligations, and second, toward the greater participation of women in the paid labor force, even women whose children are toddlers. Far more American women are working, and typically they earn a lot more than before. While the proportion of working-age men with jobs has fallen from almost 80 percent in 1960 to 70 percent in 1995, the share of women working has risen from 35 to 55 percent. By some measures, the typical man's earnings fell 7 percent between 1973 and 1993; those of the typical woman rose 11 percent (*Economist*, June 8, 1996, 27; see also Van Horn 1988; Blackwelder 1997). Similarly, in 2001 over 12 percent of corporate seats were held by women, up from near zero only thirty years before. In effect, if opportunities for women to earn improve, then the costs of giving up work to have children or of staying home with children already born become greater. As parenting becomes more a conscious choice, those who have children may invest more in them, even though both women and men are generally more likely to start their families later (or not at all) and to have fewer children when they do. Moreover, as more women have their own incomes and as gender roles converge the reduced specialization of men and women, as men and women means that the "gains of trade," or relative advantages of reciprocity in marriage, are now reduced, making marriage a less attractive alternative than formerly in America (or than in more patriarchal societies or enclaves today). Thus it is not surprising that highly patriarchal enclaves in America, such as the Mormons, Orthodox Jews, or evangelical Christians, have high rates of marriage and low rates of divorce (Becker 1981; Blossfield 1995).

As early as 1917, Arthur W. Calhoun argued that women's access to industry must be a prime factor in offering a woman the possibility of separation from her husband. Studies since the 1970s show that married women with jobs are more likely to divorce or separate than those who stay home. As female economic dependency lessens and as relatively safe sex is available without marriage thanks to contraception, divorce becomes an easier option for women. At the same time, however, potential benefits of marriage, such as emotional support or help in the home, became more important, and marriages truly based on equality and esteem become more possible (Schwartz 1994; K. Gerson 1993).

These changes affect children. Though the performance of children is more related to class than to family structure, children of divorce more frequently drop out of high school; marry during their teens or become unmarried teenage mothers; divorce; are jobless; or land in jail (McLanahan and Sandefur 1994). Perhaps half of these consequences are related to the poverty of single-parent families. But the rest do indeed seem to be the consequences of divorce. The rates of performance of children of stepfamilies are not much better (Beer 1988; Holloway et al. 1997; Booth and Dunn 1994).

Divorce also has unequal economic consequences for men and women. Men may actually see their disposable incomes rise, especially if they pay little or no child support. Separated and divorced women suffer an average fall of about 30 percent in their incomes the year after their marriage breaks up, and even greater drops occur for middle-class wives without careers. "Only one in four lone mothers in the United States regularly receives the full amount of child support owed to the family each month. Although a number of federal reforms to improve child support collection were established in the 1980s, there is still little uniformity in state laws regarding divorce, child support, and custody, and the obstacles confronting interstate collection efforts are enormous" (McFate 1991, 20). Divorce and lone parenthood also increase female and child poverty (Ermisch 1991; Acock and Demo 1994) and tend to leave children without a model of successful marriage, thereby inclining them more toward cohabitation rather than marriage and toward higher rates of divorce if married. Today one-third of all babies are born to unmarried mothers, who tend to be younger, less educated, from minority groups, and living separately from their child's father (Wu and Wolfe 2001).

Other analysts, such as Lenore Weitzman (1985), note that radical subjectivism, an ideology of love, and the freedom to "grow as a person" have contributed to the "divorce revolution." The pop-therapeutic vision of love, which fuels the divorce revolution, is vaporous and infinitely expanding. One never knows if one is *really* in love or if one has realized one's true nature or how much or for how long. Indeed, one is always searching, and if the search leads one away from spouse and children, so be it. Yet the freedom sought through divorce is elusive. Indeed, with disputes about custody and scheduling and vacations and who drives which child, divorced spouses are often more entangled with one another than before—and more exhausted. One result is that two of three adults who were children of divorce decide not to have children of their own (Wallerstein 2000, 67).

Secularization and individualism also seem to play a role in the declining stability and centrality of the family. As work shifted from the extended family to the factory or the state, the primary structures of lineage, patronage, and clan gave way to the primacy of atomized individuals, on the one hand, and rationalized firms, bureaucracies, and markets, on the other. Thus modernity itself devalues the family as the dominant source of identity, particularly among the middle classes, where effort and talent are relatively more important than solidarity of lineage or work group and where the family group itself has fewer members and generations. Indeed, with the advent of nuclear and subnuclear families, the family's claims on individuals are no longer social, economic, professional, or entrepreneurial so much as emotional. Ancestors and descendants become less important as secular individuals are both freed and exiled from claims of prior and subsequent generations, as well as from the possibility of deep collective narrations. Even widowhood has come to be seen as a transitional status (Lopata 1996).

In sum, one might say that patriarchy has not been eliminated so much as reorganized to operate structurally rather than personally, through institutional arrangements that secure male privileges indirectly. For example, although female labor has increasingly been incorporated into capitalist economic production, most occupational categories remain coded by gender, with secretaries and nurses still being largely female and managers and surgeons remaining mostly male. Male and female career trajectories also are radically separated insofar as women often forego career advancement for childbirth and motherhood without provision for time off or day-care facilities for children.

With industrialization and modern state formation, families proved inadequate for the reproduction of both labor power and citizens in the new societies. Thus socialization came to be increasingly directed by the state through schooling and other activities that provided jobs specifically designated for women in "caring" occupations such as nursing, teaching, or social work. The state also began to regulate biological reproduction through sponsorship or medical agencies, family planning, and legalized abortion, as well as policies of taxation or subsidies, especially for poor unmarried mothers. Thus gender relations moved from the private to the public sphere as families and single mothers became more dependent on the state (Laslett and Brenner 1989; Waters 1989).

These changes parallel the general historical process of increasing individuation, on the one hand, and increasing abstraction of social institutions, on the other. The rationalized system becomes more remote and uncontrollable by individual actors; the lifeworld, more encapsulated, powerless, and radically subjective (Habermas 1987, 356). Thus the new relations between genders and generations can be understood as part of a larger segregation of self and system, a bureaucratization and commercialization of functions formally conducted by extended groups of kin and community, and a simultaneous release of persons into a radically subjective individualism.

DEBATES OVER THE AMERICAN FAMILY

While many Americans "see the unsettlement of family life as a calamity, others see it as a liberation, holding that the nuclear family was always a sweatshop for the wives, a private brothel for the husbands, and an emotional ghetto for the children. No matter where we look, what some will call a crisis others call an awakening, or a liberation, or a step toward dignity and truth" (Schaar 1981, 332). Such debates over the American family usually miss the larger trend away from "families" and toward "lifestyles" as a way of organizing daily activities and primary relations. This movement away from the families also reflects the increased longevity of postindustrial persons. People may have engaged in family pursuits for much of their lives but still live long enough to lead other kinds of "postfamily" lives. Nonetheless, public debates over family policy focus on the tenuousness of marriage and the increase in paid workforce participation among mothers, particularly mothers of young children. As noted, female workforce participation is linked with divorce insofar as single women who work may feel less compelled to marry, wives may more easily divorce, and husbands may feel less guilty or financially vulnerable in leaving a wife who has an independent income. Conversely, as marriage becomes less secure, women wish to maintain their ties to the labor market and are often forced to work or keep on working when a marriage ends.

The therapeutic orientation to relationships that Cancian (1987), Illouz (1997a, 1997b, 1997c), and others have studied represents one side of the debate over the family, as well as a profound conflict between two different social classes and moral orders that are rivals in their perceptions of womanhood, marriage, work, and morality, with one side stressing duty and obligation and the other side emphasizing love and feelings. In effect, the "culture of abundance" (Susman 1984) is in conflict with the cultures of nineteenth-century Puritan capitalism and twentieth-century immigrant Catholicism and Judaism. "Placed in this context, what 'love' in America means and represents is not principally about relationships and self-development; it also is something men and women and social classes fight over. In that struggle, androgynous love is becoming a new standard, a moral vision that proposes an entirely new feminist language and technology of the self and the body" (McCarthy 1988, 828; see also Swidler 2001). Overall, while men and women continue to have different styles of loving, images and ideals are shifting toward androgynous love and self-development for both men and women.

In both the patriarchal and modern family ideals, women are expected to be nurturers and guardians of family, love, and stability, and they usually internalize these ideals themselves. Hence, criticisms of the breakdown of the family tend to be directed at females, especially those who are or would be more independent, such as the 55 percent of mothers with children under twelve months old who are working outside the home. "Conservatives often fault working women for putting their individual interests (career, personal fulfillment, and so on) above those of 'the family.' Some defenders of working mothers counter that economic necessity alone is responsible for women's increased labor force participation. Both groups tend to ignore the change in cultural expectations about women working. Today, most *men* as well as most women expect wives to contribute to the economic support of their families, especially if the children are of school age or older. In 1991, three quarters of all mothers of school-aged children, 60 percent of mothers of preschool children, and over half the mothers of children under two were in the [paid] labor force" (McFate 1991, 19–20). Conservatives also insist that defects of individual character are the source of social ills and that character can be formed only in the family; this position for them also explains why many social problems do not respond to government intervention. Solutions offered by conservatives thus focus on reforming character by bringing the Bible into classrooms, keeping sex education out, and generally supporting motherhood and family.

Conversely, since the 1970s, feminists have criticized the ideology of the family, and sociology has moved past the Parsonian model of the nuclear family and its expressive and instrumental gender roles. Family textbooks routinely challenge the prevailing myths and point to the diversity of family forms and experiences. Even popular culture challenges the ideal in daytime TV and in programs like *Roseanne* and *The Simpsons*. Yet images of the family "continue to exercise power over American hearts, minds, and politics. This power should puzzle the alarmists who warn that family values have declined, that we live in a postmarital or postnuclear family culture. Indeed, how can the alarmists explain the emotional appeal of their own jeremiads if family values are obsolete?" (Skolnick 1998, 233; see also Gillis 1997). It may be the case, of course, that many conservatives speak the truths of their own experiences, especially insofar as cultural conservatives tend to be more working class, patriarchal, and male. For such persons, divorce can be particularly devastating. As males, they likely had limited contact with their children, largely mediated by their wives, who, according to their conservative code, must be betrayers and enemies. For such men, divorce represents a loss of family, order, power, and relations with their children (Arendell 1995).

Conservatives (for example, Whitehead 1997; Shalit 1999; M. Gallagher 1996; Mack 1997) also tend to be absolutists, and liberals (for example, Gore and Gore 2002), relativists. Under the banner of family values, conservatives wage a war not only of words, but also for the control of contemporary national culture and the consciousness of succeeding generations. Liberals respond not with absolutes or threats of apocalypse, but more often by exposing the assumptions, misconceptions, and historical inaccuracies that mark the neoconservative campaign to redeem an imagined past and colonize the future with a moral and political commitment to the "traditional family." Contesting the neoconservative assumption of a natural relation between a historically constant traditional family and a strong civic life, scholars like Michael Shapiro (2002) show how the situation of the family in relation to public life has emerged differently in different historical periods. Indeed, moral or theological assertions often are opposed to public attachments, revealing that "the family" appears as a contingent cultural and historical process (for overviews see Wilson 1993; Marshall and Boles 1991; Eisenstein 1982).

The work of sociologist Talcott Parsons supported advocates of "family values" by arguing that only one kind of family was functionally adequate for modern societies and, furthermore, that the uniquely legitimate model was the male-dominated nuclear family. By contrast, the work of Stephanie Coontz presents a conflicting viewpoint, "asserting that many forms of families are effective and laudable, and that our values and our social institutions should be organized in ways that help them all to flourish" (Aulette 1998, 236). Debates over stepfamilies run along similar axes. Conservative critics embrace the indictment of stepfamilies proposed by evolutionary psychologists, who contend that parents have evolved over eons to care about the welfare of only their genetic offspring. Such critics use this (dubious) science as ammunition to lobby for "pro-family" social policies. In this logic, if stepfamilies are so unnatural from a genetic point of view that they imperil children's welfare, everything should be done to prevent divorce (and thus remarriage).

By contrast, liberal critics contend that genetic predispositions are no more than predispositions and are not cast in bronze. In this view, social policies that keep unhappy families trapped together are far more risky psychologically than life in a stepfamily. "What is needed, they argue, is not more stigmatizing of stepfamilies, but rather policies that strengthen stepfamilies and reduce any risks that might exist. True, various studies show that stepkids do more poorly on a variety of measures than do kids who live in two biological parent families, even adjusting for income level. [Indeed] stepchildren do about as well as kids who live with a single parent, which is to say much worse than kids in traditional nuclear families. Moreover, stepfamilies are expected to outnumber biologically parented families by 2007. But the proper response, say liberals, is not to condemn stepfamilies but to support and strengthen them. For example, in studies that asked people to rank the roles that were most important to them, 'parent' topped the list, but 'stepparent' ranked extremely low" (*U.S. News and World Report,* November 29, 1999, 61). Such results suggest that stepparents, lacking a clear mandate or authority in the new family, often are passive or ineffective at parenting. Moreover, like domestic partners, stepparents currently have almost no legal standing in most states; even when they assume responsibility for their stepchildren, such as providing emotional and financial support, they have no corresponding rights. If the marriage ends, the stepparent has no legal grounds to ask for custody or visitation. Similarly, stepchildren rarely have rights—to life insurance benefits, for example—or, if the marriage ends, to continued support or inheritance. For liberals, the policy response is obvious: changes in the legal status of stepparents would improve these conditions (*U.S. News and World Report,* November 29, 1999; see also Barnes et al. 1998).

Similarly, while many liberals and feminists celebrate the autonomy and power gained by women through greater participation in the paid labor force, conservatives emphasize the growing tension between the requirements of employers for a flexible workforce and the ability of parents and communities to nurture their children and provide for their health, welfare, and education. For example, when an infant died in the care of a hired babysitter in Massachusetts in 1996, a public debate ensued as to whether Dr. Deborah Eappen, the upper-middle-class working mother of the dead child, got what she deserved. As an ophthalmologist who continued her practice three days a week while starting her family, Eappen hired a young English au pair to care for her two diaper-age sons. According to national news accounts, many Americans rallied behind the ideology of intensive mothering and criticized the Eappens, especially the mother, for working instead of caring for the two children (Howland 1997, A6). This ideology, which demands full-time maternal care, is the standard held for middle- and upper-class women (Hays 1996), but it is contradicted by

American political and legal policies for lower-class women on governmental assistance. When mothers on welfare stay home with their children, governmental "reforms" gear them for employment. Thus, the Eappen case draws attention to how ideologies and policies concerning the socially accepted roles of women are heavily laden by the politics of class (Brommer 1998, 2).

Neither conservatives nor liberals often take account of changes in the broader political economy that might invite a more radical critique of family values and policies in light of postindustrial capitalism. Global competition and the spread of information technology are forcing businesses to engage in rapid, worldwide production changes, customized marketing, and just-in-time delivery. They are reorganizing work around decentralized management, task differentiation, and short-term and part-time employment. Increasingly, workers must be able to move across firms, and even across types of work, as jobs get redefined. But there is a stiff price being paid for such flexibility in the labor market. It separates workers from the social institutions—family, long-term jobs, and stable communities—that sustained economic expansions in the past and supported the growth and development of the next generation. Such costs are exacerbated by the continuing movement of women into paid work, which puts a greater strain on the family's ability to care for and rear children (Carnoy 2000).

Indeed, some observers argue that the workplace has become a kind of "home" in itself, with clear tasks, order, and recognition, whereas the home has become "work," requiring endless emotional effort, unlimited demands, and few rewards. Consider, for example, the care of children among dual-earner couples, one-third of whom have preschool children and work split shifts, with one spouse employed in the daytime and the other employed evenings, nights, or on rotating schedules. On the positive side, for liberals, in virtually all such cases fathers become primary caregivers with children when their wives are employed. However, these gains may be more than offset by the longer-term costs to the marriage. Among couples with children, for example, when men work nights (and have been married less than five years) the likelihood of separation or divorce five years later is some six times greater than for men who work days. When women work nights (and have been married more than five years), the odds of divorce or separation are three times as high. Moreover, the data suggest that the increased tendency for divorce is not because spouses in troubled marriages are more likely to opt for night work; the causality seems in the opposite direction (Presser 1999, 1779).

Another aspect of the debates about the family involves the "basic nature" of men and women, with conservatives stressing nature (for example, Tiger 1999;

Gligliere 1999) and liberals emphasizing nurture. However, "difference feminists," such as Carol Gilligan (1993), deem certain (for them negative) traits such as competitiveness as inherently male, whereas (positive) traits such as nurturance or emotional expressiveness are viewed as inherently female. This question of biology and gender was raised by Betty Friedan in 1963, and it has been central to public discussions of the family and the role of women since the founding of the women's movement in the mid-nineteenth century.

> Is anatomy destiny? . . . Do women have a special responsibility for children—or just half a responsibility? Should they be allowed to struggle in the workplace or forced to stay home (debated, despite the fact that most women today have no choice but to work)? And how do their decisions affect children and men? Finally, who will control their reproductive decisions—men or themselves? Above all, does society have a right to legislate the behavior of women as a special class defined by their biological attributes? Corollary issues like . . . female sexual freedom, sexual harassment, and male violence are explained . . . as the reaction of threatened, testosterone-poisoned males to the upheaval around all these questions, with the implication either that men would stop being violent toward women if women would behave subserviently, or that many men are innately violent, or both" (Johnson 1996, 22; see also Maccoby 1998).

Despite their more complicated logistics and time constraints, however, mothers with careers tend to be happier, with more cheerful and competent children and with husbands more engaged in family life (Rivers and Barnett 1997). Such findings corroborate Betty Friedan's image of frustrated American housewives, but they apply mainly to more educated women with careers, not to the great majority of working women who are in low-paying jobs. Yet other research, such as the Framingham Heart Study, shows that not only heart disease, but also depression and chronic illness are more frequent among homemakers than among working women, whether these be professional, middle, or lower-middle class (Hays 1996). Moreover, other psychological and sociological studies show no significant differences between the children of employed and nonemployed mothers according to most measures of child development and that daughters seem actually to benefit when mothers work (Johnson 1996, 26; Harvey 1999). With such studies, the discourse of childhood innocence is being superseded with that of children's competence, and teenage immaturity gives way to an image of adolescent sophistication (Elkind 1994). In light of such evidence, the ideal of the supermom of the 1960s seems to have emerged not from a biological nature of women but from various converging political, economic, and ideological forces.

The debates over family policy can be seen as a struggle over who is to control the means of reproduction and who will care for the kids. It cannot be coincidental, for example, that male-run institutions like the Catholic Church, the Japanese government, and most Islamic states outlaw or strictly control contraception (Johnson 1996, 28). In these debates, conservatives mostly assume that there is only one correct form of the family and liberals that there is a basic openness, indeterminacy, and choice in the concept of family. The former position is morally charged and somewhat authoritarian, whereas the latter is tied to individualistic and emancipatory ideas and is somewhat technicist or scientistic. For example, conservatives believe that teenage mothers reflect a larger cultural and moral failure of American society that they link to increased premarital and extramarital sexual activity, a permissive and sexually explicit culture and popular media, and the precedence of personal preference and pleasure over duty to bonds of couples, kin, and community. Conservatives also decry what they see as the loss of the privacy and autonomy of the family in the face of encroachments by the state. They oppose sex education in public schools and insist that their right to transmit moral family values is undermined by programs that pretend to be morally neutral. Conservatives also favor more patriarchal gender roles and hierarchy, public policies that reflect their religious beliefs, and a new respect for wives as homemakers and builders of families and communities (Luker 1984).

By contrast, liberals favor a more secular, managerial, and technical definition of problems of families and approaches to their solution. For example, public health and medical practitioners often assume that people act against their own best interest and thus must be guided by doctors, social scientists, or other experts. Similarly, the discourse of Planned Parenthood focuses on techniques of reproductive planning rather than on duties or traditions (Joffe 1986). Thus liberals challenge conservatives by arguing that the provision of contraceptives to students or clean needles to heroin addicts is primarily a health issue and not a moral, religious, or political one, insofar as both the contraceptive and clean needle programs aim to promote the supposedly universal values of enlightenment and health through social technologies rather than through political coercion or moral exhortation.

Liberals like Anthony Giddens (1992) assert that changes, such as the greater instability of marriage, the separation between sexuality and reproduction, or the increased number of stepfamilies and single-parent families, all have an emancipatory potential. Giddens applauds "plastic sexuality," "confluent love," and the "pure relationship" as democratic and desirable alternatives to a sexuality harnessed to reproduction, love based on addictive or codependent relationships, and the rights and obligations of traditional marriage. For Giddens and other optimists, the separation of sexuality from procreation liberates persons to cultivate their own gender and sexual identities without being hostage to traditional relationships, unless of course these further their changing narratives of the self. Thus Giddens celebrates "the pure relationship, designed to fulfill individuals' needs for intimacy (rather than societal or parental expectations) and lasting only as long as participants find it rewarding. In the pure relationship love is confluent love (i.e., contingent, temporary, based on equality and mutual satisfaction, and subject to continuous examination and negotiation)" (Gimenez 1993, 271).

Aside from being profoundly unsociological, if only in forgetting that constant negotiation seems more like work than love, Giddens fails to note that the new autonomy he heralds is available or advantageous mainly to privileged white males in advanced Western societies. The nonbinding commitment of a "pure relationship" sounds much like a male flight from deeper engagement, especially one based on moral affinities, as in Aristotle's conception of friendship. Conservatives of course would consider it disastrous. Feminists could call it a new patriarchy; Marxists could call it a glorification of privileged alienation. For people of unstable income, limited education, and modest means, the "traditional family" is often a unique source of economic and emotional stability or even survival. Giddens, it seems, is talking about an idealized, affluent lifestyle, perhaps his own, not about families and relationships as they are experienced and understood by most people. And even for the affluent, "pure relationships" are rarely if ever devoid of practical concerns and unequal power. Indeed, much sociological research (for example, Jamieson 1998) suggests that images of self-disclosure, intimacy, and growth have become much more pervasive in "public stories," in what people say but not in what they do. In everyday life, relations between parents and children or men and women are not equal, and practical help and caring usually matter more than self-disclosure and empathy.

Only a few writers have sought to recast these debates within a broader political economic context, and even these efforts have been denigrated in a report commissioned by the respected American Council of Families (Glenn 1997; per contra see Stacey 1996). One such exception is Stephanie Coontz, who shows how the myth of the "typical" family of the 1950s is better understood if we place images about it in the broader economic context of the 1950s and its connection to governmental support of households. Coontz (1998) reminds us that real wages grew faster in one year in the 1950s than in the whole decade of the

1980s. "The '50s also provided such policies as a minimum wage above poverty, a much larger proportion of federal spending on public works (schools and sewage systems), GI benefits, and home financing" (Aulette 1998, 236). With most of these policies dismantled and poverty rates growing among every kind of family, including those headed by white men, the 1950s do seem worthy of nostalgia, even though most women then were restricted to the domestic sphere. In addition to personal and political reasons for the massive entry of middle-class women into the paid labor force, as the 1950s economy began to unravel, households had to increase their number of earners to maintain a middle-class status and, perhaps, a modest amount of upward mobility. Thus, "Coontz reminds us that when family values crusaders promote nuclear households with a male breadwinner and female homemaker, they are telling us we must abandon the American dream . . . and replace it with a no-growth or declining family economy" (Aulette 1998, 236). Moreover, it turns out that families with employed adults, including employed married mothers, generally are better off economically *and* emotionally. "Women are happier, men have stronger connections to children, children do better in school, and everyone is better off financially. The bad news is that multiple-job families face new problems, like finding high-quality child care and finding enough time, especially for such emergencies as the illness of a family member" (Aulette 1998, 236). Thus, what today's families need is not a return to an idealized 1950s, but a new social context—in particular, the organization of business and government. "During the transition to a male breadwinner family during the early nineteenth century, government funded the transportation systems that were essential for the development of a national market. In today's transition to a coprovider family system, child care, paid parental leaves and family-friendly work policies are equally vital social and economic investments as were canals and railroads then" (Coontz 1998, 74). "Not surprisingly, then, those who promote the 1950s model of families also promote restrictions in birth control, abortion, divorce and welfare, and are the same people who oppose parental leaves because these inhibit the flexibility of employers" (Aulette 1998, 237).

Extending these views, we could argue that the new and problematic condition of today's families is generated by the simultaneous growth of the economy, increased labor by men and women, and the stagnation or decline of the majority's standards of living. In this view, the crux of the problem lies in the larger political economy, labor market, and government politics and not in divorced parents or unwed mothers. Instead, our focus should be on the vastly increased inequalities of income and wealth; the removal of rungs in an older ladder of social mobility; the replacement of good, stable jobs by part-time, dead-end, or low-paying ones; and the relative decline of government support for struggling families and parents. Thus, one version of American debates over the family is that between values and the economy. Those who support the traditional family argue that we need to adopt a particular set of values. Their opponents often argue that we need to change the economy (Aulette 1998, 237). But why not restructure *both* the economy *and* American values? Most pointedly, Americans might temper their therapeutic individualism in ways that broaden responsibility for taking care of each other and especially taking care of children. Such new values clearly support necessary changes in the economy to distribute its fruits more equitably in the service of new values of community responsibility.

To summarize, conservatives, who are usually pessimists, point to high rates of divorce and of single-parent or stepfamilies, and they argue that personal liberty has become license to abandon the family. Liberals, usually optimists, note that an overwhelming majority of Americans continue to marry and have children and that divorce is no more disruptive today than was death in the past. They argue that conservatives have a too narrow and idealized conception of family, which makes them confuse change with decline of the institution. Instead, liberals suggest that postindustrial society brings greater affluence and personal freedom, and, as a result, families have become more egalitarian, flexible, and intimate. A third, distinctly minority position, however, rejects conservative nostalgia as well as liberal technicism and self-absorption and instead advocates radical changes in both American values and the political economy.

A DIFFERENTIATION OF THE CRISIS

A country as large, diverse, and decentralized as the United States offers a great range of constraints and opportunities, despite the homogenizing effects of capitalism and commercialized culture. Given the many distinctions of American class, race, ethnicity and religion, portraits of the "median," the "mode," or the "average" family are necessarily ideal types. The nuclear family itself is a relatively recent creation. Far from "traditional," it was invented in the nineteenth century in the image of bourgeois property rights, with women's role defined as legitimate reproduction within middle-class families (Yeatman 1993, 538; Smart 1992; Rotundo 1993). Moreover, different family forms have flourished alongside the "traditional" one. In colonial times stepfamilies were almost as prevalent as now; Amish and Hasidim have always had large, extended families; the

Nation of Islam is endogenous; and Mormons were long polygamous and show no declines in fertility despite generally monogamous marriages and increases in wealth.

Family forms differ greatly by race and ethnicity. Whereas some 56 percent of white children live in a "traditional" nuclear family (about half of all American children), the figures for African American and Hispanic children are 26 and 38 percent respectively. Further, since 1910 more than half of black women have worked outside the home, whereas white women surpassed this mark only in the past two decades. The percent of black women over the age of fourteen who are married fell from 62 to 38 percent between 1950 and 1995, whereas the comparable figures for white women are 66 and 59 percent. Many of these disparities reflect the disadvantages of black men in the labor force. The view of the male's role as provider also makes the inability to perform it more grievous to black males than to whites. Moreover, there are half as many middle-class black men as middle-class black women (Tucker 1995). Because the relatively few middle-class black men are in high demand, they have relatively less incentive to marry or to stay married (Sterk-Elifson 1994; Taylor, Jackson, and Chatters 1997). All these factors create much greater difficulties in relations between the genders for blacks than for whites.

A further difficulty in defining "average" or "median" families is that statistical patterns relevant to family life are rarely linear and cumulative. Among other things, familial wealth and income have significant impacts on familial lifestyles only when they fall below or exceed critical thresholds. Nor are these effects evenly distributed. For example, an increase in income of 10 percent is likely to have more dramatic consequences at the bottom than at the top of the distribution. Conversely, sometimes affluence and scarcity both have negative effects on domestic structures. Indeed, for this very reason, the absence in any analysis of differences in the behaviors of distinct social groups, especially classes, or different generations or cohorts can mask highly distinct processes. This point is especially important in view of changes in the American social structure since about 1970—specifically, the drastic increase of inequality in the distributions of wealth and income—after about fifty years during which these distributions were fairly stable or becoming less unequal. Increased income inequality has been amplified by a variety of regressive tax, fiscal, and welfare policies that were conservative political responses to slowdowns in the growth rates of the American economy during the 1970s and 1980s, as well as by a 1,000 percent upswing in the stock market between 1985 and 2000 that enriched many who were already affluent. Despite the relative decline of transfer payments, America's elderly are no longer the poorest age group. Alternatively, ownership of a home (though perhaps not a condo) is much less likely for younger people than it was for their parents, since the great burst of new home ownership occurred before 1975. Similarly, dual-career couples have spread the income gap between professional and working-class families because in the latter the wife is less likely to be employed outside the home.

Such increases in class and generational inequalities have accentuated the variability of both conjugal and intergenerational relations and their respective meanings. For example, informal cohabitation of college students and other middle-class young adults may be a response to overchoice—an excessive range of options and an ensuing inability to be completely committed to any of them. But it also may reveal a lack of financial resources and the corresponding downward mobility of children compared to their parents. Indeed, the appearance of intergender "group houses" reflects both a postponement of marriage and a relative decline of income of many young persons. Likewise, falling rates of marriage suggest not only the rational fear of assuming obligations in an era of increased uncertainty, but also the postponement of adult responsibilities by eternal adolescents. Conversely, they may be due to less social pressure to marry but more pressure to pursue a career. Similarly, middle-class parents of an earlier generation felt obligated to give their children good work habits and a college education, after which the kids were on their own. But today, the escalator that carried adolescents into adulthood has broken down. Decently paid industrial or unionized jobs have become scarce, and well-paid professional positions have come to require enormous up-front costs for credentialing. The result is that many young adults often are unable to maintain or even attain a middle-class lifestyle without their parents' support. Thus, strains appear between the generations as children expect more than their parents had felt obligated to give (Millman 1991).

Depending on which specific group is involved, the increased participation of women in the paid labor force may indicate growing economic pressures on females to become employees or their growing economic freedom and social autonomy. Likewise, declining rates of birth may reflect the greater affluence of men and women who prefer to enjoy their free time or, conversely, the downward mobility of economically strapped couples who rationally restrict pregnancies because they cannot afford children. Increased rates of birth out of wedlock may result from the increased choices of affluent groups; from narcissistic feelings of omnipotence of leisured youths; and from the nihilism, carelessness, or welfare calculations of low-income persons.

The same equivocations characterize the behaviors of working mothers in relation to their children. Rates of participation in the paid labor force have climbed the most sharply among married women, but these may reflect downward mobility through declines in real family incomes as much as increases in aspirations for higher status. Either hypothesis might explain, for example, why women over the age of thirty who had a child in 1983 returned to work much faster than the preceding cohorts and why this trend continues in the present. Correspondingly, the shortening of the period of intense interaction between mother and infant reflects differing phenomena both within and between different individuals and groups. An earlier return to work may reflect a fear of losing employment due to downsizing, a commitment to higher career expectations, or the eschewal of intimacy in a culture that favors individualism. All these hypotheses may be true, but in different degrees for different groups of women.

A similar diversity exists for different age groups. At one end of the age continuum, as noted, the elderly are less poor as a group, and as a result, they less frequently depend on their adult children for material support. Persons in the middle of the age continuum are more likely to divorce and remarry and to experience the downward mobility that goes with these choices, and thus they are less often able or willing to support the higher education of their own children. Such decisions often weaken the bonds between middle-aged parents and both their children and their own parents. At the same time, if grandparents help their struggling grandchildren, the economic and emotional bonds between them may be reinforced (Bengtson and Robertson 1985). At the lower end of the age continuum, the changing mix of increased inequality and greater competition in the labor market inclines more young people to remain dependent on their parents or other kin for longer periods of time. Further, as Bengtson (2001) has argued, the importance of intergenerational, extended family ties may be increasing in response to the greater uncertainties of marriages. In any case, economic and conjugal changes have differing effects on the different generations and on their respective styles of interaction.

Finally, there are similarly ambiguous convergences in the incidence of divorce among the rich and poor. At the affluent end of the socioeconomic scale, individuals often divorce because their partners have become socially obsolete or too expensive in view of the market for eligible alternatives. Donald Trump, for example, explained that he divorced his second wife, Marla, because, had he waited five years, the price of divorce would have more than doubled. Among poor people, individuals often break their union because divorce cuts their psychological and financial burdens, especially if they are men.

In short, more detailed images of the American family may seem kaleidoscopic because they represent moments of transition in the responses of successive generations and different social groups in a fast-changing culture and political economy. As such, the situation of families today recalls Robert MacIver's statement about anomic persons who "deride the values of other men, whose only faith is the philosophy of denial, and who live on the thin line of sensation between no future and no past" (1950, 84–85). Not only are differing segments of the American population experiencing the anomie of new scarcity or sudden success, but these groups also are inwardly torn between aspirations for an unachieved future and nostalgia for an unretrieved past. For all these reasons, bonds between the genders and the generations are highly problematic, but in different ways for different segments of society.

THE PLURALIZATION OF AMERICAN FAMILY FORMS

Recent experience and statistics reveal significant diversity of American family forms, due in part to rises in rates of divorce and out-of-wedlock births. A further cause is new technologies that facilitate reproduction, just as technologies to inhibit reproduction had earlier encouraged new domestic arrangements. Today's new technologies enable couples previously diagnosed as infertile to reproduce, sometimes in surprising abundance. Mrs. Nkem Chukwu, for example, who miscarried triplets in 1998, became pregnant with injectable fertility chips called gonadotropins and gave birth to octuplets, most of whom survived (Morrow 1999).

> [New technologies] also allow third parties to become biologically involved in the making of a child; and as a result, they raise questions about what it actually means for a child to be essentially one's own. For instance, in the case of artificial insemination, a wife may be impregnated not with her husband's sperm, but with that of a donor. With in vitro fertilization, the ovum may be donated, fertilized in the laboratory, and then implanted in another woman's uterus. And in surrogate pregnancies, a third party may become biologically involved in one of two ways. If a couple's own gametes are fertilized in vitro, and the resulting embryo is implanted in the womb of another woman, that woman bears the child as a *gestational* surrogate. If, however, the surrogate is inseminated artificially with the husband's sperm, she conceives and bears the child for the couple as a *genetic* surrogate. Thus, reproductive technologies have made it possible for a child to have as many as five parents: a genetic father, a rearing father, a genetic mother, a gestational mother, and a rearing mother (Wasserman and Wachbroit 2001, 3).

Of course, most of the families created or expanded through such technologies are not so elaborate. Nonetheless, whereas there formerly were only two ways of obtaining children—natural parenting or adoption—now there are multiple possibilities, even without the direct involvement of a man. Today the anonymous "other woman" can be the surrogate co-mother of one's child. Yet cases like that of Baby M (noted above) underline the possibilities of conflicts—for example, between the biological and the adopting mothers and between them and the inseminating or adopting males, who risk becoming legally impotent fathers. Children with multiple parents also can be legally orphaned. For example, although Jaycee Louise Buzzanca, a healthy two-year-old, had six people who might qualify as her parents, a California judge ruled that she was legally parentless (Jaroff 1997). Her bizarre case is an object lesson in how far both the law and social norms have trailed behind advances in fertility science. If an egg donor is Jewish, does that ensure, under the Jewish law of matrilineal descent, that the resulting child is Jewish? Does an egg have an ethnic identity or a religious one? Is an egg donor the same thing as a mother? And what is a person—a fetus, an embryo, or a born child? Such questions challenge both the meaning and role of parent and hence the relations between generations; they also reflect "the ongoing incursions of market relations into the apparently noncommodified relations of family life. While the physical baby cannot be bought and sold, the surrogate, the adoption search, the repeated medical interventions are increasingly for sale to the highest bidder. As the moral economy comes to mimic the dollar economy, women and men who are unwilling to engage in expensive or unethical medical or social interventions are seen as lacking in real desire for a child" (D. Gerson 1996, 788). And even without new technologies, the ascendance of market and technological principles can generate moral and social ambiguities that even the sagacious cannot resolve. For example, Woody Allen's marriage to his adopted daughter, Soon-Yi, has made her the stepmother of her own siblings and Mia Farrow, Woody Allen's mother-in-law. "The catalog-style browsing for top-drawer genes and specific attributes subtly corrupts the single most significant attribute of parental love, which is that it is love for what one has been given. Its unconditionality is owed not least to the fact that the children have not been designed by the parents" (Talbot 1998, 42; see also Lemonick 1999, 56).

New family forms that appear outside of current norms further multiply as new technologies converge with alternate sexes or genders. For example, can the lesbian partner of a woman who has received donor insemination claim parental rights to the resulting child? Until recently, most courts said no, but views have been changing, especially on the West Coast. Yet in New Jersey, Superior Court Judge Vincent Gresso ruled that a lesbian's ex-partner had custody rights to their child even though she had not been legally married and was neither the father nor the birth mother (*Washington Post,* November 4, 1998; see also Bozett 1987). Alternative families such as "domestic partners" also are gaining recognition from employers, insurers, and government agencies, as well as assistance from courts in defending their rights and arrangements. The possibility of sex change operations, at least for the affluent, further complicates what it may mean to be a man or a woman. Indeed, categories that formerly appeared given in nature and provided an assumedly biological basis for family life and intergender relations are now subject to conscious choice. Moreover, the relatively greater financial independence of women and the elderly, along with new cultural norms and practices, has encouraged a proliferation of relations for sex, child making, and cohabitation.

This proliferation of new gender, sexual, and family forms suggests that the modern nuclear family is no longer the primary family form, thanks to the emergence of what some researchers describe as the postmodern family (see Cheal 1991; Stacey 1990). For Stacey the term "postmodern family" means that there are "competing sets of family cultures [and no] single culturally dominant family pattern, like the modern one, to which the majority of Americans conform and most of the rest aspire" (1990, 93). Instead, as the metanarrative of progress collapses, the norms of modernity are challenged by the diversity and fluidity of contemporary family life, and evolutionary histories of an ideal nuclear family are cast in doubt.

Not only are families changing their structure and composition demographically, but they also are recasting their values and aspirations, albeit often without conscious intention. For example, of a group of young mothers interviewed several times between 1962 and 1977, half at first agreed that "When there are children in the family, parents should stay together even if they don't get along." But the women who agreed were almost as likely to divorce in the following fifteen years as those who disagreed (Cherlin 1981). Twenty years later, however, many fewer women would recommend staying together. Thus, pleas by political figures for a return to "traditional family values" may serve as a palliative for seemingly intractable personal problems, economic changes, or status frustrations, but they have little to do with the actual conditions, causes, and, increasingly, the norms of American family life today. Nevertheless, despite certain radical changes, the "traditional" or "nuclear family" retains its appeal as a myth of harmony and personal integration (Weeks 1991, 21; Press 1991;

Stacey 1990). In sum, the diversity of family forms does not entail a collapse of the ideological primacy of the "normal family." Indeed, this very breach between a dominant modernist ideology and a fragmented postmodern experience is itself a typically postmodern condition.

Postmodern, postindustrial society is also a postkinship and even a postproduction society, in the sense that people are relatively more oriented toward personal consumption and pleasure than toward duty, production, and work. Postindustrial persons are more focused on self and peers than on older or younger generations, more neutral concerning gender, and more concerned with personal choices than with what is given by birth or obligation. They are, in short, less familial. In premodern and modern families, work and economic dependency were central forces shaping relations of genders and generations, with elder males controlling both the means and the fruits of economic production and biological reproduction. In postindustrial societies, however, proportionately fewer people work than formerly and do so for a smaller part of their lifespans, whereas a greater amount of lifespace is devoted to personal consumption. Relationships among genders and generations based on production are declining as people are linked more directly and individually to mass markets as consumers. Thus an orientation toward families as units of production is shifting toward an orientation toward individuals as units of consumption, as advertisers well know.

One can see the change in orientation in the softening of distinctions between informal cohabitation, extramarital affairs, and early married life among both straights and gays.

> Young married couples conduct themselves more and more like cohabitants. They postpone having a child; they are fairly permissive about each other's behavior; they [may] tolerate occasional infidelity, or experiment with conventional forms of it (within a basic fidelity). . . . Others, after a life of random affairs, decide they have had enough and try to organize a retreat into something like cohabitation, for example shacking up with their most favored connection, though not necessarily for good. The life style of young homosexual couples is rather like that of heterosexual cohabitants of their generation. What is the difference? A child? But . . . the heterosexual relationship, at least in the start [also] is based on mutual attachment rather than on a child or the desire for one (Béjin 1985, 167).

The same ambiguity is seen within the category "informal cohabitation," in contrast to the distinct residential and sexual arrangement inherent in the notions of concubine or common-law spouse, on the one hand, and roommate, on the other. The choice of such vague terms as "living together" or "significant other" obscures the conflict between the romantic desire for "illegitimate" romance and the positivist temptation to hide or routinize its expression. This ambiguity is augmented by variations in the descriptive terms used by different relevant actors—the cohabitants themselves, their friends, their parents, or even ostensibly objective social scientists, who often eschew critical analysis in favor of complicitous redescriptions of the actors' garbled version of what is going on. Expressions like "open marriage" or "alternative lifestyle" and their implicit sexual connotations also illustrate the range of new and still ambiguous (post)family forms (O'Neil and O'Neil 1972). On the one hand, these expressions highlight romanticism and also the difficulties of sustaining intense emotions and peak experiences, ascertaining the contribution of others to them, and, hence, knowing one's "true" self. On the other hand, these expressions belong to a technicist grammar since they raise the question of whether the self can find uniformities underlying its various performances and create order and predictability in social interactions.

Until around 1970, cohabitation was illegal in almost all American states. Now it is routine. More than half of all first marriages are preceded by cohabitation, and one-quarter of unmarried women between twenty-five and thirty-nine are cohabiting. Whereas only 2 percent of U.S. women born during 1928–1932 cohabited before marrying or reaching age thirty (Schoen and Owens 1992), almost half of those born between 1963 and 1967 (49 percent) did so (Bumpass and Sweet 1995). Cohabitation is thus a central kind of relationship between adult men and women (Bumpass, Sweet, and Cherlin 1991; Schoen and Owens 1992), and as such, it constitutes a family form. As the incidence of cohabitation has increased, it also has spread to a wider diversity of population groups: young and older adults, those previously married or those never married, those with coresident children, those with less than a high school degree, and those with college degrees or higher (Bumpass and Sweet 1995). "Long-term cohabitors may differ in important ways from those who live together with definite plans to marry, or those couples who cohabit and then break up. . . . Our knowledge about long-term cohabitors is quite limited" (Sassler, McNally, and Schoen 1998, 3). Yet, we no longer can assume that cohabitation will eventually lead to marriage (Sassler, McNally, and Schoen 1998, 2; see also Clarkberg, Stolzenberg, and Waite 1995; Raley 1996; Sassler and Goldscheider 1997; Thornton, Axinn, and Teachman 1995; Manning and Smock 1995; Smock and Manning 1997).

We thus should consider cohabitation, with or without children, as a new or postfamily form, more akin to peer relations than to older familiar groupings. Cohabitors, more than married couples, are likely to share achieved characteristics (Schoen and Weinick 1993). Yet this does not seem to affect the longevity of their cohabitation or the likelihood of their eventual marriage. "Cohabitation, then, does not appear to be accomplishing its role as a 'testing ground' for possible marriage, or as an arrangement that will reduce the likelihood of divorce" (Sassler, McNally, and Schoen 1998, 19). Instead, it has become a lifestyle choice of its own.

Such shifts are also from committed cross-gender and cross-generational relations toward personal freedom to choose and change in the here and now— that is, shifts from "family" to "lifestyle." The shifts also reflect, on the one hand, structural changes toward consumption in a highly rationalized late capitalism and, on the other hand, complementary cultural and psychological changes toward extreme subjectivism. Whereas families are collective and oriented toward production, lifestyles are individuated and oriented toward consumption. Similarly, families are given, whereas lifestyles are chosen. Kin are acquired by birth, not by choice, with the exception of marriage, which until recently was arranged by elders (Hunt and Hunt 1987, 441; per contra, see Berger 2002). In this sense, families are relatively more stable, whereas lifestyles are more fluid because, unlike kin relations, they are conditional, voluntary, and, hence, revocable. Although the desires that motivate choices of lifestyles are shaped by mass advertising, they still are experienced and perceived as voluntary. Even in "peer marriages" (Schwartz 1994), the commitment of both partners is to their relationship first, even if this means sacrificing time with their children. All these trends make relations between genders and generations more tentative and labile. Further, because families are explicitly transgenerational, whereas lifestyles usually are specific to peer groups or age cohorts, the multiple generations that connect people to a past and a future become less important, and the largest time horizon becomes a single life. And whereas "family" used to imply the values of continuity and stability and the "home" that one never fully leaves, lifestyles are oriented toward change and pleasure, toward oneself and one's own experiencing of the here and now.

Families also are based on some form of cooperation between the genders, whereas lifestyles tend to be gender neutral. Indeed, most lifestyles can be pursued with men, with women, alone, or in an affinity group, with little obligation or continuing ties to one's lifestyle mates. One indication of this gender neutrality is the shift in rhetorics governing divorce, from images of sin and defilement to concerns for liberty for men and equality for women. In effect, both marriage and divorce have become signs that mark crucial steps in one's career or one's life cycle. As the song says, "I'll love you forever, tonight." Similarly, instead of the old expression, "Tom and Mary are splitting" or "Tom is divorcing Mary," people are more likely to say, "Tom is getting a divorce," thereby defining divorce as a service available in the appropriate market.

Perhaps this is the major shift in relations between genders and generations. As marriage becomes less a lifetime commitment and more a lifestyle option, divorce rates increase, and even within marriages children become less important because lifestyles are centered on adults. "Families invest in children; individuals with life-styles invest in themselves. At first, this takes the form of guarding personal time by buying market substitutes for motherwork. But the logic also extends to saving the time and money by not having children. . . . [Birth] rates are up among poor, unmarried teens (for whom a baby is one of the few life-style options available) and down among the affluent, educated elite (for whom the opportunity costs of children are becoming too great)" (Hunt and Hunt 1987, 443; see also Mintz and Kellog 1988).

In sum, the transition to postindustrial, postmodern society has profound implications for families. Families are still a major source of identity, they set limits on children, and they "produce" the next generation. Yet there also are shifts from families toward peers as sources of identity, from patriarchy toward greater gender equality, from stern paternal authority toward preoccupation with a child's proper feelings and development, and from the family as a unit of production toward lifestyle groups or individuals as units of consumption. Moreover, because newer or more postmodern forms occur more frequently among the upper-middle or professional groups and among older persons who are in a "postfamily" stage of life, these social distributions also reflect and contribute to political and cultural divides. Thus, rural and lower- or working-class persons, who cannot afford to divorce, are more often conservative on value issues, whereas professionals generally are liberal. Yet even working-class conservative groups seem to be assimilating upper-middle-class values and behaviors. Thus many fundamentalist religious groups mix feminist and conservative Christian gender ideologies (Ammerman 1987; Beaman-Hall 1996; Gallagher 1996; McGuire 1987; Rose 1987; Stacey 1990). The particular ways in which feminist norms are absorbed into ideologies differ, however, across groups. Some groups incorporate contemporary feminist ideas because of economic necessity; for example, the groups studied by Nancy Ammerman (1987) and Susan Rose (1987) had to adapt to women's paid employment as an economic imperative, although their rhetoric still asserted the centrality of women's domestic roles. In contrast, Judith Stacey's (1990) study found that Global Ministries of Love (GML) offered its members a more flexible gender ideology and promoted a variety of postmodern family structures and emphasized the inherent value of women's employment (Jenkins n.d., 1).

HISTORICAL AND CURRENT TENSIONS
BETWEEN ROMANTIC SUBJECTIVISM
AND RATIONAL CALCULATION

Since the colonial period in America, the conflict between residential segregation by ethnicity or race and social and residential mobility by class have created tensions and unpredictability in social relations. Like many other peoples, various American groups like to live among themselves and avoid being exposed to polluting and disruptive others. While this desire is fostered by immigration and the persistence of ethnic communities, it has been counterbalanced by social mobility and assimilation into a broader, more Anglo-Saxon national culture.

This balance has changed over time. During the early days of colonization, settlements were more internally homogeneous, but the difference in their respective forms of life made it difficult to describe a singular "American" family. New York and Virginia, for example, had differing populations, religions, and cultures, and the vast majority of people lived in villages or isolated homesteads or plantations. In both cases, relatively high rates of cultural and geographic endogamy helped to reproduce existing family patterns.

To be sure, English common law almost everywhere formed the legal basis of social relations and infused them with the norm of fairness (Horwitz 1977), however stratified and unequal these relations might have been. For example, the notion of fair price governed economic transactions within and between familial groups. Injunctions such as "Honesty is the best policy" or "Love thy neighbor as thyself" made practical sense to the extent that, first, risks were seen as circulating evenly among all segments of one's family and community groups and, second, people's "contracts" with each other were broader in scope and longer in duration than any particular deal on which they might be tempted to cheat.

Within this framework, social and psychological distinctions between males and females were paralleled by distinctions of both domestic tasks and types of capital. In addition to "women's work" and "men's work," more easily movable personal property (monies, kitchenwares, furniture, silver, jewelry) was inherited by daughters and wives (though controlled by their husbands), whereas land, the major form of capital, went to sons. Daughters occupied a position below sons, and their marriage dowries preempted bequests to which they were entitled as heirs. A wife was similarly subordinate to the authority of a husband; she assumed power only during his absence or after his death (Greven 1970; Wyatt-Brown 1982). In general, different local interpretations of English common law and precedents paralleled differences in the economic bases of the various colonies, in the relative isolation of settlements, and in the control exerted by men over women and by elders over young. This variety still persists in the differences among state laws concerning marriage, divorce, and inheritance.

The closing of the frontier, the advent of railroads and the telegraph, population growth, and a stronger nation-state—all reduced residential isolation and also jeopardized the predictability of conjugal and intergenerational bonds. Industrialization during and after the Civil War fostered greater social mobility of individuals rather than geographic mobility of families and thereby undermined the earlier, more familial and communal bases of rights and obligations. By the end of the nineteenth century, mobility came to refer to individuals rather than families or groups. Self-interest more and more became the guide and the rationale of persons' behavior both outside and within families. Theodore Dreiser's *Sister Carrie,* Sinclair Lewis's *Babbitt,* and F. Scott Fitzgerald's *The Great Gatsby* present the sometimes tragic consequences of the ethos and efforts of "making it" for Americans of various social ranks. Indeed, "women adrift" was the popular label for wage-earning women who lived on their own in boarding and rooming houses in the industrializing urban settings of the United States at the turn of the century. This is the social history of garment workers, laundresses, saleswomen, clerks, cabaret dancers, teachers, and nurses who first migrated to Chicago between 1880 and 1930 to search for work or to escape oppressive family circumstances (Meyerowitz 1988).

In the twentieth century, the intrusion of capitalist ideology and behavior into the family realm again fostered changes in familial values and the instability and atomization of the family unit. Yet it is less the uncertainty of behavior than the underlying celebration of personal choice that affects American families. American ideology has always frowned on any form of stable commitment. It has always been ambivalent about aristocracy, as suggested by the derogatory connotations attached to "elitism" or to any transcendental standards, including substantive definitions of justice. In this context, the preference of Americans for personal mobility rather than collective solidarity—for liberty rather than equality—creates tensions in all social groups, including the family. This preference helps to explain the success of neoclassical economists, who write about familial relations exclusively in terms of individual and nonreciprocal choices. Gary Becker (1981), for example, writes about the economic trade-offs between having more vacations or having another child. Such rational calculation of one's choices in the matrimonial or domestic markets reinforces the loneliness one experiences, whether one is a winner or a loser in the quest for personal status advancement. American novels are replete with stories of lonely winners and abandoned losers, whether these happen to be husbands, wives, or children. For the same reasons, opportunistic achievers often seem pathetic, even when extremely successful.

The importance that Americans have attached to escaping from political, religious, or economic oppressions and their corresponding attachment to liberty are at the very core of American individualism, which stresses the need to escape the threats of others and to overthrow social boundaries (Anderson 1971). To be sure, the continuous migrations, the immensity of the land, and the myth of the frontier have always encouraged an image of a self that moves easily through space and time. But American individualism (and implicit antifamilism) also has been fostered by an unbridled capitalism, which legitimates material self-interest and, later, satisfaction through consumption as a moral basis of society.

The American values of romantic subjectivism and rational calculation and the tensions between them shape American marriages in contradictory ways. For example, although single persons are inclined to consciously calculate their options within the marriage market, they still disdain prenuptial agreements, which they consider as crass and unbecoming to a supposedly total and spontaneous conjugal commitment. The very personalization of "commitment" as a subjective choice, however, renders it fragile. Moreover, subjective freedom also means a lack of social support and hence an ensuing increase of burdens on the conjugal union that may overwhelm both the romantic and the utilitarian intentions of the spouses. Thus, prenuptial decrees are less unpopular among candidates for a second marriage because experience has taught them that they need to protect the dependents of their earlier unions and that freedom may require more safeguards for the end than the beginning of their marriage. Meanwhile, the costs to children, if there are children, pile up (USDA 2000). American society has declining fertility rates and concomitant aging, and each new generation of families has little temporal continuity, security, or social support. Moreover, every indicator suggests that this situation will continue (Sweet and Bumpass 1987). Fewer younger people will be expected to support more older ones while receiving less support themselves.

The resolution of tensions between romantic subjectivism and rational calculation varies according to class, ethnic group, and gender. For example, while many Americans still marry partners who live close to their parents, such endogamy (whether residential, religious, ethnic, educational, or socioeconomic), has been most typical of persons located at the two opposite ends of the social spectrum, the highest and lowest classes (Mindel and Habenstein 1981). These two groups have the most at stake in marriage, either because of the wealth and power they hold and want to keep or because of the threats to which they are exposed. In these groups mobility through marriage, as in the films of Betty Grable or Mae West, is largely a myth. In contrast, those in between the high and the low have practiced exogamy as a reflection of their real and hoped-for status mobility. Even this tendency is variable by ethnicity and generation, however. For example, first-generation "NewYorRicans," despite jobs, greater resources, and broader residential options, nevertheless marry more often among themselves than those who have just arrived from Puerto Rico.

For "successful" men, social and psychological mobility has meant advancement through a career, with residence and matrimonial status serving more as symbols than as instruments of occupational mobility. Wives may be "trophies," markers more than means of advancement. In American bourgeois ideology, women, children, houses, and cars are part of the self-image that men have been expected to acquire and project as part of their occupational pursuits; the very existence, profile, and notably the dependence of these markers on the male have epitomized how well males have done in the world of work. Women were sexual or material objects for men; men were providers or status objects for women.

This system has required a strict separation between occupational and familial emotional investments, at least since the Industrial Revolution, when paid work for most persons was separated from home. Whereas work was for money and family was for love, most men made a greater investment in work. Since about 1970, however, both occupational and familial investments have become more labile within larger and more inclusive markets. Conversely, with telecommuting and other such arrangements, there has been a countermovement, among knowledge workers at least, of reconnecting the places of family and work. Yet these new arrangements may mean greater social isolation, as suggested by people increasingly shopping for both mates and jobs on the Internet. Indeed, with an increase in the population of singles and a decrease of neighborly and familial ways for people to meet, dating services, the Internet, and other new markets for meeting ideal others are expanding. And in comparison to the pre-AIDS bar culture, emotional intimacy (of a sort) on the Net is more likely to precede physical mingling. Similarly, serial monogamy suggests that successive spouses and children can be engaged or divested according to one's own market value and one's needs at successive stages of the life cycle.

For women, social and psychological mobility through careers has been obstructed by structural and cultural factors. Whereas the expression "Try everything at least once during your lifetime" had an occupational undertone for males, until recently it had a sexual one for females (Bellah et al. 1985). Because marriage was the main path to mobility for American females, as mythologized in such films as *The Solid Gold Cadillac* (1956, with Judy Holliday) or *How to Marry a Millionaire* (1953, with Marilyn Monroe), women more than men have sought to wed higher in class or ethnic hierarchies. Since social status for men increases sharply with financial success and hence usually with age, one side effect of this pattern was to strain relations between men and women of the same birth cohorts, as well as between successive generations of mothers and children. For example, sons and daughters of first marriages may be close in age to stepmothers of their fathers' later unions. Moreover, the matrimonial mobility of women through exogamy or remarriage continues to threaten the integrity of their families of both origin and destination. As a result, women have often been suspected of betraying their earlier families and unsettling their new ones. Accordingly, stepmothers have a much harder time in new marriages than stepfathers, especially as they are expected to be more engaged emotionally in the new familial unit. Popular media have documented the contradictory feelings and behaviors caused by female matrimonial mobility, but there has been no clear cultural vision that would help newly formed "mixed couples" to define themselves. Such conflicts are elided in the film *My Big Fat Greek Wedding* (2002), but only because the groom is totally absorbed in his new family and his parents are cyphers. Actual Cinderellas are as rare as the myth is benevolent, insofar as Cinderella is both happy with her prince and remains kind to her mother and sisters.

We have noted that as females enter the paid labor market and gain greater financial independence, their interests have shifted from issues of family loyalty toward those of career advancement. No longer so in need of providers, these women seek in their mates the qualities of companionship that might alleviate the pressures they experience on the job. In this sense, professional women are now akin to their male counterparts in treating the work and domestic lives as two separate compartments. Indeed, such women need less a providing husband than a nurturing wife or, almost as rare, an equal partner, day-care provider, and live-in maid.

As women entered the middle rungs of the labor market, advice to job seekers was modified accordingly: "Every woman for herself and no holds barred in the pursuit of male approval. . . . To be a pleaser and a charmer is not *selling out;* it is *investing* in happiness (yours). . . . If you can make a man (boss, client, employee) feel more masculine and confident because of the way you look at him when he talks, then do" (H. Brown 1982, 50; emphasis added). Here the moves of romantic subjectivism are subsumed under the rules of rational calculation. In the expanded labor marketplace, men and the ways to please them provide the opportunities for another sale or investment of the every-woman-for-herself road to success.

Despite tactics like those recommended by Helen Gurley Brown in *Cosmopolitan,* however, contradictions between the romantic ideals of femininity and the calculations of career weigh heavily on American women. At work they are expected to be both competitive and comely, aggressive yet deferential. They are both contenders and prizes in wars between the genders. And as the major actors of family socialization, they also are expected to nurture the family and manage tensions between the generations. These tensions also exist within the role of homemaker. That is, the family still expects the woman to be the housewife who cooks, cleans, and looks after the children, all while maintaining a youthful appearance and remaining sexually attractive to her husband. Most popular media reinforce this image, however different it may be from women's actual living arrangements. Yet some TV shows have responded to these changes: At the end of the series *Thirtysomething* in 1992, a main character who was well married left her husband to advance her career in New York, explaining that she just could not do the "family thing" any more (Bonner and DuGay 1992). At the same time, liberal feminism, with its focus on the individual woman and her advancement, is easily coopted by the media, as in the TV show about a postfeminist lawyer, *Ally McBeal.* In one episode, "Love Unlimited" (January 18, 1999), Ally is happily in love with a handsome doctor, Greg, only to sabotage her contentment by kissing an ex-boyfriend and thereby losing her current love. The lesson she learns seems to be that professional success and happiness in love do not mix (Dubrofsky n.d.), all because of her own ineptness.

The ethos of rational calculation and romantic subjectivism, of efficiency and love, of the "divorce culture" and the "marriage culture," also is distributed unequally by gender. This inequal distribution contributes to unequal power relations within marriage. To the extent that women in particular believe in traditional marital values, such as family, security, love, and romance, and view marriage as forever and divorce as a last resort, their husbands can "use the threat of divorce" to wield power. Women may be disempowered not only because they are loath to see their marriages end, but also because the social-scientific findings about how divorce hurts women have become part of our divorce-culture lore. As Karla Hackstaff (1999) points out, women who are "traditionalist" about marriage are less likely to share equal power with their husbands in the first place, so a culture of divorce ends up making that imbalance even more pronounced. She also notes that while most couples tended to espouse some form of gender egalitarianism, those who more fully embraced the tenets of the divorce culture—that is, those who saw marriage as contingent and optional with divorce being an option—were more able to create egalitarian marriages. "[These findings] seem to support feminist critiques of marriage. With little evidence that men are embracing the traditionally feminine domains of relationships and familial love, it would seem that the best way for women to achieve some measure of equality in their relationships with men would be to abandon the ideals of traditional marriage" (Hopper 2000, 849; see also Nock 1998).

The same principle holds in divorce or abandonment before marriage. Miss Havisham, in Dickens's *Great Expectations,* had been left at the altar many years before. She stopped the clocks, shut herself in the ruins of her nuptial hope, and trained the lovely Estella to take her revenge upon men. A contrasting, contemporary American version of Miss Havisham is Nicole Contos, whose intended husband took his honeymoon without her as she awaited him and their marriage in church. Instead of withdrawal, however, Ms. Contos actively sought media publicity for her trauma and turned her shame into triumph. Her broken dream was a ticket not to seclusion but to (momentary) stardom (Morrow 1997, 114).

The tensions between an ethos of rational calculation and romantic subjectivism also can be seen in American films and TV, which show how the search for the perfect mate has become less believable than formerly. The scariest scene in Alfred Hitchcock's *Vertigo* (1956) is when Kim Novak presents her remade self to Jimmy Stewart, who does not yet know that she is in fact the supposedly dead woman he loved. By scrupulously making her over, he thinks that he has bought a second chance at happiness when he really has doomed them both. The counterpoint assumption behind television sitcoms contemporaneous with *Vertigo,* such as *Father Knows Best* and *The Adventures of Ozzie and Harriet,* was that the husbands and wives were uniquely perfect for each other, which is why they married.

By contrast, the assumption behind current shows, like *Friends* and *Seinfeld,* as well as countless films, is that perfection is rare or only apparent and that changing partners is at least as normal as changing selves. The romantic illusion of perfection is waning, only to be supplanted by a new one—that the quest for romance can go on forever and is at least as satisfying and certainly more interesting than "settling down." "One of the final episodes of . . . *Seinfeld* revealed the sad consequences of this theory. Jerry Seinfeld, who is to antiromance what Don Quixote was to the real thing, is suddenly converted to the prospect of a permanent attachment when he meets Janeane Garofalo, who is, in every way but the anatomical, Seinfeld himself. Seinfeld immediately falls shallowly in love with himself, and is prepared to marry himself when the inevitable question arises: Who would marry someone like him?" (Rosenblatt 1996, 91). From *Vertigo,* where a man loves a woman and loses, to Seinfeld, where a man loves or despises himself too much and loses, we see the progress of romance in the late twentieth century. In both cases—loving too much an idealized image of the other or loving oneself too much—the contradictions between rational calculation and romantic subjectivism render intimacy and familial solidarity highly problematic.

Typically, as there is more anomie and confusion in the personal lifeworld, the capitalist market system enters to assist. In 1996, for example, the Disney Company launched its redesigned, multiply linked, interactive website, Family.com, joining the growing list of sites backed by such high-profile companies as Starwave, Time Warner, and Procter and Gamble. Such sites are attractive to corporations because they draw women—the minority on the Internet but usually in charge of the household budget. "Publishers with a steady female audience can find major advertisers willing to support the sites, which are still mostly free to users. Big corporations also get to showcase related products. For example, ParentTime, a new partnership between Time Warner and Procter and Gamble, incorporates content from family-oriented Time-Life books and such Time Warner publications as *Baby Talk* and *Time for Kids*" (*Newsweek,* December 16, 1996, 71; see also Steinberg and Kincheloe 1997).

The fusion of self-absorbed subjectivity and rational calculation of expected benefits against proposed investments is seen in other supposedly intimate areas of the lifeworld, including sexuality. For example, "the whole concept of 'perversion' has been changed. The words 'illegitimate' and 'perverted' now apply to orgasms obtained by an individual in an 'inegalitarian' relationship, particularly if achieved by force. As 'normality' means regarding one's body as a property of which one can 'dispose freely,' henceforward the standing form of perversion is rape, i.e. grabbing one's pleasure and breaking the rule of fair exchange" (Béjin 1985, 205). "So one finds oneself instructed to distance oneself from one's body by means of the mind, the better to coincide with the sensations that arise spontaneously in it, to be a spectator of the sexual act without ceasing to take part in it, to be overwhelmed by stimuli while at the same time activating them through the fantasies one has evoked oneself and mastered, expressing oneself 'spontaneously' in the course of actions which have to be programmed and controlled yet in the grip of external forces. One is expected to be ascetically hedonistic . . . to be both performer and spectator, to be spontaneous while never ceasing to program each step in one's behavior, to be independent yet conform with other people's norms," to be simultaneously egoistic and altruistic (Béjin 1985, 211–212). Likewise, though William Masters and Virginia Johnson's clinical therapy was mainly for couples, not individuals, Masters asserted that "A moment's reflection is enough to convince one that for the male, no less the female, orgasm is an entirely egocentric affair." That is, one should selfishly give to one's partner in order to get something for oneself in exchange (quoted in Béjin 1985, 211–212).

Another sign of the new egalitarianism and instrumentalization of sex is shifts in the meaning of the term "nymphomaniac," which today falls somewhere between a joke and a compliment, whereas formerly it was a term of extreme censure. At the same time, a new term, "sex addict," is applied censoriously, mostly to men, suggesting greater equality in the social disciplining of sexual conduct (Mead 2000, 148). Indeed, we may be returning to a pre-Victorian view of female lasciviousness. For example, women's magazines advocate "Six Guys to Do before You Say I Do" and advise on the best available vibrators on the market (Mead 2000, 148). Yet the older gender ideology persists, as seen in the film *Fatal Attraction,* in which an unmarried woman is portrayed as a violent threat to a traditional conjugal relationship after a brief affair with the "innocent" husband (Brittain 1989, 178–204).

Another example of the tension between sentiment and calculation is the case of Adam Nash, a Colorado infant and "first test-tube baby from an embryo screened and selected for implantation from among several competing embryos," in this instance to provide an umbilical cord with tissue for an ailing older sibling. The Nash family's decision prompts questions about the ethics of parents choosing their offspring's features as if they were options on a car. But even as the issue is debated, the practice is growing. More than three hundred in vitro fertilized babies already have been born in the United States with the help of the same genetic screening techniques. So far the instrumental goal has been to save an older sibling or to avoid extreme defects (Park 2000, 102). But why not create a child to save or improve a parent or simply to optimize one's utilities in the baby-making market? Because such medical procedures are quite expensive, class differences may come to be encoded in genes.

Such activities can be seen as an extension of the market system into the most personal spheres of the lifeworld. They also appear in the domestic outsourcing business, which offers to do what formerly were sentimental tasks and performs them better than parents could, even if parents had the time and desire to do them. Script 'n Scribble, a firm in the suburbs of Washington, D.C., will send care packages to a child at camp that look as if they came from his or her parents but in fact are designed and targeted to current kid tastes. The gifts prepared by the company's owner, Shana Collidge, "may not be personal but they are personalized: she'll put the child's name on stickers, notepads, stationery, photo albums" (Talbot 1997, 207). Such offerings go far beyond nannies or cleaning services, deep into the rarefied realms of personal organizers, professional family-meal planners, freelance educational advisers, children's birthday consultants, and play-group coordinators. Moreover, because such services are now available for an hourly fee, they are no longer out of the reach of the middle class. In fact, as noted, big corporations like Xerox, Hewlett-Packard, and Mariott offer on-site versions of some of these services—for example, personal shopping or dry cleaning—to all their employees at company headquarters. "It is hard to say, in the end, whether the new domestic services will enhance or further erode family life in the post-wife era. Certainly when corporations offer so many benefits—a nurse dispatched to your house to take care of a sick child, takeout meals 'home-cooked' at the employee cafeteria—the subtle effect is to undermine legitimate family-oriented excuses for limiting your hours at work" (Talbot 1997, 207).

Intimacy has become such a strenuous business partly because love, family, and parenthood are increasingly organized by and around the market, as Beck and Gernsheim-Beck (1995) have noted. But a market-oriented life is difficult to sustain. For one thing, tradition becomes less useful as a guide to conduct as the market requires greater time and psychic investments and as our social moorings in community and kin decrease. Intimacy in a primary love relationship promises to relieve us from these demands and tensions, "but the same forces that make intimacy a much needed substitute for the fading community and tradition also make intimacy an ever more elusive goal. Because the individual engineered by the welfare state and the market is called upon to 'stage manage' her biography and to compulsively plan her moves," she must turn herself into the calculating center of her life plan (Illouz 1997b, 79). Such willful forces that drive people to seek intimacy are also those that undermine it. Thus intimacy calculation can make intimate relationships the "battlefield on which daily wars are waged over an equal sharing of domestic chores, geographical relocations, and child care. From this basic tension evolves the new and 'normal chaos of love': We must achieve separation yet strive for intimacy, we have an ever-growing need of true emotions, yet the market dictates that we protect our self-interest and be competitive. Love for children is supposed to consolidate intimacy, yet it pulls us farther apart as it drains all of our energy and leaves little to share with our partner" (Illouz 1997b, 79).

This "normal chaos of love" was ushered in by women's massive (re)entry into the paid labor force and their claim to equality, which have marked the crumbling of the castelike gender relationships of an earlier industrial capitalism. Women are no longer vassals in the domestic sphere. The gender hierarchy of the capitalist economy is laid bare, and the contradictions between the nuclear family, on the one hand, and the market and the welfare state, on the other, are revealed. Yet in the effort to overcome these contradictions through a free and equal love, no relationship of intimacy—whether parenthood, sex, or marriage—can any more be taken for granted. Gender roles and identity are constantly negotiated and always up for grabs. Parenthood and family are no longer predicated on biology and marriage respectively, thus allowing for more fluid and improvised varieties of relationships. This incertitude and chaos have become "normal" insofar as the market demands that men and women alike be independent, economic earners, and calculators, thus turning the family into one more domain of bargaining and contention, a new lifestyle arena of individualized interests and options. Romantic subjectivism thus erects a new divinity that we worship but that can give us little reward. "Love has become our private god, yet the majestic divinity quickly crumbles under the daily struggles fought in our kitchens and bedrooms" (Illouz 1997b, 79).

Intimacy and equality are likely to remain elusive goals as long as the classic nuclear family remains at the heart of our vision of intimacy and as long as we do not restrict the penetration of the market. This issue is much more than a matter of who cleans the toilet or carries out the garbage. Instead, it implies a complete rethinking of the institutions that have been tailored to cater to the diminishing nuclear family. At the same time, the dual-income marriage is the royal road to middle-class social mobility and in that respect may often unite economic interests and intimacy. In other words, the market *also* can bring people together, especially those persons who are more marginal and vulnerable in

American society. Thus the circumstance that generates a centrifugal range of choices available to more privileged members of society can have a centripetal effect on those who live their lives in terms of necessity more than choice. It is true that women's claim to equality raises historically unprecedented challenges to the family. But these challenges intersect with, rather than subvert from within, the still formidable inequalities of cultural, social, and economic resources.

In sum, the mass uniformity, market segmentation, and individual mobility of late capitalism help to explain how both romantic subjectivism and rational calculation affect current relations among and within families. The very notion of subjectivity ceases to refer to the actions of persons who resist being treated as objects. Rather, subjectivity has become synonymous with the ephemeral and the particular and the unreliability of personal tastes. Such a reduction renders romantic subjectivism far from the individualism that Thoreau thought indispensable to democracy. Instead contemporary subjectivism, or even cultural rebellion, becomes harmless to the system insofar as it is now expressed through consumer choices among prepackaged images of different personas, products, or services that the system is able to provide.

CHANGING CONFLICTS BETWEEN GENDERS

We noted that romantic love became a central ingredient of marital unions in the United States only in the twentieth century. With it, little by little, the body emerged as the site of sensual pleasure, accompanied by a culture of eroticism and a science of sexual pathology, usually with men as the agents and women as the objects. Sex came to be viewed as a domain or expression of love that both legitimated and elevated carnal joy. In the post–World War II period, especially since the 1960s and the advent of the contraceptive pill, this linkage of sex to love weakened among younger persons as sex in itself was validated as a form of pleasure, expression, and discovery. With the deromanticization of femininity and the assertion of "rights" to orgasm, the romantic and the erotic aspects were separated further (Maines 1999; Ericksen and Steffen 1999).

These changes generated new tensions concerning sex, love, and marriage and different gender codes for each of them. Many of these tensions are highly visible in the American institution of "dating" since about 1955, when it moved from the front porch to the back seat but had not yet arrived at the Internet (Bailey 1988; Dillon 1997). Functionalist writers have described relations between male and female adolescents or young adults as anticipatory socialization, a preparation for adult roles. But such writers rarely note that both the practices and feelings of dating have reflected the same intrusion of capitalism in the personal and cultural sphere that we have sketched above (Wallard 1937; see also Bailey 1988). For males, the winning market strategy in dating was to offer minimal material or symbolic favors in exchange for maximal sexual privileges. For females, it was the opposite: they were to concede as little sex as possible in exchange for maximal material or symbolic rewards. In caricatured terms, the male ideal implied by dating was the rapist or trickster, who takes sex while giving nothing of value in exchange. The ideal female was frigid or chaste; she seduced in order to reject, in the process receiving gifts and proposals of marriage.

The institution of dating served two functions simultaneously. It enabled young men and women to evaluate their market moves in relation to the supply of goods they were interested in obtaining. It also enabled them to rank themselves in the hierarchy of their own genders. Like the stock market, dating was a cultural world that shaped the expectations and practices of individual investors and institutionalized the terms of their exchanges. The verbal form, dating, and its distinction from the nominative concept of appointment, hinted at the challenges underlying the seemingly informal encounter between two persons. To say "I have a date with Jean (or Jack)" not only announced one's position in the status ranking within the genders, but it also made public that one's date was the target of specific strategies in the sexual (male) or marital (female) markets. Similarly, the terms "coffee date," "blind date," or "double date" evoked the limited investments to be made in the transaction and also the windfall profits that might occur. Finally, vocabularies surrounding "putting out" defined explicit differences among "necking," "petting," "heavy petting," and "going all the way," and each could then be compared with dollar costs of the date, thereby clarifying the comparative values exchanged.

As Fleming and Fleming put it, "After kissing came touching. First we'd touch through the clothes. You'd let a boy hold your ribs and maybe his thumb would be touching the edge of your breasts and you'd think, 'Well, okay, tonight I'll let him.' Then the next night his hand would go higher. When he reached your nipple you knew you had to make a decision. He'd either have to stop and start all over again at the ribs, or the next thing was to lift the shirt up and let him work through your bra" (1975, 182–183). Female adolescents adopted ground rules concerning how far tactile foreplay might go, offering in effect an implicit road map of their bodies, with "Road Closed" and "Detour" clearly indicated, though the signpost could change on subsequent journeys.

Male adolescents tried to stretch these rules as far as possible and often de-scribed their progress in terms of sports metaphors (getting to first base, second base, a home run, etc.) Much of this behavior continues, of course, though it now begins at younger ages than formerly. Adolescents still often work after school, boys to pay for a car (a key instrument of sexual action), girl to pay for clothes (crucial equipment of allure).

Dating was structured not only by its own internal codes, but also by its in-stitutional contexts. For example, insofar as much dating was and remains a fix-ture of American campuses, its rituals are both stimulated and thwarted by academic regulations and such concepts as "in loco parentis" or "parietals." University authorities used to, and some are beginning again, to restrict the hours during which persons of opposite genders were allowed to visit, the per-missible deployment of bodies during these visits, the degree to which doors of students' bedrooms might be shut, or the minimal number of feet to remain on the floor. At the same time, university administrators sponsor both organiza-tions (like fraternities and sororities) and rituals (like homecomings) most likely to stimulate the dating-rating system.

One consequence of this style of social interaction for women was that both autoeroticism and frigidity became appropriate market tactics, with some girls turning to obesity to exit the system. By reducing the overt expression of "need" for heterosexual sex, these tactics allowed young women to bargain more effec-tively and to maximize their own gains vis-à-vis both their partners and other girls. Of course, these strategies had costs, such as anorexia or bulimia, which can be understood as ways to resist the use of one's body as an object of calcu-lated market speculation and, indeed, to become aggressively asexual and with-draw from the dating-rating system (Blumberg 1988). For example, in Philippe Labro's novel, *The Foreign Student,* the main female character finally has to be resocialized by her parents, who remind her of the matrimonial dividends to which they feel entitled because of the sacrifices they made for her education.

Contradictory messages were and still are part of female socialization in America. Girls are taught to strive and achieve but generally not beyond what is appropriate "for a girl." Rubin notes that "such parental and social ambivalence leaves its mark, producing women who are cleft in two—torn between the in-tellectual and intuitive parts of self, between the need to achieve in the larger worlds and the need for human relatedness" (1981, 49). These experiences leave achieving women with "two selves," one for the world of work and a contradic-tory one for the world of family. It may be that identity ambivalence of this kind is experienced more deeply by women than by men, but as male gender roles change to include stronger norms of sensitivity and nurturance, establishing a consistent male identity also becomes more difficult (Weigert and Frank n.d., 16).

In short, the very institution of dating has marked the difficulties of developing intimate relations between the two genders. In socializing young men and women to the instrumental or manipulative roles expected of them throughout their lives, it has not prepared them to share feelings and obtain emotional support from one another. Thus "The Little Pub," a short story by Patricia Zelver, evokes the loneliness of the wife of an upwardly and geographically mobile corporate executive; she cannot get committed to any kind of cause and falls prey to boredom and vacuity, with their accompanying symptoms. In its own ways, dating has been a preparation to this type of psychological destruction, not only because it has preceded logically and chronologically the sharp gender segregation of domestic roles, but also because it has limited the psychological worth of participants to their exchange value in a market.

The animality of the male was supposed to be transformed into a caring commitment by the affection and the ongoing relationship leading to marriage that would ideally accompany the act of intercourse (Nock 1998). Passion was always associated with violence, domination, loss of the will, hunger—animal characteristics. Since men are animals, or at least more animalistic, they need sex more than women, whose basic instincts are to nurture. Yet women are potentially more animalistic than men, which is why they need to be controlled. Thus women who enjoy sex are "wildcats" or "savage beasts," or at least "foxes"—bad girls suitable for fun but not for marriage (Brienes 1992; Groneman 2000). At the same time, sexual sharing in marriage, especially in its early period, was thought to express and cement bonds of love, though older persons were thought to need and want sex less or not at all. The wife should be a virgin and the husband, more experienced, should be an authoritative guide and teacher mediating between his wife and the outside world, even in bed. During the honeymoon the newlyweds should "get used to each other" sexually until "the honeymoon is over," and sex and its mysteries are pushed aside by more practical matters. All these images were represented in media and conversations of postwar American culture. As Lowery and Defleur put it, "The movies taught a generation of males how to light a cigarette in a 'manly' manner, how to tip one's hat to a lady in a gallant way, or how to offer one's arm properly. They taught girls how to purse their lips coyly; how to lower their eyelids enticingly; how to sit gracefully; or how to shed a dainty tear for maximum effect" (1995, 36). Although this ideology lingers, it has faded somewhat (and moved to younger age cohorts) with the emergence of other options and the decline of dating and, indeed, of honeymoons as institutions. Today there is more financial and sexual equality of the genders, women more frequently are willing to pay for their share of an outing *and* enjoy sex, more people live together, and most people sleep together before marriage. Indeed, it now can be asked whether extramarital loves are a sign of confident autonomy or conjugal betrayal.

Today young people not only date, but also hang out together as friends, lovers, or crews. As women's economic autonomy undermines the dyads of both work versus home and male versus female, there also emerges a new area of freedom and affirmation for women and self-reflection and potential renewal for men. One sees this in shifts of attitudes toward sexuality, particularly homosexuality, pornography, and adultery, although they remain deeply grounded in structural variables (for example, Klassen, Williams, and Levitt 1989; Pallone 2002; Dank and Refinetti 1999). Before the AIDS epidemic, there was a legitimation of open marriage, swinging, and, hence, a relative devaluation of exclusive domestic intimacy. Experts of the time warned that guilt inhibited sexual pleasure, argued the relative merits of clitoral versus vaginal orgasm, provided norms concerning their optimal frequency, and offered techniques designed to improve the participants' performance.

Yet change has not necessarily improved relations between the genders. As courting behavior declines, so does the distinction between friends and lovers, causing new stresses and role conflicts in relations. As noted, the ambiguous category of "informal cohabitation" itself suggests a blurring of gender roles. Moreover, questions such as "Who pays?" or "Will she (or he) put out?" have become fraught with ambiguity and, hence, may be greater potential sources of conflict than the formal rules, which, though restrictive, were fairly clear. As shown in the film, *When Harry Met Sally* (1989), friendship between men and women is still a terrain of struggle between older values of courtship and newer ones of gender equality.

Conflicts, fears, and aspirations about class are a taboo subject in America and so often get coded by gender, thereby generating sociostructurally driven conflicts between men and women (Ortner 1991). Working-class persons, for example, tend to categorize their own members as middle class or lower class—that is, "respectable" or "bums" (Hannerz 1969, 34–35, 97–99); "college boys" or "streetcorner boys" (Whyte 1943); "routine seekers" or "action seekers" (Gans 1962), and the like. Such categories within the working class are also coded by gender, with women holding or seeking respectable or middle-class identities and status and men identifying themselves, in their maleness, with the action seekers, which are seen by working-class women as dangerously lower class.

This coding is clearly related to the world of work. Working-class women's jobs are in the office—clean, closer to management, with separate lunch areas and bathrooms. Working-class men more often are in the factory or yard. Their work is physical, sweaty, more removed from the bosses, and sometimes dangerous. Thus working-class male identities are often tied to the "manliness" of their (increasingly scarce) labor and to the men or the "mates" with whom they work. Yet this male identity and culture is seen as threatening by working-class women, especially those with strong aspirations to join the middle class. It is only through marriage to a "good girl" that the working-class male can be "saved" from his wayward (and manly) ways. This comes at a cost. Not only must he at least partly abandon his pals, but he also is faced with his wife's emotional and status expectations, which he is most unlikely to be able to fulfill. Middle-class jobs are largely unavailable to persons of his competencies and limited educational credentials, and his wife's expectations of feminized love are almost sure to be beyond his emotional range and a threat to him as a man. Hence, the displacement of class relations onto gender relations breeds conflict and tensions between men and women, especially for members of the working class.

Continuing intergender conflicts also are suggested in the frequency of both practices and charges of sexual harassment and perhaps more dramatically in the lack of consensus on the meaning of the term and its ethical connotation. "Date rape" has a similar ambiguity. The fact that colleges and corporations publish manuals devoted to sexual harassment out of fear of legal action reflects not only the increased power of women, but also the growing amorality of gender relations—amorality rather than immorality, since such publications imply that their readers do not know what is proper or improper and that for the sponsoring institutions morality is merely a legal or instrumental problem. Indeed, the official policy goal of a "gender-neutral workplace" is a way of negating difference. Even today, American feminists have little positive to say about the nurturance of intimacy between the genders. Instead, some feminists seek to create sex-blind macroeconomic policies that would make the fate of women a variant of the fate of workers in general. Bizarrely, many women today are like most men were in the 1950s. Their issues often are ones of money and power, whereas many men today focus more than before on feelings and relationships. Thus new gender choices have emerged that are broader than the prior ones yet not altogether heartening. At the extreme, for women the choice is to be an empty-headed housewife or an empty-hearted professional; for men it is to be macho or a wimp (Font and Tantillo 1993; Faludi 1999). None of these choices is realistic in practice or necessarily more satisfactory than the older, more rigid gender roles and presumptions.

The temporal dimension of paired gender conceptions from the 1950s to the 1990s was displayed in American television and film. One of the strongest representations of the dangers of female independence was *Sunset Boulevard* (1950), whose protagonist, Norma Desmond, played by Gloria Swanson, is a faded silent screen star whose insistent devotion to a career leads her to maniacal homicide. As Stanford Lyman points out,

> [Actresses such as] Joan Crawford, Olivia de Haviland, Rosalind Russell and Ginger Rogers [also] portrayed professional career-oriented women, and were depicted as less than women, as willful or pathological opponents of the received cultural imperative that a man should be both husband and provider. No matter how successful or how independent, these films argue, a woman cannot be truly happy, cannot achieve a wholesome female existence, without a man, love, marriage, and family. In *Lady in the Dark* (1944), Ginger Rogers portrays a successful fashion editor whose aspiration for an independent career is professionally diagnosed as a symptom of mental illness. Troubled by nightmares that psychotherapy ultimately reveals to be the after-effects of an unhappy childhood, Rogers' character seeks help from a male analyst who redefines her careerism as an unhealthy compensatory device:
>
> PSYCHOANALYST. You've had to prove you were superior to all men; you had to dominate them.
>
> CHARACTER. What's the answer?
>
> PSYCHOANALYST. Perhaps some man who'll dominate you (1987, 79–81).

At the same time that women are shown to ideally submit to the husband/provider, the world of the husband is shown to pitilessly grind him down, reducing his masculine independence to a mere cog in the mechanism of commerce. In these representations, things have not changed much since Henry James's *The Bostonians* (1886), in which the feminist lion becomes the wifely mouse, or Charlotte Gilman's *The Yellow Wallpaper* (1899), in which a wife's efforts to be a writer are diagnosed by her doctor/husband as the symptoms of a derangement that they finally become.

American films of the 1950s also depict men as solitary wanderers, whether pioneers, warriors, or cops or "in the company of other men equally dedicated to the male life. From this point of view, women occupy an ambiguous place in a man's life. They need defense, deserve respect, give comfort—but they expect marriage. Thus, women are necessary for a man's ego and sexual demands, but insufficient to satisfy his basic needs. More to the point, the good woman, precisely because she demands marriage, threatens to destroy once and for all men's basic source of masculinity—the free, roving, irresponsible life. The battle between the sexes is also, then, a struggle within each of them over which principle—the free masculine or the fettered feminine—will triumph and how it will do so" (Lyman 1987, 85–86). In most Westerns (now a passé genre), the masculine principle wins. The hero resists the will of other strong men, but he resists as well the domestication of his will that marriage would entail. And so he rides off like Shane or the Lone Ranger to his next lonely (or homoerotic) adventure.

Other films of the period represented these opposing principles in the hero's love of both a good (marriageable) girl and a bad (independent, adventuresome) one, with the hero finally choosing the good girl and sealing his presumably happy fate with a conjugal rather than passionate kiss. For many men and women today, the good girls of yesterday seem silly and insipid, however seductively and asexually sweet. By the 1970s and 1980s, screen heroines often sought passionate romance *and* careers of their own, thus relocating the battle between two women for the heart of a man to open warfare between the genders. This shift is portrayed in *Kramer vs. Kramer* (1979), *Ordinary People* (1980), and *The War of the Roses* (1989). Mrs. Kramer (Meryl Streep) chooses to abandon her son in pursuit of a career that, by the end of the film, is more successful than her husband's, whereas the husband becomes a sweeter person with a lesser career. Less benignly, in *The War of the Roses* Mr. and Mrs. Rose, in the process of divorcing, end up killing each other.

Parallel dramas play out in the political theater of Washington. Mrs. Clinton was long attacked for signs of autonomy such as using her premarital name, Rodham, but was later forgiven by some antifeminists because she stood by her man during the Lewinsky scandal and impeachment hearings. Now a senator from New York, still married, apparently a good mother, and emerging as one of the shrewdest players in the Senate, Hillary Clinton may become an icon of a new gender type. Similarly there are new images of female warriors—television heroines such as Xena or karate queens like Michelle Yee. Even the independent "material girl," Madonna—despite her recent foray into motherhood and marriage—exemplifies this aggressive, independent image. Even when successfully adapted, however, new gender ideals are ambiguous and amorphous. For example, although women have enacted real changes in gender practices and their emotional and normative meanings, have claimed more choices, and have validated female sexual pleasure, they still participate in the beauty and sex systems that merchandise their bodies and erotic affect in the markets for status, career, and marriage. Similarly, though men can now more easily experience and display a wider range of emotions, including tender and romantic ones, these often are mixed with or subordinated to an orientation favoring dominance, performance, and instrumental control (Seidman 1987, 721).

Another expression of new ambiguities about gender is the emergence of more than two of them. In addition to male and female, there now are also straight, gay, bisexual, and transsexual varieties, plus other groups that advance alternative sexual identities and protest that they are misrepresented or excluded from both the heterosexual hegemony and the gay and lesbian alliance. Indeed, sex roles in America have become so labile that the question asked of children, "What do you want to be when you grow up?" can now include sexual orientations. Even "straight" men are becoming more androgynous as economically more independent women desire them for love, sex, or companionship. Her shopping for furnishings is now his consumerism of sports gear; her wonder bra is now his gym-enhanced pecs; her silicone, his steroids; her earrings, his earring (Connell 1995; Faludi 1999).

Many of these new choices and confusions can be interpreted in terms of the intrusion of late capitalism into the most intimate spheres of life. For example, postmodern capitalism assigns greater value to consumption and redefines marriage from a way of life into a lifestyle. Men now consume gadgets and gear like women buy clothes, and both do so more for themselves than, as formerly, for their families. This loosens roles that formerly were more strictly coded by gender, thereby rendering gender roles more porous. Such rejections of fixed roles and standards challenge people to discover or impose meanings on quotidian yet protean situations, even as they inflate the demands on the self to be all things to everyone and hence nothing in particular to anyone.

The increased participation of women in the paid labor force also represents an extention of the capitalist ethos into the family sphere and the shift of domestic life from private into public forms. Not only has cooking by women been branded by some as a symbol of male oppression, but also there has been a corollary increase in the use of commercial fast-food and other eating facilities by families with small children (Burros 1988). Food preparation and housework are not the only familial functions to have shifted, however selectively, from private to public forms. The same holds true of leisure, which often entails public spectacles or purchased entertainment, as when commercial firms are contracted to organize reunions of extended families or alumni classes. Even romance is linked to consumption, as in a candlelit dinner at a fine restaurant, a love weekend at a country bed and breakfast inn, or honeymoon or anniversary vacation in Aruba (Illouz 1997a). It is thus harder to know whether vacations are a form of pleasure or a new kind of work or whether eating out is a public celebration or merely a substitute for the domestic labor of cooking at home.

From the romantic subjectivist viewpoint, marriage and divorce are purely personal choices. By contrast, in preceding periods the legal definition of marriage as a social institution required couples who wished to divorce to justify their separation in terms of the values and interests of the larger community. Starting with California, however, a number of states enacted no-fault divorce laws that allowed either spouse to leave a marriage at his or her discretion, regardless of the partner's or anyone else's wishes. While no-fault divorce is often seen as an advance of subjective freedom in the pursuit of personal happiness, it can also be viewed as a triumph of system rationalization since it improves administrative speed and efficiency at lower costs. Moreover, it appears as another invasion of old and new forms of capitalism into the private sphere. In the same way that employers can peremptorily fire workers who generate insufficient surplus value, divorcing spouses are now entitled to reject their partners as redundant. Indeed, the very term "no-fault divorce" construes marriage to be like a morally neutral car accident from which all parties may walk away uninjured, or at least unblamed. Just as the freedom of employers was not restricted by the costs of their decisions about rejected workers, so new divorce laws have modified alimony as having been unduly punitive, thereby sparing the economically dominant (usually male) spouse from responsibility for the sudden impoverishment of the former partner. In the same way that laws encourage retraining programs for displaced workers, recent divorce laws specify that the indemnities paid to separating spouses are temporary and contingent on their preparation for a new occupational role. Finally, while the new laws favor the splitting of conjugal property, divorcing couples often have little to divide but their debts, since the consumer culture discourages saving and favors spending on credit (Weitzman 1985). The unjust effects of such legislation have been masked by ideologies of both rationality and subjectivism, as well as an emphasis on due process and the contract laws of the late nineteenth century. The result is that most of the burdens and risks inherent in conjugal relations are allocated to the weakest parties, usually children and women.

TENSIONS IN RELATIONS AMONG
GENERATIONS

The conflicts between ideological orientations that stress rational calculation and those that emphasize romantic subjectivism also affect bonds between the generations (Bengtson and Achenbaum 1993). At the macro level, functionalist theorists have castigated the extended family as dysfunctional to modern economic growth. In such a perspective, the privations of the working class are seen as caused by their failure to limit the number of their children and to relinquish ties with siblings and parents in favor of individual occupational and status mobility. The American Dream was expected to be inward-oriented, and little was said about class inequalities; collective action for group mobility; or the restraints imposed on individual advancement by patriarchy, racism, or the overall structure of occupations. In this functionalist view, the fulfillment of the American Dream required few children, a full-time homemaker, and the abandonment of one's family of origin. Likewise, the misfortunes of lower classes and minorities (and of so-called underdeveloped societies abroad) were attributed implicitly to their women, who reproduced their cultures of poverty directly through their bodies and indirectly through their ways of child rearing and their unsevered links with their extended kin.

Whatever it did explain, this perspective left out a lot. For example, "fictive kin" bound African Americans together in resistance to both the institution of slavery and, later, discrimination, and such bonds made the formation of "normal families" extremely difficult. Arrangements in which grandmothers or aunts often were central were criticized as "too familistic," even though they supported both family and community life. The lack of social progress of such marginalized groups was then attributed to a culture of poverty that kept them tied, however dysfunctionally, to large, intergenerational families rather than to values and family forms that could foster individual advancement.

Other models of appropriate child rearing carry different ideological loads. For example, American mothers have been expected to develop independence in their children, but the recommended length of breast feeding has varied with shifts in the theories concerning the links among maternal bonds, children's independence, the nature of "independence" and "emotional growth" themselves, and their relation, if any, to suckling. These shifts have been linked to parallel changes in the aesthetic and sexual appreciation of large, small, soft, or hard breasts and, more generally, to shifts in the social and economic status of women. For example, Marilyn Monroe, the sex goddess of the 1960s, would be too plump to make it in movies today. The ideal female body for many is now shaped by workouts, preferably supervised by a personal trainer, but still with an ample bosom. This shape seems to appeal both to many women, for whom in-shape athleticism is a sign of independence, and to many men, whose fear of independent women is assuaged by an androgynously slim body with reassuringly maternal breasts. Similarly, the supposedly negative effect of maternal employment on child development may have had less to do with the loneliness of the child than with ideological efforts to limit the occupational aspirations of women and to reassure threatened patriarchal men.

In short, bonds between American mothers and children are continuously subjected to two distinct but simultaneous attacks. Positivist ideologies that emphasize rationality and individual achievement have marginalized such bonds (Burkett 2000), whereas romantic subjectivism has underscored their importance. The result is that intimacy between generations is highly problematic—first, because the dominant positivist language of rationality and calculated achievement omits or dismisses subjective emotional life and, second, because the stress on individual self-interest invalidates affective commitments, whatever they are, and particularly feelings of altruism and dependence that are central to parent-child relations. The overt discourse that emphasizes the need to stimulate children's independence clashes with the desire to nurture our young. Often this conflict is resolved by using parental love and approval instrumentally, as an incentive or payment for children's achievement.

In effect, we have official pieties about two opposed principles—love and success, or familial solidarity and personal independence. The first is expressed in right- and left-wing ideologies of family values or community; the second is exploited by consumer capitalism and advanced by its neoliberal and libertarian ideologies. Thus one can simultaneously decry the use of nursing homes as storage bins for the aged and applaud the success of retirement communities, whose inmates indulge in voluntary age segregation. One can condemn the phenomenon of latchkey children but celebrate two-career marriages. In the midst of this value confusion, the lonely crowd often begins at home.

Extreme subjectivism also lessens the need for intersubjective confirmations of experiences and perceptions and thereby contributes to the reality anemia of postmodern society. This tends to lower barriers among fantasies, phantasms, and actual experience of family life. Thus it is difficult to determine how much the rise in reported incidents of domestic violence, molestation, and incest reflects an increase in their occurrence, an increase in the rates of reporting, or a more subtle blurring of experience with individual or collective imaginations.

To what extent does rising spousal violence reflect new resentments caused by the declining rewards from new or lost careers, new status competition between spouses, or frustrations caused by social mobility or the lack of it? Does increased reported domestic molestation correspond to a general moral numbness associated with the diffusion of narcissism, the turmoil caused by the demise of traditional forms of patriarchy, or the increased circulation of psychoanalytical myths in the population at large that enables real or imaginary victims to impute their real or imaginary shortcomings to real or imaginary aggressors? Or could all these be characteristic responses to an age of both liberation and narcissism?

Reality anemia and the exaltation of feelings also make it difficult to distinguish between the frequency of incestuous practices as opposed to incestuous fantasies or "recovered memories." The diffusion of Freudian ideology also makes it easier to impute one's own failings to childhood traumas caused by parental pathologies. Thus, it often is unclear whether children (or "adult children") who report having been abused by their fathers or teachers recount a true experience, the product of their own imaginations, or the coaching of a therapist or parent. The reverse also is true: deeply held personal feelings are less connected to publicly verifiable experience. Indeed, as the separation of Woody Allen and Mia Farrow and the sentimental adventures of Michael Jackson attest, such personal feelings may become transformed into vicariously available public spectacles. In sum, we know little of the extent to which the reports and the effects of the seduction of children by parents derive from corporal intercourse or are generated by symbolic interaction or psychic intra-action.

Another factor contributing to incomprehension or confusion between parents and children is the "postrevolutionary" sexuality of twenty-first-century children. Television, advertising, and the Internet have made the secrets of adulthood available to children, and their carnal awareness has little in common with the earnest or joyous liberating sexual ideology or experience of their parents. "Parents can search all they want for common ground with today's kids, trying to draw parallels between contemporary carnal knowledge and an earlier generation's free-love crusades, but the two movements are quite different. A desire to break out of the old-fashioned strictures fueled the '60s movement, and its participants made sexual freedom a kind of new religion. That sort of reverence has been replaced by a more consumerist attitude. In a 1972 cover story, *Time* declared, 'Teenagers generally are woefully ignorant about sex.' Ignorance is no longer the rule. As a weary junior high counselor in Salt Lake City puts it, 'Teens today are almost nonchalant about sex. It's like we've been to the moon too many times'" (*Newsweek,* March 25, 2002). With this, sex increasingly is assumed to be engageable without emotional consequences. At age fifteen, nearly 50 percent of girls have had intercourse at least once; for eighteen-year olds the figure is 70 percent.

Later in the life cycle, the joint effects of personal freedom and market calculation allow parents and children to disengage from one another in the same way that spouses uncouple from unwanted partners. A child may be treated like a much-loved but dispensable or replaceable pet, a mere extension of, or vehicle for, the changing needs or feelings of its owners. Similarly, many adult children consign older relatives to the aging crowd of nursing homes. In reciprocation, one sees elderly parents in fine cars with bumper stickers gleefully announcing, "I am spending my kids' inheritance!" (Rosenfeld 1979). Financial advisers help rich clients not only to avoid inheritance taxes, but also to reduce their estates by spending more now for their own pleasure. To die broke and leave nothing to one's offspring increasingly is an option for estate planning. Half the adult children with parents who die after the age of seventy inherit zero. Parents are living longer, with more health expenses, and the first thing to go is bequests to children. These developments dramatize a weakening of intergenerational commitments.

The shift in power to younger generations is especially hard for baby boomers, those born in the decade after 1945 who are now entering middle age—about seventy-six million by most counts, not including eight million immigrants of this age cohort. This has been a self-absorbed and entitled generation that has defined itself not through sacrifice (as its parents had), but through indulgence. Boomers still are a potent group, effecting changes at every turn in the way Americans think and act. When they smoked dope, its possession was decriminalized or soft-pedaled; when they protested the Vietnam War, the country changed its policies; when their incomes increased and their lives settled, menus that previously included only the basics began to diversify and mention fat content. But now their careers have likely hit a brick wall. They have not saved enough, their pensions are underfunded, their health is deteriorating, and their political power is waning. Boomers also are unprepared for retirement. "They don't hold nearly as much stock as their parents do, and . . . they saved for retirement much less conscientiously than their Gen X counterparts are doing today. As a result, a full 40% of boomers, and 30% of those nearest to retirement, have less than $10,000 in personal savings. That's more than 30 million people who are no better prepared for retirement than they are for a couple of weeks with the family at Disneyworld" (Okrent 2000, 68–74).

The size of the boomer generation, its relative lack of savings and increasing need for care, and the tendency of the elderly to vote in greater percentages than any other age group are likely to converge to create extreme intergenerational conflicts. For example, since it costs between $35,000 and $50,000 a year to support one person in a nursing facility, middle-aged boomers increasingly have to choose between caring for their children or their parents. Divorce also has consequences on the comity or tensions among the generations. Formerly, when divorce statistics first began to rise, many Americans comforted themselves with the belief that parents and children shared the same interests and that a child in an unhappy home would surely suffer from it. What was right for parents—including divorce—was right for children. But today that seems to be a self-serving myth. For example, Wallerstein, Lewis, and Blakeslee (2000) find that today one-quarter of all adults under the age of forty-four come from divorced homes, and for many of them divorce was and remains a life-transforming event. "The myth that if the parents have a poor marriage the children are going to be unhappy is not true," they say bluntly. Either way—a glass half empty (Wallerstein, Lewis, and Blakeslee) or three-quarters full (Hetherington 2002), a good enough marriage, a marriage without violence or martyrdom or severe disorder will do for the children. Thus divorce remains the collision point between our belief in the pursuit of happiness and our desire to protect children, another unresolved legacy passed to the next generation (Goodman 2000, A21; see also Hareven 1996).

Many of the conflicts between parents and children are greater for the middle class, both because the economic consequences of divorce are not as great for them as for working- or lower-class persons and because class tensions *within* the middle class often play out between parents and children, particularly between parents' fear that they or their children will descend into the working class and childrens' typical desire to live more in the now. Thus the "class struggle" that goes on between working-class men and women plays out intergenerationally between middle-class parents and children. Will the children reproduce the class position that they have been given by achieving through education, choosing and making the right career, and selecting the right mate? Enormous pressures are placed on middle-class children to comply with their parents' demanding expectations, pressures that they resist through displays of green hair, dating downward, smashing daddy's car, getting pregnant, or a liking for working- or lower-class music and other cultural items. By contrast, working-class parents generally do not attempt to impose such controls, nor do they expect their children to invest years of monklike behavior in professional training and apprenticeship.

The current travails of the American family originate in two distinct forces. In the short term, they reflect structural shifts toward postmodern capitalism—to wit, changes in employment opportunities and economic constraints on different family members according to their age, gender, and marital status. These short-term effects are amplified by longer-term tensions between rational calculations made to adapt to and reproduce the system and the romantic subjectivism involved in resisting or withdrawing from it. Yet these tensions are themselves shifting as the system enters more deeply into the lifeworld and as subjectivity itself is increasingly defined instrumentally in terms of lifestyles and consumption.

Advanced capitalism has brought economies of scale and high turnover to producers, even while providing sufficient differentiation to satisfy the symbolic requirements of social stratification for citizens to become consumers. Goods and services in the consumer economy are marketed to highly specified social groups, each of which marks its identity and status with different styles of consumption that, like higher status itself, are increasingly based on waste and obsolescence.

The ethos of consumerism may encourage either passivity or innovation, as long as these are expressed through purchasing goods or services. But this ethos also fosters invidious comparisons among families and within the family itself. For example, children, men, and women are segmented into discrete markets, as though they were completely autonomous of each other and constantly evolving in different directions. As families have fewer meals together, home refrigerators or the local Roy Rogers have become the privileged places for eating alone or with peers. Parents and children may even avoid one another in response to their different tastes in clothing, food, or music; their conflicting rhythms of leisure and work; and their differing styles of speech. In short, peer group lifestyles triumph at the expensive of solidarity among genders and generations.

Responses to these broad conditions are shaped by the peculiarities of intergender and intergenerational bonds in specifically American contexts. For example, much of the American public and its social science gurus still cherish an optimistic faith in both progress and rationality. This faith obscures the fact

that progress, rationality, personal choices, and modernity all have their contradictions and their points of entropy and reversal. Indeed, all these values,
like the broader liberal ideology of which they are a part, today are deeply
threatened, while each of the alternatives advanced to replace them is limited or
undermined by the others.

Chapter 8 The Postmodern Transformation of Art: From Production of Beauty to Consumption of Signs

Art has moved from craft production of beauty to mass consumption of signs. It is not made for use or delight so much as it is purchased as a sign of status and identity. No longer merely aesthetic, political, or commemorative, art has become an investment in an ever more fragmented selfhood, with profound changes ensuing for art worlds and artists. The artist today is neither the craftsperson of preindustrial times nor the seer or desperado in the romantic counterimage of the industrial era. The new market for art has created a star system in which the successful artist has become a reproducer of salable icons and is himself a salable icon or, in Hollywood parlance, a bankable star.

In this chapter we show how the emergence of postindustrial social structures and postmodern ideological orientations has facilitated the intrusion of capitalistic behaviors and attitudes in the cultural sphere. We first characterize the earlier conflict between commerce and high culture and then show how, in the postindustrial and postmodern period, art became thoroughly commercialized, even when artists tried to resist being reduced to commodities. We also show how postmodernity has transformed American cultural scenes in the major artistic disciplines. We then turn to contemporary art works, which we evaluate in light of three criteria of postmodernity formulated by Frederic Jameson (1983). The remaining dilemma, however, is to ascertain whether the postmodern aesthetic generates liberating heterogeneity and difference or whether it is a new avatar of capitalism that imposes the segmentation of art markets and the flexible commodification of artistic objects and values.

THE CREATION OF "ART" AS A
PRIVILEGED CATEGORY

The ambivalence that many people feel toward art—as a source of freedom and pleasure or as an enemy of ethics—also can be understood as a tension between the conspicuous consumption discussed by Thorstein Veblen and the Protestant ethic described by Max Weber. Veblen's (1899) theory of the leisure class seeks to understand why the very bases of human life and the central means and ends of capitalist society—that is, labor and wealth—ultimately were not regarded as worthy of honor. By contrast, Weber (1992, 14–15) introduces his study of the Protestant ethic with remarks on music and architecture that he presents as examples of the pervasive rationalism of Western society, notably in the domain of art and not just in business firms and state bureaucracies.

The social definition of art as a distinct and universal category of experience was a first step in this long process of transforming aesthetic creations into exchangeable commodities. To be exchanged for cash, art first had to be apprehended as independent of its contexts of use and assessed in terms of some nonlocal value. Painting on canvas was a step in this direction since it made the artwork more removable from its initial milieu. In the aesthetic theories of Enlightenment Europe, the value in art that transcended all contexts was beauty, and it remained so during the initial stages of industrialization, until art was later reduced to another universal value—money. The postmodern period may be characterized as the latest stage in this transformation. Now beauty, money, art, and even anti-art are all fragmented into interchangeable signs. Indeed, postmodernization has not merely eroded the experience of culture as an integrated unity by confronting each lived unity with many others. More, art itself is no longer seen as a domain of unity, however ideally conceived, but rather as a fragmentation of forms in response to various emerging and changing taste cultures and semiotic orders.

In all these transformations, "art" operates as an ideological construction rather than as any kind of natural category. In its modern usage, to call an object or activity "art" is to bestow upon it an apparently inherent, quasi-sacred value, while withholding this value from other often similar activities. The term "art" then functions as a category of distinction that assists in the construction and maintenance of a hierarchy of values and, thence, of persons; the hierarchy, once constructed, can be made to appear natural and inevitable (Bourdieu 1996; Kelly 1986, 9). Although "the arts" are taken to fall within a broader category of "pleasure," they invoke a specific sort of contemplative appreciation that associates contemporary cosmopolitan elites with earlier aristocrats and nobles. Indeed, from this viewpoint, "the arts" as revered yet pleasurable objects and activities are due as much to the status of their current patrons and their association with leisured, courtly taste as to any intrinsic moral or spiritual properties that they may embody (Bourdieu 1984).

Earlier generations of Americans, like Europeans, bought paintings for pleasure, status, or commemoration but not for investment. Here Veblen's dictum that waste is efficient as a display of wealth is apt, for a century ago art was bought more to lose money than to gain it. Moreover, rich Americans could not get tax writeoffs by giving their collections to museums because there was no personal income tax and few public museums. People applauded extravagant purchases not as shrewd investments, but rather as elitist acts of commercial indifference.

The "sacralization" of cultural objects began in the United States in the 1870s with the creation of large, prestigious institutions and the mystification of artistic production. At midcentury John Singleton Copley complained that painters had a social status similar to that of tradesmen (in Hughes 1997), but by the end of the century the artist had been separated from his or her publics and mythologized as a crazed demigod or desperado. Similarly, by the outset of the twentieth century "the previously commonplace practice of performing Shakespeare along with a farce, a comic dance, and a trained animal act had disappeared, the rowdy audience behavior in public performances had been eliminated (no more crunching peanuts during a concert or hissing inept actors), and newcomers were convinced to value, if not share, the aesthetics of the elite" (Griswold 1990, 509). The modern conception of "the arts" was universalized in both time and space so that artifacts from ancient Greece or other cultures could be revered as art (Kelly 1986, 9).

In the economic and social realms, things were thought to be better because newer, as opposed to the aesthetic realm, where they remained better because older. Thus, American elites continued to validate their economic success by reaffirming the past and its artistic masterpieces, especially "Old European Masters." Likewise, movies were not at first considered a highbrow aesthetic form precisely because of the newness of the cinema and its association with technological progress. Even though this particular medium earned the label of "seventh art form," the image of Hollywood often connoted vulgarity or naïveté. "Cinema" still is more European, connoting art, whereas "movies" are more American, connoting entertainment.

POSTINDUSTRIAL AND POSTMODERN
COMMODIFICATIONS OF ART

The barrier between artistic and economic values and pursuits began to crumble as the market absorbed more and more areas of life and as capital became increasingly liquid. With mass communication, marketing, and spectacles, capitalistic ventures since the mid-twentieth century have further invaded the cultural realm. The greater volume of cash and credit, the abstraction of things into interchangeable commodities generally, laws permitting art to be used as a tax deduction, and the abstract qualities of modern finance—all favored the swift convergence of one commodity into another and of liquid assets into art. Thus, we have come to think of works of art themselves as investments, assets, or collateral for debt. Further, as the number of executive, professional, and technical workers has grown, along with their discretionary income, the ideology extolling consumption has claimed a larger social territory. Indeed, the blurring of criteria used to distinguish consumption and investment has facilitated the invasion of various art scenes by purely commercial interests. In contrast to the earlier period, when the arts were considered more as a grace note to industrial rhythms or an emotional escape from them, the arts have become another kind of commodity subject to the logic of profit. New taste makers and shapers of desire—whether they be curators, media moguls, gallery owners, or theater critics—shape culture markets as protean places for the consumption of new lifestyles and identities through the consumption of art.

Since the latter decades of the twentieth century, capitalism has become more global and driven by electronic information. As a result, space-time experience has become more compressed and turnover more accelerated. Flexible accumulation, short production runs, and rapid market shifts now characterize art as much as other advanced economic sectors. There is a speedup in the workshops of symbolic production. The transactions involving artworks, their financial values, and their rates of turnover all have accelerated. Innovations and obsolescence of art are more rapid and their market cycles shorter (Moulin 1987; Reitlinger 1961). Even though there have always been cycles in the values assigned to distinct genres, artists, or individual pieces, the time interval separating peaks from nadirs keeps getting shorter, with avant-gardes succeeding one another with blurring speed. As a result, prices reached in art auctions have both soared and dived. As the arts have become another form of flexible accumulation, magazines such as *ARTnews* compile an "investor's guide" to the art market and issue newsletters that highlight trends in auction prices, tax legislation, and other topics relevant to those who consider cultural capital a subcategory of economic capital. Similarly, *Connoisseur* magazine featured an investor's file that reviewed newly discovered schools, periods, or artists that had good price/equity ratios and upside potentials. The *Times/Sotheby* art index reports putative statistics on the price movements of art objects from Tibetan bronzes to Italian Bronzinos. Of course, even with information arriving electronically from all over the globe, like most stock market news, these tips are usually obsolete before they reach their readers.

The rise of mass media as a dominant cultural factor also affects the commercialization of art and the condition of the artist. In a dialectical fashion, the culture industry thrives on what it fears, and it is nourished by what it excludes—free creativity (Gouldner 1979). The industry seeks to transform an earlier role of the artist or intellectual into that of a contract worker, to turn art and ideas into novelty items or spectacles for sale. As the industry defangs autonomous creators through promises of wealth, the "success" of works of high culture becomes defined by money. Great books are known as such by becoming best-sellers, "masterpiece" art shows are called blockbusters, "classical" movies are supposed to be Oscar winners, and "best" musical scores are expected to win golden or platinum recordings. Similarly, indigenous or communal traditions are folklorized to become more easily vended (Widmer 1975; Peterson 1972). For example, formerly autochthonous country music is now remade for mass presentations by media stars.

As audience reception becomes disconnected from shared conceptions of aesthetic merit or communal traditions, fame based on recognizable achievement is replaced by celebrity based on image recognition. Postmodern artists embrace the very celebrity and commercialization that modernists tended to eschew. Even literary or visual artists perform themselves. They and their works are known for being known, purchased because of their names in a celebrity system that offers a market price and legal brand name protection for personalities, even though it is acknowledged that the fame they enjoy is transient

(Thompson 1979). As high modernism was absorbed as the formal aesthetics of corporate capitalism and the bureaucratic state, postmodernism integrates high and popular culture in the eclectic and short-lived consumerism of the new global economy.

CORPORATIONS, AUCTION HOUSES, DEALERS, CRITICS, AND MUSEUMS AS COMMODIFIERS OF ART

Since the 1980s, large corporations and auction houses have increasingly taken control of art. Corporations have become the major patrons of art in every respect. They form private collections, sponsor every major museum exhibition, and coopt or marginalize works that have critical bite. Similarly, auction houses have become financial and brokerage institutions, thereby revaluing art as collateral. Perhaps the avant-garde American artists of the 1940s were the last generation that, without cynicism, considered art a heroic undertaking. They felt acute tension between the spiritually elevated character of their endeavor and the commercialism that increasingly surrounded the display and sale of what they produced. While they resented the market, however, they also accepted it as a reliable indicator of the value of their work.

As corporations buy in high volume and at low cost, however, old masters become blue chips and young artists become penny stocks that, if properly nurtured, hopefully will rise (Crimp 1987, 85). Thus the art market divides into two major segments—blue chip and speculative. Blue chips are works for which a market has been solidly established, with relatively stable prices and, hence, an easier association of aesthetic excellence and market value; most collectors will not pay vast sums for works whose aesthetic reputations could possibly be doubted. Speculative works are those by "new" or "undiscovered" artists or those that fit no established market category, artists whose works and reputations may or may not be hugely appreciated. Critical and monetary success are closely related since each tends to create, or at least confirm, the other (Moulin 1987, 113). It thus seems that, at least in speculative markets for art, the economists have it wrong. Rather than a commodity's value determining its price, here it is price—set by dealers or produced at auctions—that establishes value.

Dealers, critics, and museums also have helped to turn art into a commodity. From being midwives for creators and educators of patrons, contemporary dealers have become financial advisers, confidence men, and weathervanes of art market futures. Like brokers in hogbacks, they counsel clients to buy today in order to profit by selling or donating tomorrow. Artists of course are aware of such advice, so they try to manipulate the art market by marketing themselves through dramatically artistic personae; by starting, naming, or promoting circles, movements, or manifestos; and by cultivating and affiliating themselves with prestigious critics or galleries (Balfe and Wyszomirski 1985). Often, too, they simply cut a deal, taking 15 percent on sales of their work by a high-volume global art merchandiser rather than 40 percent on fewer sales from a local gallery.

Dealers also become confidence men by providing not only surety of provenance, but also, more important, assurance that the market will rise. In New York, for example, the informal circles of artists that formerly were so important in the establishment of new schools and approaches are no longer crucial (Bernier 1977; Simpson 1981). Instead, dealers have come to take the role of taste makers because adoption by a leading dealer is the artist's ticket to exposure in the market (Peterson 1987; Zukin 1982). Often dealers are quite explicit about their role in making the market for an artist. "'A client comes in and wants to know what that's worth,' said one dealer pointing to a lithograph hanging in his office. I'll tell him $2,500. If he asks me why, the real answer, the bottom line, has to be 'because I say so'" (Trustman 1979, 77). Further, galleries become not only more specialized, but also more stratified. Some fortunate few—Castelli having been the most famous—open branches in the metropolitan centers of the developed world that are most likely to attract patrons, but the majority of galleries barely survive and often do not. The same holds in literary, musical, or theatrical disciplines, where the gap between the most and the least successful gets wider. Of the $7.8 million total sales for works of living artists in the mid-1970s, more than half went to ten big-name artists (Kernan 1988). In the past three decades, this concentration of attention and money has greatly increased.

The growth of dealers has been paralleled by the enhanced functions performed by art critics, who began to function as publicists for art in the early twentieth century. Like stock market investment, art market investment depends on the creation of another cultural product: confidence. This product is perhaps an even more subtle artifact than the artworks that it serves to validate, and critics help to produce it. The first modern confidence men of art were probably Bernard Berenson and Lord Duveen, who often "made," or even made up, artists (Behrman 1952, 156–157). Once the older artifacts had been cleaned up and marketed, attention was directed to "lesser known masterpieces" and to unknown (that is, not yet marketed) contemporary artists. Such promotion today has become pervasive, further stimulating demand for art and further expanding the market. Scholars and museums help in the production of confidence by providing pedigrees and shrines for the selected works, whose sister and cousin artworks then enjoy price inflation through family resemblance and the secondary celebrity of sameness. During the New York City Armory show in 1913, reviewers first assumed their new role as instruments of self-fulfilling prophecies. Whether damning or adulatory, their reviews invariably boosted attendance, because all of them promoted the importance of what was shown. Today there are monthly openings in several hundred galleries in New York City alone. The decision by individual critics and magazines to cover a show thus becomes crucial to its success.

As criticism more and more operates as promotion, artists come to be the topic of reviews more than the art, through articles, reviews, interviews, and profiles that appear not only in art journals, but also in magazines of style such as *Vogue* or *Vanity Fair*. "What matters in the art world publicity machine is the media exposure, and the content of attention seems to be less important than the attention itself. A well-known critic [Hilton Kramer] commented on this mechanism ironically: 'The best publicity for a new artist would be an article that said the artist murdered his mother, married his sister, raped his father, and did the painting in between and that is the real story of the painting. That would be a great sell'" (Warchol 1992, 29). Some artists have called such promotion the "column-inch effect" or the Julian Schnabel phenomenon: even negative criticism helps as long as a lot of space has been devoted to it. For example, "serious" critics love to attack Schnabel, but this only makes him more celebrated, famous for having been written about and heatedly discussed. For this reason critiques or evaluations of artworks themselves become commodities of considerable value. As Gary Indiana said, "The problem comes when you see that no matter how critical you are, what is really important is the fact that the picture is in the magazine or the newspaper." He further commented on the commercial exploitation of his own writing, which reflects a more general trend: "The magic of the word in mass media is simply that the name gets spelled right—your writing is going to be used as a commodity as much as the work of art is. I have tried all kinds of ways to booby trap the process: I have written pornographic columns where the last paragraph is simply a mention of a show I happened to like; I have tried humor, which was not always understandable. And yet, the review still will be put in the plastic and laid on the gallery counter" (quoted in Warchol 1992, 27–28).

The movement of art from object of appreciation to equity for investment is perhaps most energetically undertaken precisely in that preserve against commercial values, the museum. The fiscal crisis of the state in the 1970s and 1980s led to cutbacks in public support of museums, which then began acting more like market-oriented firms seeking more visitors/customers in order to enhance receipts and impress their donors/investors. The young John Carter Brown, a former director of the National Gallery of Art, prepared for his museum career by first taking courses in business. Similarly, a former director of New York's Metropolitan Museum of Art bragged that he tried to blend almost everything he thought of or looked at into a business (Hoving 1993). The transformation of museums into sales emporiums, brokerage houses, and art theaters is reflected in the Chicago Art Institute's choice to copyright the maquette of a statue donated by Picasso and seek revenues from its reproduction (Clignet 1985). Similarly, the Dalí museum in St. Petersburg, Florida, sells reproductions of Dalí printed on T-shirts, contributing to a new genre of artistic communication and blurring the distinction between "original" and "copy" in an entrepreneurial spirit worthy of Dalí himself. Museums also influence the resale market by purchasing and exhibiting the works of older or dead artists; when they buy and show those of younger painters, they can make both the artists and the market for their works, a market in which museum trustees often hold important stakes (Becker 1982; Crane 1987; Peterson 1987, 7; Meyer 1979; Zolberg 1984). One example is a 1999 show, "Sensation," at the Brooklyn Museum of Art, which was alleged to be a "scam" involving Christie's auction house, the Brooklyn Museum, and Charles Saachi, the advertising mogul and owner of the art, in order to raise the value of his collection (Levine 2000, 19; Rothfield 2001). Of course, curators also can use shows to assist original and serious contemporary artists (Metcalf 1985; Whitt 1987). But either way, boundaries between public museums and private art firms have become as porous as those between the public and private profit sectors of the general economy.

Perhaps the current phase began several decades ago, when the Metropolitan Museum paid $2.3 million for Rembrandt's *Aristotle Contemplating a Bust of Homer* and put a red velvet sash around it. *Time* magazine printed the painting on its cover with a gold border, thereby suggesting the embrace of art by wealth. Big loan exhibits often serve as the promotional efforts of their sponsors: "The Treasures of the Vikings" promoted tourism for Norway; a show on Coco Chanel's fashions advertised that house's often second-rate designs. One big exhibit from China was financed in part by Charles Bloomingdale of the department store chain. Beforehand, Bloomingdale had American designers invent yuppie chinoiserie based on motifs from the show, then had the designs turned into mass-produced, "handmade" decorative items in China, to be reimported and sold by Bloomingdale's as authentic Chinese *objets d'art* drawn from (and promoted by) the show. In the same spirit of commercial egoism, the Lehmann Collection in the Metropolitan Museum is housed in a specially built wing that is a shrine to the memory and money of the eponymous banker, a sacral place with scant wall space. The whole gallery has little or no relation to the museum's regular holdings but much relation to avarice in acquiring splendid works, regardless of the cost in principles of aesthetic intelligence or display. Indeed, the collection has no business there (or rather, only business put it there).

Since 1990 shows have served even more blatantly as extensions of corporate advertising. In June 1998 the SoHo Guggenheim opened an exhibit on "The Art of the Motorcycle," sponsored by BMW. Naturally the show had a good sampling of BMW motorcycles but, as a corporate press release announced, "only the ones which are really considered art." Cash-hungry museums readily comply with corporate requirements to use their public spaces as private showrooms. For example, the Los Angeles County Art Museum and Chicago's Museum of Contemporary Art both agreed as a condition of funding by Lexus to showcase Lexus's cars.

The East Wing of the National Gallery in Washington gives out a similar message of what art is and is for—magnificence for mass consumption. The very sumptuousness of the East Wing suggest an ultrachic shopping mall. The blockbuster shows seem to overwhelm the visitors, to send them reeling out of each exhibit. And the shows themselves carry such titles as "The Splendors (of Dresden, etc.)" or "The Treasures (of Tutankhamen et al.)" (Withers 1981). Of course, many big exhibitions have displayed the highest standards of connoisseurship and scholarly acumen and also have been huge popular successes. One thinks of the 1980 Picasso retrospective at the Museum of Modern Art and its superb successor or the 1998 Van Gogh exposition at the National Gallery seen by five hundred thousand visitors (*Economist,* March 6, 1999.) But the megashows are often not of such quality, and they create a public impression that the only two kinds of important art are "Masterpieces" and "Treasures." This notion tends to undermine loyalty to the museum as an institution, "since the people who flocked to 'Gold of the Gorgonzolas' could no more be counted on to be loyal to the museum than those who attend a hit movie may be assumed to be 'loyal' to the movie theater in which it is screened" (Hughes 1993, 13). It also makes it harder for smaller museums that now aspire to blockbuster shows but lack the resources and influence to do the necessary borrowing. Although many commentators insist that the age of the blockbuster show is over, museums continue to evaluate shows by the number of visitors they draw.

The Boston Museum of Fine Arts (BMFA) engages in the same processes, though its endowment insulates it somewhat from popularization (Gusek 1992). The BMFA is one of America's oldest museums, formed by the emerging nineteenth-century Boston elite to coopt the concept of "fine art" and thereby establish and control more cultural capital and social esteem. The BMFA continues to show art objects, but now they are framed toward more popular and engaging contexts (DiMaggio 1987). Moreover, the number of its shows not entirely focusing on art, such as "Greater Boston Looks Ahead" (1945), has increased significantly since 1970. The BMFA established its first publicity department in 1982, and the use of the word "treasure" and colors to dramatize exhibition titles increased, as did corporate sponsorship, government funding, and the relative power of trustees over curators' decisions (Gusek 1992).

Museum shows are accompanied by aggressive marketing campaigns, the introduction of specialty items in the institution's shops, and package travel deals. All such efforts suggest that museums are eager participants in the consumer culture and ready when sufficiently paid to be used for corporate promotion. There is also, of course, an aesthetic and political narrowing in this process, since organizational survival over time requires the exclusion of artists and themes whose works, reputations, or personalities might be unwelcome to corporate or government sponsors. California's Republican congressperson Brian Bilbray, who votes to fund the National Endowment for the Arts (NEA), stressed that public funds cannot be used on the cutting edge because artists have to be responsible to those who pay the bills (in Jones 1998). This sentiment is even truer for corporate funding. Since corporations associate their names with shows for reasons of status and prestige, those shows must be above criticism, safe in all respects, without aesthetic or political challenges—in other words, "timeless." Correspondingly, as culture is brought to the masses (or at least the middle classes), both "high" and "popular" art are merged as commodities.

POSTMODERNITY AND THE CHANGING
RELATIONSHIP BETWEEN THE ARTS AND
SOCIAL STRATIFICATION

In America as elsewhere, there has always been a close relation between culture and social class. Various social groups use differing criteria to place objects in the distinct categories of the aesthetic. They distinguish between traditional and contemporary; low-, middle-, and highbrow objects; and the durable, transient, and trash (Thompson 1979). Not only do different social groups have different versions of these categories, but the categories also change at different rates and are justified by different rationales.

Such contrasts also vary across nations. What is considered highbrow and used as a marker of class distinction in one place may be considered popular culture in another (Katz-Gerro 1998, 18). For example, unlike France, with its academy and historic governmental sponsorship of a secular cosmopolitan and national culture (Brown 1995; Bourdieu 1984), Americans have a highly diverse and labile cultural pluralism. Thus in the United States there is more frequent display of nonelite cultural forms, which most people do not rank in a single hierarchical order. Grandma Moses remained popular with almost all groups as an icon of a lost America, if not for the formal properties of her art. Likewise, even though bathtub madonnas are peculiar to traditionally Catholic rural southern Indiana, they are experienced by many as just another variety of artistic production. Driving through the countryside, one is frequently struck by religious art of the front yard—"brightly painted two- or three-foot Madonnas . . . sheltered by . . . up-standing bathtubs buried halfway in the ground" (Smith-Shank 1996, 2). Such variability in the relationship between art consumption and social position is not explained by aesthetic universals. Another instance of "blue-collar art" is velvet paintings, often hung on laundry lines outside of gas stations, "so that when you stop for gas, you can also browse through the gas-gallery." Portraits of mythic heroes have always been popular forms of art and one of the most popular of the gas-gallery paintings is that of the King—Elvis—on velvet" (Smith-Shank 1996, 2). One such art entrepreneur is David J. Potter, who explained his wares to a reporter: "But I tell ya, these things really do communicate, through symbolism. That one communicates Elvis, that one a black jaguar. . . . This is blue collar art. I, like most Americans, can't afford to drop $5,000 at the local gallery" (quoted in Snyder 1989, E2). Yet "vulgarity" also can be expensive, as are the neon whales or female buttocks for sale in the "art galleries" of Las Vegas.

In short, just as "high" art has always undergone processes of commercialization downward, so "low" art often experiences mobility upward. Sociologically, there is no inherent difference among works of folk, popular, or mass culture, even though the cultural context or aesthetic status denoted by these terms may differ radically (Becker 1982). Thus collectors have turned "primitive" or "folk" art into a "fine" art, whereas the costumes of the eighteenth-century French court are now worn, in modified form, by country and western singers, whose main appeal is to a working-class public. Similarly, though ice skating is generally classified as entertainment or sport whereas dance is considered art, this classification could change with shifts in their characteristic patterns of presentation, consumption, and assessment and their use as markers of status (Peterson 1972, 1987; DiMaggio 1987). In the visual arts the emergence of photography as a significant medium in its own right and also as an effect on pop art or photorealism suggests a merging of popular and classical forms. In music Peterson (1975) showed how "country music" shifted from a regional and rural cultural form to the preferred music of the white working class in the first two decades after World War II. By the 1980s it had become thoroughly commercialized but nonetheless was played and appreciated by many American academic leftists and European intellectuals. American jazz has a similar history of redefinition from folk to popular music to high art or, sometimes with different venues and publics, all of these at once. It seems, in a postmodern fashion, that people are increasingly able to switch aesthetic codes with ease, enjoying classical, country, or jazz depending on their mood and circumstances. Indeed, postmodern artists no longer "quote" the images or motifs of a mass or popular culture, as Flaubert and Dostoyevsky did. Instead, they incorporate them so fully that older critical and evaluative categories, which presumed a radical differentiation of high and low or of modernist and mass culture, are no longer useful.

To summarize, the loss by old cultural elites and even the wealthiest individuals of their historic ability to define genres, subjects, and methods has reinforced postmodern flexibility and encouraged more democratic access to various cultural forms. During the Reagan and the second Bush administrations the National Endowment for the Humanities and the NEA both decided to emphasize late-nineteenth-century humanistic ideals. But unlike government agencies or corporations, wealthy individuals have a stronger interest in maintaining the arts as high culture and markers of high status. The tendency of a corporate or government sponsor is to evaluate the success of a museum show by how many people have seen it, rather than whether the right people appreciated it. Government involvement thus reduces the ability of wealthy individuals to directly control high culture as the reserve of those endowed with cultural capital. The conjunction of such forces has accelerated the turnover and mobility of artistic objects over time, in space, and across aesthetic categories (Crane 1987, 142; Tuchman 1988, 9).

THE EXPANSION OF THE ARTIST AND ART
PUBLIC AS INVESTORS-CONSUMERS

Changes in artists and the art public have been accompanied by shifts in the demographic and class structure of all cultural actors, who, like their products, have grown in scale, rate of turnover, and heterogeneity. The number of painters, actors, and musicians has increased dramatically since the material basis of their occupational lives has become cheaper and since the expanded culture industry has employed many more of them in largely technical or commercial roles. Further, as the average income per capita has grown in the upper service sector of employment, more Americans have been able to directly or indirectly support a higher number of dependents, including aspiring artists and performers.

American art teaching swelled in the late 1960s and 1970s as children of the postwar baby boom began moving through art schools like a pig through a python, arriving in the world of would-be professional artists at the end of the 1970s. "Every university had to have its art department, and that department had to be full. The National Association of Schools of Art and Design guesses that about 900 institutions offer fine-arts degree programs; its own 138 member schools had 45,000 students in the fall of 1982, of whom some 8,500 graduated with B.F.A. degrees in the spring of '83" (Hughes 1985, 78). American art schools of various sorts now graduate over forty thousand persons per year—about as many adults as there were in Florence around 1500. Growth in the volume of artworks produced also has been phenomenal. For example, in New York in 1945, there were a handful of galleries and a score of artists regularly exhibiting, rather than hundreds of galleries and many thousands of persons who call themselves artists in New York today.

The growth has been accompanied by a growing differentiation of the occupational structure among art producers, creating unemployment at the bottom and a star system at the top. As supply exceeds demand in the expanded art market, brand name recognition becomes more important. A minority of "recognized" painters or performers are able to demand extraordinarily high fees for works that are shown in a few geographically scattered and socially prestigious places, on television, or on mass-marketed compact discs. The fabulous prices for celebrity works and the fabulous incomes of star artists are much touted in the press. With this separation of value from worth, the notion of performance in the artistic disciplines become increasingly like that of professional sports. A soprano is evaluated by the highest notes she can reach; a pianist, by the speed with which he can run the keyboard. As a result, symptoms of "art fatigue" appear among art publics and within distinct art communities. With these changes, there has been an erosion of the aesthetic and social control that used to be exercised by practitioners and patrons. Instead, success is more exclusively defined by a nonaesthetic value—money.

At the same time, the overwhelming majority of artists cannot live from their art and are obliged to work part-time in nonartistic jobs—baritones as bartenders and cellists as checkout clerks. Government data on "various artists' occupations" for 1970 and 1980, for example, revealed that the number of art workers had increased by 48 percent, whereas their earnings during this period had decreased by 37 percent (NEA 1988). The number of American citizens who call themselves artists more than doubled between 1970 and 1990—from 720,000 to 1,671,000, with the largest percentage increase, bizarrely, in Alaska (Alper et al. 1992, 3). Moreover, few other occupations have such highly trained people who must earn most of their incomes outside their chosen fields. This large component of bottom-income artists also participates in the expanded art market as consumers with more taste than money. The opposite is true of the middle and the top: new money, new collections, newly old masters, little taste. Rich and tasteless collecting of course is not new—as is attested in the collections of John Pierpont Morgan, William Randolf Hearst, and James Hirshhorn, the discoverer and merchant of uranium. What is new today is the vastly increased scale of investment in art, in terms of both dollars and investors.

With the growth of cultural consumption there has been an expansion of what Daniel Bell (1973, 20) called the cultural mass—not the creators of culture but the transmitters. These are people who work in higher education, publishing, the broadcast media, films, theater, and museums. They constitute an important market for more serious culture themselves, even as they edit, repackage, interpret, and transmit high culture for a wider mass audience.

With the vastly increased and largely uncritical demand for culture, the art industry has become like the fashion industry. In the 1940s and 1950s, for example, there was a new avant-garde every three years. The contrived succession of artistic fads has become much more self-consciously engineered since then, and the turnover of avant-gardes has become faster (Crane 1987; Simpson 1981; Peterson 1987, 8; Wolff 1981). New brand name styles must be produced each season and in volume. With associations of galleries selling one star simultaneously in New York, London, Zurich, Paris, Tokyo, and Milan, art stars must work at production runs that match other flexible postindustrial sectors, with a minimum of two paintings a week. "We look to the collector who spends $50,000 a year as a vital clientele," says a representative of Christie's. "The secret," adds a colleague, "is that the market is international. If the dollar is down, the yen and Deutsche mark are up" (quoted in Ames 1988, 72). Globalization, speedup, and flexible production are features of art as they are for other sectors of late capitalism.

One consequence of these features is that bad art is not what it used to be. "Tradition" and "academic practices" are distrusted because these were what modernism had overthrown. Now, aesthetic entropy pervades the booms and busts for "hot" new paintings. The weakening of self-disciplining artistic communities softens their internal aesthetic standards, which have been partly replaced by an increased quasi-therapeutic regard for the "individuality" or "struggles" of newly marketed artists, along with a rejection of gendered and Eurocentric canons. Expressing their contempt for metanarratives, revolting art students and instructors of the 1960s massacred plaster casts and disdained drawing from life in most art schools of the United States, since taking photos rather than making sketches was so much easier. In America as elsewhere, high art was once viewed as a refuge from mass culture. The culture industry could produce schlock for the masses, but "we" could rent a Bergman video or visit Rubens or Rothko in the museum (Hughes 1985, 79–80). But for people born after 1960, this attitude often seems elitist or irrelevant. Clarity of form is replaced by hybrids, depth by quick cuts, unity of image by pastiche. High and low easily commingle. Philip Glass noted of his opera, *Christopher Columbus,* that he wanted people to come to the performance in tennis shoes.

In sum, the public as producers, investors, and consumers of art has expanded greatly with the growth of upper-service-sector employment, the creation of new fortunes, and the enlargement of the numbers of producers, interpreters, and transmitters of art. The expansion of the market for art has generated new income for the arts, though relatively little of it goes to most artists. Instead, a star system has emerged in which most income goes to a few and much less to the many. As this pattern tends to break down minimal aesthetic and social standards within specific artistic communities, what art is and means also change. "Art" is now less an object of beauty, or even excellence of craft, and more a sign for investment or consumption.

ARTISTIC DISCIPLINES IN POSTMODERN AMERICA

Although the postmodern and postindustrial shifts that we have described all are characterized by the abandonment of stable paradigms, essences, or foundations, they have not occurred at the same times and rates across different artistic genres and disciplines because of contrasts in each discipline's organizational structure, costs of production, and internal patterns of development.

Postmodern Visual Arts

With the loss of shared exemplars in the visual arts of sculpture and painting, representation becomes both more personal and more depersonalized. In modernist terms, we have an increase in both idiosyncratic freedom and collective alienation. On the one hand, there is the inflationary emotionalism of artists like Chris Burden, who "have themselves shot in the arm because one cannot know what it feels like to be shot if one is not shot" (Gablik 1985, 49–50). For some artists, such antimaterialist performances were attractive precisely because they seemed to resist commodification. On the other hand, we find manifestos of depersonalization for a new aesthetics of exclusion, as in Mark Rothko's twelve rules for a new academy: "no texture, no brushwork or calligraphy, no sketching or drawing, no forms, design, color, light, space, time, movement, size or scale; no symbols, images or signs; neither pleasure nor pain" (quoted in Clignet 1990b, 240). Similarly, in an interview in *ARTnews* in 1983, Roy Lichtenstein insisted that he and his art were "anti-contemplative, anti-nuance, anti-getting-away-from-the-tyranny-of-the-rectangle, anti-movement and light, anti-mystery, anti-paint-quality, anti-Zen, and anti- all of those brilliant ideas of preceding movements which everyone understands so thoroughly." Such anti-establishment pronouncements, along with his comic strip lampoons of artistic classics, quickly made Lichtenstein a darling of the art establishment, secured by the promotional efforts of Leo Castelli, and made Lichtenstein himself an instant classic.

All these interventions erode not only the orthodox boundaries between simulation and stimulation, creators and publics, presence and representation, but they also subvert the very understanding of what "art," "realism," or "beauty" could possibly be. When the meaning or message of a work of art becomes impossible to decipher, when it becomes hard to tell *what* is a work of art, the notion of the artist's intent also loses any meaning. For example, a collector who bought a work by the sculptor George Segal of two life-size figures lying on a bed removed the figures and placed them on pedestals. The artist's recourse to get the figures back in bed was limited to friendly persuasion. Similarly, a black Alexander Calder mobile was bought by a Pittsburgh man and donated to the local airport. It was repainted green and gold, the county colors, and fixed in a rigid position because the new owners were unaware that a mobile is supposed to move (Kernan 1988). More generally, eclecticism of styles, media, and images is now the convention, even within a single painting. What is new and postmodern is that the process now presupposes a discontinuity of traditions, not extensions of them, since in the new channel-surfing approach to painting, no image is presumed to have authority over any other. In this way postmodern art reflects the new mode of information: instant reproduction.

By deconstructing and juxtaposing different aesthetic orders, by refusing to take any one of them as ultimately adequate, postmodern works of visual art present multiple masks whose interplay unmasks regimes of signification that seek to impose a unitary structure to experience. In the postmodern moment, "the real is no longer what it used to be. . . . There is an escalation of the true, of the lived experience; a panic-stricken production of the real and the referential. . . . The very definition of the real becomes: that of which it is possible to give an equivalent reproduction" (Baudrillard 1983, 12–13, 146). Sometime the vacuity of the display is a comment on what is absent, as in Charles Ray's 1998 show at the Whitney Museum of American Art. The very solemnity of the display's triviality, the grand presentation of empty gestures, seems to criticize the sacred importance attributed to art itself. Something similar occurs with Claes Oldenburg's sculptures. The spaces for which they are commissioned are almost always crushingly mediocre, not public spaces in a formerly social, civil, or political sense. Hence, they cannot properly contain "monuments"—that is, sculpture that expresses some public purpose or endeavor. And since there can be no believable public monuments, Oldenburg invents believable unbelievable ones—private objects (like a lipstick) that in their gargantuan scale both mock and provide shared public meanings (Van Bruggen 1997).

In this situation the only realism that is plausible is deconstructive verisimilitude (Denzin 1994). That is, the artist can only produce a work that reproduces these multiple versions of the real, showing how each version impinges on and shapes the phenomenon being represented. A work's verisimilitude is given in its ability to reproduce and deconstruct the reproductions and simulations that structure what, for the moment, is taken as real. Modern copies, or copies of copies, are reproductions in which no attempt is made to mark an original. The result is a pastiche of styles. Because copies are "keyed" to other copies rather than to an original, reproduction attains the status of parody (Manning 1991, 18; see also Goffman 1974, 156–157). For example, Umberto Eco discovered Leonardo's painting of *The Last Supper* in a roadside museum in Santa Cruz, California: "Between San Francisco and Los Angeles I was able to visit seven wax versions of Leonardo's Last Supper. . . . Each is displayed next to a version of the original. . . . The waxwork scene is compared to a reduced reproduction carved in wood, a nineteenth century engraving . . . and against such insufficient models, the waxwork, of course, wins" (1986, 16–17). The wax copy is viewed as more real, appealing, and vibrant than the copy (or copies) to which it is compared. Such a display also has a commercial purpose—to encourage the viewer to desire and buy (a copy of) the most real copy (Manning 1991, 8–9).

When the uniqueness and, hence, the scarcity of an item cannot be controlled or when there is more profit in multiples than in singles, copies are manufactured. This manufacture is especially true in an age of electronic (and not merely mechanical) reproduction. Sounds can be electronically produced, remastered, taken from TV, and "converted to colors, colors to lights, lights to pictures, pictures back to sounds. What code organizes this sythesthesia? Digitally remastered compact discs are sold as more original than an analogically produced original performance of an artist. . . . Similarly, it will soon be possible through laser technology to produce a Mona Lisa that appears as 'original' as the 'original'" (Manning 1991, 17). All these practices put in disarray those metasigns that serve to discriminate among copies, fakes, and doubles and to create invidious rankings and evaluations.

Postmodern Cinema

The rejection of the modernist movement takes a specific form in films as art forms. For example, in *The Long Goodbye* (1973), director Robert Altman uses whispered voiceovers and superimposed dialogues to symbolize the reduced understanding that we have of our surroundings. Scratching and sculpting the physical surface of the celluloid, as in the animated films of Norman McLaren, are another example of a postmodern transformation of reality into images. The older *Hellzapoppin'* (1941) pursued the same goal by underlining the relativity of images in a slapstick fashion. Here the main characters speak to one another vertically, from one frame of the film to the next one just below. In the film *Blue Velvet* (1986), the protagonist moves between two utterly distinct worlds—that of an idealized small American town of the 1950s and sexual dementia. These two worlds exist in the same space-time, each suggesting the unreality of the other (see Harvey 1989, 48; Denzin 1994). Similarly, in Quentin Tarantino's film *Pulp Fiction* (1994), a number of apparently unrelated episodes are presented in an apparently arbitrary series. This antinarrative weirdness is naturalized through dialogue, which often is a philosophic or deliberative discourse spoken in the most everyday idioms and style, though it remains a protest against any imposition of coherence or history or identity. Only in the last episode, perhaps a concession to modernism, do we see how all the characters and episodes are related to each other in an almost unified flow.

These examples highlight only a few of the issues raised by postmodernism in cinema, even as they suggest that postmodern themes are not necessarily exclusive to a particular era. For example, one can argue that the coloring of formerly black-and-white classics should be read in more deconstructive terms. If all statements are viewed as representations without corresponding essences or foundations, how might valid aesthetic arguments be invoked against the creation of a newer, colored version of a black-and-white film, even against the wishes of its maker? Is the video version the same film as the big screen "original"? Or is the original the book? Or is it an earlier film, of which the present film is a remake? Or is the original the actual events upon which the film was based, events that are now understood mainly through their cinematic expression? Are the themes of ambiguity, hyper-reality, and absence simply the recycling of film noir, or do they express a new postmodern sensibility, or is this rapid recycling itself a sign of the postmodern?

Postmodern Architecture

In the field of architecture, the modernist belief in linear progress, universal truths, and rational planning became a built environment designed by avant-garde planners and architects in the service of a new social order. For example, the early high modernism of Frank Lloyd Wright or the international styles of Le Corbusier and Mies van der Rohe guided efforts to revitalize war-torn or aging cities in Europe and America and to create transportation systems, factories, hospitals, schools, and housing for workers. Yet the design imaginary of modern architects soon devolved into literally concrete images of power and prestige for publicity-conscious corporations and governments and into dehumanizing housing projects for workers (Harvey 1989, 35; Huyssens 1984, 14; Frampton 1980). Such projects, along with new technologies of rapid transport and high-rise construction, contributed to postwar social stability and economic growth.

Following Virginia Woolf's specification of the birth of modernity in literature, Charles Jencks (1977) dated the demise of modernism on July 15, 1972, when several blocks of the Pruitt-Igoe Housing Project in St. Louis were dynamited. This event marked the death of Bauhaus functionalism and Le Corbusier's "modern machines for living." Against the hidden and ahistorical dependence of modernism on the machine metaphor and the production paradigm of an earlier capitalism, postmodern architects favor the reintroduction of multivalent symbolic dimensions and the mixing of codes, much as assembly-line industrial production is shifting to postindustrial flexible accumulation. Against a failed, sleek modernism, postmodern architecture offers humor, more humane scale, less giganticism, bleek rationality, and a greater diversity of spaces. Rather than building for uniformity and homogeneity, the postmodern architect designs for a wide array of taste cultures whose relation to each other only the market researcher or scholarly critic can decode.

On the one hand, postmodern architects use—and often help to invent—the most advanced construction materials and techniques. On the other hand, they advocate the reappropriation of slow-changing historical forms and patterns, as well as their eclectic recombination. Thus Philip Johnson's high-rise building for AT&T in New York City has a neoclassical midsection, Roman colonnades at the street level, and a Chippendale pediment at the top. These citations may be tenderly ironical, as is the use of ruins and other fragments of Greco-Roman architecture by the Poiriers, the French couple who wink in the direction of Romantic artists who first invented this type of reference. Such admixtures remind inhabitants and visitors of the relativity of history, the ephemeral quality of human endeavors, and the flexible appropriation of alternative pasts.

Postmodern architecture issues from a critique of the rigidity of architectural modernism and the terrifying mediocrity of suburban sprawl, which together were accused of tearing the social fabric of the traditional cities and neighborhoods with isolating freeways and high-rises, all under the imperious aegis of a charismatic master (Jameson 1991, 2; Berman 1982; Jacobs 1992). By contrast, postmodern architecture displays aesthetic populism that effaces the earlier high-modernist barriers between high culture and mass, commercial, or processed culture with works that jumble, transform, and thereby appropriate the categories and contents of the very culture industry that was so passionately denounced by modernists at least since the Frankfurt School.

One striking example of wry yet passionate eclecticism is Frank O. Gehry's Guggenheim Museum in Bilbao, Spain, which locals call the metallic artichoke (Van Bruggen 1997). Gehry draws inspiration from postmodern artists such as Claes Oldenburg, Richard Serra, and Frank Stella, as well as from the artist Gordon Matta-Clark, who exhibited wall segments he had cut from a condemned house. Gehry literally deconstructed his own house in Santa Monica (1977–1978), exposing wooden lathes, beams, joists, and plumbing; adding wood-framed skylights; and wrapping the exterior in corrugated steel and chicken-wire glass (Dal Co and Forster 1998). Gehry insisted that his roadside vernacular fit the boats and campers that were parked in the driveways of his outraged neighbors. Such a mixing of industrial materials and pop fantasy offers both a paean to and a critique of American values.

Postmodern Literature

Similar processes are occurring in literature and the book industry. In an earlier bourgeois era, culture critics (including Karl Marx) once championed the transcendent value or liberating power of great authors and works. By contrast, contemporary culture operates within a field of stylistic and discursive heterogeneity with few if any consensual norms. Literary masters have been replaced by writers (often in-house staff writers) who no longer can or must impose "high" forms of speech in an increasingly postliterate era. Whereas modernists abhor these changes, postmodernists have "been fascinated precisely by this whole 'degraded' landscape of schlock and kitsch, of TV series and *Reader's Digest* culture, of advertising and motels, of the late show and the grade-B Hollywood film, of so-called paraliterature, with its airport paperback categories of the gothic and the romance, the popular biography, the murder mystery, and the science fiction or fantasy novel" (Jameson 1991, 2–3). Authors of more complex texts no longer simply "quote" such materials as Dostoyevsky or Joyce once did but incorporate them into the very substance of their writings.

Most consequentially, book making has been reorganized into new social-technical systems. For example, computers make layout and compositing a new job for the writer, though formerly they were done by the publisher, much as McDonald's turns customers into busboys. Book distribution also is computerized and dominated by book chains, with the result that supply is now the slave of immediate, media-generated demand. Moreover, book publishing and selling have themselves been taken over largely by international corporate conglomerates. One cause and result is that national literary boundaries are becoming more porous, with American products increasingly important in global popular culture. Unlike earlier writers of trash fiction, such as Harold Robbins or Jacqueline Suzanne, today's Stephen King, Sidney Sheldon, and Danielle Steel are international literary stars. Jay McInerney's *Bright Lights, Big City* set off a fad in Italy for yuppie novels. The flow also is inbound, as marked by Bertelsmann's purchase of Random House in 1998. In 1986 the British John le Carré's *The Perfect Spy* sold 285,600 copies in America, and the Italian Umberto Eco's *The Name of the Rose* sold 320,000, thereby marking the emergence of an international market in popular books led by the United States.

Publishing in America today is dominated by a clutch of giant companies that often are parts of even larger domestic empires or are owned by foreign conglomerates and that include smaller publishing houses with their own imprints. In June 2000, for example, BarnesandNoble.com invested $20 million in and became a major partner of MightyWords, a Web company that lets readers download e-books onto their own computers. When publishing houses, news magazines, Internet sales networks, TV programs, entertainment firms, and other media are all owned by the same corporation, books are no longer merely books. The focus instead is on copyrighted material that can be marketed in many different forms and venues—pocketbook and hardcover editions; with and without illustrations; for book clubs or part of a series; as film, video, or TV; in various languages and forms to various sectors of a now multinational market. Persons, viewpoints, and works not amenable to this system tend to be excluded.

These changes often quash editorial discretion. As an example, a book by Seymour Hersh that criticized the media was reviewed negatively, and nervously, by *Time,* which was owned by the same conglomerate as Hersh's book publisher. An equally big change has occurred in the retailing of books by major discount chains. For example, Barnes and Noble (which bought B. Dalton in 1986) together with Waldenbooks accounted for about half of over-the-counter book sales in America in 1990. "The discounting of books led to increased sales, even though the number of new titles did not change—about 50,000 a year around 1990. Yet the range of titles stocked and their length of time on shelves has plummeted. As a result, in the late 1970s a book could get into the American bestseller lists if it sold 50,000 copies; now it needs to sell over 300,000" (*Economist,* 1987, 111).

During the same period, however, as in some of the other disciplines, new technologies have emerged that permit a democratization of literary production by reducing the costs and time of publication and distribution and making possible the "sixty-second book." For example, technologies such as print-on-demand enable the low-cost and almost instantaneous production of books in customized lots as small as one. These trends promote anti-oligopolistic business practices and more access and diversity for writers and readers. For about $400 you can publish your own book and sell it through Amazon.com, BarnesandNoble.com or Borders.com. Similarly, through a process called collaborative filtering, computerization can identify microreaderships interested in nonstandard "product," readerships that have always been essential to nurturing as yet little-known authors (Gladwell 1996). The Internet also helps to crystallize microreaderships because visitors to literary chatrooms can share information in an easy, disinterested way. Sites of high-frequency interchanges serve litnetsters, like Alternative-X from Boulder, Colorado. The publishing community also has been a part of the explosion in desktop publishing, personal computers, Internet use, information exchange, and the publication of information through electronic books, compact discs, and World Wide Web pages. Such advanced technologies and methods enable the profitable mass production of paperback books within minutes. They allow booksellers to respond to micropublics not only because of fast, flexible production, but also because production on demand can eliminate, or at least reduce, the 30–40 percent bulk returns that publishers traditionally have had to absorb.

With these innovations and in the market spaces overlooked by the big discount chains, little bookstores, often electronic, are resurging. The average American buys more than twice as many books today than at midcentury, and there are nearly ten times as many bookstores. The innovations tend to support "special-interest" authors and publications, including those in literature and scholarship. Thus, as in the other artistic fields, technological changes and marketing innovations in the book industry are Janus-faced (Peck and Newby 1996). On the one hand, they induce authors to become cultural promoters and publishers to represent or create stars who write blockbuster books. Those whose work does not appeal to a mass readership or who write for and build smaller publics become much less attractive to both publishers and sellers of books. On the other hand, technologies also may foster greater independence for some writers and readers and thereby serve as a source for antihegemonic art.

Along with such changes, the very meaning of what is a "book" is being transformed. Books formerly were stable physical items. One could touch or smell them or know that they were located on one's desk or in the library's stacks. Moreover, for the past five hundred years or so in the West, it usually has been clear that there were correct, authorized, or definitive versions of any book. Today computerized texts are reversing this tradition. With their virtual character, such texts can easily be altered, and, hence, readers find it increasingly difficult to know what version they are reading or who is (or are) its authors. The modern text gives way to the postmodern hyper-text, in which the "real" or "original" text and various "performances" of the text become indistinguishable.

Moreover, like quick cuts and broken narratives in such films as *Pulp Fiction*, electronic narratives can be cut and sliced, with audio or with visuals or without, almost at the reader's will, and the reader/author may be in Singapore or

Sausalito. Other sub- and hyper-texts also can be added or subtracted. Cut the footnotes, add the photos, change the headers, mix in a little *Crime and Punishment* to add spiritual or existential depth to *Les Misérables*. Alice Randall's *The Wind Done Gone* as a version of *Gone With the Wind* or Sena Jeter Naslund's *Ahab's Wife* as a remake of *Moby Dick* are just a beginning, as modern linear narrative presentation gives way to postmodern flexible performance.

ARTISTIC POSTMODERNISM: SOME GENERAL FEATURES

While there have been diverse changes in specific artistic disciplines, postmodern ideology has affected aesthetic orientations generally. Frederic Jameson (1983) identified three criteria of postmodern art forms: the death of the subject, the transformation of a concrete reality into a world of images, and the fragmentation of time into a series of perpetual presents. Regardless of the discipline or the date at which its postmodern forms emerge full-fledged, the thrust of postmodernism is to reject all codified meanings and methods as ideological or oppressive. Concepts like truth or beauty are thought to have died, first as givens, then as possibilities, and finally as significant categories of human experience. The last step in this decay of absolutes is the collapse of oppositions that had been previously considered essential to the production of culture—fact and fiction, author and text, essence and appearance, reality and its representations. Past (causality and motivation) and future (telos and destiny) are collapsed into the present (acceptance of absurdity and choice).

Under these conditions, postmodernity marks not only the decline of the subject and its linear temporal development, but also the emergence of juxtaposed fragments that symbolize the equivocations that stand between decay and promise, regret and hope, or beginning and end. In postmodern antinovels, such as those of Nathalie Sarraute or Alain Robbe-Grillet, for example, the characters are often less befuddled than the author as to what is going on. Postmodern music and other art forms increasingly rely on random occurrences or on machines. Locations of distinct objects and oppositions in space and time also are disordered. Such disorders are seen in the speedup and flexible accumulation of images and the breakup of clear narrative life cycles and plotlines and in the rapid movement of objects back and forth between à la mode and retro, or high and low, or folk and fine art.

As we noted, such relativization of formerly fixed categories comes with the proliferation of new art worlds and market sectors and the ensuing profusion of competing avant-gardes, each with a shorter life span than the last. The simultaneous multiplication of schools or avant-gardes and the blurring of rules also erode the professional solidarity of artists to one another, since each group is responsive to a different market sector. For example, Abstract Expressionism in the 1940s and Minimalism in the early 1960s were supported by academic critics and the curators of New York museums. Pop and Photorealism of the early 1970s and Neo-Expressionism of the early 1980s were patronized by dealers, investors, and collectors. Figurative and pattern paintings of the early 1970s were purchased by regional museums and corporate art acquisition managers (Crane 1987, 41).

In such a situation, art readily becomes fashion, and fashion becomes the latest consumer preference of different groups, each with its own tastes, each nullifying claims of the others to any more general aesthetic judgment. With a large-scale culture industry catering to increasingly diversified market sectors and with a parallel fragmentation of various art worlds, existing rules of aesthetic propriety and rights to artistic property die young, while newer ones are born in such a profusion that each tends to suffocate its siblings. This profusion of definitions encourages an inflation of the interpretations offered of existing artworks, even as their respective turnovers and life cycles are accelerated. The abandonment of one single and stable paradigm (such as that which European masters formerly exemplified for Americans) in turn generates numerous coexisting aesthetic paradigms, cultural proprieties, legal properties, and canons of realism. And as with the fragmentation of political legitimation, in the multiplicity of aesthetic and anti-aesthetic legitimations each tends to negate the others.

Though often celebrated as a liberating multivocality, the anti-aesthetics of "anything goes" in the art market is akin to "everything comes and goes" in the stock market, in nostalgia, in relationships, and in everyday life. In the absence of reliable aesthetic criteria, people more readily assess the value of works of art (or anything else) according to their monetary value or return on investment. Whereas formerly the currency of art was beauty, increasingly it is simply currency. Such "realism" accommodates all tendencies, just as capitalism accommodates all "needs," provided only that the tendencies are marketable and the needs have purchasing power. Thus pop artists break with the austere canons of high modernist paintings and embrace the consumer culture as their inspiration. What Madison Avenue was for Andy Warhol, the neon landscape of Las Vegas was for Robert Venturi and other postmodern architects, who celebrate fantasy and eclecticism against the rectilinear realism of modernism. We learn, in *Learning from Las Vegas* (Venturi et al. 1972), to glorify the billboard strips, schlock spectacles, and pop aesthetics of casino culture. Venturi also tells us that Disneyland is "the Symbolic American Utopia . . . nearer to what people want than what architects have ever given them" (Goldberger 1972, 41). Critics who defend high culture and loathe its Disneyworld debasements (for example, Bell 1973, 20; Marcuse 1978) nonetheless agree with Venturi and others that the boundaries between high and popular art increasingly collapse under the aegis of capitalist commodification and mass consumerism.

The commodified realism of "anything goes" also involves contradictions in the role and expectations of the artist. Ideologies of art simultaneously stress the depersonalization of the creative process and the glorification of self-images (Gablik 1985, 38–40; Lasch 1978; Lichtman 1982, 225). But these self-images are not enactments of identities so much as creations of the market. On the one hand, art products are depersonalized; on the other, artists themselves assume the posture of flamboyant narcissists. For example, Rothko's depersonalized art operates by extolling the principles of a new aesthetics that excludes any hint of human sensibility. At the other end of the continuum are artists who make themselves and their emotions the product—literatis like Truman Capote or Norman Mailer or visual artists like Mike Parr, who use violence to "get the public implicated" (Gablik 1985, 49–50).

In all these changes, the instrumental calculation of modernity is blatantly exhibited and ironically contradicted. Postmodern "architects, painters, sculptors, film makers, novelists, performance artists and others meticulously duplicate, magnify and complicate the drift of industrial society. . . . Duplicating the implicit structure of modernity, postmodernist practitioners are universal levelers. They strive for inclusiveness even though, paradoxically, only the culturally competent can spot their references. By mixing genres and styles, reversing established plots and sequences, and disabling authoritative texts, voices and persons, their open-ended projects readily include trash, kitsch, clichés, throwaways and outcasts. They appropriate, salvage and recycle the past and present while painstakingly they eroticize and refine the routines and artifacts of modernity" (Kariel 1990, 96). For example, David Salle's collages impose no unity or choice among the incompatible source materials from which they are assembled (Taylor 1987, 8), and Frank Stella's painted reliefs seek to represent all the garish and mundane aspects of New York City, from subway cars to the holiday light on the Empire State Building. The "spiritual qualities" of such art are greedy vitality, trashy materialism, and complacent sensationalism—qualities of the world that they sardonically applaud. In many ways, then, one can describe the postmodern aesthetic as devouring itself, in this sense corresponding to the mythical beast evoked by the Beatles in *Yellow Submarine,* a beast that swallows everything on its path and, as it runs out of things to swallow, ends up swallowing itself.

Thus aesthetic ironies of the dominant system are not necessarily a threat to it. Instead, the system that commodifies art preserves itself by turning even protest into an item of display, celebration, and consumption, especially when the rebels are without a cause. The skepticism and irony of postmodernism can be read as caused by disillusion with the utopian projects and protests of modernism. Yet postmodern irony also is defeated by cooptation even as it succeeds by imitation. Thus postmodern representations may be seen as signs of the diffusion of postindustrial capitalism within the cultural community itself. Whereas modernist artists sought to shock the bourgeoisie, their postmodern successors aestheticize politics and accept the economization of art. They still shock the bourgeoisie, but now with schlock that becomes stock in celebrity and sales.

In such a context, Lichenstein's mocking aesthetics of newsprint and comics; Warhol's art of Campbell's soup cans; or the minimalist and ironic works of playwrights such as Samuel Beckett or composers such as Cage or Glass—all are reflections both on and of late capitalist society. It does not mean that the older canons of beautiful or realistic representation have been supplanted. On the contrary, they remain significant because the vast majority of popular and even many high cultural expressions still conform to realistic codes of representation, however brutal, self-mocking, or phony these may have become. More significant, these older codes continue to condition the reception of sur-, neo-, hyper-, and antirealist works. This cacophony of conflicting codes is itself emblematic of postmodern society.

The postmodern collapses not only the distinction between the old and the new or the model and the copy, but also the gap between the ugly and the beautiful. Instead of the purity and refinement of modernism, postmodernism favors parody, pastiche, kitch, camp, or generally ironical comments about the relativity of taste and its subservience to money and power. With the derealization of canons, paradigms are viewed more as social and historical conventions to be deconstructed to reveal their ideological exclusions. But because there is nothing outside such constructions, such ideological unmasking reveals itself as implying yet another construction. Such analyses thereby enhance rhetorical and critical awareness but may also serve as implicit apologies for the status quo.

The postmodern era also is frequently characterized by the fragmentation of one single paradigm and the collapse of boundaries among genres or, even more important, among cultural realms deemed to be distinct. In this context the artist's goal is not to represent truth or beauty but to contest multiple aesthetic verisimilitudes, multiple versions of the beautiful and the true—in effect, to bring chaos to order. For example, in his postmodern multicultural sculpture, Michael Lucero draws on various styles of pre-Colombian arts, such as the Colima, Nayarit, and Maya. Yet the painted and glazed surfaces of these "pre-Colombian" forms refer to different European traditions such as Abstract Expressionism and European modernism, and the work incorporates scenes reminiscent of the Old Masters. Similarly, David Foster Wallace's story "Westward the Course of Empire Takes Its Way" (1989) satirizes avant-garde literary techniques by being a virtuoso compendium of them. There are "authorial intrusions in the manner of John Barth; whimsical collages of wild fabulation and deadpan realism that recall Richard Brautigan, or maybe middle-period Kurt Vonnegut; and long, long sentences in the style of Donald Barthelme. The proceedings are shot through with an air of wild Pynchonian intrigue" (Scott 2000, 39). The result in both Lucero's sculpture and Wallace's novella is not a "comment" on their various sources but a deconstruction and recreation of them into something wholly new. This new form is also evident in the shows or events mounted by Christo and Krzysztof Wodiczko (Clignet 1990b). Both of these artists have changed what a work of art is to be taken to be—Christo, by wrapping islands off the Florida coast or hanging a curtain in a Colorado canyon, Wodiczko by projecting selected large-scale images directly onto the facades of public buildings and the walls of monuments. The works by Christo underline the implicit statements present in a natural or artificial landscape by changing its relationship with the background. They also radically undermine the conception of the artist as lonely demi-urge or the artwork as eternal form. Instead, the wrapping of the Pont Neuf in Paris, for example, was a temporary happening that involved about one thousand persons possessed of multifarious skills, including those of sixty-five alpinists. The shows by Wodiczko protest the politics of monuments that literally pour dominant capitalist ideologies in cement. Instead he emphasizes their contradictions by contrasting the fake solemnity imputed to the past with economic or political scandals of the present. Thus Wodiczko renders transparent the ideological function of architecture and challenges the regimes that it celebrates and depends on. Above all, these two artists also have modified the legal terms governing relations between artists and their audiences, between artists and their support personnel, between art and politics, and between public and private facets of art worlds. Thus, as Wodiczko's art subverts the seeming permanence of the surface of buildings by projecting contemporary images on them, he challenges the interaction between the past and the present and between the building and the politics that built it or among the architect, his or her client, and the artist who comments on these relations. Similarly, whereas Christo seeks private and public sponsorship of his projects, he does so in ways that challenge existing arrangements. In short, postmodernism not only modifies the definitions of specific works, methods, and publics, but it also alters the economic, legal, and space-time definitions that frame aesthetic communication. Both artists are in the modern heroic mode, taking art out of the galleries and into the streets, yet both use postmodern techniques to achieve their aesthetically or politically radical effects.

IMPLICATIONS, EQUIVOCATIONS, AND CONCLUSIONS

We have argued that the postmodern celebration of heterogeneity and difference is intimately connected to increased commodification of aesthetic objects and values in advanced capitalism, and we have noted that many postmodern artists have failed to adopt a critical posture toward the pro-market ideology that appears to be assumed in contemporary expressions of artistic heterogeneity and difference. Of course, one could argue that art has been a commodity since at least the eighteenth century, as Brewer and Bermingham (1995) show in discussing the social and economic networks of British culture during that period. Artists, for their own reasons, have generally denigrated any economic valoration of their production. Perhaps what is different now is the nakedness of the discussion of art as a commodity. Or more exactly, art has long been a form of investment in cultural capital; recently it has become an investment in economic capital as well. The fragmentation of art worlds and the transformation of beauty into signs also has multiplied and dramatized conflicts about the property rights that can be claimed on art works, as well as about the proprieties demanded of them (Clignet 1985, 1990b). Thus, there has been a sharp rise in the frequency and visibility of legal actions concerning fakes and forgeries, plagiarism, art thefts, and obscenities. For example, forgers may be recognized by modernists as criminals and by postmodernists as a genuine variety of artists, as illustrated by the fortunes and misfortunes of writer Clifford Irving. Irving's "authorized" biography of recluse Howard Hughes was widely celebrated but ultimately proven to be fake, costing Irving $756,000 and fourteen months in jail. Similarly, whereas obscenity or pornography used to be clear-cut social problems defined by dominant groups to protect and discipline others, in the postmodern era boundaries among acceptable and deviant behaviors, subject matters, and genres have become porous and malleable. While modernists might chart the objective devolution of a specifc art work from sin to crime to error to a mere example of an alternative style, postmoderns argue for their dramaturgic coexistence.

The controversy surrounding the show of Robert Mapplethorpe's photos in the late 1980s is a case in point. The publicity generated by both the champions and the opponents of the late photographer ensured high attendance for the exhibition and high prices for his works. The protagonists also helped erode boundaries among culture, state, and market by quarreling over, without distinguishing among, several different questions: (1) what was the aesthetic value of these photographs; (2) were they obscene; (3) if so, was this assessment sufficient cause for canceling subsidies by the NEA; (4) was such a cancellation a form of censorship; and (5) was the alleged obscenity a sufficient cause of forbidding the show altogether? Moreover, few people noticed that the positions of fundamentalists and multiculturalists, who respectively condemned and defended Mapplethorpe, both derived from the American Puritan assumption that art must have a moral meaning. Chris Ofili's painting of a Madonna made partly of elephant dung and Renée Cox's photomontage titled "Yo Mama's Last Supper," which substituted her nude frontal self for Jesus, in Brooklyn Museum of Art shows of 1999 and 2001 elicited similar challenges, debates, and confusions as to what may be taken as art and what kinds of art are permissible.

In short, such confusions suggest that intrusions of capitalism and the state into the cultural sphere have blurred both the boundaries between the public and private facets of artistic communities and the responsibilities of each cultural actor. For example, full control by market forces would preclude any public subsidy because the invisible hand would be expected to direct artistic outcomes. By this logic, the first issue underlying the Mapplethorpe controversy was to determine whether the state should subsidize the arts because such support violates libertarian ideology. Conversely, there may be something special about art that justifies an intervention that is disallowed in other arenas. And if the state is to intervene, should not its subsidies be contingent on the works' meeting certain formal and substantive standards, as is the case with most other forms of assistance? Yet many artists took the refusal to subsidize the Mapplethorpe show as political censorship, in spite of the legal distinction between forbidding a show or performance and refusing to fund it. In this logic, passive failure to provide monies is equivalent to active suppression, or the "terror" of silencing the other, to use Lyotard's (1984) term. Yet many artists agree to have such decisions taken by a panel of artistic "experts" appointed by the NEA. Others argue that such exclusive control by specialists is undemocratic and that expenditures of public funds require the participation of elected individuals who represent taxpayers.

In this sense, the Mapplethorpe show and other postmodern breaches of modernist canons reactivate debates as to the respective roles and rights of citizens; their official representatives; and curators, artists, and other experts. They exacerbate the equivocations in the notion of "representation," which is used to refer at once to the normative content of artworks and the normative delegation of both aesthetic and political decisions. Indeed, the social rebellions and resistance going on today, in America and elsewhere, may not be about class struggle, the ownership of property, or the means of production so much as they are about the struggle for meaning and the control of the means of representation.

Whether in painting, architecture, or other postmodern art forms, artists change the size of their works, the raw materials used, the very production process, or the conditions under which these works can be experienced in response or in resistance to market forces. In so doing, artists challenge reigning definitions of the singularity of aesthetic production and the canons for assessing artistic worth. The key question is no longer what is universal, real, beautiful, or true. Instead, the focus is on how reality and truth are constructed, both aesthetically and socially, in specific historical contexts and who will control these processes of symbolic (re)production. The issues appear within a larger political economy and collective consciousness that works of art at once express, legitimate, challenge, and transform.

Yet postmodernism is not only about the emergence of new relations of "cultural superstructures" and their appropriate "material bases." It also is about interactions of distinct sets of ideological or cultural constructs, such as the arts and the law, the arts and language, or the arts and political belief. Seen in this light, postmodernist discourse is more useful than an older Marxist style of analysis. But it remains analytically suspect on at least two counts. First, the deconstructive stance taken by many postmodern analysts toward the systemic properties of time and history limits the reflexivity of their own approach. Since the notion of "post" involves definite time-space references, any analysis implies a historicity that many postmodern theorists explicitly reject. This rejection also leads to problems or omissions in dating the presumed cleavage or overlaps between modern and postmodern practices (Clignet 1985). From this vantage, the claims of a new postmodern era are exaggerated or at least unspecified. For example, postmodern art recombines old elements into new totalities, but so did Cubism. It also claims to be antihierarchical and ironic, but so was Dada and, indeed, so were Cervantes and Rabelais. Correspondingly, many of the features imputed to postmodern art may be less typical of a specific historical period than of a transition and competition between older and newer types of social organization, psychological responses, and cultural forms. Thus the very term "postmodernism" may be limiting and contradictory, for it reintroduces surreptitiously a linear, narrative sense of time and history that it claims to have dismissed. This and other subjectivisms also are at odds with claims concerning the death of the subject.

Further, to the extent that analysts emphasize the philosophical or literary properties of postmodernism without rooting them in the activities of the communities that adopt the relevant practices, they run the risk of idealist, antisociological theorizing, of advocating or criticizing rather than explaining, and of inviting an apolitical nihilism or aestheticism. Such theorizing raises the issue of who benefits most of all from the intellectual constructions made around postmodern art forms. Could it be that the example and defense of postmodernism provide an implicit justification of the newest forms of capitalism, a perverse if unconscious alliance between some segments of the economic and cultural elites? Or is postmodernism still a source of critique, innovation, and freedom? The variety of forms taken by postmodern artistic expressions and the advocacy of heterogeneity by some of its theorists may be construed as a commitment to political pluralism. But they also may reflect the intrusion of late capitalism into the domain of cultural production and consumption. Indeed, these alternate interpretations are central in debates among theorists of the postmodern. Given limited resources and competing constituencies, these issues are not merely academic.

For a first group, the term "postmodern" refers to a reaction against the excesses of a functionalism that sought exclusively to enhance productivity and usefulness. Thus, theorists like Gilles Deleuze, Felix Guattari, Jean Baudrillard, or Jean-François Lyotard celebrate postmodernism for liberating desire, play, or pluralism from the oppressions of Enlightenment reason and capitalist calculation. Lyotard welcomes the death of any orthodoxy and envisions artists and writers "working without rules in order to formulate the rules for what will have been done" after the event has happened (1984, 81). Thus he hopes that free creativity can resist capture by any ideology. By contrast, Habermas (1987a) criticizes postmodernists for overlooking the constraints of political economy and for drifting, however unwittingly, into the neoconservative camp. Similarly but from a Marxist perspective, Frederic Jameson (1983, 125; 1991) and David Harvey (1989) see the movement as reinforcing the logic of consumer capitalism. In this view, the pluralism generated by postmodernism rationalizes and stimulates the segmentation of markets while trivializing the political process.

Drawing on both postmodernism and its critics, we could say that the emphasis on deconstruction and on the openness of all interpretations encourages a multiplicity of local discourses and a more rapid turnover in the most popular ones. As different groups have their own codes and truths, the shared experience and solidarity of the working class is undermined. However, as we have argued, this solidarity already has been undermined, long before postmodernists arrived on the scene, by shifts in the political economy itself. Indeed, as Marxists like Jameson and Harvey assume a "natural" development of working-class solidarity and resistance, they tend to use the deus ex machina of "culture" to explain their unexpected withering away. By contrast, many postmodernists and poststructuralists have accepted the challenge of representing or understanding these new conditions, often in ways that appear to be non-, anti-, or postmodern. The resulting cacophony of language games tends not only to delegitimate hegemonic discourses and create space for new ones, as postmodernists argue, but it also tends to accentuate the consequences of economic shifts of late capitalism, as well as the fragmentation of shared paradigms for any public discourse, as critics of postmodernism have insisted. These are not contradictory positions, however, if we see them as expressions of the simultaneous hyper-rationalization and radical subjectivism that characterize contemporary American life.

References

CHAPTER 1

Alba, Richard. 1990. *Ethnic Identity: The Transformation of White Identity.* New Haven and London: Yale University Press.

Albrow, Martin. 2001. "Society as Social Diversity: The Challenge for Governance in the Global Age." *Governance in the Twenty-First Century.* Paris: Organization for Economic Co-Operation and Development.

Ansell, Amy Elizabeth. 1997. *New Right, New Racism: Race and Reaction in the United States and Britain.* New York: New York University Press.

Bensman, Joseph. 1988. "The Crisis of Confidence in Modern Politics." *International Journal of Politics, Culture, and Society* 2, no. 1 (fall): 15–35.

Berlin, Ira. 1998. *Many Thousands Gone: The First Two Centuries of Slavery in North America.* Cambridge, Mass.: Belknap Press.

Brodkin, Karin. 1998. *How Jews Became White Folks and What That Says about Race in America.* New Brunswick, N.J.: Rutgers University Press.

Brown, Richard Harvey, and George V. Coelho, eds. 1986. *Tradition and Transformations: Asian Indians in America.* Williamsburg, Va.: College of William and Mary. Studies in Third World Societies.

Brulle, Robert J. 2000. *Agency, Democracy, and Nature: The U.S. Environmental Movement from a Critical Theory Perspective.* Cambridge: MIT Press.

Butler, Jon. 2000. *Becoming America: The Revolution before 1776.* Cambridge: Harvard University Press.

Castells, Manuel. 1996. *The Rise of the Network Society.* Cambridge, Mass.: Blackwell.

Crèvecoeur, J. Hector St. John de. 1782. *Letters from an American Farmer.* London: Printed for T. Davies.

Dashefsky, Arnold. 1976. *Ethnic Identity in Society.* Chicago: Rand McNally.

Deetz, Stanley. 1995. *Democracy in an Age of Corporate Colonization: Developments in Communication and the Politics of Everyday Life.* Albany: State University of New York Press.

Delbanco, Andrew. 1989. *The Puritan Ordeal.* Cambridge: Harvard University Press.

———. 1995. *The Death of Satan: How Americans Have Lost the Sense of Evil.* New York: Farrar, Straus, and Giroux.

Donahue, John D. 1992. "The Devil in Devolution." *American Prospect* 32 (May-June): 42–47.

Edgell, Stephen, Sandra Walklate, and Gareth Williams, eds. 1995. *Debating the Future of the Public Sphere: Transforming the Public and Private Domains in Free Market Societies.* Brookfield, Vt.: Arbury.

Fields, Barbara. 1990. "Slavery, Race, and Ideology in the Unites States of America." *New Left Review* 181:95–118.

Flournoy, Don M. 1992. *CNN World Report: Ted Turner's International News Coup.* London: J. Libbey.

Foucault, Michel. 1977. *Discipline and Punish: The Birth of the Prison.* Trans. Alan Sheridan. New York: Random House.

Fossett, Mark A., and M. Therese Seibert. 1997. *Long Time Coming: Racial Inequality in the Nonmetropolitan South, 1940–1990.* Boulder, Colo.: Westview.

Fox, Russell Arben. 2001. "Tending and 'Intending' a Nation: Confecting Visions of American National Identity." Manuscript. Washington, D.C.: Catholic University of America.

Frederickson, George M. 1997. *The Comparative Imagination: On the History of Racism, Nationalism, and Social Movements.* Berkeley: University of California Press.

Friedman, Bernard. 1970. "The Shaping of Radical Consciousness in Provincial New York." *Journal of American History* 56, 4:781–801.

Fuchs, L. H. 1990. *The American Kaleidoscope: Race, Ethnicity and the Civic Culture.* Hanover, N.H.: University Press of New England.

Gans, Herbert J. 1988. *Middle American Individualism: The Future of Liberal Democracy.* New York: Free Press.

Giroux, Henry A. 1993. *Theory and Resistance in Education: A Pedagogy for the Opposition.* South Hadley, Mass.: Bergin and Garvey.

Greider, William. 1992. *Who Will Tell the People? The Betrayal of American Democracy.* New York: Simon and Schuster.

Hall, John A., and Charles Lindholm. 1999. *Is America Breaking Apart?* Princeton, N.J.: Princeton University Press.

Hartigan, John. 1999. *Racial Situations: Class Predicaments of Whiteness in Detroit.* Princeton, N.J.: Princeton University Press.

Herman, Simon N. 1977. *Jewish Identity: A Social Psychological Perspective.* Beverly Hills, Calif.: Sage.

Hochschild, Arlie Russell. 1983. *The Managed Heart: Commercialization of Human Feeling.* Berkeley: University of California Press.

Horwitz, Morton J. 1977. *The Transformation of American Law.* Cambridge: Harvard University Press.

Ignatiev, Noel. 1995. *How the Irish Became White.* New York: Routledge.

Jacobson, Matthew Frye. 1998. *Whiteness of a Different Color: European Immigrants and the Alchemy of Race.* Cambridge: Harvard University Press.

Kanter, Rosabeth, B. Stein, and T. Jick. 1992. *The Challenge of Organizational Change.* New York: Free Press.

Kingsbury, S. 1906–1935. *The Records of the Virginia Company of London.* Washington, D.C.: U.S. Government Printing Office.

Kolko, Gabriel. 1967. *The Triumph of Conservatism: A Re-Interpretation of American History, 1900–1916.* Chicago: Quadrangle Books.

Korgen, Kathleen O'Dell. 1998. *From Black to Biracial: Transforming Racial Identity among Americans.* Westport, Conn.: Praeger.

Kubler, G. 1963. *Shape of Time: Remarks on the History of Things.* New Haven: Yale University Press.

Lasch, Christopher. 1978. *The Culture of Narcissism: American Life in an Age of Expectations.* New York: Norton.

Lieberson, Stanley, and Mary C. Waters. 1988. *From Many Strands: Ethnic and Racial Groups in Contemporary America.* New York: Russell Sage Foundation.

Lindorff, David. 1992. *Marketplace Medicine: The Rise of the For-Profit Hospital Chains.* New York: Bantam Books.

Lipset, Seymour Martin. 1979. *The Third Century: America as a Post-Industrial Society.* Stanford, Calif.: Hoover Institution Press.

Lundberg, Ferdinand. 1969. *The Rich and the Super-Rich.* New York: Lyle Stuart.

Lyman, Stanford M. 1998. Gunnar Myrdal's "An American Dilemma after a Half Century: Critics and Anti-Critics." *International Journal of Politics, Culture and Society* 12, 2:327–389.

———. 2001. "The Assimilation-Pluralism Debate: Toward a Postmodern Resolution of the American Ethnoracial Dilemma." Manuscript. Boca Raton: Florida Atlantic University, College of Social Sciences.

Mayer, Arnoj. 1981. *The Persistence of the Old Regime: Europe to the Great War.* New York: Pantheon Books.

Mills, Charles W. 1997. *The Racial Contract.* Ithaca, N.Y.: Cornell University Press.

Min, Pyong Gap, ed. 2001. *The Second Generation: Ethnic Identity among Asian Americans.* Lanham, Md.: Rowman and Littlefield.

Morgan, E. 1975. *American Slavery, American Freedom: The Ordeal of Colonial Virginia.* New York: W. W. Norton.

Naisbitt, John, and Patricia Aburdene. 1990. *Megatrends 2000: Ten New Directions for the 1990's.* New York: Morrow.

Nixon, Ron. 2000. "Letter from South Carolina." *The Nation,* May 15, 21–23.

Olzak, Susan. 1992. *The Dynamics of Ethnic Competition and Conflict.* Stanford, Calif.: Stanford University Press.

Osborne, David, and Ted Gaebler. 1992. *Reinventing Government: How the Entrepreneurial Spirit Is Transforming the Public Sector.* Reading, Mass.: Addison-Wesley.

Paine, Thomas. 1984. "The American Crisis." In *The Writings of Thomas Paine,* 4 vols. Ed. M. D. Conway. New York: Knickerbocker Press.

Parenti, Christian. 1996. "Making Prison Pay." *The Nation,* January 29, 11–14.

Patterson, Orlando. 1997. *The Ordeal of Integration: Progress and Resentment in America's "Racial" Crisis.* Washington, D.C.: Civitas/Counterpoint.

———. 1998. *The Rituals of Blood.* Cambridge: Harvard University Press.

Persell, Caroline Hodges. 1994. "Robin McWilliams Lecture: Taking Society Seriously." *Sociological Forum* 9, 4:641–657.

Pessen, Edward. 1990. *Riches, Class, and Power before the Civil War.* Piscataway, N.J.: Transaction Publishers.

Peters, T. 1992. *Liberation Management.* Basingstoke: MacMillan.

Pressley, Sue Ann. 2000. "S. Carolina's House Votes to Move Flag: Rebel Banner Compromise Fails to Sway the NAACP." *Washington Post,* May 11.

Ritzer, George. 1999. *Enchanting a Disenchanted World: Revolutionizing the Means of Consumption.* Thousand Oaks, Calif.: Pine Forge Press.

Root, Melissa, ed. 1992. *Racially Mixed People in America.* Newbury Park, Calif.: Sage.

Ryan, Alan. 1989. "Tocqueville in Saginaw." *London Review of Books,* March 2, 19–21.

Salamon, Sonya. 1980. "Ethnic Differences in Farm Family Land Transfers." *Rural Sociology* 45:109–119.

———. 1994. "Territory Contested through Property in a Midwestern Post-Agricultural Community." *Rural Sociology* 59, 4 (winter): 636–654.

Schor, Juliet. 1998. *The Overspent American: Upscaling, Downshifting, and the New Consumer.* New York: Basic Books.

Sclar, Elliot D. 2000. *You Don't Always Get What You Pay For: The Economies of Privatization.* Ithaca, N.Y.: Cornell University Press.

Sider, Gerald M. 1993. *Lumbec Indian Histories: Race, Ethnicity, and Identity in the Southern United States.* Cambridge: Cambridge University Press.

Smaje, Chris. 2001. "Re-Thinking the 'Origins Debate': Race and Political Formations in England's Chesapeake Colonies." Manuscript. University of Surrey, Department of Sociology, UK.

Spencer, Michael. 1997. *The New Colored People: The Mixed Race Movement in America.* New York: New York University Press.

Stark, Andrew. 1999. "Flying the Flag." *Times Literary Supplement,* April 30, 6.

Takaki, Ronald. 1989. *Strangers from a Different Shore: A History of Asian Americans.* Boston: Little Brown.

Tally, Margaret. 2001. "The Illness of Global Capitalism: Female Employees on 'Sick Leave' and the Social Meaning of Pain." In *The Politics of Selfhood: Bodies and Identities in Postmodern Capitalism.* Ed. Richard Harvey Brown. Minneapolis: University of Minnesota Press.

Taylor, Alan. 1995. *William Cooper's Town: Power and Persuasion on the Frontier of the Early American Republic.* New York: Knopf.

Tocqueville, Alexis de. 1945 [1835]. *Democracy in America.* London: Saunders and Otley.

U.N. Human Development Programme. 1997. *United Nations Human Development Report 1997.* "Human Development to Eradicate Poverty." New York: United Nations.

Vidich, Arthur J., and Joseph Bensman. 1971. *The New American Society: The Revolution of the Middle Class.* Chicago: Quadrangle Books.

Waters, Mary C. 1990. *Ethnic Options: Choosing Identities in America.* Berkeley: University of California Press.

Williams, Eric. 1961. *Capitalism and Slavery.* New York: Russell and Russell.

Williams, Richard. 1990. *Hierarchical Structure and Social Value: The Creation of Black and Irish Identities in the United States.* Cambridge: Cambridge University Press.

Wolfe, Alan. 1990. "The Return of the Melting Pot." *New Republic,* December 31, 27–34.

Wong, Paul. 1998. Race, Ethnicity, and Nationality in the United States: Toward the Twenty-First Century. Boulder, Colo.: Westview.

Wood, Gordon S. 1980. "Democracy and the Constitution." Ed. Robert A. Goldwin and William Schambia. Washington, D.C.: American Enterprise Institute.

———. 1992. *The Radicalism of the American Revolution.* New York: Knopf.

CHAPTER 2

Adonis, Andrew, and Stephen Pollard. 1998. *A Class Act: The Myth of Britain's Classless Society.* London: Penguin.

Baran, Paul, and Paul Sweezy. 1967. *Monopoly Capital: An Essay on the American Economic and Social Order.* New York: Monthly Review Press.

Bendix, Reinhardt. 1956. *Work and Authority in Industry.* New York: John Wiley.

Bensel, Richard Franklin. 1990. *Yankee Leviathan: The Origins of Central State Authority in America, 1859–1877.* New York: Cambridge University Press.

Berger, Peter. 1986. *The Capitalist Revolution: Fifty Propositions about Prosperity, Equality, and Liberty.* New York: Basic Books.

Berlet, Chip, and Matthew Lyons. 2000. *Right-Wing Populism in America.* New York: Guilford.

Birnbaum, Norman. 1971. *The Crisis of Industrial Society.* New York: Oxford University Press.

Blackburn, McKinley, et al. 1990. "The Declining Economic Position of Less Skilled American Men." In *The Future of Lousy Jobs.* Ed. Gary Burtless. Washington, D.C.: Brookings Institution.

Blau, Joel. 2001. *Illusions of Prosperity: America's Working Families in an Age of Economic Insecurity.* New York: Oxford University Press.

Bourdieu, Pierre. 1984. *Distinction: A Social Critique of the Judgment of Taste.* Cambridge: Harvard University Press.

———. 1991. "Political Representation." In *Language and Symbolic Power,* 171–202. Cambridge: Harvard University Press.

Brown, Cliff. 2000. "The Role of Employers in Split Labor Markets: An Event-Structure Analysis of Racial Conflict and AFL Organizing, 1917–1919." *Social Forces* 79, no. 2 (December): 653–681.

Brown, Richard Harvey. 2002. "Global Capitalism, National Sovereignty, and the Decline of Democratic Space." *Rhetoric and Public Affairs* 5, no. 2 (summer): 347–357.

Bruce-Briggs, B., ed. 1979. *The New Class?* New Brunswick, N.J.: Transaction Books.

Brulle, Robert J. 2000. *Agency, Democracy, and Nature: The U.S. Environmental Movement from a Critical Theory Perspective.* Cambridge: MIT Press.

Burnham, Walter Dean. 1973. *Politics/America: The Cutting Edge of Chance.* New York: Van Nostrom.

Chandler, Alfred D., Jr. 1977. *The Visible Hand: The Managerial Revolution in American Business.* Cambridge: Harvard University Press.

Cherry, Robert. 2001. *Who Gets the Good Jobs? Combating Race and Gender Disparities.* New Brunswick, N.J.: Rutgers University Press.

Conto, Richard A. 1999. *Making Democracy Work Better: Mediating Structures, Social Capital, and the Democratic Prospect.* Chapel Hill: University of North Carolina Press.

Davis, Mike. 1986. *Prisoners of the American Dream: Politics and Economy in the History of the U.S. Working Class.* London: Verso.

Deetz, Stanley. 1992. *Democracy in an Age of Corporate Colonization: Developments in Communication and the Politics of Everyday Life.* Albany: State University of New York Press.

Djilas, Milovan. 1957. *The New Class: An Analysis of the Communist System.* New York: Praeger.

Domhoff, William G. 1972. *Fat Cats and Democrats: The Role of the Big Rich in the Party of the Common Man.* Englewood Cliffs, N.J.: Prentice Hall.

Drew, Elizabeth. 2001. "Bush's Weird Tax Cut." *New York Review of Books,* August 9, 50–52.

Drucker, Peter F. 1989. *The New Realities: In Government and Politics/In Economics and Business/In Society and World View.* New York: Harper Collins.

Dubofsky, Melvin. 1974. *Industrialism and the American Worker.* Arlington Heights, Ill.: AHM Publishing.

Epstein, Jason. 1996. "White Mischief." *New York Review of Books,* October 17, 30–32.

Fink, Leon. 1985. *Workingmen's Democracy: The Knights of Labor and American Politics.* Urbana: University of Illinois Press.

Forbath, William. 1991. *Law and the Shaping of the American Labor Movement.* Cambridge: Harvard University Press.

Fuchs, Lawrence H. 1994. Review of Massey and Denton's *American Apartheid. American Journal of Sociology* 99, no. 5:1342–1343.

Gates, Jeffrey R. 2000. *Democracy at Risk: Rescuing Main Street from Wall Street.* Cambridge, Mass.: Perseus.

Gerteis, Joseph. 1998. "Political Alignments and the American Middle Class, 1974–1994." *Sociological Forum* 13, no. 4:639–667.

Giddens, Anthony. 1971. *Capitalism and Modern Social Theory: An Analysis of the Writings of Marx, Durkheim and Weber.* Cambridge: Cambridge University Press.

———. 1991. *Modernity and Self-Identity: Self and Society in the Late Modern Age.* Stanford, Calif.: Stanford University Press.

———. 1994. *Beyond Left and Right: The Future of Radical Politics.* Stanford, Calif.: Stanford University Press.

Gilbert, Dennis. 1994. "Class Inequalities in the United States: An Examination of Recent Trends." Paper presented to the meeting of the Eastern Sociological Society, March.

Gilbert, Dennis, and Joseph Kahl. 1987. *The American Class Structure.* Chicago: Dorsey.

————. 1993. *The American Class Structure.* Belmont: Wadsworth.

Gilens, Martin. 1999. *Why Americans Hate Welfare: Race, Media, and the Politics of Antipoverty Policy.* Chicago: University of Chicago Press.

Gladwell, Malcolm. 1996. "St. Nick's Beard." *New Yorker,* November 25, 9–10.

Glassman, Ronald M. 1997. *The New Middle Class and Democracy in Global Perspective.* New York: St. Martin's.

Gouldner, Alvin Ward. 1979. *The Future of Intellectuals and the Rise of the New Class.* New York: Seabury.

————. 1980. *The Two Marxisms: Contradictions and Anomalies in the Development of Theory.* New York: Seabury.

Granovetter, Mark S. 1995. *Getting a Job: A Study of Contracts and Careers.* Chicago: University of Chicago Press.

Grimaldi, James V. 2000. "Microsoft's Lobbying Largess Pays Off: Back-Channel Effort Wins Support for Case." *Washington Post,* May 17, A1.

Gusfield, Joseph. 1963. *Symbolic Crusade: Status Politics and the American Temperance Movement.* Carbondale: University of Illinois Press.

Hacker, Andrew. 1988. "Black Crime, White Racism." *New York Review of Books,* March 3, 36–41.

————. 1997. *Money: Who Has How Much and Why?* New York: Scribner's.

Halle, David. 1984. *America's Working Man: Work, Home, and Politics among Blue-Collar Property Owners.* Chicago: University of Chicago Press.

Harrison, Bennett, and Barry Bluestone. 1988. *The Great U-Turn: Corporate Restructuring and the Polarizing of America.* New York: Basic Books.

Hartz, Louis. 1955. *The Liberal Tradition in America: An Interpretation of American Political Thought since the Revolution.* New York: Harcourt Brace.

Hechter, Michael. 1975. *Internal Colonialism.* Berkeley: University of California Press.

Higley, Stephen Richard. 1995. *Privilege, Power, and Place: The Geography of the American Upper Class.* Lanham, Md.: Rowman and Littlefield.

Hochschild, Jennifer. 1995. *Facing Up to the American Dream: Race, Class, and the Soul of the Nation.* Princeton, N.J.: Princeton University Press.

Hodgson, Godfrey. 1992. *The World Turned Right Side Up: A History of the Conservative Ascendency in America.* Boston: Houghton Mifflin.

Inglehart, Ronald. 1977. *The Silent Revolution: Changing Values and Political Styles among Western Publics.* Princeton, N.J.: Princeton University Press.

————. 1996. *Modernization and Postmodernization: Cultural, Economic, and Political Change in Forty-Three Societies.* Princeton, N.J.: Princeton University Press.

Inglehart, Ronald, and Paul R. Abramson. 1995. *Value Change in Global Perspective.* Ann Arbor: University of Michigan Press.

Joseph, Antoine. 2000. *Skilled Workers' Solidarity: The American Experience in Comparative Perspective.* New York: Garland.

Karabel, Jerome. 1979. "The Failure of American Socialism Reconsidered." *Socialist Register.* London: Merlin Press.

Katznelson, Ira. 1981. *City Trenches: Urban Politics and the Patterning of Class in the United States.* New York: Pantheon.

Keister, Lisa. 2000. *Wealth in America: Trends in Wealth Inequality.* New York: Cambridge University Press.

Kelley, Stanley, Richard Ayres, and William Bowen. 1967. "Registration and Voting: Putting First Things First." *American Political Science Review* 61:359–379.

Kenworthy, L. 1998. "Do Social-Welfare Policies Reduce Poverty? A Cross-National Assessment." Luxembourg Income Study. Working Paper No. 188.

Kerbo, Harold R. 1983. *Social Stratification and Inequality: Class Conflict in the United States.* New York: McGraw-Hill.

Kimeldorf, Howard. 1999. *Battling for American Labor: Wobblies, Craft Workers, and the Making of the Union Movement.* Berkeley: University of California Press.

Kimeldorf, Howard, and Judith Stepan-Norris. 1992. "Historical Studies of Labor Movements in the United States." *Annual Review of Sociology* 18:495–517.

Laslett, J. H. M., and Seymour M. Lipset, eds. 1974. *Failure of a Dream? Essays on the History of American Socialism.* Garden City, N.Y.: Doubleday.

Lenin, V. I. 1975 [1920]. *Selected Works in Three Volumes.* Moscow: Progress Publishers.

Lewis, Charles, and the Center for Public Integrity. 1998. *The Buying of the Congress: How Special Interests Have Stolen Your Right to Life, Liberty, and the Pursuit of Happiness.* New York: Avon.

Lind, Michael. 1996. *Up from Conservatism: Why the Right Is Wrong for America.* New York: Free Press.

Lipset, Seymour Martin. 1963. *The First New Nation.* New York: Basic Books.

———. 1979. *The Third Century: America as a Post-Industrial Society.* Stanford, Calif.: Hoover Institution.

———. 1981. *Political Man: The Social Bases of Politics.* Baltimore: Johns Hopkins University Press.

Luttwak, Edward. 1994. "Why Fascism Is the Wave of the Future." *London Review of Books,* April, 3, 6.

Lyman, Stanford M. 1972. *The Black American in Sociological Thought: A Failure of Perspective.* New York: Putman.

Manza, Jeff. 1996. Review of Seymour Lipset's *American Exceptionalism: A Double Edged Sword. Contemporary Sociology* 25, no. 6:760–761.

Marx, Karl. 1976 [1867]. *Capital.* Vol. 1. Harmondsworth, England: Penguin.

Marx, Karl, and Fredrich Engels. 1953 [1892]. *Karl Marx and Frederick Engels on Britain.* Moscow: Foreign Languages Publication House.

Massey, Douglas S., and Nancy A. Denton. 1993. *American Apartheid: Segregation and the Making of the Underclass.* Cambridge: Harvard University Press.

Meeropol, Michael. 1998. *Surrender: How the Clinton Administration Completed the Reagan Revolution.* Ann Arbor: University of Michigan Press.

Mills, C. Wright. 1956a. *The Power Elite.* New York: Oxford University Press.

———. 1956b. *White Collar: The American Middle Classes.* New York: Oxford University Press.

———. 1963. "Mass Media and Public Opinion." Pp. 577–598 in *Power, Politics and People: The Collected Essays of C. Wright Mills.* New York: Oxford University Press.

Mink, G. 1986. *Old Labor and New Immigrants in American Political Development: Union, Party, and the State, 1875–1920.* Ithaca, N.Y.: Cornell University Press.

Morgan, Edmund S. 1975. *American Slavery, American Freedom: The Ordeal of Colonial Virginia.* New York: Norton.

Naisbitt, John. 1982. *Megatrends: Ten New Directions Transforming Our Lives.* New York: Warner.

Nelson, Lars-Erik. 1998. "Democracy for Sale." *New York Review of Books,* December 3, 8–10.

Neustadtl, Alan, Dan Clawson, and Denise Scott. 1992. *Money Talks: Corporate PALs and Political Influence.* New York: Basic Books.

Nieuwbeerta, Paul. 1995. *The Democratic Class Struggle in Twenty Countries, 1945–1990.* Amsterdam: Thesis Publishing.

Ostreicher, R. 1988. "Urban Working-Class Political Behavior and Theories of Electoral Politics, 1870–1940." *Journal of American History* 74:1257–1286.

Parsons, Talcott. 1967. "Full Citizenship for the Negro American?" In *The Negro American.* Ed. Talcott Parsons. Boston: Beacon Press.

Perrucci, Robert, and Earl Wysong. 1999. *The New Class Society.* Lanham, Md.: Rowman and Littlefield.

Phillips, Kevin. 1969. *The Emerging Republican Majority.* New Rochelle, N.Y.: Arlington House.

Piven, Frances Fox, and Richard A. Cloward. 1988. *Why Americans Don't Vote.* New York: Pantheon.

Piore, Michael J. 1979. *Birds of Passage: Migrant Labor and Industrial Societies.* New York: Cambridge University Press.

Poggi, Gianfranco. 1991. "Yankee Leviathan." *American Journal (Book Review) of Sociology* 97, no. 3 (November): 855–857.

Prechel, Harland. 2000. *Big Business and the State: Historical Transitions and Corporate Transformations, 1180s–1990s.* Albany: State University of New York Press.

Rosenblum, Gerald. 1973. *Immigrant Workers: Their Impact on American Labor Radicalism.* New York: Basic Books.

Roy, William G. 1997. *Socializing Capital: The Rise of the Large Industrial Corporation in America.* Princeton, N.J.: Princeton University Press.

Schmitt, Eric. 2001. "Segregation Growing among U.S. Children." *New York Times,* May 6, 28.

Schumpeter, Joseph. 1942. *Capitalism, Socialism, and Democracy.* New York: Harper.

Schwab, Larry M. 1991. *The Illusion of a Conservative Reagan Revolution.* New Brunswick, N.J.: Transaction Books.

Shefter, Martin. 1994. *Political Parties and the State: The American Historical Experience.* Princeton, N.J.: Princeton University Press.

Skocpol, Theda. 2000. *The Missing Middle: Working Families and the Future of American Society.* New York: Norton.

Smith, Adam. 1937 [1798]. *An Inquiry into the Nature and Causes of the Wealth of Nations.* New York: Random House.

Sombart, Werner. 1976 [1906]. *Why Is There No Socialism in the United States?* Trans. Patrice M. Hocking and C. T. Husbands. London: Macmillan.

Steinfeld, Robert. 2001. *Coercion, Contract, and Free Labor in the Nineteenth Century.* New York: Cambridge University Press.

Stryker, Robin. 1995. "The Making of American Exceptionalism: The Knights of Labor and Class Formation in the Nineteenth Century." *Contemporary Sociology* 24, no. 4 (July): 369–371.

Szelényi, Ivan, and Bill Martin. 1988. "The Three Waves of New Class Theories." *Theory and Society* 17:645–667.

Takaki, Ronald. 1989. *Strangers from a Different Shore: A History of Asian Americans.* Boston: Little Brown.

Teixeira, Ruy, and Joel Rogers. 2000. *America's Forgotten Majority: Why the White Working Class Still Matters.* New York: Basic Books.

Terkel, Studs. 1980. *American Dreams, Lost and Found.* New York: Pantheon.

Tocqueville, Alexis de. 1835. *Democracy in America.* London: Saunders and Otley.

Tonelson, Alan. 2000. *The Race to the Bottom: Why a Worldwide Worker Surplus and Uncontrolled Free Trade Are Sinking American Living Standards.* Boulder, Colo.: Westview.

U.N. Human Development Programme. 2000. *United Nations Human Development Report 2000.* New York: United Nations.

Vanneman, Reeve and L. Cannon. 1987. *American Perception of Class: A Study of the American Class Structure.* Philadelphia: Temple University Press.

Vogel, David. 1978. "Two Cheers for Capitalism." *Working Papers for a New Society* 6, 5 (September–October): 68–71.

———. 1995. *Trading Up: Consumer and Environmental Legislation in a Global Economy.* Cambridge: Harvard University Press.

Voss, Kim. 1993. *The Making of American Exceptionalism: The Knights of Labor and Class Formation in the Nineteenth Century.* Ithaca, N.Y.: Cornell University Press.

Wattenberg, Ben. 1974. *The Real America: A Surprising Examination of the State of the Union.* Garden City, N.Y.: Doubleday.

Weinstein, James. 1967. *The Decline of Socialism in America, 1912–1925.* New York: Monthly Review Press.

Wolfe, Alan. 1990. "The Return of the Melting Pot." *New Republic,* December 31, 27–34.

———. 1998. *One Nation, after All: What Middle-Class Americans Really Think about God, Country, Family, Race, Welfare, Immigration, Homosexuality, Work, the Right, the Left, and Each Other.* New York: Viking.

Wolff, Edward N. 1996. *Top Heavy: The Increasing Inequality of Wealth in America and What Can Be Done about It.* New York: New Press.

Wolfinger, Raymond E., and Steven Rosenstone. 1980. *Who Votes?* New Haven: Yale University Press.

Zolberg, Aristide R. 1986. "How Many Exceptionalisms?" In *Working Class Formation: Nineteenth Century Patterns in Western Europe and the United States.* Ed. Ira Katznelson and Aristide Zolberg, 397–455. Princeton, N.J.: Princeton University Press.

CHAPTER 3

Atlas, James. 1984. "Beyond Demographics: How Madison Avenue Knows Who You Are and What You Want." *Atlantic Monthly,* October, 49–58.

Baker, Melvin H. (chairman of the board of National Gypsum Company and a vice-president of the National Association of Manufacturers). 1959. Quoted in *Christian Science Monitor,* July 2, 12.

Ball, Terrence. 1984. Review of Haskell's *The Authority of Experts. Contemporary Sociology* 13, no. 6:743–744.

Barber, Bernard. 1983. *The Logic and Limits of Trust.* New Brunswick, N.J.: Rutgers University Press.

Bartel, Diane. 1996. "Cultural Movements and Legitimation Strategies." Manuscript. Department of Sociology, State University of New York, Stony Brook.

Becker, Howard. 1984. *Art Worlds.* Berkeley: University of California Press.

Bell, Daniel. 1973. *The Coming of Post-Industrial Society: A Venture in Social Forecasting.* New York: Basic Books.

———. 1991. *The End of Ideology: On the Exhaustion of Political Ideas in the Fifties.* New York: Free Press.

Beniger, James R. 1986. *The Control Revolution: Technological and Economic Origins of the Information Society.* Cambridge: Harvard University Press.

Bennett, William. 1984. *To Reclaim a Legacy: A Report on the Humanities in Higher Education.* Washington, D.C.: National Endowment for the Humanities.

Bensman, Joseph. 1988. "The Crisis of Confidence in Modern Politics." *International Journal of Politics, Culture, and Society* 2, no. 1:15–35.

Bensman, Joseph, and Robert Lilienfeld. 1985. "Law in Society: The Place of Reason and Rationality." *International Journal of Politics, Culture, and Society* 1, no. 2:58–84.

Bloom, Allan. 1986. *The Closing of the American Mind.* New York: Simon and Schuster.

Blumenberg, Hans. 1983. *The Legitimacy of the Modern Age.* Trans. Robert W. Wallace. Cambridge: MIT Press.

Bowles, Samuel, and Herbert Gintis. 1986. *Democracy and Capitalism: Property, Community and the Contradictions of Modern Social Thought.* New York: Basic Books.

Brenkman, John. 1979. "Mass Media: From Collective Experience to the Culture of Privatization." *Social Text* 1 (winter): 94–100.

Brown, Richard Harvey. 1989. *Social Science as Civic Discourse.* Chicago: University of Chicago Press.

———. 1995. "Realism and Power in Aesthetic Representation." In *Postmodern Representations: Truth, Power, and Mimesis in the Human Sciences and Public Culture.* Ed. Richard Harvey Brown, 134–167. Urbana: University of Illinois Press.

———. 1998. *Toward a Democratic Science: Scientific Narration and Civic Communication.* New Haven: Yale University Press.

Caplow, Theodore, Howard M. Bahr, John Modell, and Bruce A. Chadwick. 1991. *Recent Social Trends in the United States 1960–1990.* Montreal: McGill-Queens University Press.

Clignet, Remi. 1985. *The Structure of Artistic Revolutions.* Philadelphia: University of Pennsylvania Press.

Coleman, James S. 1982. *The Asymmetric Society.* Syracuse, N.Y.: Syracuse University Press.

Connolly, William E. 1987. *Politics and Ambiguity.* Madison: University of Wisconsin Press.

Crozier, Michael. 1984. *The Trouble with America: Why the System Is Breaking Down.* Trans. Peter Heinegg. Berkeley: University of California Press.

Cuddihy, John M. 1974. *The Ordeal of Civility: Freud, Marx, and Lévi-Strauss and the Jewish Struggle with Modernity.* New York: Basic Books.

Dahl, Robert A. 1977. "On Removing Certain Impediments of Democracy in the United States." *Political Science Quarterly* 92, no. 1 (spring): 1–20.

Davis, Mitchell P. 1988. *Directory of Experts, Authorities, and Spokespersons: Talk Show Guest Directory.* Washington, D.C.: Broadcast Interview Source.

Ditz, Toby L. 1986. *Property and Kinship.* Princeton, N.J.: Princeton University Press.

Dugger, Ronnie. 1988. "Annals of Democracy." *New Yorker,* November 7, 40–108.

Durkheim, Emile. 1964 [1893]. *The Division of Labor in Society.* New York: Free Press.

Edelman, Murray J. 1988. *Constructing the Political Spectacle.* Chicago: University of Chicago Press.

Edsall, Thomas Byrne, and Mary D. Edsall. 1991. "Race." *Atlantic Monthly,* May, 53–86.

Eitzen, Stanley D., and Doug A. Timmer. 1985. *The Sociology of Crime and Criminal Justice.* New York: Macmillan.

Entman, Robert M. 1989. *Democracy without Citizens: Media and the Decay of American Politics.* New York: Oxford University Press.

Epstein, Jason. 1996. "White Mischief." *New York Review of Books,* October 17, 30–32.

Ewen, Stuart. 1976. *Captains of Consciousness.* New York: McGraw-Hill.

Farrell, Thomas B., and G. T. Goodnight. 1981. "Accidental Rhetoric: The Row Metaphors of Three Mile Island." *Communication Monographs* 48:271–300.

Fay, Brian. 1975. *Social Theory and Political Practice.* London: Allen and Unwin.

Fisher, Walter R. 1992. "Narration, Reason, and Community." In *Writing the Social Text: Poetics and Politics in Social Science Discourse.* Ed. Richard Harvey Brown, 199–218. New York: Aldine de Gruyter.

Freidrich, Carl Joachim. 1963. *Man and His Government: An Empirical Theory of Politics.* New York: McGraw-Hill.

Fuchs, Lawrence H. 1989. *The American Kaleidoscope: Pluralism and the Civic Culture.* Middletown, Conn.: Wesleyan University Press.

Geiger, Theodore. 1969. "The Mass Society of the Present." In *Theodor Geiger on Social Order and Mass Society.* Ed. Renate Mayntz, 169–184. Chicago: University of Chicago Press.

Gerring, John. 1998. "American Political Culture: An Institutional Explanation." Paper presented to the meetings of the American Political Science Association, Boston, September.

Goldfarb, Jeffrey. 1992. *The Cynical Society: The Culture of Politics and the Politics of Culture in American Life.* Chicago: University of Chicago Press.

Gross, Alan G., and Arthur Walzer. 1997. "The *Challenger* Disaster and the Revival of Rhetoric in Organizational Life." In *From Critique to Affirmation: New Roles for Rhetoric in Creating Civic Life.* Ed. Richard Harvey Brown, 75–93. Special issue of *Argumentation* 11, no. 1.

Habermas, Jürgen. 1975. *Legitimation Crisis.* Boston: Beacon Press.

Hall, John A., and Charles Lindholm. 1999. *Is America Breaking Apart?* Princeton, N.J.: Princeton University Press.

Harrington, Michael. 1985. "Norman Thomas, Dignified Democrat: A Socialist's Centennial." *New Republic,* January 7 and 14, 16–18.

Haskell, Thomas L. 1984. *The Authority of Experts.* Bloomington: University of Indiana Press.

Hearne, Vicki. 1986. *Adam's Task: Calling Animals by Name.* New York: Knopf.

Held, David. 1982. "Crisis Tendencies, Legitimation and the State." In *Habermas: Critical Debates.* Ed. John B. Thompson and David Held, 180–195. Cambridge: MIT Press.

Heller, Agnes. 1987. *Beyond Justice.* New York: Basil Blackwell.

Hittinger, John P. 1989. "The Moral Status of the Expert in Contemporary Society." *The World and I* (August): 561–585.

Hodgson, Godfrey. 1992. *The World Turned Right Side Up: A History of the Conservative Ascendency in America.* Boston: Houghton Mifflin.

Horwitz, Morton J. 1977. *The Transformation of American Law 1780–1860.* Cambridge: Harvard University Press.

Inglehart, Ronald. 1991. "Changing Values in Industrial Society: The Case of North America, 1981–1990." Paper presented to the meetings of the American Political Science Association, Washington, D.C.

Kleinberg, Benjamin S. 1973. *American Society in the Post-Industrial Age: Technocracy, Power, and the End of Ideology.* Columbus, Ohio: Charles E. Merrill.

Krugman, Paul. 1991. *The Age of Diminished Expectations: U.S. Economic Policy in the 1990s.* Cambridge: MIT Press.

Laufer, Romain, and Catherine Paradeise. 1988. *Marketing Democracy: Public Opinion and Media Formation in Democratic Societies.* New Brunswick, N.J.: Transaction Books.

Levi, Margaret. 1998. "A State of Trust." In *Trust and Governance.* Ed. Valerie Braithwaite and Margaret Levi, 77–101. New York: Russell Sage Foundation.

Lipset, Seymour Martin, ed. 1979. *The Third Century: America as a Post-Industrial Society.* Stanford, Calif.: Hoover Institution.

Litowitz, Douglas. 1997. *Post-Modern Philosophy and Law.* Lawrence: University of Kansas Press.

Luhman, Niklas. 1982. *The Differentiation of Society.* New York: Columbia University Press.

MacIntyre, Alisdair. 1981. *After Virtue: A Study in Moral Theory.* Notre Dame, Ind.: University of Notre Dame Press.

———. 1988. *Whose Justice? Which Rationality?* Notre Dame, Ind.: University of Notre Dame Press.

Macpherson, Crawford Brough. 1962. *The Political Theory of Possessive Individualism.* London: Oxford University Press.

Merryman, John H., and Albert E. Elsen. 1987. *Law, Ethics, and the Visual Arts.* 2 vols. Philadelphia: University of Pennsylvania Press.

Miller, Arthur Selwyn. 1968. "Toward the 'Techno-Corporate' State: An Essay in American Constitutionalism." *Villanova Law Review* 14, no. 1 (fall): 1–73.

Miller, Perry. 1965. *The Life of the Mind in America.* New York: Harcourt Brace.

Mills, C. Wright. 1963. "Mass Media and Public Opinion." In *Power, Politics and People: The Collected Essays of C. Wright Mills,* 577–598. New York: Oxford University Press.

Morone, James A. 1991. *The Democratic Wish: Popular Participation and the Limits of American Government.* New York: Basic Books.

Nelkin, Dorothy. 1984. *Science as Intellectual Property.* New York: Macmillan.

Neumann, W. Russell. 1986. *The Paradox of Mass Politics: Knowledge and Opinion in the American Electorate.* Cambridge: Harvard University Press.

Neustadtl, Alan, Dan Clawson, and Denise Scott. 1992. *Money Talks: Corporate PALs and Political Influence.* New York: Basic Books.

Offe, Claus. 1984. *Contradictions of the Welfare State.* Cambridge: MIT Press.

Piven, Frances Fox, and Richard A. Cloward. 1988. *Why Americans Don't Vote.* New York: Pantheon.

Qualter, Terrence H. 1985. *Opinion Control in the Democracies.* New York: St. Martin's.

Reich, Robert B. 1991a. "Unacknowledged Legislators." *New Republic,* January 21, 38–42.

———. 1991b. *The Work of Nations: Preparing Ourselves for 21st-Century Capitalism.* New York: Knopf.

Richardson, Jeremy. 1993. *Pressure Groups.* New York: Oxford University Press.

Rosen, Jay. 1988. "Election Coverage as Propaganda." *Propaganda Review* (summer): 5–14.

Rothman, Stanley. 1979. "The Mass Media in Post-Industrial America." In *The Third Century: America as a Post-Industrial Society.* Ed. Seymour Martin Lipset, 327–344. Stanford, Calif.: Hoover Institution.

Scharr, John H. 1981. *Legitimacy in the Modern State.* New Brunswick, N.J.: Transaction Books.

Simmel, Georg. 1971 [1903]. "The Metropolis and Mental Life." In *George Simmel, on Individuality and Social Forms.* Ed. Donald Levine, 324–339. Chicago: University of Chicago Press.

———. 1978. *The Philosophy of Money.* Trans. Tom Bottomore and David Frisby. London: Routledge and Kegan Paul.

Skinner, Quentin. 1998. *Liberty before Liberalism.* Cambridge: Cambridge University Press.

Stanley, Manfred. 1981. *The Technological Conscience: Survival and Dignity in an Age of Expertise.* Chicago: University of Chicago Press.

Szabo, Denis. 1973. "The Post-Industrial Society: Deviance and Crime Diagnosis and Prognosis for the Year Two Thousand." Manuscript. Informational Centre for Comparative Criminology, University of Montreal.

Thomson, Michael. 1979. *Rubbish Theory.* New York: Oxford University Press.

Vidich, Arthur J. 1975. "Political Legitimacy in Bureaucratic Society: An Analysis of Watergate." *Social Research* (winter): 779–811.

———. 1987. "Religion, Economics, and Class in American Politics." *International Journal of Politics, Culture, and Society* 1, no. 1:4–22.

———. 1990. "American Democracy in the Late Twentieth Century: Political Rhetorics and the Mass Media." *International Journal of Politics, Culture, and Society* 4, no. 1:5–29.

———. 1991. "The End of the Enlightenment and Modernity: The Irrational Ironies of Rationalizations," *International Journal of Politics, Culture, and Society* 4, no. 3:269–284.

Weber, Max. 1978. *Economy and Society: An Outline of Interpretive Sociology.* Ed. Guenther Roth and Claus Wittich. Berkeley: University of California Press.

Wheeler, Michael. 1976. *Lies, Damn Lies, and Statistics: The Manipulation of Public Opinion in America.* New York: Liveright.

Wolfe, Alan. 1977. *The Limits of Legitimacy: Political Contradictions of Contemporary Capitalism.* New York: Free Press.

———. 1998. *One Nation, after All: What Middle-Class Americans Really Think about God, Country, Family, Race, Welfare, Immigration, Homosexuality, Work, the Right, the Left, and Each Other.* New York: Viking.

Wolff, Janet. 1981. *The Social Production of Art.* New York: St. Martin's.

CHAPTER 4

Acocella, Joan. 1998. "A Politics of Hysteria." *New Yorker,* April 6, 64–79.

Ammerman, Nancy. 1987. *Bible Believers: Fundamentalists in the Modern World.* New Brunswick, N.J.: Rutgers University Press.

———. 1990. *Baptist Battles: Social Change and Religious Conflict in the Southern Baptist Convention.* New Brunswick, N.J.: Rutgers University Press.

Anderson, Benedict. 1983. *Imagined Communities: Reflections on the Origin and Spread of Nationalism.* London: Verso.

Anderson, R. M. 1987. "Pentacostal and Charismatic Christianity." In *The Encyclopedia of Religion,* vol. 11. Ed. Mircea Eliade, 229–235. New York: Macmillan.

Ashley, David. 1997. *History Without a Subject: The Postmodern Condition.* Boulder, Colo.: Westview.

Becker, Penny Edgell, and Nancy L. Eiesland, eds. 1997. *Contemporary American Religion: An Ethnographic Reader.* Walnut Creek, Calif.: Alta Mira.

Bernstein, Mary. 1997. "Celebration and Suppression: The Strategic Uses of Identity by the Lesbian and Gay Movement." *American Journal of Sociology* 103, no. 3 (November): 531–565.

Brecher, Jeremy, and Tim Costello. 1990. *Building Bridges: The Emerging Grassroots Coalition of Labor and Community.* New York: Monthly Review Press.

Brown, Richard Harvey. 1989. *A Poetic for Sociology: Toward a Logic of Discovery for the Human Sciences.* Chicago: University of Chicago Press.

———. 1998. *Toward a Democratic Science: Scientific Narration and Civic Discourse.* New Haven: Yale University Press.

Brubaker, Rogers. 1984. *The Limits of Rationality: An Essay on the Social and Moral Thought of Max Weber.* London: Allen and Unwin.

Brulle, Robert J. 2000. *Agency, Democracy, and Nature: The U.S. Environmental Movement from a Critical Theory Perspective.* Cambridge: MIT Press.

Calhoun, Craig, ed. 1994. *Social Theory and the Politics of Identity.* Cambridge, Mass.: Blackwell.

Carpenter, J. A. 1997. *Revive Us Again: The Reawakening of American Protestantism.* New York: Oxford University Press.

Carwardine, R. J. 1993. *Evangelicals and Politics in Antebellum America.* New Haven: Yale University Press.

Cohen, Charles L. 1995. Review of Julius H. Rubin's *Religious Melancholy and Protestant Experience in America. Contemporary Sociology* 24, no. 2:184–185.

Cohen, Jean L. 1985. "Strategy or Identity: New Theoretical Paradigms and Contemporary Social Movements." *Social Research* 52 (winter): 663–716.

Crook, Stephen, Jan Pakulski, and Malcolm Waters. 1992. *Postmodernization: Change in Advanced Society.* London: Sage.

Dahrendorf, Ralf. 1988. *The Modern Social Conflict.* London: Widenfeld and Nicolson.

Dalton, Russell J., and Manfred Kuechler. 1990. "New Social Movements and the Political Order: Inducing Change for Long-Term Stability?" In *Challenging the Political Order: New Social and Political Movements in Western Democracies.* Ed. Russell J. Dalton and Manfred Kuechler. Cambridge: Polity.

Dalton, Russell J., Manfred Kuechler, and Wilhelm Bürklin. 1990. "The Challenge of New Movements." In *Challenging the Political Order: New Social and Political Movements in Western Democracies.* Ed. Russell J. Dalton and Manfred Kuechler, 3–22. Cambridge: Polity.

Davidson, J. D., R. E. Pyle, and D. V. Reyes. 1995. "Persistence and Change in the Protestant Establishment, 1930–1992." *Social Forces* 74, no. 1:157–175.

Davies, James A. 1962. "Toward a Theory of Revolution." *American Sociological Review* 27:5–19.

Davis, N. J., and R. V. Robinson. 1996. "Are the Rumors of War Exaggerated? Religious Orthodoxy and Moral Progressivism in America." *American Journal of Sociology* 102, no. 3:756–787.

Dayton, D. W. 1991. "Some Doubts about the Usefulness of the Category 'Evangelical.'" In *The Variety of American Evangelicalism.* Ed. D. Dayton and R. Johnson, 245–251. Downers Grove, Ill.: InterVarsity.

Dayton, D. W., and R. K. Johnson, eds. 1991. *The Variety of American Evangelicalism.* Downers Grove, Ill.: InterVarsity.

Durkheim, Emile. 1965 [1912]. *The Elementary Forms of Religious Life.* Trans. Karen Fields. New York: Free Press.

Duyvendak, Jan Willem. 1995. *The Power of Politics: New Social Movements in France.* Boulder, Colo.: Westview.

Eder, Klaus. 1993. *The New Politics of Class: Social Movements and Cultural Dynamics in Advanced Societies.* London: Sage.

Falk, Richard. 1988. "Religion and Politics: Verging on the Postmodern." *Alternatives* 13, no. 3 (July): 379–394.

Finke, Roger, and Rodney Stark. 1992. *The Churching of America, 1776–1990: Winners and Losers in Our Religious Economy.* New Brunswick, N.J.: Rutgers University Press.

Gerson, Ken, and Ralph Armbruster. 1997. "Beyond Old and New Social Movements." Manuscript. Departments of Political Science and Sociology, University of California, Riverside.

Gibbins, J. R. 1989. "Contemporary Political Culture: An Introduction." In *Contemporary Political Culture.* Ed. J. R. Gibbons, 1–30. London: Sage.

Gitlin, Todd. 1980. *The Whole World Is Watching: The Media in the Making and Unmaking of the New Left.* Berkeley: University of California Press.

———. 1996. Review of Michael J. Piore, *Beyond Individualism. Contemporary Sociology* 24, no. 6:736–737.

Green, John C. 1996. "A Look at the 'Invisible Army': Pat Robertson's 1988 Activist Corps." In J. C. Green, J. L. Guth, C. E. Smidt, and L. A. Kellstedt. *Religion and the Culture Wars.* Lanham, Md.: Rowman and Littlefield.

Green, John C., James L. Guth, Corwin E. Smidt, and Lyman A. Kellstedt. 1996. *Religion and the Culture Wars: Dispatches from the Front.* Lanham, Md.: Rowman and Littlefield.

Guigni, Marco G. 1998. "Structure and Culture in Social Movement Theory." *Sociological Forum* 3, no. 2:365–375.

Guth, James L. 1996. "The Politics of the Christian Right." In J. C. Green, J. L. Guth, C. E. Smidt, and L. A. Kellstedt. *Religion and the Culture Wars,* 7–29. Lanham, Md.: Rowman and Littlefield.

Guth, James L., John C. Green, Corwin E. Smidt, Lyman A. Kellstedt, and Margaret Poloma. 1997. *The Bully Pulpit: The Politics of Protestant Clergy.* Lawrence: University Press of Kansas.

Habermas, Jürgen. 1991. "New Social Movements." *Telos* 49 (fall): 33–37.

Harrison, Bennett. 1994. *Lean and Mean: The Changing Landscape of Corporate Power in the Age of Flexibility.* New York: Basic Books.

Harrison, Bennett, and Barry Bluestone. 1988. "The Growth of Low-Wage Employment: 1963–86." *American Economic Review* 78 (May): 124–128.

Harvey, David. 1989. *The Condition of Postmodernity: An Enquiry into the Origin of Cultural Change.* Cambridge, Mass.: Blackwell.

Hill, S. S. 1980. *The South and the North in American Religion.* Athens: University of Georgia Press.

Hulsberg, W. 1988. *The German Greens: A Social and Political Profile.* London: Verso.

Hunt, Stephen, Malcolm Hamilton, and Tony Walter, eds. 1998. *Charismatic Christianity: Sociological Perspectives.* New York: St. Martin's Press.

Iannaconne, L. R. 1993. "Heirs to the Protestant Ethic? The Economics of American Fundamentalists." In *Fundamentalisms and the State.* Ed. M. Marty and R. Appleby, 342–366. Chicago: University of Chicago Press.

Inglehart, Ronald. 1977. *The Silent Revolution: Changing Values and Political Styles among Western Publics.* Princeton, N.J.: Princeton University Press.

———. 1984. "The Changing Structure of Industrial Cleavages in Western Societies." In *Electoral Change in Advanced Industrial Democracies.* Ed. D. J. Dalton, S. C. Flanagan, and P. A. Beck, 25–69. Princeton, N.J.: Princeton University Press.

———. 1990. *Culture Shift in Advanced Industrial Society.* Princeton, N.J.: Princeton University Press.

Jasper, James. 1998. *The Art of Moral Protest: Culture, Biography, and Creativity in Social Movements.* Chicago: University of Chicago Press.

Jasper, James, and Dorothy Nelkin. 1992. *The Animal Rights Crusade: The Growth of a Moral Protest.* New York: Free Press.

Jelen, T. G., and C. Wilcox. 1995. *Public Attitudes toward Church and State.* Armonk, N.Y.: Sharpe.

Johnston, Hank, and Bert Klandermans, eds. 1995. *Social Movements and Culture.* Minneapolis: University of Minnesota Press.

Kellstedt, Lyman A., and Corwin E. Smidt. 1996. "Measuring Fundamentalism: An Analysis of Different Operational Strategies." In J. C. Green, J. L. Guth, C. E. Smidt, and L. A. Kellstedt, *Religion and the Culture Wars,* 193–218. Lanham, Md.: Rowman and Littlefield.

Kellstedt, Lyman A., John C. Green, James L. Guth, and Corwin E. Smidt. 1996. "Grasping the Essentials: The Social Embodiment of Religion and Political Behavior." In J. C. Green, J. L. Guth, C. E. Smidt, and L. A. Kellstedt, *Religion and the Culture Wars,* 174–192. Lanham, Md.: Rowman and Littlefield.

Klandermans, Bert. 1997. *The Social Psychology of Protest.* Oxford: Blackwell.

Kriesi, Hanspeter, Ruud Koopmans, Jan Willem Duyvendak, and Marco G. Giugni. 1995. *New Social Movements in Western Europe: A Comparative Analysis.* Minneapolis: University of Minnesota Press.

Larana, Enrique, Hank Johnson, and Joseph Gusfield, eds. 1994. *New Social Movements: From Ideology to Identity.* Philadelphia: Temple University Press.

Lichter, L. S., S. R. Lichter, and S. Rothman. 1983. "Hollywood and America: The Odd Couple." *Public Opinion* 5, no. 6:54–58.

Lichter, S. R., and S. Rothman. 1981. "Media and Business Elites." *Public Opinion* 45, no. 5:42–46, 59–60.

Lienesch, Michael. 1993. *Redeeming America: Piety and Politics in the New Christian Right.* Chapel Hill: University of North Carolina Press.

Linzey, A. 1999. *Animal Rites: Liturgies of Animal Care.* London: SCM Press.

Linzey, A., and D. Cohn-Sherbok. 1997. *After Noah: Animals and the Liberation of Theology.* London: Mowbray.

Lipset, Seymour, and Earl Raab. 1978. *The Politics of Unreason: Right-Wing Extremism in America, 1790–1977.* Chicago: University of Chicago Press.

Lo, Clarence Y. H. 1982. "Counter-Movements and Conservative Movements in the Contemporary U.S." *Annual Review of Sociology* 8:107–134.

Lowe, Brian M. 2001. "Animal Rights as a Quasi-Religion." *Implicit Religion* 4, no. 1:41–60.

Lyotard, Jean-François. 1988. *The Postmodern Condition: A Report on Knowledge.* Minneapolis: University of Minnesota Press.

MacKinnon, Catherine. 1992. "Pornography as Discrimination and Defamation." *Boston University Law Review* 793:71.

Manza, J., and C. Brooks. 1997. "The Religious Factor in Presidential Elections, 1960–1992." *American Journal of Sociology* 103, no. 1:38–81.

Marsden, G. M. 1980. *Fundamentalism and American Culture: The Shaping of Twentieth Century Evangelicalism, 1870–1925.* New York: Oxford University Press.

———. 1987. "Evangelical and Fundamental Christianity." In *The Encyclopedia of Religion,* vol. 15. Ed. Mircea Eliade, 190–197. New York: Macmillan.

———. 1991. "Fundamentalism and American Evangelicalism." In *The Variety of American Evangelicalism.* Ed. D. Dayton and R. Johnson, 22–35. Downers Grove, Ill.: InterVarsity.

McGee, Michael Calvin. 1980. "The Origins of 'Liberty': A Feminization of Power." *Communication Monographs* 47, no. 1 (March): 23–45.

———. 1983. "Social Movement as Meaning." *Central States Speech Journal* 34, no. 1 (spring): 67–82.

McLoughlin, W. G. 1978. *Revivals, Awakenings, and Reform: An Essay on Religion and Social Change in America, 1607–1977.* Chicago: University of Chicago Press.

Melling, Philip H. 2001. *Fundamentalism in America: Millennialism, Identity and Militant Religion.* Edinburgh: Edinburgh University Press.

Melucci, Alberto. 1989. *Nomads of the Present: Social Movements and Individual Needs in Contemporary Society.* Philadelphia: Temple University Press.

———. 1996. *Challenging Codes: Collective Action in the Information Age.* Cambridge: Cambridge University Press.

Misztal, B. 1985. "Social Movements against the State." In *Poland after Solidarity.* Ed. B. Misztal, 143–164. London: Transaction Books.

Moore, R. Laurence. 1994. *Selling God: American Religion in the Marketplace of Culture.* New York: Oxford University Press.

Morris, Aldon D., and Carol Mueller, eds. 1992. *Frontiers of Social Movement Theory.* New Haven Conn.: Yale University Press.

Neuhaus, Richard John. 1999. "Sacred Umbrellas." *Times Literary Supplement,* April 30.

Offe, Claus. 1985. "New Social Movements: Challenging the Boundaries of Institutional Politics." *Social Research* 52, no. 4:817–868.

———. 1990. "Reflections on the Institutional Self-Transformations of Movement Politics: A Tentative Stage Model." In *Challenging the Political Order.* Ed. R. Dalton and M. Kuechler, 232–250. Cambridge: Polity.

Oldfield, D. M. 1996. *The Right and the Righteous: The Christian Right Confronts the Republican Party.* Lanham, Md.: Rowman and Littlefield.

Olson, Mancur. 1971. *The Logic of Collective Action: Public Goods and the Theory of Groups.* Cambridge: Harvard University Press.

Parker, J. 1993. "With New Eyes: The Animal Rights Movement and Religion." *Perspectives in Biology and Medicine* 36:338–346.

Patterson, Orlando. 1998. *The Rituals of Blood.* Cambridge: Harvard University Press.

Piore, Michael J. 1995. *Beyond Individualism.* Cambridge: Harvard University Press.

Piven, Frances Fox, ed. 1992. *Labor Parties in Postindustrial Societies.* New York: Oxford University Press.

Pizzorno, A. 1978. "Political Exchange and Collective Identity in Industrial Conflict." In *The Resurgence of Class Conflict in Western Europe since 1968.* Ed. C. Crouch and A. Pizzorno, 277–298. London: Macmillan.

Poulantzas, Nicos. 1982. "On Social Classes." In *Classes, Power, and Conflict.* Ed. Anthony Giddens and David Held. Berkeley: University of California Press.

Pyle, R. E. 1996. *Persistence and Change in the Protestant Establishment.* Westport, Conn.: Praeger.

Robbins, Thomas, and Susan J. Palmer, eds. 1997. *Millennium, Messiahs, and Mayhem: Contemporary Apocalyptic Movements.* New York: Routledge.

Rothman, S., and S. R. Lichter. 1984. "What Are Movie-Makers Made Of?" *Public Opinion* 6, no. 6:14–18.

Rozell, M. J., and C. Wilcox. 1995. *God at the Grass Roots: The Christian Right in the 1994 Election.* Lanham, Md.: Rowman and Littlefield.

Rubin, Julius H. 1994. *Religious Melancholy and Protestant Experience in America.* New York: Oxford University Press.

Schmitt, Rudigen. 1989. "Organizational Interlocks between New Social Movements and

Traditional Elites: The Case of the West German Peace Movement." *European Journal of Political Research* 17, no. 5 (September): 583–598.

Shibley, Mark A. 1996. *Resurgent Evangelicalism in the United States: Mapping Cultural Change since 1970.* Columbia: University of South Carolina Press.

Singer, Peter. 1975. *Animal Liberation: A New Ethics for Our Treatment of Animals.* New York: New York Review.

Simons, Herbert W. 1991. "On the Rhetoric of Social Movements, Historical Movements, and 'Top-Down' Movements: A Commentary." *Communication Studies* 42, no. 1 (spring): 94–101.

Smidt, Corwin E., and James Penning. 1990. "A House Divided?" *Polity* 23, no. 1:127–138.

Smith, Christian. 1998. *American Evangelicalism: Embattled and Thriving.* Chicago: University of Chicago Press.

Smith, T. L. 1957. *Revivalism and Social Reform in Mid-Nineteenth-Century America.* New York: Abingdon.

Stillman, Todd. 2000. "Virtual National Movements: Palestinian Diasporic Nationalism on the Internet." M.A. thesis, Department of Sociology, University of Maryland.

Stryker, Sheldon, Timothy J. Owens, and Robert White, eds. 2000. *Self, Identity, and Social Movements.* Minneapolis: University of Minnesota Press.

Tarrow, Sidney. 1989. *Democracy and Disorder: Protest and Politics in Italy, 1965–1975.* New York: Oxford University Press.

Touraine, Alain. 1981. *The Voice and the Eye: An Analysis of Social Movements.* Trans. Alan Duff. Cambridge: Cambridge University Press.

Veen, H-J. 1989. "The Greens as a Milieu Party." In *Greens in West Germany.* Ed. E. Kolinsky, 31–60. Oxford: Berg.

Vidich, Arthur J., and Michael W. Hughley. 1988. "Fraternization and Rationality in Global Perspective." *International Journal of Politics, Culture, and Society* 2, no. 2 (winter): 242–256.

Weber, Max. 1958. *The City.* Trans. and ed. Don Martindale and Gertrud Neuwirty. Glencoe, Ill.: Free Press.

———. 1978. *Economy and Society: An Outline of Interpretive Sociology.* Ed. Guenther Ross and Claus Wittich. Berkeley: University of California Press.

Williams, Rhys, ed. 1992. *Cultural Wars in American Politics.* Hawthorne, N.Y.: Aldine de Gruyter.

Woodbury, Robert D., and Christian S. Smith. 1998. "Fundamentalism et al: Conservative Protestants in America." *Annual Review of Sociology* 24:25–26.

Woodbury, Robert D., P. Brick, and L. Babie. 1996. "Evangelicals and Politics: Surveying a Contemporary Mason-Dixon Line." Paper presented at the meetings of the American Sociological Association, New York.

Wuthnow, Robert. 1988. "Religious Discourse as Public Rhetoric; Review Essay." *Communication Research* 15 (June): 318–338.

———. 1994. *Producing the Sacred: An Essay on Public Religion.* Urbana: University of Illinois Press.

Zald, Mayer N. 1982. "Theological Crucibles: Social Movements in and of Religion." *Review of Religious Research* 23, no. 4 (June): 317–336.

———. 1988. "The Trajectory of Social Movements in America." *Research in Social Movements, Conflict, and Change* 10:19–41.

Zaretsky, Eli. 1976. *Capitalism, the Family, and Personal Life.* New York: Harper and Row.

CHAPTER 5

Abbott, Andrew Dean. 1988. *The System of Professions: An Essay on the Division of Expert Labor.* Chicago: University of Chicago Press.

Acocella, Joan. 1999. *Creating Hysteria.* San Francisco: Jossey-Bass.

Adorno, Theodor W. 1973. *The Jargon of Authenticity.* Evanston, Ill.: Northwestern University Press.

Appleby, Joyce Oldham. 2000. *Inheriting the Revolution: The First Generation of Americans.* Cambridge, Mass.: Belknap Press.

Arendt, Hannah. 1951. *The Origins of Totalitarianism.* New York: Macmillan.

———. 1970. *On Violence.* New York: Harcourt Brace Jovanovich.

Béjin, André. 1985. "The Influence of the Sexologists Second Sexual Democracy." In *Western Sexuality: Practice and Precept in Past and Present Times.* Ed. Philippe Ariès and André Béjin. New York: Basil Blackwell.

Bellah, Robert N. 1975. *The Broken Covenant: American Civil Religion in Time of Trial.* New York: Seabury Press.

Bellah, Robert N., Richard Madsen, William L. Sullivan, Ann Swidler, and Steven M. Tipton. 1985. *Habits of the Heart: Individualism and Commitment in American Life.* Berkeley: University of California Press.

———. 1991. *The Good Society.* New York: Knopf.

Belohradsky, Vaclau. 1981. "Bureaucracy and Banalization of Culture." In *American Society: Essays in the Political Economy and Cultural Psychology of an Advanced Industrial System.* Ed. Richard Harvey Brown. Washington, D.C.: Washington Institute for Social Research.

Benn, Stanley I., and G. F. Gaus, eds. 1983. *Public and Private in Social Life.* London: Croom Helm.

Bennett, Jane. 1990. "On Being a Native: Thoreau's Hermeneutics of Self." *Polity* 22, no. 4 (summer): 559–580.

Bernstein, Basil. 1971. *Class, Codes, and Control.* 3 vols. London: Routledge and Kegan Paul.

Bjorklund, Diane. 1998. *Interpreting the Self: Two Hundred Years of American Autobiography.* Chicago: University of Chicago Press.

Blumer, Herbert. 1969. *Symbolic Interactionism: Perspective and Method.* Englewood Cliffs, N.J.: Prentice Hall.

Brown, Richard Harvey. 1987. *Society as Text: Essays on Reason, Rhetoric, and Reality.* Chicago: University of Chicago Press.

———. 1998. *Toward a Democratic Science: Scientific Narration and Civic Communication.* New Haven: Yale University Press.

———. 2000. "The Erotics of Academic Conversation: Love, Ethics and Reason in Scholarly and Civic Discourse." In *Knowledge and Power in Higher Education: A Reader.* Ed. Richard Harvey Brown and J. Daniel Schubert. New York: Teachers College Press.

Burnstein, Andrew. 1999. *Sentimental Democracy: The Evolution of America's Romantic Self-Image.* New York: Hill and Wang.

Chodorow, Nancy. 1978. *The Reproduction of Mothering.* Berkeley: University of California Press.

Dickson, Lynda. 1993. "The Future of Marriage and Family in Black America. *Journal of Black Studies* 23, no. 4 (June): 472–491.

Durkheim, Emile. 1951. *Suicide.* New York: Free Press.

Erickson, Erik H. 1959. *Identity and the Life Cycle: Selected Papers.* New York: International Universities Press.

Ewen, Stuart, and Elizabeth Ewen. 1982. *Channels of Desire: Mass Images and the Shaping of American Consciousness.* New York: McGraw Hill.

Fingarette, Herbert. 1963. *The Self in Transformation: Psychoanalysis, Philosophy, and the Life of the Spirit.* New York: Basic Books.

Fox-Genovese, Elizabeth. 1993. "Beyond Individualism: Vicissitudes of the Self in a Postmodern World." Paper presented to the meetings of the American Political Science Association. September.

Foucault, Michel. 1977. *Discipline and Punish: The Birth of the Prison.* Trans. Alan Sheridan. New York: Random House.

———. 1978. *History of Sexuality.* Trans. Robert Hurley. New York: Pantheon Books.

Fromm, Erich. 1974. *The Art of Loving.* New York: Perennial Library.

Fuller, Robert. 1986. *Americans and the Unconscious.* New York: Oxford University Press.

Gans, Herbert J. 1988. *Middle American Individualism: The Future of Liberal Democracy.* New York: Free Press.

———. 1991. *People, Plans, and Policies: Essays on Poverty, Racism, and Other National Urban Problems.* New York: Columbia University Press.

Gehlen, Arnold. 1980. *Man in the Age of Technology.* Trans. Patricia Lipscomb. New York: Columbia University Press.

Georges, Christopher. 1993. "Brow Up, Crybabies, You're America's Luckiest Generation." *Washington Post,* September 12.

Gergen, Kenneth. 1991. *The Saturated Self: Dilemmas of Identity in Contemporary Life.* New York: Basic Books.

Gerth, Hans Heinrich, and C. Wright Mills. 1953. *Character and Social Structure.* New York: Harcourt.

Gup, Ted. 1985. "The Smithsonian's Secret Contract." *Washington Post Magazine,* May 12, 8–20.

Gusfield, Joseph. 1986. "I Gotta Be Me." *Contemporary Sociology* 15, no. 1:7–9.

Hall, Leslie A. 1991. *Hidden Anxieties: Male Sexuality, 1900–1950.* Cambridge, Mass.: Polity.

Halle, David. 1984. *America's Working Man: Work, Home, and Politics among Blue-Collar Property Owners.* Chicago: University of Chicago Press.

Hartz, Louis. 1955. *The Liberal Tradition in America.* New York: Harcourt Brace Jovanovich.

Hewitt, John. 1998. *The Myth of Self-Esteem: Finding Happiness and Solving Problems in America.* New York: St. Martin's.

Hirschman, Albert O. 1977. *The Passions and the Interest: Political Arguments for Capitalism before Its Triumph.* Princeton, N.J.: Princeton University Press.

Hitchens, Christopher. 1997. "This Long Drink of Water." *Times Literary Supplement,* June 6, 20–21.

Hofstadter, Richard. 1963. *Anti-Intellectualism in American Life.* New York: Knopf.

Horney, Karen. 1937. *The Neurotic Personality of Our Time.* New York: W. W. Norton.

House, James S. 1981. "Social Structure and Personality." In *Social Psychology: Sociological Perspectives.* Ed. Morris Rosenberg and Ralph H. Turner, 525–561. New York: Basic Books.

Howe, Daniel Walker. 1997. *Making the American Self: Jonathan Edwards to Abraham Lincoln.* Cambridge: Harvard University Press.

Howe, Irving. 1986. *The American Newness: Culture and Politics in the Age of Emerson.* Cambridge: Harvard University Press.

Hsu, Francis. 1983. *Rugged Individualism Reconsidered: Essays in Psychological Anthropology.* Knoxville: University of Tennessee Press.

Illouz, Eva. 2000. "A Future of the Sociology of the Emotions." Manuscript. Department of Sociology, Hebrew University, Jerusalem.

———. 2003. *Oprah Winfrey and the Glamour of Misery: An Essay on Popular Culture.* New York: Columbia University Press.

Inkeles, Alex. 1983. *Exploring Individual Modernity.* New York: Columbia University Press.

Irvine, Leslie. 1999. *Codependent Forevermore: The Invention of Self in a Twelve Step Group.* Chicago: University of Chicago Press.

Jefferson, Thomas. 1954. *Papers.* Princeton, N.J.: Princeton University Press.

Kahn, R. 1973. "The Professionals." *Wall Street Journal,* August 6.

Kohn, M. L. 1969. *Class and Conformity: A Study in Values.* Homewood Ill.: Dorsey.

Kohn, M. L., and C. Schooler. 1969. "Class, Occupation and Orientation." *American Sociological Review* 34:659–678.

Kusserow, Adrie Suzanne. 1999. "De-Homogenizing American Individualism: Socializing *Hard* and *Soft* Individualism in Manhattan and Queens." Manuscript. Department of Anthropology, St. Michael's College, Colchester, Vt.

Langman, Lauren, and Wanda Harold. 1989. "The American Midas." Paper presented to the meetings of the American Sociological Association. Manuscript. Department of Sociology, Loyola University, Chicago.

Langman, Lauren, and Leonard Kaplan. 1979. "Terror and Desire: The Social Psychology of Late Capitalism." Paper presented to the meetings of the American Sociological Association, August 27.

Langman, Lauren, and Judith A. Richman. 1987. "Psychiatry as a Vocation." *Current Research on Occupations and Professions* 4:21–67.

Lasch, Christopher. 1978. *The Culture of Narcissism: American Life in an Age of Diminishing Expectations.* New York: Norton.

Leo, John. 1992. "The Politics of Feelings." *U.S. News and World Report,* March 23, 28.

Lifton, Robert J. 1976. *The Life of the Self: Toward a New Psychology.* New York: Simon and Schuster.

Lipset, Seymour Martin. 1979. *The First New Nation.* New York: W. W. Norton.

Lyman, Stanford M. 1978. *The Seven Deadly Sins: Society and Evil.* New York: St. Martin's.

MacKinnon, Catherine. 1987. *Feminism Unmodified: Discourses on Life and Law.* Cambridge: Harvard University Press.

Marcel, Gabriel. 1962. *Man against Mass Society.* Trans. G. S. Fraser. Chicago: Regnery.

Marx, Leo. 1987. "A Visit to Mr. America." *New York Review of Books,* March 12, 36–38.

Mead, George Herbert. 1934. *Mind, Self and Society from the Standpoint of a Social Behaviorist.* Chicago: University of Chicago Press.

Melendez, Rita Maria. N.d. "The Modern Confessional: A Foucauldtian Analysis of Contemporary Confession in the Lives of Catholics and Gays." Manuscript. Department of Sociology, Yale University.

Merton, Robert K. 1957. *Social Theory and Social Structure.* Glencoe, Ill.: Free Press.

Miller, K. A., M. L. Kohn, and C. Schooler. 1977. "Women and Work: The Psychological Effects of Occupational Conditions." *American Journal of Sociology* 85:66–94.

Minson, Jeffrey. 1985. *Genealogies of Morals: Nietzsche, Foucault, Donzelot and the Eccentricity of Ethics.* New York: St. Martin's.

Nelson, Joel I. 1968. "Anomie: Comparisons between the Old and New Middle Class." *American Journal of Sociology* 74, no. 2 (September): 184–192.

Nolan, James L. 1998. *The Therapeutic State: Justifying Government at Century's End.* New York: New York University Press.

Ostereicher, Emil. 1979. "The Privatization of the Self in Modern Society." *Social Research* 46, no. 3.

Pearlin, Leonard I., and M. L. Kohn. 1966. "Social Class, Occupation, and Parental Values." *American Sociological Review* 31:466–479.

Polsky, Andrew. 1991. *The Rise of the Therapeutic State.* Princeton, N.J.: Princeton University Press.

Putnam, Robert D. 2000. *Bowling Alone: The Collapse and Revival of American Community.* New York: Simon and Schuster.

Reiff, Philip. 1990. *The Feeling of Intellect: Selected Writings.* Chicago: University of Chicago Press.

Reisman, David. 1950. *The Lonely Crowd.* New Haven: Yale University Press.

Roberts, Randy, and James Olson. 1997. *John Wayne: American.* Lincoln: University of Nebraska Press.

Rose, Nikolas. 1989. *Governing the Souls: Technology of Human Subjectivity.* London: Routledge.

Rosen, Stanley. 1985. "Post-Modernism and the End of Philosophy." *Canadian Journal of Political and Social Theory* 9, no. 3 (fall): 90–101.

Rothschild, Matthew. 1984. "Central Employment Agency: Students Respond to the CIA Rush." *The Progressive,* 18–21.

Schutz, Alfred. 1967. *The Phenomenology of the Social World.* Trans. George Walsh and Frederick Lehnert. Evanston, Ill.: Northwestern University Press.

Sennett, Richard. 1978. *The Fall of Public Man: On the Social Psychology of Capitalism.* New York: Vintage.

Shain, Barry Alan. 1996. *The Myth of American Individualism: The Protestant Origins of American Political Thought.* Princeton, N.J.: Princeton University Press.

Shils, Edward. 1981. *Tradition.* Chicago: University of Chicago Press.

Slater, Philip Elliot. 1991. *A Dream Deferred: America's Discontent and the Search for a New Democratic Ideal.* Boston: Beacon Press.

Spindler, Q. Dearborn. 1948. "American Character as Revealed by the Military: Descriptions and Origins." *Psychiatry: Journal for the Study of Interpersonal Processes* 11:275–281.

Stryker, Robin. 1994. "Rules, Resources, and Legitimacy Processes: Some Implications for Social Conflict, Order and Change." *American Journal of Sociology* 99 (January): 847–910.

———. 1995. "The Making of American Exceptionalism: The Knights of Labor and Class Formation in the Nineteenth Century." *Contemporary Sociology* 24, no. 4 (July): 369–371.

Taylor, Barbara. 1983. *Eve and the New Jerusalem: Socialism and Feminism in the Nineteenth Century.* New York: Pantheon.

Thoreau, Henry David. 2000. *Walden and Civil Disobedience.* Ed. Michael Meyer. Boston: Houghton Mifflin.

Tocqueville, Alexis de. 1945 [1835]. *Democracy in America.* New York: Knopf.

Trilling, Lionel. 1971. *Sincerity and Authenticity.* Cambridge: Harvard University Press.

Trotha, Trutz von. 1974. *Jugendliche Bandendeliquenz.* Stuttgart: Ferdinand Enke.

Valadez, Joseph, and Remi Clignet. 1987. "On the Ambiguities of a Sociological Analysis of Narcissism." *Sociological Quarterly* 28, no. 4:455–472.

Weigert, Andrew, and David D. Franks. 1989. "Ambivalence: A Touchstone of the Modern Temper." In *The Sociology of Emotions.* Ed. David D. Franks and E. Doyle McCarthy, 205–228. Greenwich, Conn.: JAI Press.

Westkott, Marcia. 1988. "Americans and the Unconscious." *Contemporary Sociology* 17, no. 2 (March): 226.

Wexler, Philip. 1992. *Becoming Somebody: Towards a Social Psychology of School.* Rochester, N.Y.: University of Rochester.

Whyte, William H. Foote. 1956. *The Organization Man.* New York: Simon and Schuster.

Wills, Gary. 1997. *John Wayne's America: The Politics of Celebrity.* New York: Simon and Schuster.

Wright, J. D., and S. Wright. 1976. "Social Class and Parental Values for Children: A Partial Replication and Extension of the Kohn Thesis." *American Sociological Review* 41:527–537.

CHAPTER 6

Abrahamson, Mark. 1995. *Urban Enclaves: Identity and Place in America.* New York: St. Martin's.

Adams, Barbara. 1990. *Time and Social Theory.* Cambridge: Polity Press.

———. 1995. *Timewatch: The Social Analysis of Time.* Cambridge: Polity Press.

Agger, Ben. 1989. *Fast Capitalism: A Critical Theory of Significance.* Urbana: University of Illinois Press.

Aminzade, Ronald. 1992. "Historical Sociology and Time." *Sociological Methods and Research* 20 (May):456–480.

Applebome, Peter. 1996. *Dixie Rising: How the South Is Shaping American Values, Politics, and Culture.* New York: Random House.

Barber, Benjamin. 1983. *The Logic and the Limits of Trust.* Piscataway, N.J.: Rutgers University Press.

Bartky, Ian. 2000. *Selling the True Time: Nineteenth Century Timekeeping in America.* Stanford, Calif.: Stanford University Press.

Baumgartner, M. P. 1988. *The Moral Order of the Suburb*. New York: Oxford University Press.

Bellah, Robert N., Richard Madsen, William L. Sullivan, Ann Swidler, and Steven M. Tipton. 1985. *Habits of the Heart: Individualism and Commitment in American Life*. Berkeley: University of California Press.

Bergmann, Albert. 1993. *The Postmodern Divide*. Chicago: University of Chicago Press.

Brown, Cliff. 2000. "The Role of Employers in Split Labor Markets: An Event-Structure Analysis of Racial Conflict and AFL Organizing, 1917–1919." *Social Forces* (December): 653–681.

Brown, Richard Harvey, and Remi Clignet. 2000. "The Commercialization of American Higher Education." In *Knowledge and Power in Higher Education*. Ed. Richard Harvey Brown and Daniel Schubert. New York: Teachers College Press.

Brown, Richard Harvey, and George V. Coelho, eds. 1986. *Traditions and Transformation: Asian Indians in America*. Williamsburg, Va.: College of William and Mary. Studies in Third World Societies.

Bukatman, Scott. 1993. *Terminal Identity: The Virtual Subject in Postmodern Science Fiction*. Durham, N.C.: Duke University Press.

Caldeira, T. 1996. "Fortified Enclaves: The New Urban Segregation." *Public Culture* 8: 303–328.

Checkoway, Barry, ed. 1986. *Strategic Perspectives on Planning Practice*. Lexington: Lexington Books.

Clignet, Remi. 1990. "L'Exceptionnalisme." In *L'Etat des Etats-Unis*. Ed. M. F. Toinet and A. Lenkh. Paris: La Découverte.

———. 1992. *Death, Deeds, and Decedents: Inheritances in Modern America*. Hawthorne, N.Y.: Aldine de Gruyter.

Crane, Diane. 1987. *The Transformation of the Avant Garde*. Chicago: University of Chicago Press.

Davis, K. 1990. *Women and Time: The Weaving of the Strands of Everyday Life*. Aldershot: Avebury.

Dickens, Charles. 1978. *On America and the Americans*. Austin: University of Texas Press.

Diner, Hasia. 2001. *Lower East Side Memories: A Jewish Place in America*. Princeton, N.J.: Princeton University Press.

Duhamel, Georges. 1931. *America: The Menace, Scenes from the Life of the Future*. Boston: Houghton Mifflin.

Duncan, James S. 1990. *The City as Text: The Politics of Landscape Interpretation in Kandyan Kingdom*. Cambridge: Cambridge University Press.

Durkheim, Emile. 1965 [1912]. *The Elementary Forms of Religious Life*. Trans. Karen Fields. New York: Free Press.

Dworkin, Ronald. 1996. "Sex, Death, and the Courts." *New York Review of Books*, August 8, 44–50.

Eliade, Mircea. 1954. *The Myth of the Eternal Return*. New York: Pantheon Books.

———. 1959. *The Sacred and the Profane*. New York: Harper and Row.

Ellin, N. 1996. *Architecture of Fear*. New York: Princeton Architectural Press.

Eltis, David. 1987. *Economic Growth and the Ending of the Transatlantic Slave Trade*. New York: Oxford University Press.

Epstein, Cynthia Fuchs, Carroll Seron, Bonnie Oglensky, and Robert Sauté. 1999. *The Part-Time Paradox: Time Norms, Professional Life, Family and Gender.* New York: Routledge.

Ferguson, Marjory. 1991. "Marshall McLuhan Revisited: 1960 Zeitgeist Victim or Pioneer Postmodernist?" *Media, Culture, and Society* 13:71–90.

Flaherty, Michael G. 2000. *A Watched Pot: How We Experience Time.* New York: New York University Press.

Foster, Stephen William. 1988. *The Past Is Another Country: Representation, Historical Consciousness, and Resistance in the Blue Ridge.* Berkeley: University of California Press.

Foucault, Michel. 1977. *Discipline and Punish: The Birth of the Prison.* New York: Random House.

Franklin, J. H. 1975. "The North, the South, and the American Revolution." *Journal of American History* 62.

Friedland, Roger, and Deirdre Boden, eds. 1994. *Nowhere: Time and Modernity.* Berkeley: University of California Press.

Fuchs, Stephan. 1988. "Tautology and Paradox in the Self-Descriptions of Modern Society." *Sociological Theory* 6:21–37.

———. 1992. *The Professional Quest for Truth: A Social Theory of Science and Knowledge.* Albany: State University of New York Press.

Fuentes, Carlos. 1986. "When Don Quixote Left His Village the Modern World Began." Book review, *New York Times,* March 23.

Fukuyama, Francis. 1992. *The End of History and the Last Man.* New York: Macmillan.

Gabel, Joseph. 1984. "The Mass Psychology of the New Federalism: How the Burger Court's Political Imagery Legitimizes the Privatization of Everyday Life." *George Washington Law Review* 52:263–271.

Garreau, Joel. 2000. "Home Is Where the Phone Is." *Washington Post,* October 17, A1–A12.

Giddens, Anthony. 1987. *Social Theory and Modern Sociology.* London: Polity Press.

Glick, James. 1999. *Faster: The Acceleration of Just about Everything.* New York: Pantheon.

Gordon, David. 1978. "Capitalist Development and the History of American Cities." In *Marxism and the Metropolis: New Perspectives in Urban Political Economy.* Ed. William K. Tabb and Larry Sauers. New York: Oxford University Press.

Gouldner, Alvin W. 1972. *The Coming Crisis in Western Sociology.* New York: Basic Books.

Gramsci, Antonio. 1959. *The Modern Prince and Other Writings.* New York: International Publishers.

Grant, Susan-Mary. 1997. "Making History: Myth and the Construction of American Nationhood." In *Myths and Nationhood.* Ed. Geoffrey Hosking and George Schöpflin, 88–106. New York: Routledge.

Greer, Scott. 1962. *The Emerging City: Myth and Reality.* New York: Free Press.

Gregory, Bruce. 1988. *Inventing Reality: Physics as Language.* New York: Wiley.

Grimsley, Kirstin Downey. 2000. "Creative Perks for the Frazzled: Firms Hire Cooks and Convinces to Ease Home Life for Employees." *Washington Post,* February 25, A1–A16.

Griswold, Wendy. 1992. Review of *Commonplaces: Community, Ideology, and Identity in American Culture,* by David M. Hummon. *American Journal of Sociology* 97, no. 6 (May): 1752–1754.

Gurvitch, Georges. 1964. *The Spectrum of Social Time.* Dordrecht, Netherlands: D. Reidel.

Hacker, Andrew. 2000. "The Case against Kids." *New York Review of Books,* November 30, 12–18.

Hage, Jerald, and Charles H. Powers. 1992. *Post-Industrial Lives: Roles and Relationships in the 21st Century.* Newbury Park, Calif.: Sage.

Halbwachs, Maurice. 1950. *La Mémoire collective.* Paris: Presses Universitaires de France.

Hanawalt, Barbara, and Michal Kobialka, eds. 2002. *Medieval Practices of Space.* Minneapolis: University of Minnesota Press.

Harvey, David. 1989. *The Condition of Postmodernity: An Inquiry into the Origins of Cultural Change.* Oxford: Basil Blackwell.

Heidegger, Martin. 1980 [1927]. *Being and Time.* Trans. J. Macquarrie and E. Robinson. Oxford: Blackwell.

Herwison, Robert. 1987. *The Heritage Industry.* London: Methuen.

Hochschild, Arlie Russell. 1989. *The Second Shift: Working Parents of the Revolution at Home.* New York: Avon Books.

———. 1993. *The Managed Heart.* Berkeley: University of California Press.

———. 1997. *The Time Bind: When Work Becomes Home and Home Becomes Work.* New York: Metropolitan Books.

Hughes, Robert. 1993. *The Culture of Complaint.* New York: Oxford University Press.

Hummon, David M. 1990. *Commonplaces: Community, Ideology, and Identity in American Culture.* Albany: State University of New York Press.

Jacobs, Jerry. 1984. *The Mall: An Attempted Escape from Everyday Life.* Prospect Heights, Ill.: Waveland.

Jacobs, J. A., and K. Gerson. 1998. "Who Are the Overworked Americans?" *Review of Social Economy* 56, no. 4:442–449.

Jameson, Fredric. 1992. *Postmodernism, or the Cultural Logic of Late Capitalism.* Durham, N.C.: Duke University Press.

Kalleberg, Anne, and Cynthia Epstein. 2001. "Introduction: Temporal Dimensions of Employment Relations." *American Behavioral Scientist* 44, no. 7 (March): 1064–1075.

Kern, Stephen. 1983. *The Culture of Time and Space: 1880–1918.* Cambridge: Harvard University Press.

Kowinski, William S. 1985. *The Malling of America: An Inside Look at the Great Consumer Paradise.* New York: W. Morrow.

Kubler, George. 1962. *The Shapes of Time: Remarks on the History of Things.* New Haven: Yale University Press.

Kundera, Milan. 1983. "Et si le roman nous abandonne." *Le Nouvel observateur,* August 25.

Lakoff, George, and Mark Johnson. 1980. *Metaphors We Live By.* Chicago: University of Chicago Press.

Landes, David S. 2000. *Revolution in Time: Clocks and the Making of the Modern World.* Cambridge, Mass.: Belknap Press.

Liera-Schwichtenberg, Ramona. 1996. Manuscript. Center for Women's Studies, Wichita State University, Kansas.

Louv, Richard. 1983. *American II.* New York: Penguin.

Low, Setha M. 2000. "Constructing Exclusion through Gated Communities." *Social Issue.*

Lowenthal, David. 1985. *The Past Is a Foreign Country.* Cambridge: Cambridge University Press.

Lukács, Georg. 1971. *The Theory of the Novel.* Cambridge: MIT Press.

Luke, Timothy W. 2003. "From Body Politics to Body Shops: Power, Subjectivity, and the Body in an Era of Global Capitalism." In *The Politics of Selfhood: Bodies and Identities in Global Capitalism.* Ed. Richard Harvey Brown, ch. 5. Minneapolis: University of Minnesota Press.

Maines, D. R. 1983. "Time and Biography in Diabetic Experience." *Mid-American Review* 8:103–117.

Mannheim, Karl. 1936. *Ideology and Utopia.* New York: Harcourt Brace.

Marcuse, Herbert. 1964. *One Dimensional Man: Studies in the Ideology of Advanced Industrial Society.* Boston: Beacon Press.

Marx, Gary. 1997. "Social Control across Borders." In *Crime and Law Enforcement in the Global Village.* Ed. W. McDonald. New York: Matthew Bender.

Marx, Karl. 1973 [1857]. *Grundrisse.* Trans. Martin Nicolaus. New York: Vintage.

———. 1976 [1867]. *Capital,* vol. 1. Harmondsworth, England: Penguin.

Melbin, Murray. 1978. "Night as Frontier." *American Sociological Review* 43:3–22.

Merton, Robert King. 1964. *Social Theory and Social Structure.* New York: Free Press.

———. 1973. *The Sociology of Science: Theoretical and Empirical Investigations.* Chicago: University of Chicago Press.

———. 1984. "Socially Expressed Durations: A Case Study of Concept Formation in Sociology." In *Conflict and Consensus.* Ed. W. Powell and R. Robbins, 262–283. New York: Free Press.

Miller, Daniel, and Guy Swanson. 1958. *The Changing American Parents.* New York: Holt, Reinhart and Winston.

Miller, John. 2000. *Egotopia: Narcissism and the New American Landscape.* Tuscaloosa: University of Alabama Press.

Mintz, Beth, and Michael Schwartz. 1985. *The Power Structure of American Business.* Chicago: University of Chicago Press.

Moore, Wilbert E. 1963. *Man, Time and Society.* New York: Wiley.

Moscovici, Serge. 1968. *Essai sur l'histoire humaine de la nation.* Frankfurt: Surkamp.

Mumford, Lewis. 1963. *Technics and Civilization.* New York: Harcourt Brace Jovanovich.

Murphy, Jim. 1997. "The Excremental Society." Unpublished manuscript. Department of Sociology, University of Maryland, College Park.

Nadesan, Majia Holmer. 1997. "Gender and Temporality in Interpersonal Systems." *Symbolic Interaction* 20, no. 1:21–43.

Naipaul, Vidiadhar Surajprased. 1988. *A Turn in the South.* New York: Knopf.

Nasaw, David. 1993. *Going Out: The Rise and Fall of Public Amusement.* New York: Basic Books.

Nguyen, D. T. 1992. "The Spatialization of Metric Time: The Conquest of Land and Labour in Europe and the United States." *Time and Society* 1, no. 1:29–50.

Nowotny, Helga. 1994. *Time: The Modern and Postmodern Experience.* Cambridge, Mass.: Polity Press.

O'Malley, M. 1992. "Standard Time, Narrative Film and American Progressive Politics." *Time and Society* 1, no. 3:341–358.

Persell, Caroline Hodges. 1994. "Robin McWilliams Lecture: Taking Society Seriously." *Sociological Forum* 9, no. 4:641–657.

Peyser, Marc. 1997. "Time Bind? What Time Bind?" *Newsweek,* May 12, 69.

Piore, Michael, and Charles Sabel. 1984. *The Second Industrial Divide.* New York: Basic Books.

Poster, Mark. 1990. *The Mode of Information: Poststructuralism and the Social Context.* Chicago: University of Chicago Press.

Prigogine, V., and Isabelle Stengers. 1979. *La Nouvelle alliance.* Paris: Gallimard.

Robinson, John, and Geofrey Godbey. 1999. *Time for Life: The Surprising Ways Americans Use Their Time.* University Park: Pennsylvania State University Press.

Rochberg-Halton, Eugene. 1986. *Meaning and Modernity: Social Theory in the Pragmatic Attitude.* Chicago: University of Chicago Press.

Rogers, Stacy J., and Paul R. Amato. 2000. "Have Changes in Gender Relations Affected Marital Quality?" *Social Forces* 79:731–753.

Rosenzweig, Roy, and David Thelen. 1998. *The Presence of the Past: Popular Uses of History in American Life.* New York: Columbia University Press.

Roth, Julius A. 1963. *Timetables.* New York: Bobbs-Merrill.

Rouse, Joseph. 1987. *Knowledge and Power: Toward a Political Philosophy of Science.* Ithaca, N.Y.: Cornell University Press.

Ryder, Norman. 1965. "The Notion of Cohort in the Study of Social Change." *American Sociological Review* 30:840–861.

Sack, Robert David. 1986. *Human Territoriality: Its Theory and History.* Cambridge: Cambridge University Press.

St. Clair, Robert N. 2002. *Social Metaphor: Essays in Social Epistemology.* New York: Mellen.

Salman, Jacqueline. 1998. "'Hi Dad! Bye Mom': Couples Try Parenting in Shifts." *Washington Post,* August 2, A1, A27.

Schor, Juliet. 1999. *The Overworked American.* New York: Basic Books.

Schwartz, Barry. 1975. *Queuing and Waiting: Studies in the Social Organization of Access and Delay.* Chicago: University of Chicago Press.

Sennett, Richard. 1970. *The Use of Disorder: Personal Identity and City Life.* New York: Knopf.

Shapiro, Laura. 1997. "The Myth of Quality Time." *Newsweek,* May 12, 62–68.

Shearing, Clifford, and Philip C. Stenning. 1983. "Private Security: Implications for Social Control." *Social Problems* 30:493–506.

Shelton, Alan. 1993. "Writing McDonald's, Eating the Past: McDonald's as a Postmodern Space." *Studies in Symbolic Interaction* 15:103–118.

Smith, Mark M. 1997. *Mastered by the Clock: Time, Slavery, and Freedom in the American South.* Chapel Hill: University of North Carolina Press.

Sontag, Susan. 1977. *Illness as Metaphor.* New York: Farrar, Strauss, Giroux.

———. 1989. *AIDS and Its Metaphors.* New York: Farrar, Strauss, Giroux.

Sorokin, Pitrim. 1943. *Sociocultural Causality, Space, and Time.* Durham, N.C.: Duke University Press.

Spain, Daphne, and Suzanne Bianchi. 1996. *Balancing Art: Motherhood, Marriage, and Employment among American Women.* New York: Russell Sage Foundation.

Specter, Michael. 2000. "Search and Deploy: The Race to Build a Better Search Engine." *New Yorker,* May 29, 88–100.

Talbot, Margaret. 1997. "Dial-A-Wife: The Next Domestic Solution." *New Yorker,* October 20–27, 196–208.

Taylor, William R. 1979. *Cavalier and Yankee: The Old South and American National Character.* New York: Oxford University Press.

Thompson, E. P. 1967. "Time, Work Discipline, and Industrial Capitalism." *Past and Present* 38:56–97.

Thompson, Michael. 1979. *Rubbish Theory: The Creation and Destruction of Value.* New York: Oxford University Press.

Tocqueville, Alexis de. 1945 [1835]. *Democracy in America.* New York: Knopf.

Turnbull, Colin M. 1983. *The Human Cycle.* New York: Simon and Schuster.

Turner, Ralph H. 1960. "Sponsored and Contest Mobility and the School System." *American Sociological Review* 25, no. 6:855–867.

———. 1976. "The Real Self from Institution to Impulse." *American Journal of Sociology* 81:989–1075.

Vidich, Arthur, and Joseph Bensman. 1958. *Small Town in Mass Society: Class, Power, and Religion in a Rural Community.* Princeton, N.J.: Princeton University Press.

Waits, William B. 1993. *The Modern Christmas: A Cultural History of Giftgiving.* New York: New York University Press.

Walker, Katherine D. 1998. "Identity and the Internet: The Cyber-Self in an Emerging Virtual Realm." Manuscript. Department of Sociology, University of Massachusetts, Amherst.

Waller, Willard. 1937. "The Dating and Rating Complex." *American Sociological Review* 2, no. 5:727–734.

Walzer, Michael. 1986. "Pleasures and Costs of Urbanity." *Dissent* 33, no. 4 (fall): 470–475.

Watson, James L., ed. 1997. *Golden Arches East.* Stanford, Calif.: Stanford University Press.

Weber, Max. 1958 [1904–1905]. *The Protestant Ethic and the Spirit of Capitalism.* Trans. and ed. Talcott Parsons. New York: Scribner's.

Wexler, Philip. 1983. *Critical Social Psychology.* Boston: Routledge and Kegan Paul.

Whitehead, Alfred North. 1953. *Science and the Modern World.* New York: Free Press.

Whyte, William H. 1943. *Street Corner Society.* Chicago: University of Chicago Press.

Yakura, Elaine. 2001. "Billables: The Meaning of Time in Consulting." *American Behavioral Scientist* 44, no. 7 (March): 1076–1095.

Young, Michael. 1988. *The Metronomic Society: Natural Rhythms and Human Timetables.* Cambridge: Harvard University Press.

Zelinsky, W. 1988. *Nation into State: The Shifting Foundations of American Nationalism.* Chapel Hill: University of North Carolina Press.

Zerubavel, Eviatar. 1977. "The French Republican Calendar: A Case Study in the Sociology of Time." *American Sociological Review* 42:868–877.

———. 1981. *Hidden Rhythms: Schedules and Calendars in Social Life.* Chicago: University of Chicago Press.

Zukin, Sharon, Robert Baskerville, Miriam Greenberg, Courtney Guthreau, Jean Halley, Mark Halling, Kristen Lawler, Ron Nerio, Rebecca Stack, Alex Vitale, and Betsy Wissinger. 1998. "From Coney Island to Las Vegas in the Urban Imaginary: Discursive Practices of Growth and Decline." *Urban Affairs Review* 33, no. 5 (May): 627–654.

CHAPTER 7

Acock, Alan C., and David H. Demo. 1994. *Family Diversity and Well-Being.* Thousand Oaks, Calif.: Sage.

Ammerman, Nancy. 1987. *Bible Believers: Fundamentalists in the Modern World.* New Brunswick, N.J.: Rutgers University Press.

Anderson, Quentin. 1971. *The Imperial Self: An Essay in American Literary and Cultural History.* New York: Knopf.

Arendell, Terry. 1995. *Fathers and Divorce.* Thousand Oaks, Calif.: Sage.

Ariès, Philippe. 1979. *Histoire des populations françaises et de leurs attitudes devant la vie depuis le XVIIIè siecle.* Paris: Editions du Seuil.

Aulette, Judy Root. 1998. "The Way We Really Are: Coming to Terms with America's Changing Families." Review essay. *Contemporary Sociology* 27, no. 3 (May): 235–237.

Bailey, Beth L. 1988. *From the Front Porch to the Back Seat: Courtship in Twentieth-Century America.* Baltimore: Johns Hopkins University Press.

Barnes, Gill Gorell, Paul Thompson, Gwyn Daniels, and Natasha Burchardt. 1998. *Growing Up in Stepfamilies.* New York: Clarendon Press.

Basch, Norma. 1999. *Framing American Divorce: From the Revolutionary Generation to the Victorians.* Berkeley: University of California Press.

Beaman-Hall, L. 1996. "Family at Any Cost? Evangelical Ideology and the Response to Wife Abuse." Paper presented at the American Sociological Association meeting, New York.

Beck, Ulrich, and E. Gernsheim-Beck. 1995. *The Normal Chaos of Love.* Cambridge: Polity.

Becker, Gary. 1981. *A Treatise on the Family.* Cambridge: Harvard University Press.

Beer, William A., ed. 1988. *Relative Strangers: Studies of Stepfamily Processes.* Totowa, N.J.: Rowman and Littlefield.

Béjin, André. 1985. "The Decline of the Psychoanalyst and the Rise of the Sexologist." In *Western Sexuality: Practice and Precept in Past and Present Times.* Ed. Philippe Ariès and André Béjin. New York: Basil Blackwell.

Béjin, André, and Michael Pollak. 1977. "La rationalisation de la sexualité." *Cahiers internationaux de sociologie* 24, no. 62 (January–June): 110–125.

Bellah, Robert N., Richard Madsen, William M. Sullivan, Ann Swidler, and Steven M. Tipton. 1985. *Habits of the Heart: Individualism and Commitment in American Life.* Berkeley: University of California Press.

Bengtson, Vern L. 2001. "Beyond the Nuclear Family: The Increasing Importance of Multigenerational Bonds." *Journal of Marriage and Family* 63, no. 1 (February): 1–16.

Bengtson, Vern L., and W. Andrew Achenbaum, eds. 1993. *The Changing Contract across Generations.* New York: Aldine de Gruyter.

Bengston, Vern, and Joan Robertson, eds. 1985. *Grandparenthood.* Beverly Hills, Calif.: Sage.

Berkin, Carol. 1996. *First Generations: Women in Colonial America.* New York: Hill and Wang.

Berger, Brigette. 2002. *The Family in the Modern Age: More than a Lifestyle Choice.* New Brunswick, N.J.: Transaction Books.

Blackwelder, Julia. 1997. *Now Hiring: The Feminization of Work in the United States, 1900–1995.* College Station: Texas A and M University Press.

Blossfield, Hans-Peter. 1995. *New Roles for Women: Family Formation in Modern Societies.* Boulder, Colo.: Westview.

Blumberg, Joan Jacobs. 1988. *Fasting Girls: The Emergence of Anorexia Nervosa as a Modern Disease.* Cambridge: Harvard University Press.

Bonner, Francis, and Paul DuGay. 1992. "Representing the Enterprising Self: Thirtysomething and Contemporary Consumer Culture." *Theory, Culture and Society* 9, no. 2 (May): 67–92.

Booth, Alan, and Judy Dunn. 1994. *Stepfamilies: Who Benefits? Who Does Not?* Hillsdale, N.J.: Lawrence Erlbaum.

Bozett, Frederick W. 1987. *Gay and Lesbian Parents.* New York: Praeger.

Brienes, Wini. 1992. *Young, White, and Miserable: Growing up Female in the Fifties.* Chicago: University of Chicago Press.

Brittain, A. 1989. *Masculinity and Power.* Oxford: Blackwell.

Brommer, Stephanie J. 1998. "The Mommy Wars: Conflicting Ideologies of Motherhood in the United States." Manuscript. Department of Anthropology, University of California, Santa Barbara.

Brown, Clair. 1994. *American Standards of Living, 1918–1988.* Cambridge: Blackwell.

Brown, Helen Gurley. 1982. *Having It All.* New York: Simon and Schuster.

Bumpass, Larry L., and James A. Sweet. 1995. *Cohabitation, Marriage, and Union Stability: Preliminary Findings from NSFH2.* Madison: University of Wisconsin, Center for Demography and Ecology. NSFH Working Paper No. 65.

Bumpass, Larry L., James A. Sweet, and Andrew J. Cherlin. 1991. "The Role of Cohabitation in Declining Rates of Marriage." *Journal of Marriage and the Family* 53:913–927.

Burkett, Wynn Mclanahan. 2000. *Life after Baby: From Professional Woman to Beginner Parent.* Berkeley, Calif.: Wildcat Canyon Press.

Burros, Marian. 1988. "Women: Out of the House but Not out of the Kitchen." *New York Times,* February 24, A1, C10.

Calhoun, Arthur Wallace. 1917. *A Social History of the American Family from Colonial Times to the Present.* Cleveland: Arthur H. Clark.

Cancian, Francesca. 1987. *Love in America: Gender and Self-Development.* Cambridge: Cambridge University Press.

———. 1994. "Romantic Longings." Book review. *Social Forces* 42, no. 3 (March): 907–908.

Carnoy, Martin. 2000. *Sustaining the New Economy: Work, Family, and Community in the Information Age.* New York: Russell Sage Foundation.

Casper, Lynn M., and Suzanne M. Bianchi. 2002. *Continuity and Change in the American Family.* Thousand Oaks, Calif.: Sage.

Chambers, Deborah. 2001. *Representing the Family.* London: Sage.

Cheal, David. 1991. "Unity and Difference in Postmodern Families." Manuscript. Sociology Department, University of Winnipeg.

Cherlin, Andrew J. 1981. *Marriage, Divorce, Remarriage.* Cambridge: Harvard University Press.

Clarkberg, Martin, R. Stolzenberg, and L. Waite. 1995. "Attitudes, Values, and Entrance into Cohabitational versus Marital Unions." *Social Forces* 74:609–634.

Clement, Wallace, and John Myles. 1994. *Relations of Ruling: Class and Gender in Postindustrial Societies.* Montreal: McGill University Press.

Connell, R. W. 1995. *Masculinities.* Berkeley: University of California Press.

Coontz, Stephanie. 1988. *The Social Origins of Private Life.* London: Verso.

———. 1998. *The Way We Really Are: Coming to Terms with America's Changing Families.* New York: Basic Books.

Daily, Nancy. 1998. *When the Baby Boom Women Retire.* Westport, Conn.: Praeger.

Dank, Barry, and Roberto Refinetti, eds. 1999. *The Politics of Sexuality.* New Brunswick, N.J.: Transaction Books.

Dayton, Cornelia Hughes. 1995. *Women before the Bar: Gender, Law, and Society in Connecticut, 1639–1789.* Durham: University of North Carolina Press.

Degler, Carl N. 1980. *At Odds: Women and the Family in America from the Revolution to the Present.* New York: Oxford University Press.

D'Emilio, John, and Estelle B. Freedman. 1989. *Intimate Matters: A History of Sexuality in America.* New York: Perennial.

DeMunck, Victor C., ed. 1998. *Romantic Love and Sexual Behavior.* New York: Praeger.

Dillon, M. C. 1997. "SexLove: Marginality and Rectitude." Manuscript. Department of Philosophy, Binghamton University, New York.

Dubrovsky, Rachel. N.d. "Ally McBeal as Postfeminist Icon: The Aestheticizing and Fetishizing of the Independent Working Woman." Manuscript. Institute of Communications Research, University of Illinois, Urbana-Champaign.

Eisenstein, Zillah. 1982. "The Sexual Politics of the New Right: Understanding the 'Crisis of Liberalism' for the 1980s." *Signs: Journal of Women in Culture and Society* 7, no. 3:567–588.

Elkind, David. 1994. *Ties That Stress: The New Family Imbalance.* Cambridge: Harvard University Press.

Ericksen, Julia, and Sally Steffen. 1999. *Kiss and Tell: Surveying Sex in the Twentieth Century.* Cambridge: Harvard University Press.

Ermisch, John F. 1991. *Lone Parenthood: An Economic Analysis.* New York: Cambridge University Press.

Faludi, Susan. 1999. *Stiffed: The Betrayal of the American Man.* New York: Morrow.

Farley, Reynolds. 1996. *The New American Reality: Who We Are, How We Got Here, Where We Are Going.* New York: Russell Sage Foundation.

Fleming, Karl, and Anne Taylor Fleming. 1975. *The First Time.* New York: Simon and Schuster.

Font, John C., and Maura Shaw Tantillo, eds. 1993. *American Sexual Politics: Sex, Gender, and Race since the Civil War.* Chicago: University of Chicago Press.

Fuchs, Victor R. 1988. *Women's Quest for Economic Equality.* Cambridge: Harvard University Press.

Gallagher, Maggie. 1996. *The Abolition of Marriage: How We Destroy Lasting Love*. Washington, D.C.: Regnery.

Gallagher, S. 1996. "Symbolic Traditionalism and Pragmatic Egalitarianism: Contemporary Evangelicals, Families, and Gender." Paper presented at the American Sociological Association meeting, New York.

Gans, Herbert. 1962. *The Urban Villagers: Group and Class in the Life of Italian-Americans*. New York: Free Press.

Garey, Amita. 1998. *Gender Vertigo: American Families in Transition*. New Haven: Yale University Press.

Gay, Peter. 1986. *The Bourgeois Experience: From Victoria to Freud*. Vol. 1: *The Education of the Senses*. New York: Oxford University Press.

Gerson, Deborah A. 1996. "Barren in the Promised Land." *Contemporary Sociology* 25, no. 6 (November): 788–789.

Gerson, Kathleen. 1993. *No Man's Land: Men's Changing Commitments to Family and Work*. New York: Basic Books.

Giddens, Anthony. 1992. *The Transformation of Intimacy: Sexuality, Love and Eroticism in Modern Societies*. Stanford, Calif.: Stanford University Press.

Gilligan, Carol. 1993. *In a Different Voice: Psychological Theory and Women's Development*. Cambridge: Harvard University Press.

Gillis, John R. 1997. *A World of Their Own Making: Myth, Ritual, and the Quest for Family Values*. Cambridge: Harvard University Press.

Gimenez, Martha. 1993. "The Transformation of Intimacy." Book review. *Social Forces* 72 (September): 271–272.

Glenn, Noval D. 1997. *Closed Hearts, Closed Minds: Textbook Story of Marriage*. New York: Institute for American Values.

Gligliere, Michael P. 1999. *The Dark Side of Man: Tracing the Origins of Male Violence*. Reading, Mass.: Perseus.

Goodman, Ellen. 2000. "A Self-Serving Divorce Myth?" *Washington Post*, September 30, A21.

Gordon, M. 1978. *The American Family: Past, Present, and Future*. New York: Random House.

Gore, Al, and Tipper Gore. 2002. *Joined at the Heart: The Transformation of the American Family*. New York: Henry Holt.

Greven, Philip J. 1970. *Four Generations: Population, Land, and Family in Colonial Andover, Massachusetts*. Ithaca, N.Y.: Cornell University Press.

Griswold, Robert L. 1982. *Family and Divorce in California, 1850–1890: Victorian Illusions and Everyday Realities*. Albany: State University of New York Press.

Groneman, Carol. 2000. *Nymphomania: A History*. New York: Norton.

Habermas, Jürgen. 1987. *The Philosophical Discourse of Modernity: Twelve Lectures*. Trans. Frederick G. Lawrence. Cambridge: MIT Press.

Hacker, Andrew. 1997. "The War over the Family." *New York Review of Books*, December 4, 34–38.

Hackstaff, Karla B. 1999. *Marriage in a Culture of Divorce*. Philadelphia: Temple University Press.

Hall, Leslie A. 1991. *Hidden Anxieties: Male Sexuality, 1900–1950*. Cambridge, Mass.: Polity.

Hannerz, Ulf. 1969. *Soulside: Inquiries into Ghetto Culture and Community.* New York: Columbia University Press.

Hareven, Tamara. 1996. *Aging and Generational Relations.* New York: Aldine de Gruyter.

Hartog, Henrick. 2000. *Man and Wife in America: A History.* Cambridge: Harvard University Press.

Harvey, Elizabeth. 1999. "Short-Term and Long-Term Effects of Early Parental Employment on Children of the National Longitudinal Survey of Youth." *Developmental Psychology* 35, no. 2 (March): 445–459.

Hays, Sharon. 1996. *Culture Contradictions of Motherhood.* New Haven: Yale University Press.

Hetherington, E. Mavis. 2002. *For Better or for Worse: Divorce Reconsidered.* New York: Norton.

Holloway, Susan, Bruce Fuller, Marylee Rambaud, and Costanza Eqqers-Pierolea. 1997. *Through My Own Eyes: Single Mothers and the Culture of Poverty.* Cambridge: Harvard University Press.

Hopper, Joseph. 2000. "Marriage in a Culture of Divorce." Book review. *American Journal of Sociology* 106, no. 3 (November): 848–850.

Horwitz, M. 1977. "The Transformation of American Law, 1780–1860." Book review. *University of Pennsylvania Law Review,* 241.

Howland, Dave. 1997. "Au Pair Gets a Life Term." *Ventura County Star,* October 24, A1, A6.

Hunt, Larry L., and Janet G. Hunt. 1987. "Here to Play: From Families to Lifestyles." *Journal of Family Issues* 8, no. 4 (December): 440–443.

Illouz, Eva. 1997a. *Consuming the Romantic Utopia: Love and the Cultural Contradictions of Capitalism.* Berkeley: University of California Press.

———. 1997b. "The Normal Chaos of Love." Review essay. *Contemporary Sociology* 26, no. 1 (January): 78–80.

———. 1997c. "Who Will Care for the Caretaker's Daughter? Toward a Sociology of Happiness in the Era of Reflexive Modernity." *Theory, Culture and Society* 14, no. 4 (November): 31–66.

Jamieson, Lynn. 1998. *Intimacy: Personal Relationships in Modern Societies.* Cambridge, Mass.: Polity.

Jaroff, Leon. 1997. "Six Parents, One Orphan." *Time,* December 1, 45.

Jenkins, Kathleen. N.d. "Shifting Subjects of Female Submission: A Comparison of Postfeminist Gender and Family Ideology in Fundamentalist/Charismatic Christian Communities." Manuscript. Department of Sociology, Brandeis University.

Joffe, Carole. 1986. *The Regulation of Sexuality: Family Planning Workers.* Philadelphia: Temple University Press.

Johnson, Diane. 1996. "The Cultural Contradictions of Motherhood." *New York Review of Books,* November 28, 22–26.

Juster, Susan Maris, and A. Vinovskis. 1987. "Changing Perspectives on the American Family in the Past." *Annual Review of Sociology* 13:193–216.

Klassen, Albert, Colin Williams, and Eugene Levitt. 1989. *Sex and Morality in the U.S.: An Empirical Inquiry under the Auspices of the Kinsey Institute.* Middletown, Conn.: Wesleyan University Press.

La Rossa, Ralph. 1997. *The Modernization of Fatherhood: A Social and Political History.* Chicago: University of Chicago Press.

Laslett, Barbara, and Johanna Brenner. 1989. "Gender and Social Reproduction: Historical Perspectives." *Annual Review of Sociology* 15:381–404.

Laumann, Edward, John Gagmon, Robert Michael, and Stuart Michaels. 1994. *The Social Organization of Sexuality: Sexual Practices in the United States.* Chicago: University of Chicago Press.

Lemonick, Michael. 1999. "Hot Genes for Sale?" *Time,* November 9, 56.

Lopata, Helena Znaniecka. 1996. *Current Widowhood: Myths and Realities.* Thousand Oaks, Calif.: Sage.

Lowery, Sharon A., and Melvin Defleur. 1995. *Milestones in Mass Communication Research: Media Effects.* White Plains, N.Y.: Langman.

Luker, Kristin. 1984. *Abortion and the Politics of Motherhood.* Berkeley: University of California Press.

Lupton, Deborah, and Lesley Barclay. 1997. *Constructing Fatherhood: Discourses and Experiences.* Thousand Oaks, Calif.: Sage.

Lyman, Stanford. 1987. "From Matrimony to Malaise: Men and Women in the American Film." *International Journal of Politics, Culture, and Society* 1, no. 2 (winter): 73–100.

Lystra, K. 1989. *Searching the Heart.* New York: Oxford University Press.

Maccoby, Eleanor E. 1998. *The Two Sexes: Growing Up Apart, Coming Together.* Cambridge Mass.: Belknap Press.

MacIver, Robert. 1950. *The Ramparts We Guard.* New York: Macmillan.

Mack, Dana. 1997. *The Assault on Parenthood: How Our Culture Undermines the Family.* New York: Simon and Schuster.

Maines, P. Rachel. 1999. *The Technology of Orgasm: "Hysteria," the Vibrator, and Women's Sexual Satisfaction.* Baltimore: Johns Hopkins University Press.

Manning, Wendy D., and Pamela J. Smock. 1995. "Why Marry?" Race and the Transition to Marriage among Cohabitors." *Demography* 32, no. 4:509–520.

Marshall, Susan E., and Janet K. Boles. 1991. "Who Speaks for American Women? The Future of Antifeminism." In *American Feminism: New Issue for a Mature Movement.* Ed. Susan E. Marshall and Janet K. Boles. Newbury Park, Calif.: Sage.

May, Elaine Tyler. 1995. *Barren in the Promised Land: Childless Americans and the Pursuit of Happiness.* New York: Basic Books.

McCarthy, E. Doyle. 1988. "Love in America: Gender and Self-Development." Review essay. *Contemporary Sociology* 17, no. 6 (November): 827–828.

McFate, Katherine. 1991. *Poverty, Inequality, and the Crisis of Social Policy.* Washington, D.C.: Joint Center for Political and Economic Studies.

McGuire, M. 1987. *Religion: The Social Context.* Belmont, Calif.: Wadsworth.

McLanahan, Sara, and Gary Sandefur. 1994. *Growing Up with a Single Parent: What Hurts, What Helps.* Cambridge: Harvard University Press.

Mead, Rebecca. 2000. "Sex and Sensibility." *New Yorker,* September 18, 146–148.

Melody, M. E., and Linda M. Peterson. 1999. *Teaching America about Sex: Marriage Guides and Sex Manuals from the Late Victorians to Dr. Ruth.* New York: New York University Press.

Meyerowitz, Joanne. 1988. *Women Adrift: Independent Wage Earners in Chicago, 1880–1930.* Chicago: University of Chicago Press.

Millman, Marcia. 1991. *Warm Hearts and Cold Cash: The Intimate Dynamics of Families and Money.* New York: Free Press.

Mindel, Charles H., and Robert W. Habenstein, eds. 1981. *Ethnic Families in America: Patterns and Variations.* New York: Elsevier.

Mintz, S., and S. Kellog. 1988. *Domestic Revolutions: A Social History of American Family Life.* New York: Free Press.

Morgan, Edmund S. 1996. "First Generations: Women in Colonial America." *New York Review of Books,* October 31, 66–69.

Morrow, Lance. 1997. "Goodbye, Miss Havisham: A Non-Wedding Turns into a Defining Moment in the Battle of the Sexes." *Time,* December 8, 114.

———. 1999. "Is This Right? Who Has the Right to Say?" *Time,* January 11, 41.

Nock, Steven. 1998. *Marriage in Men's Lives.* New York: Oxford University Press.

Norton, Mary Beth. 1996. *Founding Mothers and Fathers: Gendered Power and the Forming of American Society.* New York: Knopf.

Okrent, Daniel. 2000. "Twilight of the Boomers." *Time,* June 12, 68–74.

O'Neil, Nena, and George O'Neil. 1972. *Open Marriage: A New Lifestyle for Couples.* New York: M. Evans.

Ortner, Sherry. 1991. "Reading America: Preliminary Notes in Class and Culture." In *Recapturing Anthropology.* Ed. Richard G. Fox, 163–189. Santa Fe, N.M.: School of American Research Press.

Pallone, Nathaniel, ed. 2002. *Love, Romance, Sexual Interaction.* New Brunswick, N.J.: Transaction Books.

Park, Alice. 2000. "Designer Baby: Parents Use Genetic Testing to Get the Baby They Need." *Time,* October 16, 102.

Popenoe, David. 1988. *Disturbing the Nest: Family Change and Decline in Modern Societies.* New York: Aldine de Gruyter.

Press, Andrea Lee. 1991. *Women Watching Television: Gender, Class, and Generation in the American Television Experience.* Philadelphia: University of Pennsylvania Press.

Presser, Harriet B. 1999. "Toward a 24-Hour Economy." *Science* 284 (June 11): 1778–1779.

Raley, R. K. 1996. "A Shortage of Marriageable Men? A Note on the Role of Cohabitation in Black-White Differences in Marriage Rates." *American Sociological Review* 61:973–983.

Rivers, Caryl, and Rosalind Barnett. 1997. "Bashing Working Mothers." *Dissent* 44 (fall): 13–15.

Robinson, Paul. 1976. *The Modernization of Sex: Havelock Ellis, Alfred Kinsey, William Masters and Virginia Johnson.* New York: Harper and Row.

Rose, Susan D. 1987. "Women Warriors: The Negotiation of Gender in a Charismatic Community." *Sociological Analysis* 48, no. 3:245–258.

Rosenblatt, Roger. 1996. "My One and Only Love." *Time,* October 21.

Rosenfeld, Jeffrey P. 1979. *The Legacy of Aging: Inheritance and Disinheritance in Social Perspective.* Norwood, N.J.: Ablex Publishing.

Rotundo, Anthony E. 1993. *American Manhood: Transformations from the Revolution to the Modern Era.* New York: Basic Books.

Rubin, Lillian B. 1981. *Women of a Certain Age: The Midlife Search for Self.* New York: Harper and Row.

Sassler, Sharon, and Frances Goldscheider. 1997. "Revisiting Jane Austen's Theory of Marriage Timing: Union Formation among American Men in the Late 20th Century." Paper presented at the meeting of the Population Association of America, Washington, D.C.

Sassler, Sharon, James McNally, and Robert Schoen. 1998. "Long-Term Consensual Unions: Cohabitation and the Transformation of the Institution of Marriage in the United States." Manuscript, Brown University.

Schaar, John. 1981. *Legitimacy in the Modern State.* New Brunswick, N.J.: Transaction Books.

Schoen, Robert, and Dawn Owens. 1992. "A Further Look at First Marriages and First Unions." In *The Changing American Family: Sociological and Demographic Perspectives.* Ed. S. J. Southa and S. E. Tolnay, 109–117. Boulder, Colo.: Westview.

Schoen, Robert, and R. Weinick. 1993. "Partner Choice in Marriages and Cohabitations." *Journal of Marriage and the Family* 55:408–414.

Schur, Edwin. 1988. *The Americanization of Sex.* Philadelphia: Temple University Press.

Schwartz, Pepper. 1994. *Peer Marriage: How Love between Equals Really Works.* New York: Free Press.

Seidman, Steven. 1987. "Pornography: Marxism, Feminism, and the Future of Sexuality." *Contemporary Sociology* 16, no. 5 (September): 719–724.

———. 1991. *Romantic Longings: Love in America, 1830–1980.* New York: Routledge.

Seligman, Adam B. 1992. *The Idea of Civil Society.* New York: Free Press.

Shalit, Wendy. 1999. *A Return to Modesty: Discovering the Lost Virtue.* New York: Free Press.

Shapiro, Michael J. 2002. *For Moral Ambiguity: National Culture and the Politics of the Family.* Minneapolis: University of Minnesota Press.

Simon, William. 1991. "Sex and Morality in the U.S." Book review. *Social Forces* 69, no. 4 (June): 1299–1300.

Skolnick, Arlene. 1991. *Embattled Paradise: The American Family in an Age of Uncertainty.* New York: Basic Books.

———. 1998. "A World of Their Own Making." Review essay. *Contemporary Sociology* 27, no. 3 (May): 233–235.

Smart, Carol. 1992. *Regulating Womanhood: Historical Essays on Marriage, Motherhood and Sexuality.* New York: Routledge.

Smith-Rosenberg, Caroll. 1986. *Disorderly Conduct: Visions of Gender in Victorian America.* New York: Oxford University Press.

Smock, Pamela J., and Wendy D. Manning. 1997. "Cohabiting Partners' Economic Circumstances and Marriage." *Demography* 34, no. 3:331–341.

Stacey, Judith. 1990. *Brave New Families: Stories of Domestic Upheaval in Late Twentieth Century America.* New York: Basic Books.

———. 1996. *In the Name of the Family: Rethinking Family Values in the Postmodern Age.* Boston: Beacon Press.

Stearns, C., and Peter Stearns. 1986. *Anger: The Struggle for Emotional Control in American History.* Chicago: University of Chicago Press.

Steinberg, Shirley, and Joe Kincheloe. 1997. *Kinderculture: The Corporate Construction of Childhood.* Boulder, Colo.: Westview.

Sterk-Elifson, Claire. 1994. "Sexuality among African-American Women." In *Sexuality across the Life Course.* Ed. Alice S. Rossi. Chicago: University of Chicago Press.

Sullivan, Andrew. 1998. *Love Undetectable: Notes on Friendship, Sex, and Survival.* New York: Knopf.

Susman, Warren. 1984. *Culture as History: The Transformation of American Society in the Twentieth Century.* New York: Pantheon.

Sweet, James A., and Larry L. Bumpass. 1987. *American Families and Households.* New York: Russell Sage Foundation.

Swidler, Ann. 2001. *Talk of Love: How Culture Matters.* Chicago: University of Chicago Press.

Talbot, Margaret. 1997. "Dial-a-Wife: The Next Domestic Solution." *New Yorker,* October 20 and 27, 196–208.

———. 1998. "The Egg Women." *New Republic,* March 15, 42.

Taylor, Robert Joseph, James S. Jackson and Linda M. Chatters, eds. 1997. *Family Life in Black America.* Thousand Oaks, Calif.: Sage.

Thornton, A., W. Axinn, and J. Teachman. 1995. "The Influence of Educational Experiences on Cohabitation and Marriage in Early Adulthood." *American Sociological Review* 60: 762–774.

Tiger, Lionel. 1999. *The Decline of Males.* New York: Golden Books.

Tucker, M. Belinda. 1995. *The Decline of Marriage among African Americans: Causes, Consequences, and Policy Implications.* New York: Russell Sage Foundation.

USBC (U.S. Bureau of the Census). 2000. *Statistical Abstract of the United States: 2000.* Washington, D.C.: Government Printing Office.

USDA. Center for Nutrition Policy and Promotion. 2000. "Expenditures on Children by Families." *1999 Annual Report.* March.

Van Horn, Susan. 1988. *Women, Work, and Fertility, 1900–1986.* New York: New York University Press.

Wallard, Willard Walter. 1937. "The Dating and Rating Complex." *American Sociological Review* 2:727–734.

Wallerstein, Judith, Julia Lewis, and Sandra Blakeslee. 2000. *The Unexpected Legacy of a Divorce: A 25 Year Landmark Study.* New York: Hyperion.

Wasserman, David, and Robert Wachbroit, eds. 2001. *Genetics and Criminal Behavior.* Cambridge: Cambridge University Press.

Waters, Malcolm. 1989. "Patriarchy and Viriarchy: An Exploration and Reconstruction of Concepts of Masculine Domination." *Sociology* 23 (May): 193–211.

Weeks, Jeffrey. 1991. *Against Nature and Other Essays on History, Sexuality and Identity.* London: Rivers Oram Press.

Weigert, John, and Arthur Frank. N.d. "Identity Ambivalence." Department of Sociology, University of Calgary, Calgary, Canada.

Weitzman, Lenore J. 1985. *The Divorce Revolution: The Unexpected Social and Economic Consequences for Women and Children in America.* New York: Free Press.

Weston, Kath. 1991. *Families We Choose: Lesbians, Gays, Kinship.* New York: Columbia University Press.

Whitehead, Barbara. 1997. *The Divorce Culture.* New York: Knopf.

Whyte, William Foote. 1943. *Street Corner Society: The Social Structure of an Italian Slum.* Chicago: University of Chicago Press.

Wilson, James Q. 1985. "The Rediscovery of Character: Private Virtue and Public Policy." *Public Interest* 81 (fall): 3–16.

———. 1993. "The Family-Values Debate." *Commentary* 95, no. 4:24–31.

Wu, Lawrence L., and Barbara Wolfe, eds. 2001. *Out of Wedlock: Causes and Consequences of Nonmarital Fertility.* New York: Russell Sage Foundation.

Wu, Zhen, and T. R. Balakrishnan. 1994. "Cohabitation after Marital Dissolution in Canada." *Journal of Marriage and the Family* 56:723–734.

Wyatt-Brown, Bertram. 1982. *Southern Honor: Ethics and Behavior in the Old South.* New York: Oxford University Press.

Yeatman, Anna. 1993. "Regulating Womanhood." Book review. *American Journal of Sociology* 99 (September): 538–540.

Zelizer, Viviana A. 1994. *Pricing the Priceless Child: The Changing Social Value of Children.* Princeton, N.J.: Princeton University Press.

CHAPTER 8

Alper, Neil O. 1981. *Artists in Massachusetts: A Study of Their Job Market Experiences.* Boston: Massachusetts Council on the Arts and Humanities.

Alper, Neil O., Gregory H. Wassal, Ruth Towse, and Abdul Khakee. 1992. *Toward a Unified Theory of the Determinants of the Earnings of Artists.* New York: Heidelberg.

Ames, Katherine. 1988. "Sold! The Art Auction Boom." *Newsweek,* April 18, 70–72.

Balfe, Judith H., and Margaret J. Wyszomirski. 1985. "Introduction." In *Art, Ideology, and Politics.* Ed. J. H. Balfe and M. J. Wyszomirski. New York: Praeger.

Baudrillard, Jean. 1983. *Simulations.* New York: Semiotext(e).

Becker, Howard S. 1982. *Art Worlds.* Berkeley: University of California Press.

Behrman, Samuel Nathaniel. 1952. *Duveen.* New York: Vintage.

Bell, Daniel. 1973. *The Coming of Post-Industrial Society: A Venture in Social Forecasting.* New York: Basic Books.

Berman, Marshall. 1982. *All That Is Solid Melts into Air: The Experience of Modernity.* New York: Simon and Schuster.

Bernier, M. 1977. *L'Art et l'argent: Le Marché de l'art au XIX siècle.* Paris: Robert Laffont.

Bourdieu, Pierre. 1984. *Distinction: A Social Critique of the Judgment of Taste.* Cambridge: Harvard University Press.

———. 1996. *The Rules of Art: Genesis and Structure of the Literary Field.* Trans. Susan Emanuel. Stanford, Calif.: Stanford University Press.

Brewer, John, and Ann Birmingham, eds. 1995. *Consumption of Culture, 1600–1800: Image, Object, Text.* New York: Routledge.

Brown, Richard Harvey. 1989. "How Art Became a Commodity." In *The Modern Muse: Condition and Support for Individual Artists.* Ed. Richard Swaim, 13–26. New York: American Council for the Arts.

————. 1995. "Realism and Power in Aesthetic Representation." In *Postmodern Representations: Truth, Power, and Mimesis in the Human Sciences and Public Culture.* Ed. Richard Harvey Brown, 134–167. Urbana: University of Illinois Press.

Clignet, Remi. 1985. *The Structure of Artistic Revolutions.* Philadelphia: University of Pennsylvania Press.

————. 1990a. "L'Exceptionnalisme." In *L'Etat des Etats-Unis.* Ed. M. F. Toinet and A. Lenkh. Paris: La Découverte.

————. 1990b. "On Artistic Property and Aesthetic Propriety." *International Journal of Politics, Culture, and Society* 4, no. 2:229–248.

Crane, Diana. 1987. *The Transformation of the Avant-Garde: The New York Art World.* Chicago: University of Chicago Press.

Crimp, D. 1987. "Art in the 80s: The Myth of Autonomy." *Precis* 6:83–91.

Dal Co, Francisco, and Kurt W. Forster. 1998. *Frank O. Gehry: The Complete Works.* New York: Monacelli Press.

Davis-Brown, Beth, and David Williamson. 1996. "Cataloging at the Library of Congress in the Digital Age." *Cataloging and Classification Quarterly* 22, nos. 3/4.

Denzin, Norman. 1994. *Blue Velvet.* Thousand Oaks, Calif.: Sage.

DiMaggio, Paul J. 1982. "Cultural Entrepreneurship in Nineteenth-Century Boston." *Media, Culture, and Society* 4:33–50 and 303–322.

————. 1987. "Classification in Art." *American Sociological Review* 52:440–455.

Eco, Umberto. 1986. *Travels in Hyperreality.* New York: Harcourt Brace Jovanovich.

Frampton, K. 1980. *Modern Architecture: A Concise History.* New York: Oxford University Press.

Gablik, Suzi. 1985. *Has Modernism Failed?* New York: Thames and Hudson.

Gladwell, Malcolm. 1996. "St. Nick's Beard." *New Yorker,* November 25, 9–10.

Goffman, Erving. 1974. *Frame Analysis.* New York: Basic Books.

Goldberger, Paul. 1972. "Mickey Mouse Teaches the Architects." *New York Times Magazine,* October 22, 40–41, 92–99.

Gouldner, Alvin. 1979. *The Future of Intellectuals and the Rise of the New Class.* New York: Seabury.

Griswold, Wendy. 1990. "The Culture of Capital: Art, Power and the Nineteenth Century Middle Class." *Contemporary Sociology* 19, no. 4 (July): 508–511.

Gusek, Jodi. 1992. "Museum Approaches to Marketing Art to the Public." Manuscript. University of Pennsylvania, Philadelphia.

Habermas, Jürgen. 1987a. *The Philosophical Discourse of Modernity: Twelve Lectures.* Trans. Frederick Lawrence. Cambridge: MIT Press.

————. 1987b. *The Theory of Communicative Action.* Vol. 2: *Lifeworld and System: A Critique of Functionalist Reason.* Trans. Thomas McCarthy. Boston: Beacon Press.

Harvey, David. 1989. *The Condition of Postmodernity: An Enquiry into the Origin of Cultural Change.* Cambridge, Mass.: Blackwell.

Hoving, Thomas. 1993. *Making the Mummies Dance: Inside the Metropolitan Museum of Art.* New York: Simon and Schuster.

Hughes, Robert. 1985. "Careerism and Hype amidst the Image Haze: American Painters of the 80s Are Buffeted by Cultural Inflation." *Time,* June 17, 78–83.

———. 1993. *Culture of Complaint.* New York: Cambridge University Press.

———. 1997. *American Visions: The Epic History of Art in America.* New York: Knopf.

Huyssens, André. 1984. "Mapping the Post-Modern." *New German Critique* 33:5–52.

Jacobs, Jane. 1992. *The Death and Life of Great American Cities.* New York: Vintage Books.

Jameson, Frederic. 1983. "Postmodernism, or the Cultural Logic of Late Capitalism." *New Left Review* 146:53–92.

———. 1991. *Postmodernism, or the Cultural Logic of Late Capitalism.* Durham, N.C.: Duke University Press.

Jencks, Charles. 1977. *The Language of Postmodern Architecture.* New York: Pantheon.

Jones, Welton. 1998. "Pro-NEA Bilbray Got What He Lobbied For." *San Diego Union-Tribune,* July 28.

Kariel, Henry S. 1990. "The Endgame of Postmodernism within the Momentum of Modernity." *Features* 22, no. 1 (January/February): 91–99.

Katz-Gerro, Tally. 1998. "Leisure Activities and Cultural Tastes as Lifestyle Indicators: A Comparative Analysis of Germany, Sweden, Italy, Israel, and the U.S." Manuscript. University of California, Berkeley.

Kelly, Owen. 1986. "The Economic Position of the Artist in Society." *A Series of Letters to . . . a Conference.* New York: New York Foundation for the Arts.

Kernan, Michael. 1988. "The Great Debate over Artists' Rights." *Washington Post,* May 22.

Lasch, Christopher. 1978. *The Culture of Narcissism.* New York: Norton.

Levine, Peter. 2000. *The New Progressive Era: Toward a Fair and Deliberate Democracy.* Lanham, Md.: Rowman and Littlefield.

Lichtman, Richard. 1982. *The Production of Desire.* New York: Free Press.

Lyotard, Jean-François. 1984. *The Postmodern Condition: A Report on Knowledge.* Minneapolis: University of Minnesota Press.

Manning, Peter K. 1991. "Copies." Manuscript. School of Criminal Justice, Michigan State University, East Lansing.

Marcuse, Herbert. 1978. *The Aesthetic Dimension.* Boston: Beacon Press.

Metcalf, Gene. 1985. "Black Folk Art and the Politics of Art." In *Art, Ideology, and Politics.* Ed. Judith H. Balfe and Margaret J. Wyszomerski, 169–194. New York: Praeger.

Meyer, Karl E. 1979. *The Art Museum: Power, Money, Ethics.* New York: William Morrow.

Moulin, Raymonde. 1987. *Le Marché de la peinture en France.* Paris: Editions de Minuit.

NEA (National Endowment for the Arts). 1988. "Labor Force Data on Various Artists' Occupations." Washington, D.C.: Research Division, National Endowment for the Arts, March.

Peck, Robin P., and Gregory Newby, eds. 1996. *Scholarly Publishing: The Electronic Frontier.* Cambridge: MIT Press.

Peterson, Richard A. 1972. "A Process Model of the Folk, Pop, and Fine Art Phases of Jazz." *American Music: From Storyville to Woodstock.* New Brunswick, N.J.: Transaction Books.

———. 1975. "From Region to Class, the Changing Locus of Country Music: A Test of the Massification Hypothesis." *Social Forces* 53:497–506.

———. 1987. "The Sociology of Art and Culture in America." Manuscript. Department of Sociology, Vanderbilt University, Nashville, Tenn.

Reitlinger, Gerald. 1961. *The Economics of Taste.* London: Barrie and Rockliff.

Rothfield, Lawrence, ed. 2001. *Unsettling "Sensation": Art Policy Lessons from the Brooklyn Museum of Art Controversy.* New Brunswick, N.J.: Rutgers University Press.

Scott, A. O. 2000. "The Panic of Influence." *New York Review of Books,* February 10, 39–43.

Simpson, Charles R. 1981. *SoHo: The Artist in the City.* Chicago: University of Chicago Press.

Smith-Shank, Deborah. 1996. "Art Trash/Trash Art/Cultural Trash." Manuscript. Indiana University.

Snyder, R. 1989. "Selling Velvet Paintings Brings Bucks." *Indiana Daily Student,* E2.

Taylor, Brandon. 1987. *Modernism, Post-Modernism, Realism: A Critical Perspective for Art.* Winchester: Winchester School of Art Press.

Thompson, Michael. 1979. *Rubbish Theory: The Creation and Destruction of Value.* New York: Oxford University Press.

Trustman, Deborah. 1979. "The Art Market: Investors Beware." *Atlantic Monthly,* January, 73–77.

Tuchman, Gaye. 1988. "The New Sociology of Culture." Manuscript. Department of Sociology, Queens College, Flushing, N.Y.

Van Bruggen, Coosje. 1997. *Frank O. Gehry: Guggenheim Museum Bilbao.* New York: Abrams.

Veblen, Thorstein. 1899. *Theory of the Leisure Class: An Economic Study of Institutions.* New York: Macmillan.

Venturi, Robert, D. Scott-Brown, and S. Izenour. 1972. *Learning from Las Vegas.* Cambridge: MIT Press.

Warchol, Krystina. 1992. "The Market System of the Art World and New Art: Prices, Roles, and Careers in the 1980s." Ph.D. diss., University of Pennsylvania.

Weber, Max. 1992. *The Protestant Ethic and the Spirit of Capitalism.* Trans. Talcott Parsons. New York: Routledge.

Whitt, J. Allen. 1987. "Mozart in the Metropolis: The Arts Coalition and the Urban Growth Machine." *Urban Affairs Council* 23:15–36.

Widmer, Kingsley. 1975. "On Processed Culture: In Praise of Waste." In *The End of Culture: Essays on Sensibility in Contemporary Society.* San Diego, Calif.: San Diego State University Press.

Withers, Josephine. 1981. "In Search of the Magic Kingdom." *New Art Examiner* 9, no. 1 (October).

Wolff, Janet. 1981. *The Social Production of Art.* New York: St. Martin's.

Zolberg, Vera. 1984. "American Art Museum: Sanctuary or Free-for-All." *Social Forces* 63.

Zukin, Sharon. 1982. *Loft Living: Culture and Capital in Urban Change.* Baltimore: Johns Hopkins University Press.

Index

African Americans: cultural traits of, 20–21; lynching of, 105; Negroes transformed into, 21; race and democracy, 36–41, 43; use of term, 16

AIDS, 77, 117, 206, 210

Alcoholics Anonymous (AA), 116, 154, 155

Alger, Horatio, 196

Allen, Woody, 230, 259

Altman, Robert, 282

America: early government in, 7–8, 43; expansionism in, 99, 194; frontier myth in, 200–201; influence of England on, 43; land distribution in, 7, 9; natural resources of, 19; rebels against authority in, 83–84; unlimited potential in, 194–197, 200–201; *see also* United States

"American creed," 42

American exceptionalism, 42–52; class politics and, 48–50; immigrants and ethnic groups in, 45–47; individualism and, 42–43, 48, 52; oligopolistic capitalism and, 46–48, 50–52, 91–92; religion and, 138; working-class consciousness and, 43–48, 51–52

Americanization, 2–6; and globalization, 2–3; of immigrants, 18–19; meanings of term, 6, 19; moral dimension of, 3, 11

American Medical International, 34

"American way of life," 83

Ammerman, Nancy, 235

Anderson, Benedict, 128

Animal rights movement, 135–136

Anti-intellectualism, 10

Aramony, William, 156

Architecture, postmodern, 283–285

Arendt, Hannah, 96, 156, 163

Aristotle, 223

Art, 264–297; aesthetic and artistic property, 78; commodification of, 267–274, 278, 289–291, 293; conclusions, 293–

Art (*continued*)
297; deconstructionism in, 87, 280–281, 292–297; as ideological construction, 265–266; markets for, 269–274; media as, 267, 268; postmodern disciplines of, 279–288; postmodern features of, 288–293; as privileged category, 265–267; production of, 277–279; social definition of, 265; social stratification and, 274–276; as tax deduction, 267
Artificial semination, 229
AT&T, divestiture of, 28
Autonomy, American ideology of, 10

Baby boomers, 260–261
Baby M, 75, 230
Barshevsky, Diane, 4
Baudrillard, Jean, 296
Beard, George Miller, 147
Beaumont, Gustave de, 23
Becker, Gary, 238
Beckett, Samuel, 291
Bell, Daniel, 96–97, 278
Bellah, Robert, 147–148, 153
Bengtson, Vern L., 228
Bensel, Richard, 50, 51
Berenson, Bernard, 270
Berger, Peter, 60
Berrigan brothers, 114
Best, Thomas, 13
Biden, Joseph, 108
Bilbray, Brian, 274
Bill of Rights, U.S., 10
Biotechnology, 77
Bjorklund, Diane, 144–145
Blair, Tony, 5, 65
Bloom, Allan, 87
Bobbitt, John Wayne, 149
Bork, Robert, 104, 108
Bourdieu, Pierre, 59
Bradshaw, John, 155
Brown, Cliff, 40
Brown, Helen Gurley, 241

Brown, John Carter, 272
Brown v. Board of Education, 76
Bruce-Briggs, B., 60–61
Brzezinski, Zbigniew, 96
Buchanan, Patrick, 65
Burden, Chris, 280
Burke, Edmund, 71
Burton, Mark, 70
Bush, George H. W., 3, 29, 41, 54–55, 65, 100
Bush, George W., 4, 5, 29, 82; election 2000 and, 25, 57, 76, 79, 94, 100, 105, 106, 108, 136–137; political campaigns of, 18, 94, 107; Star Wars and, 30; wealth gap and, 55
Bushnell, Horace, 146
Buzzanca, Jaycee Louise, 230

Cage, John, 291
Calder, Alexander, 280–281
Calhoun, Arthur W., 213
Campaign financing, 56, 62–64, 106
Cancian, Francesca, 208, 216
Capitalism: consumption and, 90, 150, 191–193, 238, 262; contemporary, 88–92; globalization of, 133, 193; individualism and, 238; postmodern, 139, 167, 255, 262; social control in, 107; spatiality in, 185–189; temporality and, 179–185
Carter, Jimmy, administration of, 55
Challenger space shuttle, 82–83
Child labor, 211
China, market economy in, 31
Chodorow, Nancy, 150
Christian Coalition, 117
Christo, 292–293
Chukwu, Nkem, 229
CIA, covert operations of, 101–102
Citizenship: abstract notion of, 74; diminishing habits of, 92, 98, 129; meaning of, 66, 103; obligations of, 8, 67–68, 75–76
Civic activism, 73, 76

Civil Rights Movement (1960s), 8, 10, 30, 39, 40, 69, 117, 131, 133, 136

Civil society, 120–121

Civil War, U.S., 12, 50, 51

Class politics: decline of, 7, 52–62, 66, 116, 121, 126, 128–129; family values and, 220; globalization and, 52–54, 66; identity politics and, 126; middle class identity and, 58–61; national organization of, 119; weakness of, 41–52, 54, 55; wealth gap and, 41–42, 49–50, 52–56

Clinton, Bill: administration of, 3–4, 5, 29, 55, 95, 108; election of, 106; health care reform and, 100; impeachment of, 57, 104, 110; personal qualities of, 81–82, 85, 104; Star Wars and, 30; Third Way and, 65

Clinton, Hillary Rodham, 254

Codependents Anonymous (CoDa), 155

Coleman, James, 96

Collidge, Shana, 245

Collins, Judy, 147

Columbine High School, 70

Commerce: American ideology of, 10; bottom line as basis of, 80, 103; corporate power, 31–35, 91–92; division of labor in, 41–42, 49, 95, 162–164, 186; employment contracts, 100, 164; entrepreneurship and, 10, 31–32; federal vs. state jurisdiction in, 25–26; financial politicians in, 26; globalization and, 62, 126; hours of work in, 32–33, 182; innovations in, 12; integration of state and, 89–90; international, *see* Globalization; interstate, 25; market competition in, 26, 28, 46, 53–54, 75, 89, 97, 179–180, 185; mass production in, 10, 12, 46, 50; oligopolization in, 46–48, 50–52, 91–92; outsourcing jobs in, 18, 30, 31, 54, 123, 126, 180, 193; productivity in, 48, 49, 62, 180, 193; profitability in, 77, 81, 84, 89, 186, 193; service sector in, 48, 54, 61, 125, 193

Communities of similarity, 81, 162, 190, 198

Comstock Law (1879), 75

Comte, Auguste, 96

Confederate flag, 200

Conservatives, 31, 43, 45, 61–62; as absolutists, 218; contradictions of, 89; family values and, 217–218, 219–222; religious right, 134–135; rugged individualism and, 149–150; selfhood of, 144

Constitution, U.S.: freedoms under, 91, 110, 187; interpretations of, 86, 201; legitimacy and, 69, 71–76, 77, 91; public space and, 187; on separation of powers, 71–72, 73; voting rights and, 105

Consumption: capitalism and, 90, 150, 191–193, 238, 262; consumerism and, 107, 148, 169, 182, 186; environmentalism vs., 126; identity through, 57–58, 66, 140; shift from production to, 120; space-time and, 190–193

Contos, Nicole, 242

Coontz, Stephanie, 218, 223–224

Copley, John Singleton, 266

Corporate power, 31–35, 56, 62, 66, 148, 150; in bureaucratic politics, 129, 130; in oligopolies, 46–48, 50–52, 91–92; supercorporations and, 88–92; technicism in, 92–98

Corporate state, 27–29, 62–66, 89, 122

Corrections Corporation of America, 31

Crèvecoeur, J. Hector St. John de, 10, 12

Crime, 85–86

Daimler-Chrysler, 2

D'Alema, Massimo, 65

Dalí, Salvador, 272

Dashefsky, Arnold, 21

Davis, Mike, 52

Deaver, Michael, 108

Debs, Eugene V., 45

Declaration of Independence, U.S., 3

Deconstructionism, 81, 87, 280–281, 292–297

Deindustrialization, 53–54

Deleuze, Gilles, 296

DeMille, Cecil B., 192

Democracy: capitalism and, 88–92; individualism and, 9, 10–11, 42–43, 146–147; mandates in, 109; participation in, 7, 35, 64, 92, 98, 129; populist, 89; in postmodern society, 165; potential for mob rule in, 90; power derived from the consent of the government in, 91; race and, 36–41, 43; rights and obligations in, 67–68, 75–76, 126; secular, 84–85, 128; wealth gap and, 64–66, 97–98

Denton, Nancy, 38

Descartes, Rene, 176

Development, metaphor of, 203–204

Dickens, Charles, 194

Diner, Hasia, 177

Dix, Dorothea, 146

Djilas, Milovan, 60

Dole, Robert, 107

Douglass, Frederick, 146, 166

Dreiser, Theodore, 237

Dubofsky, Melvyn, 49

DuBois, W. E. B., 37, 156

Due process, 99–104

Duhamel, Georges, 194

Durkheim, Emile, 49, 77, 80, 115, 116, 148, 166, 173

Duveen, Lord Joseph, 270

Eappen, Deborah, 219–220

Eco, Umberto, 281–282

Eder, Klaus, 114

Education: adult, 156; as continuous process, 196–197; costs of, 227, 228; decentralization of, 23–24, 25; human capital in, 25; market forces in, 33; military contracts and, 30; race and, 39, 76

Edwards, Jonathan, 146, 151

Egalitarianism, 77

Elections: legitimation by mandates of, 104–107, 108–111; popular vs. electoral vote in, 106; presidential (2000), 25, 57, 76, 79, 94, 100, 105, 106, 108, 136–137, 200, 201

Emancipation Proclamation, 10, 105

Emerson, Ralph Waldo, 146, 152

Employment: contracts of, 100, 164; decline of industrial workers, 126; hours of work, 32–33, 182–183; job satisfaction and, 59, 80; legislation, 90, 181; middle class and, 56, 58, 133; outsourcing jobs, 18, 30, 31, 54, 123, 126, 180, 193; part-time or seasonal, 180, 220; racism and, 38–41, 47; in supercorporations, 92; unemployment and, 103, 213, 226; wages and, 61

Engels, Friedrich, 46, 48

England: aristocratic statism in, 43; common law of, 86, 236–237; empire of, 48; influence on America, 43; wealth gap in, 53

Enlightenment, 85, 165, 174, 175

Entitlement, politics of, 126, 154, 260

Entrepreneurship, 10, 31–32, 58, 149

Environmentalism, 59, 60, 77, 126, 134, 135

Equality, limited use of term, 145

Ethical relativism, 77

Ethnicity, 12–22; assimilation and, 14–17, 18–19; economic components of, 20; group identification and, 21–22; hierarchy of, 195–196; identity and, 14–15, 18, 19, 21–22, 56, 118; immigration and, 12–16, 21–22, 46, 195–196; intermarriage and, 15–16; multiculturalism in, 18, 19, 22, 57; political nature of, 20, 30, 56–57, 118; racism and, 17–18, 118, 236; social class and, 16–17; voting and, 20; wealth gap and, 30

Etzioni, Amatai, 96

Europe: economic recovery of, 61; ideologies in, 73; socialism in, 5–6, 11, 45, 48, 50–51; social stratification in, 11, 12; Western, as norm, 138

Fair Housing Act (1968), 39

Fair Labor Standards Act, 181

Falwell, Jerry, 65, 117, 131, 132

Families: diversity of forms, 209–213, 226, 229–236; identity based on, 215, 235; lifestyles and, 234–236; new social context for, 224; nuclear, 205, 215, 216, 217, 225, 226, 231, 246; one-parent, 212, 214, 222; postmodern, 231–236, 262; socialization of, 215; stepfamilies, 218–219, 222, 225; as units of consumption, 232, 234, 235, 255, 258

Family relations, 205–263; abuse in, 105, 139, 206, 258–259; children and, 214, 216, 259; cohabitation, 211–212, 232–234; debates about, 216–225; differentiation of, 225–229; divorce, 159, 211–214, 218, 220, 228, 229, 231, 234–235, 242, 256, 261; domestic services, 183, 245; family planning, 88; gender conflicts in, 240–247, 247–256; gender roles in, 206–211, 215–217, 220–221, 225, 241, 246, 255; generation gaps in, 257–263; historical patterns in, 206–216; market forces in, 246–247, 248, 255, 260; marriage, 15–16, 209–212, 213–214, 216, 228, 234, 237, 239–242, 250, 251, 256; out-of-wedlock births, 229; regulation of, 68, 74, 209; reproductive technologies, 229–230, 244–245; romantic subjectivism vs. rational calculation in, 236–247; state control of, 209, 237; surrogate mothers, 75, 87, 229–230; Victorian ideal in, 207–208; working mothers, 33, 191, 205–206, 209, 213, 215, 216–217, 219–220, 224, 228, 235–236, 240, 255

Family values, 209, 217–218, 219–222, 224, 225, 231–236, 237–242, 258

Fanon, Frantz, 119

Farrow, Mia, 230, 259

Federalism, 90

Federalist Party, 10

Finance: global capital markets in, 4, 32, 62; time and, 180, 186, 194–195

Fitzgerald, F. Scott, 237

Forbath, William, 51

Forbes, Malcolm, 106

Forbes, Steve, 107

Foucault, Michel, 153, 167, 175

Framingham Heart Study, 221

Franklin, Benjamin, 10, 146, 179

Freedom, definitions of, 98, 161

Freud, Sigmund, 151, 152

Friedan, Betty, 221

Fromm, Erich, 152, 167

Fuchs, Lawrence, 13

Fuller, Margaret, 146

Fuller, Robert, 167

Gans, Herbert, 168

Gehlen, Arnold, 167

Gehry, Frank O., 284–285

Gender: dating and, 247–252; family vs. lifestyle, 234–236; "men's" and "women's" work, 236–237; as postmaterialist value, 59; sex change operations, 231; trends in relations between, 206–216, 247–256

General Electric, 4

Generation gap, 257–263

Gen Xers, 260–261

Gergen, Kenneth, 167

Ghazali, Abu Hamid Al, 88

Giddens, Anthony, 59, 222–223

Gilligan, Carol, 221

Gilman, Charlotte, 253

Giroux, Henry, 18

Glass, Philip, 279, 291

Globalization, 2–6; of capitalism, 133, 193; class politics and, 52–54, 66; competition and, 19, 31, 53–54, 61, 88, 122–123, 124; economic shifts and, 3–4, 6, 61–62; emerging nations and, 66, 126; isolationism and, 57; multinational corporations and, 6, 24–25, 29, 56; op-

Globalization (*continued*)
ponents of, 65; outsourcing jobs in, 30,
31, 126; political changes and, 5–6, 24,
56, 77; racism and, 41; role of the state
in, 29–30; of social movements, 115;
wealth gap and, 53, 62
Godbey, Geofrey, 184
Goetz, Bernard, 151
Gompers, Samuel, 44, 47
"Good government" movement (1920s),
55–56
Gorbachev, Mikhail, 107
Gore, Albert, 25, 65, 76, 79, 82, 104
Gouldner, Alvin, 60
Government, *see* State
Granovetter, Mark, 38
Great Depression, 28, 85, 89
Greenpeace, 135
Gresso, Vincent, 231
Guattari, Felix, 296
Gulf of Tonkin resolution, 101
Gurvitch, Georges, 174

Habermas, Jürgen, 96, 165, 297
Hackstaff, Karla, 242
Hamilton, Alexander, 71
Hartigan, John, 16
Hartz, Louis, 42, 45, 146
Harvey, David, 297
Health care, corporate control of, 33–34
Herman, Simon, 21
Hersh, Seymour, 286
Hill, Anita, 108
Hills, Carla, 3
Hispanic, use of term, 16
Ho Chi Minh, 143
Hochschild, Jennifer, 37, 183
Hoffman, Abbie, 127
Hofstadter, Richard, 168
Homosexuality, 78, 114, 118, 131, 152–153,
161, 206, 210, 212, 231
Honda Corporation, 4
Horney, Karen, 152, 167

Hospital Corporation of America, 34
Household debt, 182–183
Humana, 34
Human rights, biotechnology and, 77
Hussein, Saddam, 103
Hyper-rationalization, 159–166

IBM Corporation, 4, 31
Identity, 142–145; ambivalence about,
144; in consumption, 57–58, 66, 140;
ethnicity and, 14–15, 18, 19, 21–22, 56,
118; focus on feelings, 164; focus on self,
154–159, 162, 168, 171; new, 168, 210; social distinctions, 162; stable core, 144;
unconscious and, 151; work and, 162–
164
Illouz, Eva, 164–165, 216
Immigration: and American dream of
ownership, 10; assimilation and, 14–17,
18–19, 195, 239; descendants of, 20–22;
ethnicity and, 12–16, 21–22, 46, 195–
196; focus on future, 158; homosexuality and, 78; labor market and, 8, 13, 45–
46; legislation, 13–14; limits sought for,
14; loosened ties to old country, 9, 10,
20, 195; to Lower East Side, 177–178;
nativists vs., 12, 14, 22; religion and, 60
Indiana, Gary, 271
Individualism, 142–171; acquisitive, 100,
148, 150, 166; ambivalence about, 197;
American exceptionalism and, 42–43,
48, 52; American ideology of, 9, 10–11,
42, 84, 98, 166–171; assessment of,
166–171; capitalism and, 238; civic, 147,
148, 171; concepts and values of, 145–
148; democracy and, 9, 10–11, 42–43,
146–147; identity and, 142–145, 168,
171; independent, 146; mobility and,
166, 237–239; moral principle of, 145–
148; postmodern, 159, 166–167, 168–
169; rationalization and, 159–166;
rugged, 149–151, 171; self-absorption
and, 81–82, 154–159, 162, 166–167,

169, 232, 237–238; self-reliance and, 9, 168; social class and, 168, 169–171; state vs., 22–23, 73–74; subjective, 169; therapeutic, 170–171; unconscious and, 151–159; violence and, 70; withdrawal and, 161–162, 166

Industrialization: contracts and, 100; demographic changes and, 4–5, 237; of emerging economies, 61, 66; labor movement and, 114, 122; revolution and, 49; urbanization and, 119; wealth gap and, 101

Industrial Revolution, 11, 12, 42, 48, 239

Inglehart, Ronald, 59, 134

Inheritance, 196

Innovation, disruptions of, 77–83

International Court of Justice, 3

International Monetary Fund (IMF), 96, 124

Internet, 239–240, 247

In vitro fertilization, 229, 244–245

Iran-Contra scandal, 86, 100, 104, 108, 109, 160

Iraq, invasion of (1990s), 103

Irving, Clifford, 293–294

Jackson, Andrew, 10, 85

Jackson, Michael, 259

James, Henry, 253

James, William, 151, 152

Jameson, Frederic, 288, 297

Japan, economic recovery of, 61

Jaynes, Gerald, 37

Jefferson, Thomas, 7, 10, 143, 145

Jencks, Charles, 283

Johnson, Virginia, 244

Jones, Paula, 109

Jospin, Lionel, 5, 65

Justice, and law, 80, 99–100

Kant, Emmanuel, 173

Karabel, Jerome, 52

Kefauver, Estes, 157

Kennedy, John F., 106

Kissinger, Henry, 149–150, 151

Know-Nothing party, 46

Kondratieff cycle, 176

Kovic, Ron, 149

Kusserow, Adrie, 169

Labor market: competition in, 228; hours of work, 32–33, 182; immigration and, 8, 13, 45–46; two-tiered, 46–48, 123; women in, see Women

Labor movement, 11, 42, 44–48, 51–52, 55, 57, 66, 115; business unionism and, 114, 122–123; membership decline in, 126, 181, 182

Labro, Philippe, 249

Lasch, Christopher, 154, 167

Law: arbitration in, 93; changing nature of, 78–81, 85; of contracts, 101; due process of, 101, 104; English common, 86, 236–237; ethics and, 79, 80; interpretations of, 87; justice and, 80, 99–100; legitimacy and, 101–102; in litigious society, 79; and order, 101–102; outdated, 230; precedent in, 86, 87–88; system maintenance in, 83; in various states, 72, 74, 105

Le Corbusier, 283

Left: liberation espoused by, 61; "Old," productivist model of, 125; postmaterialist writings of, 60–61; secular, 135; weakness of, 58

Legitimacy, 67–112; as authority to rule, 68–69, 83–88; Constitution and, 69, 71–76, 77, 91; cost-benefit aspects of, 80; crisis of, 68, 69–71, 85, 86, 97–98, 111–112; of experts, 93–97, 102, 150; fragmentation of the concept of, 67, 68–71, 100; law and, 101–102; mandate as basis of, 104–107, 108–111; moral framework of, 67–68, 80, 83, 85, 102; national sovereignty and, 77; pluralism and, 99–104; in postmodern society,

Legitimacy (*continued*)
111–112; of precedent, 86–88; results as basis of, 101–104; social and technical innovations and, 77–83; supercorporation and, 88–92; technicism and, 92–98; of tradition, 158; universality and, 74

Lenin, V. I., 49

Lewinsky, Monica, 75, 109, 110, 254

Lewis, Sinclair, 237

Liberalism: collapse of, 61; contradictions in, 89; identity politics and, 62; relativism and, 218–219, 222–223; religion and, 128; social welfare and, 73, 127

Liberty Foundation, 117

Lichtenstein, Roy, 280, 291

Lifestyle: consumption and, 57–58, 124, 140, 148, 191; families and, 234–236; legitimacy undermined by, 67–68; quality of life and, 59–60

Lincoln, Abraham, 146

Lipset, Seymour Martin, 42, 45, 50, 60, 146

Literature: modernity in, 283; postmodern, 285–288

Locke, John, 42, 50, 91

Lombardi, Vince, 102

Lott, Trent, 17

Lucero, Michael, 292

Luhman, Niklas, 96

Lundberg, Ferdinand, 26

Lyman, Stanford, 37, 253

Lyotard, Jean-François, 57, 127, 165, 296

MacIver, Robert, 229

MacKinnon, Catherine, 155

Madison, James, 71

Madonna, 254

Mafia, 101, 106

Malcolm X, 195

Mandate: engineered participation and, 106–107; legitimation by, 104–107, 108–111; representativeness of, 105–108

Mann, Horace, 146

Manufacturing: American system of, 10; economic shifts and, 3–4; employment in, 48, 54; globalization of, 62; wealth gap and, 101

Manza, Jeff, 42

Mao Tse Tung, 105

Mapplethorpe, Robert, 294–295

Marx, Karl, 45–46, 48, 116, 143, 173, 285

Marxism, 119, 121, 297

Massey, Douglas, 38

Masters, William, 244

Matta-Clark, Gordon, 284

Mayflower Compact, 84

McCain, John, 18, 107

McCartney, Bill, 117

McDonald's, 92, 192–193

McDougall, Susan, 110

McFarlane, Robert, 70

McGee, Michael Calvin, 114

McLaren, Norman, 282

Media: as art, 267, 268; campaign influence from, 107–111; and freedom of speech, 110; gender relations depicted in, 241, 242–243, 250, 251, 253–255, 259–260; image building by, 109, 110–111; manipulation of, 108, 110–111; opinion polling by, 107–108, 110; ownership of, 3, 34, 109, 127; postmodern, 282–283, 286–288; religion and, 127; social movements and, 127–128, 139, 140, 141; spin in, 108, 110

Melendez, Rita, 152

Melville, Herman, 3, 22

Men: patriarchy, 215, 222, 223, 235; roles of, 209, 210, 220, 236–237, 253; unemployed, 213, 226

Merton, Robert, 170

Mesmerism, 151

Mexico: border of, 175; NAFTA and, 14

Microsoft, 28, 63

Middle class: economic decline of, 64–65; in emerging nations, 66; fuzziness of concept, 58–61; generation gap in, 261–262; use of term, 58–59

Mies van der Rohe, Ludwig, 283

Militias, private, 69–70, 89, 118

Mill, John Stuart, 115

Mills, C. Wright, 58–59

Minson, Jeffrey, 167

Mobility, 196–197, 200–201, 237; individualism and, 166, 237–239; marriage and, 237, 239–240, 256

Modernity: capitalist forms of, 166; as differentiation, 143; rebirth of, 127; secularization and, 138; social complexity of, 78–79, 98, 142–143; social movements and, 116–117, 121–122, 134, 139–141

Monroe, Marilyn, 257–258

Moral construct, 67–68, 80, 83, 85, 102

Morality, feelings as basis of, 154–159

Moral Majority, 60, 117, 123

Morris, Dick, 108

Mosbacher, Robert, 3

Moses, Anna Mary Robertson "Grandma," 275

Motorola, Inc., 4

Multiculturalism, 18, 19, 22, 57, 66

Multiple personality disorder (MPD), 138–139

Mumford, Louis, 179

Napoleonic Code, 81

Nash, Adam, 244

Native Americans, 86–87

Neoliberal capitalism, 66

New Age spirituality, 117, 138, 152, 169

Newclassical economists, 237–238

New Deal, 28

New Right, 127, 134–135

Nixon, Richard M., 85, 106

Nongovernmental organizations (NGOs), 115

Noriega, Manuel, 108

North, Oliver, 86, 108, 110

North, Simon, 10

North American Free Trade Agreement (NAFTA), 14

Nowotny, Helga, 185

Offe, Claus, 114

Oldenberg, Claes, 281, 284

Ownership, rights of, 74–75, 77, 78

Packwood, Robert, 106

Paine, Thomas, 8, 71

Parsons, Talcott, 36–37, 218

Pereira, Fernando, 135

Perot, Ross, 65, 106

Personhood, legal status of, 230

Piore, Michael, 46–47

Pledge of Allegiance, 84

Pluralism, 14, 22, 84, 99–104

Poindexter, John, 70

Political Action Committees (PACs), 24

Political parties: electoral college and, 120; funding of, 119–120; as managerial apparatus, 129–130; weakness of, 72, 73–74, 76

Politicians: access to, 73; financial, 26; funding of, 24, 56, 62–64, 106

Populism, 9–10, 11, 43, 89

Pornography, 138–139

Postindustrialization: demographic changes and, 4–5; end of ideology in, 96–97; political economy of, 168–169; technicism and, 96

Postmaterialist values, 59–60, 62, 121–122

Postmodern societies: American, 122, 129, 167; artificial constructs of, 81; as capitalism, 139, 167, 255, 262, 296; collapse of boundaries in, 292, 294–297; individualism in, 159, 166–167, 168–169; legitimacy in, 111–112; secular left in, 135; time and history in, 296

Prisons, privatization of, 31

Privacy: concept of, 74–75; right of, 86

Privatization, 5, 31, 62

Progressives, selfhood of, 144

Promise Keepers, 117

Property: crimes of, 85–86; rights of ownership, 74–75, 77, 78, 91

Protestantism, *see* Religion

Psychotherapy, 153–154, 156, 167, 169

Racism: backlash from, 17–18; cultural, 17–18; delegitimation of, 133; democracy and, 36–41, 43; drug laws and, 17; education and, 39, 76; employment and, 38–41, 47; ethnicity and, 17–18, 118, 236; indirect forms of, 17–18; institutionalized, 18, 66, 125; narrowing of focus in, 16, 30; and politics of assertion, 18, 57, 59; segregation and, 38, 39, 40, 76, 236; slavery and, 12–13; social class and, 16–17

Rainbow Warrior, 135

Rationality, 77, 84–85, 98, 116, 134

Rationalization: division of labor in, 162–164; subjectivism vs., 159–166, 236–247, 257–258, 262

Ray, Charles, 281

Reagan, Ronald, 5, 150; administration of, 19, 29, 34, 41, 53, 54–55, 70, 100, 104, 108, 159, 187; election of, 106, 107; Iran-Contra and, 100, 104, 108, 160; Star Wars and, 30; union busting and, 123; wealth gap and, 54–55, 65, 187

Reality anemia, 160–161, 168, 259

Regan, Donald, 108

Rehr, David, 63

Reich, Robert, 157–158

Reisman, David, 167

Religion: and anti-Semitism, 20; Catholic confession, 152–153, 157; evangelicalism, 131–132, 138; evolution theory and, 86; family planning and, 88; fundamentalist, 57, 60, 117–118, 127–128, 130–133, 138–139; immigration and, 60; individualism and, 145, 146, 147; New Right, 134–135; as postmaterialist value, 59;

privacy of, 11–12; Protestant revival, 59, 60, 131, 137; Puritanism, 171; secularization of, 83–85, 133–141; selfhood and, 117; separation of church and state, 11–12, 84, 128, 131; social movements and, 116–118, 122, 125, 128, 130–139, 162; zealotry in, 84

Repressed memory syndrome (RMS), 138–139

Republican Party: chambers of commerce and, 56; corporate influence on, 129; economic shifts and, 61–62; formation of, 10; homophobia of, 114; religious right and, 132, 135, 136–137; xenophobia of, 62, 149

Retirement, extended, 181–182, 260–261

Rice, Condoleezza, 18

Rieff, Philip, 154

Robertson, Pat, 117, 131, 132

Robinson, John, 184

Rogers, William, 83

Rohatyn, Philip, 96

Romantic subjectivism vs. rational calculation, 236–247, 257–258, 262

Roosevelt, Franklin D., 26, 28, 85, 95

Roosevelt, Theodore, 28

Rorty, Richard, 165

Rose, Nikolas, 167

Rose, Susan, 235

Rothko, Mark, 280

Sadlowski, Ed, 44

Saint-Simon, Henri de, 113

Salle, David, 290

Salvation Army, 31

Schnabel, Julian, 271

Schroeder, Gerhard, 5, 65

Schumpeter, Joseph, 60

Secularism, 77, 138

Segal, George, 280

Sennett, Richard, 167, 187

September 11 attacks, 131

Serra, Richard, 78, 284

Sexuality, 243–246, 247–252, 259

Shapiro, Michael, 218

Shultz, George P., 70

Simmel, Georg, 79

Singer, Peter, 136

Skinheads, 118

Slater, Philip, 154

Slavery, 8–9, 13, 23, 38, 40; abolitionists and, 116, 199; Emancipation Proclamation and, 10, 105; family relations in, 257; impacts of, 12–13, 16, 76; time and, 180, 200

Smelser, Neil, 115

Smith, Adams, 49, 51

Smith, Christian, 132, 138

Snyder, Gary, 135

Social contract, limitation of, 100

Social control, 107

Social Darwinism, 101, 144

Social democracy, use of term, 11

Socialism: American working class and, 43–45, 47–49, 51–52, 115; in Europe, 5–6, 11, 45, 48, 50–51; inverted, 91

Social movements, 113–141; adversarial mode of, 140; changing focus of, 122–130; collective behavior as, 113; community and, 117–120, 121–122, 134, 138, 140; definitions of terms, 113–116, 120–121; democracy and, 89; framing in, 137; globalization of, 115; iconic nature of, 140–141; identity-based, 121, 162; Internet and, 119; language of, 140–141; modernity in, 116–117, 121–122, 134, 139–141; movement politics and, 128; "new" (NSMs), 113, 114–116, 117, 120–130, 132–133, 139–141; occupational structure and, 124–125; organizational structure of, 130; postideological, 134; religion and, 116–118, 122, 125, 128, 130–139, 162; value rationality of, 123–124; wealth gap and, 124–125

Sombart, Werner, 19, 52

Sony Corporation, 4

Sorokin, Pitrim, 174

Southern U.S., space-time in, 198–200

Soviet Union, collapse of, 31

Space, 172–204; in corporate capitalism, 185–189; diversity and contradictions in, 197–204; policing of, 186; public vs. private, 186–189; social character of, 173–178; social mobility and, 190–193; stabilization of, 202–204; in suburbia, 186–189; territorial rights in, 175

Sports, commercialization of, 34

Stacey, Judith, 231–232, 236

Stanley, Manfred, 96

Starbucks, 5

Starr, Kenneth, 75, 110

Star Wars nuclear defense system, 30

State: accountability and, 72, 76, 85, 91; ambiguous status of, 23–30, 66; antigovernment sentiments, 68, 69, 72, 74, 76, 102, 129; bureaucracies of, 26, 27, 70, 82–83, 85, 148, 160–161; capitalism and, 88–92; changing functions of, 5, 19, 28–29, 31, 71–72, 150; Civil War and, 50, 51; corporate welfare and, 27–29, 62–66, 89–90; corporations undermining legitimacy of, 34–35, 88–92; court-made law and, 25, 51, 72; decentralization and, 22–30, 70, 72–76; decline in trust of, 69, 70–71; as defender of property, 91; demystification of, 97; globalization and, 29–30, 62; incompetence of, 72; individualism vs., 22–23, 73–74; legitimacy of, see Legitimacy; limiting the power of, 102; management of the economy by, 90; militarization of, 29–30; privatization vs., 31; role and image of, 22–23, 27, 28–30, 156; special interests and, 27; visible hand of, 97; wealth gap and, 50, 91

States: as administrative districts, 90; decentralized governments of, 72–76; in electoral college system, 73, 105; multi-

States (*continued*)
    plicity of jurisdictions, 75; sovereignty
    of, 72, 74; variability of laws among,
    72, 74, 105
Stella, Frank, 284, 290
Supreme Court, U.S.: on desegregation,
    76; on domestic violence, 105; on elec-
    tions, 76, 79, 201; presidential nomi-
    nees to, 104, 108, 159
Surrogate mothers, 75, 87, 229–230

Tarantino, Quentin, 282
Technicism, 92–98, 107, 124, 134
Technology: coining of term, 10; impact
    of, 143, 167; innovations in, 77–83, 158,
    186; Internet, 239–240, 247; law out-
    dated by, 230; reproductive, 229–230,
    244–245; time-saving, 184–186
Television, talk, 164–165
Terrorism, 30, 86, 135
Testing, pervasiveness of, 94
Texaco, 40–41
Thatcher, Margaret, 5, 65
Third Way, 65
Thomas, Clarence, 18, 57, 108
Thoreau, Henry David, 146–147, 158,
    166, 171
Time: corporate capitalism and, 179–
    185; discretionary, 181–184; eschatolog-
    ical, 177; and faith in the future, 192,
    194–197; global standardization of,
    174, 179–180, 198; here and now, 176,
    191–193, 202, 234; history and, 177–
    178, 192, 194–195, 202; multitasking
    and, 184–185; nostalgia and, 191–192,
    200, 202; planning, 209; seasonal,
    203–204; social character of, 173–178;
    social mobility and, 190–193; stabi-
    lization of, 202–204; in 24/7 society,
    183
Tocqueville, Alexis de, 11, 23, 41–42, 146,
    147, 166, 168, 184, 194
Torricelli, Robert, 157

Touraine, Alain, 120
Transcendentalism, 146, 147–148, 151
Tri-Lateral Commission, 96
Tripp, Linda, 75
Trump, Donald, 228

Unconscious, 151–159
United States: anti-intellectualism in, 10;
    checks and balances in, 76; conserva-
    tive politics in, 31, 43, 45; decentralized
    government in, 7–8, 11, 22–30, 70, 72–
    76; ethnic and racial diversity in, 7, 12–
    22; founding of, 84; money as measure
    of success in, 10, 19, 80, 103–104, 144,
    184, 191; national identity in, 19; pre-
    industrial modernization of, 7–12; sep-
    aration of church and state in, 11–12,
    84, 128, 131; separation of powers in,
    71–72, 73, 76; slavery in, 8–9; social
    mobility in, 10–11; social stratification
    in, 8–9, 10, 12–15; transitional stages
    of, 1–2; unifying political culture in, 19
Urbanization, 4–5, 9, 119, 186, 189
Urban renewal, 39

Valenti, Jack, 107
Valéry, Paul, 19
Veblen, Thorstein, 265, 266
Veen, H.-J., 134
Ventura, Jesse, 65
Vietnam War, 101, 103, 163
Virtual reality, 160
Voss, Kim, 51
Voter participation, 20, 42, 56, 58, 70,
    106, 120, 123, 188, 261
Voting rights, 39, 104–105

Wackenhut Corporation, 31
Waldheim, Kurt, 108
Wallace, David Foster, 292
Walsh, Lawrence, 110
Walzer, Michael, 186
War, civilian casualties of, 86

Warhol, Andy, 291

War on Poverty, 114

Washington, George, 9, 71, 180

Watergate scandal, 104, 109

Wayne, John, 149–151, 165, 168, 169, 170

Wealth gap: class politics and, 41–42, 49–50, 52–56; deindustrialization and, 53–54; democracy and, 64–66, 97–98; ethnicity and, 30; families and, 224–225, 226–227; globalization and, 53, 62; industrialization and, 101; mobility and, 239; postmaterialist values and, 59–60; Reagan administration and, 54–55, 65, 187; social movements and, 124–125; state protection and, 91; supercorporations and, 91–92

Weathermen, 89, 102

Weber, Max, 37, 80, 85, 101, 115, 116, 127, 155, 159, 173, 265

Weinberger, Caspar W., 70

Weitzman, Lenore, 214

Welfare system: changing focus of, 115, 213; corporations and, 89; creation of, 59, 85, 124; expansion of, 133; weakness of, 42–43, 52, 55, 133; women and, 169, 220, 227

Wexler, Philip, 167–168

Whitehead, Mary Beth, 75

Whitewater scandal, 100, 109

Whitman, Walt, 146

Whitney, Eli, 10

Whyte, William, 167

Williams, Eric, 16

Williams, Jody, 119

Williams, Montel, 153

Williams, Rhys, 114

Williams, Robin, 37

Wills, Garry, 149, 158

Wilson, Woodrow, 90

Winfrey, Oprah, 153

Wobblies (WWW), 49

Wodiczko, Krzysztof, 292–293

Women: health of, 221; in paid labor force, 32, 33, 40, 182, 191, 205–206, 209, 213, 215, 216–217, 219–220, 224, 227–228, 235–236, 237, 240–241, 246, 255; radical feminism, 138–139; rape of, 105, 252; right to vote, 105; roles of, 205–206, 208, 217, 219–222, 236–237, 241, 246, 252–253; stepmothers, 240; on welfare, 169, 220, 227; widowhood, 215

Women's movement, 10, 59, 69, 117, 133, 190, 207, 217, 221, 235, 241

Woods, Tiger, 15

Woolf, Virginia, 283

Work: clock time and, 180–181; hours of, 32–33, 182; identity through, 162–164; inherent value of, 104, 115, 163, 232; language of, 162, 163; *see also* Employment

World Bank, 96, 124

Wright, Frank Lloyd, 283

Zald, Mayer, 137

Zaretsky, Eli, 114

Zelver, Patricia, 250